CW00382497

TANK TACTICS

0 11557 03559 9

The Stackpole Military History Series

THE AMERICAN CIVIL WAR

Cavalry Raids of the Civil War
Ghost, Thunderbolt, and Wizard
Pickett's Charge
Witness to Gettysburg

WORLD WAR I

Doughboy War

WORLD WAR II

Armor Battles of the Waffen-SS, 1943–45
Armoured Guardsmen
Army of the West
Australian Commandos
The B-24 in China
Backwater War
The Battle of Sicily
Beyond the Beachhead
The Brandenburger Commandos
The Brigade
Bringing the Thunder
Coast Watching in World War II
Colossal Cracks
A Dangerous Assignment
D-Day Deception
D-Day to Berlin
Destination Normandy
Dive Bomber!
A Drop Too Many
Eagles of the Third Reich
Eastern Front Combat
Exit Rommel
Fist from the Sky
Flying American Combat Aircraft of World War II
Forging the Thunderbolt
Fortress France
The German Defeat in the East, 1944–45
German Order of Battle, Vol. 1
German Order of Battle, Vol. 2
German Order of Battle, Vol. 3
The Germans in Normandy

Germany's Panzer Arm in World War II
GI Ingenuity
Goodwood
The Great Ships
Grenadiers
Hitler's Nemesis
Infantry Aces
Iron Arm
Iron Knights
Kampfgruppe Peiper at the Battle of the Bulge
Kursk
Luftwaffe Aces
Massacre at Tobruk
Mechanized Juggernaut or Military Anachronism?
Messerschmitts over Sicily
Michael Wittmann, Vol. 1
Michael Wittmann, Vol. 2
Mountain Warriors
The Nazi Rocketeers
On the Canal
Operation Mercury
Packs On!
Panzer Aces
Panzer Aces II
Panzer Commanders of the Western Front
The Panzer Legions
Panzers in Normandy
Panzers in Winter
The Path to Blitzkrieg
Penalty Strike
Red Star under the Baltic
Retreat to the Reich
Rommel's Desert Commanders
Rommel's Desert War
Rommel's Lieutenants
The Savage Sky
A Soldier in the Cockpit
Soviet Blitzkrieg
Stalin's Keys to Victory
Surviving Bataan and Beyond
T-34 in Action
Tank Tactics

Tigers in the Mud
Triumphant Fox
The 12th SS, Vol. 1
The 12th SS, Vol. 2
The War against Rommel's Supply Lines
War in the Aegean
Wolfpack Warriors

THE COLD WAR / VIETNAM

Cyclops in the Jungle
Expendable Warriors
Flying American Combat Aircraft: The Cold War
Here There Are Tigers
Land with No Sun
Phantom Reflections
Street without Joy
Through the Valley

WARS OF THE MIDDLE EAST

Never-Ending Conflict

GENERAL MILITARY HISTORY

Carriers in Combat
Desert Battles
Guerrilla Warfare

TANK TACTICS

From Normandy to Lorraine

Roman Jarymowycz

STACKPOLE
BOOKS

Copyright © 2001 by Lynne Rienner Publishers, Inc. This edition is published by arrangement with Lynne Rienner Publishers, Inc.

Published in paperback in 2009 by
STACKPOLE BOOKS
5067 Ritter Road
Mechanicsburg, PA 17055
www.stackpolebooks.com

All rights reserved, including the right to reproduce this book or portions thereof in any form or by any means, electronic or mechanical, including photocopying, recording, or by any information storage and retrieval system, without permission in writing from the publisher. All inquiries should be addressed to Lynne Rienner Publishers, Inc., 1800 30th Street, Suite 314, Boulder, Colorado 80301.

Cover design by Tracy Patterson

Printed in the United States of America

10 9 8 7 6 5 4 3 2 1

ISBN 0-8117-3559-1 (Stackpole paperback)
ISBN 978-0-8117-3559-9 (Stackpole paperback)

The Library of Congress has cataloged the hardcover edition as follows:

Jarymowycz, Roman Johann, 1945–
    Tank tactics : from Normandy to Lorraine / Roman Johann Jarymowycz.
      (The art of war)
Includes bibliographical references and index.
ISBN 1-55587-950-0 (alk. paper)
1. World War, 1939–1945—Tank warfare. 2. World War, 1939–1945—
    Campaigns—France. 3. United States. Army-Armored troops. 4. Canada.
    Canadian Army—Armored troops. I. Title. II. Series.
D793.J37 2001
940.54'214—dc21
                  00-062628

To Sandra

Contents

Foreword

John A. English

Roman Johann von Hugel Jarymowycz, Austrian by birth, follows in the footsteps of fellow countryman General Ludwig Ritter von Eimannsberger in writing about tank warfare. Eimannsberger was an important if long forgotten tank pioneer, and his 1934 *Der Kampfwagenkrieg* (The Tank War) gained a wide professional readership in Germany. In fact, the man most credited with the formation of German armored forces and doctrine, General Heinz Guderian, relied heavily upon Eimannsberger's work in writing his better known and more influential *Achtung! Panzer!* during 1936–1937.

Recently awarded the Order of Military Merit, Roman Jarymowycz is uniquely qualified to write a book on comparative tank tactics and the operational level of war. A life-long student of war, and of armored operations in particular, he attained his Ph.D. in history from Canada's prestigious McGill University in Montreal. Functional in French and German and capable of reading Russian, he completed his thesis under the supervision of Desmond Morton, one of Canada's most distinguished military historians. During 35 years of service with the reserve component of the Canadian armored corps, in which he commanded the Royal Canadian Hussars, Jarymowycz also acquired a matchless practical knowledge of tanks and armored fighting vehicles. In contrast to those who continue to spread the myth that French tanks were superior to German panzers in 1940 because of heavier armor and armament alone, he reminds us of the critical importance of radio and teamwork (hardly enhanced by the one-man turret in the French tank, which required one person to carry out the functions of gunner as well as commander, giving decided advantage to German tanks with three-man turrets).

Tank Tactics: From Normandy to Lorraine is probably the most comprehensive work yet produced that compares the armored forces of the United States, Britain, France, Germany, and Russia in terms of their development, organization, equipment, training, doctrine, and actual operations in Europe. The inclusion of the Canadians and Poles within the scope of this study is warranted because the former provide a second North American perspective and the latter an "operational lab study" of Allied approaches to armored warfare. Such focus further reinforces the point that the war on the Western Front was very much a coalition struggle. Twenty percent of the forces that participated in the Normandy invasion were Canadian, and without their continued presence during the Northwest European campaign Field Marshal Sir Bernard Montgomery's voice would necessarily have been more muted (80 percent of naval forces in the Normandy invasion were also British and Canadian, and their preponderance in the Atlantic enabled the U.S. Navy to concentrate against the Japanese in the Pacific). Up to mid-September 1944 roughly half the divisions on the Western Front were non-American, and even in May 1945 when U.S. strength surpassed 60 divisions, allied nations fielded 30, about the same number that the United States sent against Japan. Without non-American forces in Europe there could have been no broad front.

As Jarymowycz's substantial research of U.S., British, Canadian, German, and Russian sources reveals, there was indeed a critical interconnection between Allied ground operations in the Normandy campaign. Operation Cobra, for example, did not occur in an operational vacuum as many historians seem to suggest. Montgomery did try to launch Operations Goodwood and Cobra concurrently, and, as Jarymowycz so tellingly points out, General Fritz Bayerlein of the Panzer Lehr Division observed that, through "strong attacks . . . around Caen in the first half of July . . . the Allied Command succeeded in completely veiling from the German Supreme Command the preparations for the breakthrough at St. Lô." In putting the various pieces of the Normandy clash of armor together in integrated form and focusing on the development of operational maneuver in uncommon detail, Jarymowycz does military history a great service. His treatment of General George Patton's dash into Lorraine and his personal musings about how the Russians might have fought on the Western Front are especially illuminating. Not everyone, of course, will agree with all that he says; like Canada's wartime Prime Minister W. L. Mackenzie King, he may assume the best of the Americans and the worst of the British. Both Montgomery and Canadian General Guy Simonds may have been far better generals than as portrayed by his pen. His emphasis on the operational effectiveness of Soviet artillery offensives as part of a combined arms rather than armored approach to warfighting may also hint as much. That said, however, *Tank Tactics* in its grand sweep "from Normandy to Lorraine" offers an even-handed critical analysis and thrust of argument that, for the most part, remains both persuasive and thought provoking. Regardless of how one views the controversies that continue to swirl around the performance of Allied armies on the Western Front during World War II, and they are legion, this substantial scholarly contribution by an acknowledged tank expert will provide a new and valuable perspective. In originality and sheer depth of inquiry it constitutes a formidable tour de force by a brilliant *beau sabreur* that deserves to be studied as well as read.

—John A. English

Acknowledgments

I am indebted to the encouragement and sage advice of many. This has been a lonely trek for a Canadian and taken me through a dozen centers of learning in the United States and Canada. I don't think I could have begun this effort if not for my good fortune in meeting David A. Keough, chief archivist at the U.S. Army Military History Institute, Upton Hall, Carlisle Barracks, Pennsylvania, who patiently guided me toward discovering the U.S. Army in its most esthetic and important years. Upton Hall's librarian, D. Slonaker, took me into dusty dungeons and pointed out armored studies that gave substance to theory. The director of the Patton Museum Library, John M. Purdy, was a gracious host, and ensured that I left Fort Knox with enough data and insight from the manuscript collection to do U.S. armor justice. Reginald Roy's generosity in sharing the Marshal Stearns Papers allowed me to begin with an early insight into Lt. Gen. G. G. Simonds and his peers. Colleagues in the military have offered support and opportunity. Former commanders of Canadian Forces Staff College at Fort Frontenac, Brig. Gen. Clive Milner and Bob Alden, ensured that I participated in college field studies in France and Germany. Lt. Col. John A. MacDonald kindly shared his notes and manuscript on Canadian senior generalship. Col. David M. Glantz offered encouragement and direction in my attempts to understand the Soviet army. Despite my seeming reserve toward the artillery, I am grateful to two gunner officers, Lt. Col. Peter Kraemer and David Patterson, for access to their libraries and collection of military documents. Brian McKenna provided the initial occasion when I both rediscovered military history and my hunger to write about past battles.

I was fortunate to receive early academic guidance from Robert Vogel and then given both my reins and the whip by Desmond Morton. My research in the Canadian Department of Military History was enthusiastically aided by Steven Harris, while Canada's grand vizier of the people's military history, Terry Copp, provided encouragement, advice, and opportunity to present my ideas before critical audiences. John English offered faith and support when I needed it most; his splendid Renaissance approach to military history, particularly when I disagreed with him, encouraged me to attempt this work. Finally, my wife, Sandra, whose sublime patience and good nature permitted me to complete this. I shall treasure those exhausting but happy days as she beavered away on her computer attempting to bring sanity to my style, her faithful budgie, Maxi, chatting contentedly on her shoulder.

—Roman Johann Jarymowycz

Introduction

The aims of this work are twofold: to explain cavalry's status and raison d'être within the evolution of armor as the essence of maneuver and creativity on the battlefield, and to examine the doctrinal evolution of North American armor—that of Canada and the United States. Despite a very obvious kinship and disarming similarity between their societies, the two countries' armies have evolved separately—the Canadian force suspected of being little more than an annex of British traditions, mannerisms, and tactical opinion (which it mostly was).

The arrival of thousands of American Empire Loyalists from the independent thirteen colonies resulted in a host of Canadian units with southern antecedents: the Queen's York Rangers, for example, are also known as the Royal Americans. The War of 1812 and a surrogate Fenian invasion in 1866 sharpened the zealousness for things British and political caution toward things American. Canadian arms' gradual maturity from the Boer War to the taking of Vimy Ridge in 1917 was virtually ignored by an army whose traditions then included the Civil War.

Like the newly arrived Canadian Expeditionary Force, the American Expeditionary Force was met with European reserve—or even, it may be argued, snotty superiority. Like the Canadian, the U.S. Army was torn between British and French influences. Its lineage readily encouraged the embrace of French doctrine and equipment. Similarly, the Canadian field force (with less freedom of choice) mirrored the British influence rather than the French, although both had played fundamental roles in its origins.

Dismissed by each other, the two North American armies developed doctrine in their own two solitudes. One was decidedly more continental than the other, or so it would appear. In fact, U.S. military missions followed technical and tactical evolutions with careful interest, and the U.S. Army mirrored the cavalry-mechanization debates that raged on the Continent. Both suffered from the economic constraints of the 1930s,

1

although cavalry pioneers in the United States managed to produce an experimental tank force despite internal opposition. Meanwhile the two cultures, increasingly affected by geographic reality and modern communications, particularly cinema and radio, grew closer together. Despite the appurtenances of the British regimental system and assumed loyalist traditions, the officers and men that made up the Canadian army were far closer in spirit and temperament to their stateside neighbors than to British Tommies, particularly as war began and hundreds of thousands of civilians filled the ranks. Such natural familiarity and similarity have been overlooked.

European campaigns are regularly studied using British or German armor as the measuring stick. Canadian campaigns are considered an adjunct to British (and by that one must read "Montgomery's") aspirations. They were. But so were American operations. Montgomery was the operational *mikado* in Normandy and ensured that a wary Bradley and Crerar conform to his obstinately imposed grand vision.

I have selected specific tactical contests from the Normandy theater. Montgomery's attempts to break out of the beachhead featured four strategic offensives: Goodwood, Cobra-Spring, Totalize, and Tractable. The first was a British-Canadian effort, the remainder were U.S.-Canadian. They are important in that they were to conclude with the first and greatest example of North American armored competence—the Battle of Cannae that was the Falaise Gap—which somewhat overshadowed the remaining two Allied armored operations of the war, Patton's counterstroke against the German Ardennes offensive and U.S. armored operations in Lorraine.

The Normandy campaign offered North American tank commanders the only opportunity to demonstrate the validity of armor as an arm of operational and strategical decision. Further, it pitted an inferior armored force against a technologically vastly superior enemy. My inquiry specifically focuses on five important examples: Operations Goodwood and Atlantic, July 1944; Cobra and Spring, July 1944; Totalize, August 1944; Tractable and Cobra's pursuit, August 1944; and the Arracourt battles in Lorraine, September 1944. I believe these operations serve to demonstrate both the status quo of Allied doctrine as well as the cultural and technical differences, and similarities, of the armies.

This selection is made with the recognition that these, and some might argue more deserving contests, have been already superbly treated elsewhere by respected historians (albeit separately). Investigation of German archives and battlefield reconnaissance with battle veterans has uncovered interesting insights, and I have revised some generally accepted views.

I have taken for my theme the words of one of the distinguished and, unhappily, mostly unrecognized apostle of maneuver, Gen. Robert W. Grow. The review of the evolution of operational maneuver is taken from a cavalry perspective, and I attempt to demonstrate that the cavalry, rather than suffer exclusion, enjoyed a renaissance with the tank since its specific traditions were both maneuver and shock. The *marriage de raison* of cavalry with artillery (the gun being a successor to the lance) added firepower.

My inquiry has evolved into a perhaps too stern examination of leadership, particularly Montgomery's—and an enthusiastic recognition of the operational legacy of Soviet Russian arms. I maintain that the roots of the AirLand Battle 2000 concept begin with Soviet Marshal Tukhachevskii. In the end, this is may well be a parting salute to the armored-cavalry resurgence. As wheeled vehicles proliferate in the West and cavaliers dread the inevitable domination of the battlefield by sentient robotic armor, the modern *beau sabreur* is more content to look to the past. In the end this is, I hope, a tribute to brothers-in-arms.

A Sherman "Firefly" with 17-pounder gun—the best Allied tank in Normandy
*(Bell, National Archives of Canada, Wilfred Laurier University, Laurier Centre for
Military Strategic and Diasarmament Studies)*

CHAPTER 1

Cavalry and Mechanization, 1918–1930

Without cavalry, battles are without results.

—Napoleon[1]

The history of armor is the history of cavalry. The mechanization of the *arme blanche* was achieved after bitter debate with opponents from the infantry, the artillery and, unfortunately, the cavalry itself. Most zealous were the British officers[2] who formed the guiding light of the Royal Tank Corps and predicted a new type of warfare based entirely on the tank that not only promised to revolutionize battle but to eliminate the traditional arm associated with maneuver and attack.

The refusal of the cavalry to embrace mechanization may be dismissed as shortsighted and parochial. This is both unfair and inaccurate. The cavalry's position, apparently anchored in rustic simplicity, cloaked a complex and sophisticated arm: "Cavalrymen require to be more intelligent and better drilled than in the other forces. On outpost duty, patrolling, and reconnoitering, the men are often obliged to be self-reliant and to use their own judgement. This does not occur to anything like the same extent in the infantry or artillery."[3] The prospect of mechanization appeared as nothing less than an attempt to remove the raison d'être of the mounted arm and thus signal its elimination from the order of battle. The clash between the "apostles of mobility" and the cavalry was basically an argument over doctrinal interpretation. Throughout history the evolution of cavalry doctrine was spurred on by technology. The invention of the stirrup permitted the creation of "heavy" cavalry: armored men on horseback capable of delivering the shock of a mounted attack. The introduction of the pike and the longbow appeared to doom the mounted force. On each occasion the cavalry survived through deft cooperation with other arms, but primarily because it was the only force capable of maneuver. Cavalry continued to dominate European battles even after the appearance of musket and cannon because heavy cavalry[4] was the only arm that could deliver the armored shocks that shattered battle lines and, as a corps, pursue a withdrawing field force. Despite the innovations of Napoleonic warfare—maneuver by massed batteries, corps-level battle formations, rifle brigades, and even tactical rockets—cuirassiers and line cavalry continued to influence operational and strategic operations.[5] As long as the enemy's heavy cavalry was a force in being, a field force had little initiative.

Cavalry was distinct, kept apart from the army administratively and sequestered in the order of battle primarily to deliver the final blow. By its mere appearance, a division of heavy cavalry would force the enemy army to take complicated precautions. A cavalry force "fixed" an enemy corps and compelled commanders to bring up mounted reserves or form squares, which normally could withstand such unsupported attacks as those by the Mamalukes at the Battle of the Pyramids, Ney's charges at Waterloo, or the desperate *totenritt* by both French and Prussian armies during the battle at Sedan in 1870.[6] A poorly timed attack misused an expensive arm: its once threatening mass quickly became an impotent rabble that helplessly flailed against squares. Horses would simply not storm, jump, or trample into steady ranks with fixed bayonets: "The horses . . . resisted all attempts to force them to charge the line of serried steel."[7] The central question of what breaks lines remained. Massed artillery attack—Napoleon's grand battery—was one solution. This was the sudden grouping of all available guns before a selected point of main force to tear the enemy line to pieces.[8] However, once bombardment ceased or the target retired into dead ground (the "reverse slope"), an accelerated attack was required to close with the enemy before he recovered. If the enemy did rally or form squares, the cavalry division's horse artillery battery was presented with a dream target: an immobile mass of packed infantry. A series of volleys was sufficient to wreck the square, at which stage the waiting *sabreurs* would fall upon the hapless survivors. An orthodox cavalry attack was simply the last act of a combined-arms attack. No line could withstand the shock of a cavalry charge.

> Not a man present who survived could have forgotten in after life the awful grandeur of that charge. You perceived in the distance what appeared to be an overwhelming, long moving line, which, ever advancing, glittered like a stormy wave of the sea when it catches the sunlight. On came the mounted host until they got near enough, while the very earth seemed to vibrate beneath their thundering tramp. One might have assumed that nothing could resist the shock of this terrible moving mass.[9]

The mounted attack demanded controlled maneuver and precise supporting fire. Initially the aim was, through deceptive maneuver, to position a body of cavalry close enough to strike the enemy during his decision cycle, that is, before he had no time to form a square. The attack was a well-controlled, carefully graduated affair. Distance was divided into thirds: an initial phase conducted at the walk, a second phase at the trot, perhaps the canter. The aim was to develop enough momentum to create shock yet arrive fresh enough to conduct a furious hand-to-hand melee. Control was difficult during the gallop; most experienced cavalry commanders favored mass over speed and "charged" at the trot for the entire approach, only reaching a gallop in the last few dozen meters: "Not one of the horsemen in these masses would have been able to give his horse another direction had he wished to do so. . . . Murat attacked at the trot to preserve the close formation."[10] Surviving cavalry fell upon the defenders in a blood rage. Correctly sprung, a cavalry attack could wreck an infantry corps (Uxbridge's charge against d'Erlon's Corps at Waterloo) or destroy an entire army (Marlborough at Ramillies, "the largest cavalry battle of which there is any trustworthy account," and Marat at Eylau.)[11] If the advance was conducted at a fast trot for more than 1,000 meters, the attacking horsemen would take about three and a half minutes to reach the target. This gave the defenders enough time to fire their artillery at least five times: three volleys of solid shot, shrapnel, or grape, and two volleys of cannister (case shot) at point-blank range. The first volleys, if gunners estimated the range correctly, might disrupt the formation, while the last two would tear great holes in the attacking line and might stop the charge. Defending infantry might fire twice: once at maximum range, about 100 yards, and the last (if they did not break, though most infantry in line did) at point-blank range. Maneuver was controlled by trumpet calls that excited both men and horses.[12] Only the best disciplined regiments could be reformed directly after a charge: "*Le Cavalerie parait, de toutes les armes, le plus difficile à manier*" ("Of all the arms, Cavalry is the most difficult to control"). As Jacquenot de Presle noted, cavalry demanded dynamic leadership, an innate sixth sense that is only found in the experienced officer. Marat, LaSalle ("A hussar who is not dead at thirty is a blackguard."), and Cardigan ("Stay, sir! How dare you attempt to ride before your commanding officer!") all may have been a bit mad but they knew how to lead horsemen—a vocation not for the timid.[13] The bold cavalier was rewarded by a proficiency and élan not usually found in the other arms.

Operational limitations for massed cavalry were imposed by physical obstacles: terrain or prepared defenses. Cavalry units did not enter heavily wooded areas, avoided towns and cities, and did not attack redoubts, fortifications, or even light field defenses: "Cavalry is a very difficult arm to handle in the field; it easily gets out of hand and becomes dispersed. It can only be deployed mounted where the ground is favourable."[14] Students of the operational art will quickly recognize that massed cavalry behaved exactly as modern massed armor. Balaclava is one example. The battle featured two charges. In the first, General Scarlett's Heavy Brigade, fighting in open ground, won a stunning victory against a superior force of Russian cavalry mostly through élan. In the second, Lord Cardigan advanced through frontal and flanking artillery fire against prepared, albeit light, field defenses. Surprisingly, the Light Brigade actually reached the Russian battery and sabered most of the gunners, but only at the cost of the entire brigade. A similar attack by the 4th Australian Light Horse Brigade succeeded in Palestine during Allenby's 1917 campaign and swept through to capture Beersheba.[15]

The Napoleonic wars perfected the all-arms *groupement tactique* (battle group). Cavalry brigades often fought much like infantry, with skirmishers forward, horse artillery deployed, and a main maneuver force.[16] Light cavalry was closely trained in stalking and behaved exactly like elite jägers or voltigeurs. Fighting "on foot" was not new; it simply was not the preferred option. The American Civil War[17] and the Franco-Prussian War made dismounted carbine-equipped cavalry an absolute necessity, but despite tactical practicality even the most veteran cavaliers never abandoned their heritage:

> Union Cavalry did much of its fighting on foot, it never ceased to be cavalry properly speaking, capable, and proud of it, of charging the enemy with the saber, mounted. The same regiments that advanced on foot, with their carbines blazing to attack and breach the Selma fortifications on April 2, 1865, had charged with the saber, mounted, and driven back Confederate infantry and dismounted cavalry deployed behind field fortifications at Montevallo on March 30 and at Ebenezer Church on April 1.[18]

The introduction of quick-firing artillery and automatic weapons forced the cavalry toward what seemed to be its last evolutionary doctrinal change. Maxim machine gun fire and shrapnel defeated mounted troops well before they could close to shock their opponents: "Even the infantry found that the old *charge en masse* was virtually redundant."[19] The alternative was to revert to classic dragoon tactics: that is, as rifle-equipped, mounted infantry. Although this was accepted in principle, in practice the cavalry dismissed it as irrelevant to its principal missions. Machine guns and the 75mm cannon are bagatelle within operational maneuver. The tactical vulnerability of a cavalry squadron versus automatic fire was waived as the arm concentrated on its "traditional" roles: strategic reconnaissance, the covering force battle, the pursuit and the deep battle (*manoeuvre sur les derrières*). Nevertheless, to effectively enter the modern age of warfare, the cavalry was forced to reexamine its very reason for existence, the horse having to be seen in the light of the growing threat of motorization. Like any great church faced with a reformation, the cavalry began by denying the obvious and excommunicating revisionists from its ranks. To begin, the arm refused to acknowledge the technical superiority of the rifle over the spiritual ascendancy of the saber. U.S. Army Cavalry Regulations of 1907 stated: "It must be accepted as a principle that the rifle, effective as it is, cannot replace the effect produced by the speed of the horse, the magnetism of the charge and the terror of cold steel."[20] The essence of the mounted arm was the cabalistic confidence between man and horse and a sense of superiority—élan—that translated into aggressiveness and victory in battle. The cavalry was a combination of two weapons: the trooper and his mount. Napoleon's hussars enjoyed retelling how Capt. Marcellin de Marbot's mare Lisette saved his life at Eylau: "She sprang at the Russian and at one mouthful tore off his nose, lips, eyebrows and all of his face, making him a living death's head, dripping with blood."[21] The partnership between man and horse transcended the cavalry's eccentric habits that other arms looked at askance. The horse was more partner than battle taxi. Despite the popular romantic representations, the cavalry walked about as much as it rode.[22] A normal route march required the troopers to walk their mounts at least half the time:

> Sore backs were common with the hardships of campaigning, and one of the first lessons taught the inexperienced trooper to take better care of his horse than he did of himself. The remedy against the recurrence of sore backs was invariably to order the trooper to walk and lead the disabled animal.[23]

Horses were looked after first, watered, inspected, and policed: "The stable Piquet was doubled in strength for the first night and had a difficult task, as the horses took the opportunity to settle many old scores with one another."[24] The cavalry argued that unlike the infantry and artillery, it was a sophisticated arm committed to a partnership with a living thing.

The cavalry's decisiveness was nevertheless continually marginalized by competing arms. The only aspect of mounted operations that was clear to civilian and soldier alike was the knee-to-knee charge. The fact that it was done rarely and properly limited to heavy cavalry was usually ignored. The cavalry's hostility to technical advances was to remain consistent through to the middle of the twentieth century. Paramount was the refusal to accept the reduction in status to a "lesser arm." Still, the continental debate persisted in focusing particularly on the tactical, small-unit encounter.

> It is perhaps but natural that the training of cavalry should have been almost exclusively devoted to shock tactics and the use of *L'Arme*

blanche, in spite of the recognized fact that for many years past it had not
been possible for cavalry to act effectively against unbroken infantry. . . .
It means that instead of the firearm being an adjunct to the sword, the
sword must henceforth be an adjunct to the rifle.[25]

The argument was patent, and the proposed answer was to force cavalry to fight on foot, that is, become infantry![26] The official British attitude
was dominated by artillery and infantry generals and conformed with
German thinking.

The same pressure in the German army had led to the cavalry being
trained for dismounted action and to propose to arm it with a new rifle
superior to the Mauser . . . to increase its fire-power the German cavalry
division had been provided with Jaeger battalions in mechanized transport
each with a machine-gun company. The French cavalry was unreformed
having refused to hold or take ground.[27]

Despite the embarrassing surprise of long-range Mauser and Krupp fire
during the South African War, British cavalry continued to rely on shock
tactics,[28] much of the doctrinal debate at the turn of the century centering
on the usefulness of the lance in regard to its cutting edge. In fact, the only
technical advance introduced in the British cavalry after the Boer War was
the 1908 pattern cavalry sword—the finest thrusting sword ever invented—
that appeared to end the controversy over point and slash.

The cavalry's determination to flaunt its mystical difference with exaggerated style was resented by the rest of the army. But an army needs an
effective mounted force, popular or not, to complete a victory. Although it
was increasingly difficult to rationalize the superiority of cold steel over a
Maxim, in an age when the airplane and motorcar were still obscure play-
things for the rich the cavalry corps remained the only de facto theater-
level maneuver force. The first enemy troops in Paris in 1815, 1870, 1940,
and 1944 were the cavalry—mounted or mechanized.

Cavalry and the Great War:
Niederwerfungsstrategie Unattained

Schlieffen's goal was to create the highest achievement of generalship—a
perfect modern Cannae, or ultimate battle of annihilation. The German military philosopher, Hans Delbrück, daring to introduce objective criticism
(*sachkritik*) into military history, identified two types of strategies, *niederwerfungsstrategie,* or battle of annihilation, the complete destruction of the
enemy mass, and *ermattungsstrategie,* the battle of exhaustion that is subdivided "into two poles: battle and maneuver."[29] The choice was between

strategic maneuver leading to one decisive battle and attrition warfare. Schlieffen's try at a bold strategic maneuver—the annihilation of French land forces in a swift campaign—would allow imperial Germany to survive a war on two fronts.

The Schlieffen plan used in 1914 needed cavalry—lots of it.[30] Every army corps required at least a brigade of cavalry for screening and reconnaissance. Further, an army reserve was required to develop the covering force battle, exploit gaps, and establish effective pursuit. "German cavalry were used as the main reconnaissance force of the army, and although still trained for mounted shock action, they were moving toward being used as mounted infantry by 1914."[31]

Heavy cavalry divisions were held ready to defeat counterstrokes by the Allied mass of maneuver (the British Expeditionary Force and French Fifth Army, which were to bear the brunt of the 1914 attack and had four cavalry divisions between them).[32] At H-hour von Moltke's vanguards slipped across the frontier and penetrated Belgian territory in much the same way German uhlans had when Blücher crossed the Rhine in 1815. An aggressive screening force shielded the marching corps from nosy French Chasseurs Ardennais. When finally confronted with prepared defenses supported by artillery and machine guns, the cavalry behaved as predicted.

By the end of the summer 1914, the Western Front had become one continuous trench line. Moltke had fumbled in achieving strategic victory, and the Great War was reduced to attrition warfare, the bloody antithesis of maneuver. Although *ermattungskrieg* allowed both attrition and maneuver, tactical movement was terminated by barbed wire and machine guns. The main battle cavalry was put out to rear pastures while the general staffs figured out how to penetrate a "modern defense." Because it had become quite impossible for infantry to advance in close order, massed-infantry or mounted assaults supported by artillery *rafales* failed dramatically. As one Canadian quipped: "We were to gallop through the 'G' in 'Gap.' They might as well have aimed for the dot in 'Futile.'"[33] The cavalry could not deliver a final shock until the trench lines were penetrated, which required suppression of enemy machine guns (the presence of one or two being sufficient to stop a brigade), and there could not be a cavalry charge until the last machine gun was captured. The problem was again how to conduct a penetration battle at corps and army level. "Breakthrough always remains the most difficult form of a decision."[34]

The army required a new type of shock weapon. The gunners proposed longer preparatory fire, and eventually artillery bombardments exceeded several weeks and churned the ground into porridge but still produced no breakthrough. Success was measured by hundreds of yards. As artillery and chemicals proved incapable, the military turned to the tank.

The Advent of Armor:
Niederwerfungsstrategie Envisioned

The Battle of Cambrai when, for the first time, infantry was persuaded to work in close accord with the tanks, conceding the dominant role to the latter.

— Maj. Kenneth L. Macksey, Royal Armoured Corps

The tracked armored fighting vehicle was designed to overcome the two greatest obstacles to infantry and cavalry advance: terrain torn into muddy craters by artillery and the surviving machine gun protected by a belt of barbed wire.

Although it was a new weapon, it was soon to become pretentious enough to demand status as a new arm and impose its own particular doctrine. As early as 1914 Lt. Col. Ernest Swinton had suggested that the armored car should be fitted with caterpillar tracks to enable it to cross trenches and flatten barbed wire entanglements.[35] The idea was not encouraged. Finally, despite the support of Sir John French, the Royal Navy (Winston Churchill, first lord of the Admiralty being a keen supporter of the tank)—but not the Army—began to experiment with Swinton's concept. By the summer of 1915, the combined efforts of the War Office and the Admiralty produced the first prototypes: "Little Willie," "Big Willie,"[36] and, finally, "Mother." Trials were held in January 1916, and Gen. Douglas Haig ordered a staff report on their suitability for combat. The French, thanks to the pioneering efforts of Gen. Jean-Baptiste Estienne (the "father of French armor"), also experimented with tracked armor and may have developed the tank first (there is some debate). However, it was the British army that first introduced rhomboidal tanks into battle, and tanks attacked on the Somme in September 1916.

The tank shocked the enemy and established the fundamentals of the infantry-armor team: "Wherever the tanks advanced we took our objectives and where they did not advance we failed to take our objectives."[37] However, despite pleas from Swinton, armor was not used in mass and the surprise was wasted. British generals defended this rush to battle as a bold calculated venture rather than an attempt to outdo the French: "Thus the lesson is that if a Commander sees an invention or a new weapon which strikes at the root of his main problem and difficulties he is justified in taking the risk and employing it as a surprise and banking on it."[38]

The immediate result of the Somme was General Haig's official recognition of the tank experiment, raising its units' status from companies to full battalions, assigning a complete staff to the Heavy Branch (as it was now called) and, most important, seeing that the original order for new tanks was multiplied by ten.[39]

One of the most fervent tank advocates, John Frederick Charles Fuller, a colonel in the infantry, lobbied for a "large scale raid" by tanks on the unbroken ground near Cambrai. Fuller, who likely accomplished more than any other man to establish tanks as a main battle force, was also the principal cause of dislike and opposition to them: "Fuller repeatedly demonstrated his disrespect for parts of nearly every element of the Army's hierarchy, be they Gunners, Cavalry, Infantry or Sappers, it was against the Cavalry he railed the most because it was cavalrymen who held the top positions."[40]

His arguments made no impression until the British attacks in Flanders had failed catastrophically. Only then did an assault on a vastly greater scale envisaged by Fuller take the fancy of the high command. The first use of tanks in large numbers took place on 20 November 1917: a British force of 476 machines supported by over 1,000 guns struck the German line near Cambrai. Results were mixed: a breakthrough was not achieved, but it was still clear that armor held the answer to battlefield impasse since the action did, at one point, achieve a wide hole in one of the strongest German sectors at slight cost to the British and severe loss to the Germans.

> At 1500 hours, leading elements of the cavalry (the Canadian Fort Garry Horse) actually were riding through the 6000 yard wide gap at Masières in the direction of Cambrai, and the rest of the Cavalry Corps were to follow. But then the decision was taken to stop the mass of horsemen because conditions were not yet ripe in view of the short time remaining before dark.[41]

The opportunity for the correct use of cavalry—in mass and as operational pursuit—was missed. The Cambrai attack continued for another seven days and, as tanks were knocked out or broke down and enemy resistance stiffened, stopped altogether. The Battle of Cambrai marked a turning point in the history of war and ensured for the tank not only its own future as a dominant weapon of war but, in the British army, a place in the order of battle. The battle also demonstrated that Fuller was to be taken more seriously. The complete impact of Cambrai was the Allied decision to form a force of 10,000 tanks for 1919. The U.S. Army now reconsidered its earlier decision against armor and ordered a tank corps formed under Brig.-Gen. S. D. Rockenbach on 26 January 1918.

Although a strategic offensive designed to knock Germany out of the war in one mighty attack, the so-called Plan 1919 (a strategic offensive incorporating masses of tanks designed to overwhelm resistance "like a flood") was never attempted, a practical application of the Fuller concept was demonstrated at the Battle of Amiens on 8 August 1918, a "black day" for the German army and "its greatest reverse since the beginning of the war."[42] Over 600 British and French tanks attacked on a 20-mile front in the largest tank battle of the war. Amiens was a second massive armored blow delivered only five days after the battle at Soissons where the French army had totally surprised the Kaiserheer with 500 new tanks (most of them two-man Renaults) and cleared the Germans from the Reims pocket.

The Amiens attack represented the third complete success for the Cambrai recipe. The offensive featured such innovations as the use of heavy tanks to carry infantry machine gun teams deep into rear areas, armored cars to attack German headquarters, and armored cavalry (groupings of horsed cavalry with Whippet light tanks). The latter, an attempt at breakthrough and pursuit, failed mainly because of incompatibility: "Horsemen could not move where armored vehicles stood up to enemy fire, horsemen went too fast for Whippets when opposition ceased."[43] For the cavalry, it had the last opportunity to justify massed horsed formations as a viable operational or tactical force. Despite some minor doctrinal disappointment for Allied planners, Amiens convinced the German high command that the war was lost. The battle over mechanized doctrine had only begun.

Controlling the Arm of Decision

At the roots of Alexander's victories, one will always find Aristotle.
—Col. Charles DeGaulle, *The Army of the Future,* 1934

Previously, tank tactics had been based on theory; now working tank doctrine was to be hammered out based on after-action reports and practical experience. By 1916, it had been suggested that the infantry platoon was about the largest formation over which one could exercise direct control. Even in corps battles, actual success was achieved by platoon and section attacks that destroyed specific machine gun nests or strongpoints. The tank attack therefore had to work in concert with the infantry at its most fundamental level. The infantry attack, by its very nature, was phased and limited in scope: deliberate pace, supporting arms recoordinated, and consolidation at each captured strongpoint. The phased, set piece attack created a doctrinal environment dominated by artillery staffs. Until the Germans introduced their assault troops, the infantry was regularly ordered to occupy ground devastated by the guns, and its mission involved knocking out surviving machine gun nests and holding the ground against counterattack. Attacks planned by artillery generals featured violent torrents of fire that "prepared" the objective, then led the infantry (gunner officers encouraged foot soldiers to lean into a barrage) toward the dazed enemy. Given success, the infantry awaited the repositioning of its own artillery to continue the battle. Hence phase lines and set piece battles. The addition of tanks to the formula identified new tactical problems. Tanks initially caused shock, but enemy morale returned as armor groped about or bogged down in craters. After-action reports noted tanks' inability to fend for themselves when surrounded by aggressive enemy infantry. The solution reached was to resurrect itself later in the Normandy *bocage*. The infantry-tank combat team introduced during the Great War became the basis for all future mechanized tactics.

The cavalry attack had different parameters. Exploitation and pursuit were essential after successful penetration. The goal was to elevate a tactical success into an operational triumph. The objective was not ground but enemy reserves and the enemy command: once chaos was created in a headquarters, panic followed—a continental army, any army, then would collapse. Initial attempted solutions offered compromise: tanks and infantry were to break the line and cavalry was to pour through the rupture. In May 1916 French officers observed lancers forming to support an attack: "They're holding all these fellows back for the breakthrough that we've been waiting for for two years. . . . You know there's nothing like a lance against machine guns."[44] However, tanks carried the inherent restrictions of limited speed, maneuverability, and mechanical dependability. The other great albatross around the tank's neck was that unlike the horse, grass and water were not enough to maintain the advance.

> The tank, with her limited fuel supply, is in infinitely greater measure the child of her base. The faster she moves, the greater her consumption of that fuel which is her life blood; the slower she moves, the less her mobility. The theory of the tank careering "promiscuous-like" about the enemy's country has little relation to fact.[45]

Traditional arms attempted to impose their own doctrinal restrictions: "The new style of attack depended on artillery intelligence which took time to collect before each fresh phase in operations."[46] Despite limitations, the cross-country mobility of the tracked vehicle created new opportunities for maintaining the momentum of a successful attack: "A novel feature of the plan was the use of tanks to carry men and supplies. The most crucial aspect of this was the ability of supply tanks to eliminate the necessity for the fatiguing infantry carrying parties."[47] Combat experience proved that although the tank's armor stopped machine gun fire and shrapnel, it did not stand up to direct artillery gunfire, which created more casualties than mechanical breakdowns. "From Amiens on, tanks were to follow, not precede the infantry to try to reduce tank casualties."[48] Following the infantry was the antithesis of the cavalry approach to battle. The crawl over torn-up ground made the tank a ponderous testudo rather than a breakthrough weapon. Only after the attack reached what was to be later called "tank country" could the cavalry be set loose. The "correct" use of armor continued to be debated. Fuller and Basil Liddell Hart favored mass. The "expanding torrent" excited the tactical mind as a concept but was not the formula to overcome defense in depth. Liddell Hart eventually agreed that following a breach, the tank "should go through and push straight ahead so long as it is backed up by the maneuver body of the unit."[49] Until the 1930s this meant a division of cavalry.

The armored debate should have centered on Platonic first principles: that is, what is a tank? Is it an infantry support weapon? If so, "infantry tanks" must conform to infantry doctrine. Is the tank simply a gun platform that gives artillery more mobility and the ability to provide greater tactical support? Then, it should be controlled by the artillery. Is the tank a logical evolution of the cavalry? If so, then the need was for "cavalry tanks" designed to conform to the tactical doctrine of a cavalry corps. The French designated their armor as assault artillery (*artillerie d'assaut*) but also referred to their armored fighting vehicles as "combat tanks." Many tank officers were former artillerymen. The distinction between "self-propelled artillery" and tanks has been hazy ever since Deville mounted cannon on half-armored tank chassis. ("Inevitably the question arose whether such machines were artillery.")[50] Fuller attempted to dispose British thinking toward the acceptance of the tank as a strategic weapon. By May 1918, he had produced a long memorandum entitled "Strategical Paralysis as the Object of the Decisive Attack" that later became Plan 1919.[51] This was mechanized battle of annihilation as Delbrück had foreseen it. Its salient points were as follows:

> The fighting power of an army lies in its organization, which can be destroyed either by wearing it down or by rendering it inoperative. The first comprises killing, wounding and capturing the enemy's soldiers— body warfare; the second in rendering inoperative his power of command—brain warfare. To take a single man as an example, the first method may be compared with a succession of wounds which will eventually result in his bleeding to death; the second—a shot through the brain. The brains of an army are its staff—Army, Corps and Divisional Headquarters.[52]

Fuller's scheme did not convert his peers. By 1919 General Estienne, a gunner, whether for diplomatic reasons or lack of real vision, began to concede the tank as handmaiden to the infantry. "This criterion, accepted by all true soldiers, establishes the incomparable worth of the tank; it is not content to aid . . . the infantry's progress, it achieves it. With the tank appears a new infantry, *armored infantry* [emphasis added]."[53] Finally, there was a renegade solution that the established arms found absolutely outrageous. It was argued that the tank was so revolutionary, so different that it should be

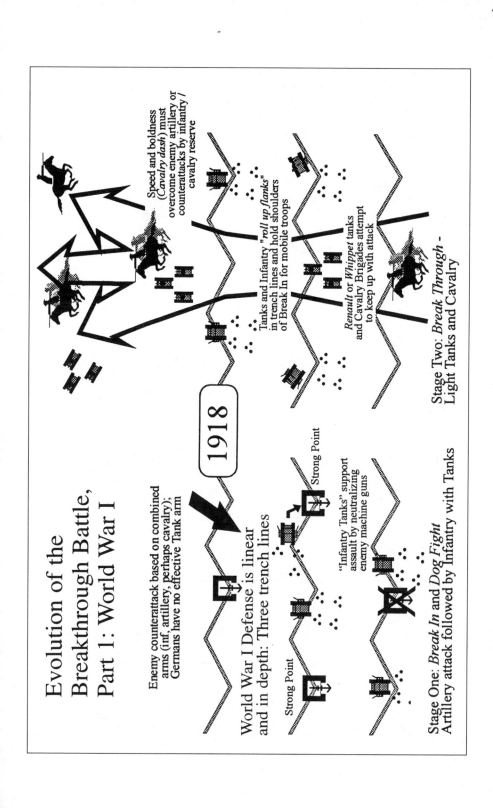

Evolution of the Breakthrough Battle, Part 1: World War I

Enemy counterattack based on combined arms (inf, artillery, perhaps cavalry); Germans have no effective Tank arm

Speed and boldness (*Cavalry dash*) must overcome enemy artillery or counterattacks by infantry / cavalry reserve

Tanks and Infantry *"roll up flanks"* in trench lines and hold shoulders of Break In for mobile troops

Renault or *Whippet* tanks and Cavalry Brigades attempt to keep up with attack

1918

World War I Defense is linear and in depth: Three trench lines

Strong Point

Strong Point

"Infantry Tanks" support assault by neutralizing enemy machine guns

Strong Point

Stage One: *Break In* and *Dog Fight*
Artillery attack followed by Infantry with Tanks

Stage Two: *Break Through* –
Light Tanks and Cavalry

recognized as a separate arm and controlled by wise men who understood its capabilities. Thus there arose the need to create a new arm and new doctrine. In Britain, this eventually became the Royal Tank Corps (RTC).

The army became concerned that the RTC's philosophy could lead to a doctrine that subordinated the other arms to "tank control." This anxiety led to predictably blustery opposition, which was not to be overcome until the winter of 1939 when panzer divisions had savaged the Polish army. The result was less the acknowledgment of a single arm's dominance but rather the acceptance of an effective method of employing the tried and true all-arms solution to winning battles (the Blitzkrieg). This was accepted in principle by 1940 but not really refined by the Allies until after 1944. The debate over what a tank is and how best to use it would continue until the end of World War II.

Notes

1. John Ellis, *Cavalry: The History of Mounted Warfare* (Devon: Westbridge, 1978), p. 139.

2. The advocates of the tank and the apostles of mobility included Winston Churchill, Ernest Swinton, Albert Stern, Murray Sueter, Tom Hetherington, William Tritton, and Walter Wilson. They were joined in 1918 by J. F. C. Fuller, B. H. Liddell Hart, H. R. Ricardo, P. C. S. Hobart, and Gifford Martel.

3. George T. Denison, *A History of Cavalry From the Earliest Times With Lessons for the Future* (London: Macmillan, 1913), p. 419.

4. Heavy cavalry (with horses 15 to 18 hands high) was armed with heavy broadswords and usually protected by body armor (the cuirass).

5. See Robert S. Quimby, *The Background of Napoleonic Warfare: The Theory of Military Tactics in Eighteenth-Century France* (New York: Columbia University Press, 1957.) Examples are Kellerman's 400 troopers hitting Zach's flank at Marengo (1800) and Murat's cuirassiers at Austerlitz and Jena (1806). The most decisive cavalry victory was Eylau (1807) where 10,700 reserve cavalry advanced 2,500 meters and shattered Russian columns. Friedland (1807) and Leipzig (1813) saw Allied cavalry quash French hopes for a last-act victory.

6. Lancers' "greatest use was as shock troops against infantry squares." Ellis, p. 40. See also the Marquess of Anglesey, *A History of the British Cavalry,* vols. I and II (London: Leo Cooper, 1973).

7. Capt. Rees H. Gronow, *The Reminiscences and recollections of Captain Gronow, being Anecdotes of the Camp, the Court, and the Clubs, and Society to the Close of the last war with France,* vol. 1 (London: 1900 – reprint of 1862 edition), p. 190.

8. The force demonstrated an impressive flexibility in an age where movement was controlled by voice, trumpet, and flag. The French were capable of maneuvering their guns as a tactical mass during a battle.

9. Gronow, p. 195.

10. "The cuirassiers laid special stress upon riding boot to boot, and never moved at a faster pace than the trot," (Bismarck). "At 150 yds from the target the

canter or trot may be increased to a gallop; the last 50 yds were at best speed. However, this was regulation—not practice," (Hohenlohe, *Conversations Upon Cavalry*).

11. Lt. Col. A. H. Burne, *The Art of War on Land.* (London: Methuen, 1950) p. 103. At Eylau (1807) as the Grenadiers à Cheval of the Imperial Guard advanced and received fire, they instinctively ducked their heads. With cavalier sang-froid their colonel shouted: "Heads up, by God! Those are bullets not turds." Ellis, p. 140.

12. When Ney ordered only Milhaud's Corps to charge, the cacophony of trumpeters sounding the advance excited both men and horses. Entire squadrons plunged forward because the horses would not be controlled. "Division after division of French cavalry were drawn into the battle, many without orders." David G. Chandler, *The Campaigns of Napoleon* (London: Weidenfeld & Nicolson, 1996), p. 148. For effect of grape shot cavalry, see Jack Coggins, *Arms and Equipment of the Civil War* (New York; Doubleday, 1962), pp. 67, 77.

13. James Lawford, *The Cavalry* (New York: Bobbs-Merrill, 1976), p. 132. Cardigan shouted at Capt Morris of the 17th Lancers during Light Brigade Charge. See Cecil Woodham-Smith, *The Reason Why* (London: Cassell, 1953).

14. Denison, p. 419.

15. "They galloped across the plain and charged the remaining Turkish trenches, using the rifle and bayonet as a lance. It was a magnificent sight to see these fellows setting their horses to jump the trenches, and at the same time lunging and thrusting with this cumbersome weapon." R. M. P. Preston, *The Desert Mounted Corps* (London: Constable, 1921).

16. "We were in fact, not infantry, but mounted riflemen." Gen. Basil W. Duke, CSA. *History of Morgan's Cavalry* (New York: Neal Publishing, 1906), p. 150.

17. Gerald F. Linderman, *Embattled Courage: The Experience of Combat in the American Civil War* (New York: Macmillan, 1987). "These cavalry fights are miserable affairs. Neither party has any idea of serious charging with the sabre. They approach one another with considerable boldness, until they get to within about forty yards, and then, at the very moment when a dash is necessary, and the sword alone should be used, they hesitate, halt, and commence a desultory fire with carbines and revolvers. . . . Stuart's cavalry can hardly be called cavalry in the European sense of the word." Ellis, p. 146.

18. Stephen Z. Starr, *The Union Cavalry in the Civil War,* vol. II (Baton Rouge: Louisiana State University Press, 1979), p. 593. "General S. D. Lee says the sword was 'little used in the late war . . . in every instance under my observation, the revolver replaced the sabre.'" "Rifle and Sabre," *Army Navy Journal* VI (11), 31 October 1868, p. 1.

19. Ellis, p. 144.

20. The American 1909 *Cavalry Journal* vowed that "the charge will always remain the thing in which it will be the cavalryman's pride to die with sword in hand."

21. Marcellin de Marbot, *Mémoires* (London: 1892). See also Brian Pohanka, "Hurricane of Sword and Horse,' *Military History,* December 1984. p. 22.

22. The artillery insisted on carrying no colors, instead it blessed its guns in formal consecrations—iron cannon became its sacred standards. The Rifle Brigade consecrates its drums.

23. Capt. C. D. Rhodes: "A normal pace in an hour was to trot for about twenty minutes, halt for ten and walk the remainder of the time. 'Walking' meant the

trooper dismounted and led his mount. It must be remembered that the troopers wore riding boots—not as comfortable as the infantry boot in a route march." Quoted in Coggins, p. 53. Maj. C. W. Devy, LSH(RC), "A Cavalry Trek Through Alberta," *Canadian Defence Quarterly* (hereafter CDQ) 3 (1934): 216. Devy records a normal hour's pace as "Halt 10 min. (loosen girth); Walk 5; Trot 10; Walk 15 (partly dismount and lead); Trot 10; Walk 10 or less."

24. "The March of A Sqn RCD from St John PQ to Petawawa Military Camp, Ontario," *Military Gazette* XV (October 1937).

25. Cavalry Training Pamphlet (Provisional) HM War Office, 1904.

26. "Doing real execution with the gun and pistol." General Duke, *History of Morgan's Cavalry.* Denison, p. 424. Also, Coggins.

27. Shelford Bidwell and Domionick Graham, *Fire Power: British Army Weapons and Theories of War 1904–1945* (Boston: George Allen and Unwin, 1985), p. 33.

28. British Cavalry Regulations of 1907 stated that "it must be accepted as a principle that the rifle, effective as it is, cannot replace the effect produced by the speed of the horse, the magnetism of the charge and the terror of cold steel."

29. Hans Delbrück, *Das Werk des Untersuchungsausschusses der Deutschen Verfassunggebendet Nationalversammlung und des Deutschen Reichstages 1919– 1926. Die Ursachen des Deutschen Zusammenbruchs im Jahre 1918,* III (Berlin, 1927), p. 346. See also Delbrück, R. H. Lutz, ed., *The Causes of the German Collapse in 1918* (Washington, D.C.: Hoover War Library Publications, No. 4).

30. Twenty-eight corps forming the German First, Second, Third, Fourth, and Fifth Armies. The northern maneuver force comprised the Second and Third Armies, containing sixteen corps, six Landwehr brigades, and five cavalry divisions.

31. Kieth Simpson, *History of the German Army* (London: Bisson, 1985), p. 82. Cavalry also conducted "colonial" operations. This included Russian and American frontier forces and British and French formations in empire service. Pershing's expedition into Mexico was more a dragoon action. British regiments in India were not trained to take on Prussian uhlans.

32. John Terraine, *Mons—The Retreat to Victory* (London: Batsford, 1960), p. 61.

33. From the South African War, in which maps did not have grid lines. A cavalry regiment was once told to ride through the "G" in "Gap" on their map. This stuck, became part of early twentieth-century cavalry banter, and was resurrected with a vengeance in the Great War. The quote is attributed to the commanding officer of the Fort Garry Horse. See Brig. Gen. J. E. B. Seely, *Adventure* (London: Hinneman, 1930). Seely commanded the Canadian 1st Cavalry Brigade in France.

34. Schlieffen, quoted in K. Krafft von Dellmensingen, *Der Durchbruch* (Hamburg: Berlin 1937), p. 405.

35. Swinton "received a brutal rebuff from generals who were not only ignorant of modern technology but were also totally committed to . . . the sanctity of personal combat." Horrific casualties and artillery's failure gave his subsequent paper, "The Armored Machine Gun Destroyer," a "more sympathetic response." Eric Morris, *Tanks* (London: Octopus, 1975), pp. 20–22. See Ernest D. Swinton, *Eyewitness: Being Personal Reminiscences of Certain Phases of the Great War, including the Genesis of the Tank* (London: Hodder & Stoughton, 1932).

36. The chosen march-past of the Royal Tank Regiment, the Royal Armored Corps, and the Royal Canadian Armored Corps is appropriately the merry English folk song, "My Boy Willie."

37. Maj. Albert Stern, quoted by Kenneth Macksey, *A History of The Royal Armored Corps and its Predecessors 1914 to 1975* (Beaminster: Newtown, 1983), p. 18.

38. Lt. Col. G. Le Q. Martel, *In the Wake of the Tank* (London: Museum Press, 1952), p. 12.

39. Macksey, p. 18.

40. Macksey, p. 19. General Robertson as commander, Imperial General Staff, General Haig as commander in chief, France, and his chief of staff, Brigadier Kiggell.

41. Macksey, p. 26.

42. *Schlachten des Weltkriegs* XXXVI (1931): 196.

43. The first reference to "cavalry tanks" originated with the Medium A or Whippet in 1917, a faster tank (8 mph versus 5 mph for the slower Mk V) was introduced as "an engineer's solution to the cavalry's insoluble problem."

44. Quoted in Ellis, p. 174.

45. V. W. Germains, *The Army Quarterly* XVI (April–July 1928): 373.

46. Dominick Graham, "Sans Doctrine: British Army Tactics in the First World War," *Technology and Tactics* (1968), p. 85.

47. W. F. Stewart, "Attack Doctrine in the Canadian Corps, 1916–1918," unpublished monograph thesis, University of Alberta, 1980.

48. Ibid., p. 199.

49. Timothy Travers and Christon Archer, eds., *The Captain Who Teaches Generals. Men at War.* p. 380. See also B. H. Liddell Hart, *Paris: or the Future of War* (New York: E.P. Dutton, 1925); *The British Way in Warfare* (London: Faber & Faber 1932); *The Future of Infantry* (London: Faber & Faber, 1933).

50. J. J. Clarke, "Military Technology in Republican France: The Evolution of the French Armored Force, 1917–1940," thesis, Duke University, 1969, and Robert Allan Doughty, *The Seeds of Disaster: The Development of French Army Doctrine 1919–1939* (Hamden: Archon Books, 1985).

51. His method was the "morcellated attack," breaking a front of 90 miles with small forces. Fuller reckoned "one tank in the attack was probably equal to 400 infantry." Macksey noted that "Fuller was an infantryman himself so he had no partisan ax to grind."

52. J. F. C. Fuller, *The Conduct of War* (London: Eyre Methuen, 1972), p. 243. Also see J. F. C. Fuller, *Lectures on FSR II* (London: Sifton Praed, 1931); *Lectures on FSR III (Operations between Mechanized Forces)* (London: Sifton Praed, 1932); *Towards Armageddon: The Defence Problem and Its Solution* (London: Lovat Dickson, 1937).

53. J. B. Estienne: *Conférence faite le 15 février 1920,* quoted in Clarke, p. 57.

A Stug III assault gun with Canadian infantry. Built on a Pz III chassis, its low silhouette made it an effective tank destroyer. *(Bell, National Archives of Canada, Wilfred Laurier University, Laurier Centre for Military Strategic and Disarmament Studies)*

CHAPTER 2

North American Tank Forces

Mechanized warfare had a natural attraction for this great nation.
—Lt. Gen. Gifford le Q. Martel[1]

In 1917, the War Department approved a U.S. Army Tank Corps of twenty-five battalions. The corps began by training at British and French schools and equipping itself with foreign machines until American factories began mass production. Despite serious attempts, only twenty-six tanks were built before war's end and none went overseas. The initial force comprised three groups, the 344th and 345th Tank Battalions and 301st Heavy Tank Battalion; by November 1918 there were four tank brigades.[2] In their first actions, the tank force experienced serious mechanical breakdown ("ditching"): at St. Mihiel, out of forty-nine U.S. tanks lost only three were attributed to enemy fire. Tanks' mechanical dependability was to remain a persistent factor in the cavalry-infantry debate over tanks' operational role.

U.S. armored doctrine was founded on British and French training and their tanks. The U.S. Army's approach to war was academically thorough: it quickly appreciated that existing doctrine simply did not fit the new war, and a Doctrinal Center was established in Chaumont, France. The term "lessons learned" was noticed in a captured German report in June 1917, translated and adopted as the best system to offer "information to all concerned."[3] The War Department immediately created a new post, assistant chief of staff, G5 Training. Its first appointee was Gen. H. B. Fiske, who insisted on "American doctrine" and "complete emancipation from Allied supervision" to create an

> entirely homogeneous American army in which the sense of initiative and self-reliance upon the part of all officers and men has been developed to the very highest degree. An American army cannot be made by Frenchmen or Englishmen. . . . The tactics and techniques of our Allies are not suited to American characteristics or the American mission in this

war. The French do not like the rifle, do not know how to use it, and their
infantry is consequently too entirely dependent upon a powerful artillery
support. Their infantry lacks aggressiveness and discipline. The British
infantry lacks initiative and resource.[4]

Fiske's headquarters translated and "Americanized" British and French
manuals (more than 100 publications before war's end) and initiated its
own lessons learned pamphlets. "Tentative Lessons Bulletins" identified
important changes in Allied and enemy doctrine and proposed recommendations to improve combat effectiveness. One early suggestion was the creation of a "mechanized corps with new antitank weapons and equipment."
The interest in "correct" doctrine created its own bureaucratic watchdogs.
The G5 shop produced "inspectors," "monitors," and, "perhaps Doctrinal
Commissars."[5]

French influence on the Americans had begun in the Revolutionary
War and was to continue. The Tank Corps quickly ordered copies of French
tanks and the U.S. artillery was soon virtually *française* in style if not temperament: 75mm (the famous *soixante-quinze*) and 155mm guns formed the
basis of the U.S. Army's direct and indirect fire to the end of World War II
and beyond. By the time the Armistice was signed the Tank Corps consisted
of 1,235 officers and 18,977 enlisted men. By May 1919 most of these
troops had been discharged. Like the French, the Americans disbanded their
tank corps in 1920 and placed the remnants under infantry command. Tank
officers attempted to propose a reasonable alternative to critics of the arm
who "denounce the tank as a freak development of trench warfare which
has already outlived its usefulness."[6] American armor had to fight a rear
guard action within the infantry branch. The more courageous ventured to
propose doctrine that while not endorsing Fuller, in effect advocated his
aim:

> All that is claimed for the Tank Corps is that it is not fettered by English
> ideas in operation which are applicable only by the English or by their
> clumsiness in design; nor by French low mechanical knowledge . . . nor
> by our own abnormal use of Tanks with the First American Army. . . . He
> [Ludendorff] is correct in stating that Tanks should be used in masses or
> not at all.[7]

That year, General Pershing testified before Congress that tanks should
remain a supporting arm of the infantry. As a result, the National Defense
Act disestablished the Tank Corps, directed that tanks be assigned to the
infantry, and denied the establishment of an armored branch (this legisla-
tion was not to be lifted until 1950). Postwar U.S. doctrine continued to
reflect French thinking. In 1920, U.S. Army Capt. Joseph Viner would state
the following thinking:

The tank should be recognized as an infantry supporting and accompanying weapon, incapable of independent, decisive, strategic and generally, tactical action. The infantry, or other formed troops, must accompany or immediately follow the tanks. Otherwise no ground will be held, as tanks can neither consolidate nor hold ground for any length of time any position taken. The tanks must operate as a result of certain decisions and plans of maneuver made by infantry or other formed troops. There is no such thing as an independent tank attack.[8]

Captain Viner's harsh evaluation was in direct contradiction of Fuller's theories but was not refuted by tank converts. Brig. Samuel Rockenback, chief of the Tank Corps and an armor pioneer wrote that "tanks should not, as a general rule, be employed in the attack of first-line positions in offensive operations."[9] The jury on U.S. armor was out and would stay sequestered until well into World War II. The army's argument against tanks was threefold: (a) tanks are of value only in trench warfare; (b) we will probably never again be engaged in truly "trench warfare"; and (c) the tank is mechanically untrustworthy and therefore unfit to be depended on in a crisis.[10]

Capt. Dwight D. Eisenhower (whose lineage was infantry and tanks) attempted a rebuttal:

Many officers who served with fighting divisions never had an opportunity to take part in an action with these machines, and their knowledge of the power and deficiencies of the tank is based on hearsay. . . . As the number of American manned tanks that actually got to take part in the fighting with American divisions was very small, the number of officers of the Army who are open advocates of this machine is correspondingly few.[11]

But in the end Eisenhower, like the majority of army tank officers, made no attempt to fight the new order and agreed that tanks were underpowered and mechanically unreliable. His response to the soundest, and therefore the most difficult to answer, of all arguments used against the tank, its mechanical inefficiency, was based on optimistic faith in the future rather than real technical breakthrough. "The clumsy, awkward and snail-like progress of the old tanks must be forgotten, and in their place we must picture this speedy, reliable and efficient engine of destruction."[12] He correctly understood that it was maneuver, not attack alone that would prove the value of the tank.

The charge of a German cavalry brigade at Vionville, in 1870, against the flank of the advancing French infantry, saved an army corps from certain annihilation. In the same battle, on another flank, the charge of a squadron saved a brigade. There is no doubt that in similar circumstances in the

future tanks will be called upon to use their ability of swift movement and
great firepower in this way against the flanks of attacking forces.[13]

The requirement for maneuver by the cavalry and the infantry's
demand for armored protection would lead to the stopgap compromise of
infantry tanks and cavalry tanks (or "combat cars" as the Cavalry was
forced to name them). Modern officers attempted to clear the air and suggest doctrinal solutions. Maj. Bradford G. Chynoweth wrote in a *Cavalry
Journal* article that "cavalry is a compounded arm—mobile yet ineffective
in combat. . . . The tank is a special, technical, and vastly powerful weapon.
It is neither a cavalryman nor an infantryman. What is wanted, then, is neither infantry tanks nor cavalry tanks, but a Tank Corps."[14]

Interestingly enough, the rebuttal was by Maj. George S. Patton, Jr.,
arguably the most experienced tank officer in the U.S. Army, but also a
confirmed cavalryman. However, despite his romanticism, Patton was a
practical soldier and would soon accept both GHQ "infantry" tank battalions and the creation of an armored force without cavalry. But in 1921 he
grumbled that "I must begin by a most vigorous dissent from the writer's
picture of a senile and impotent cavalry . . . [which] now as always must
advance by enveloping. When the ground as in France, was so limited as to
prevent this, cavalry must await the breakthrough made by tanks."[15]

Despite considerable tank experience in France, Patton preferred to
argue for retention of the horse rather than a liberation of armor from
infantry control. Unqualified faith in their chargers was to dominate U.S.
Army cavalry thinking into World War II. Surprisingly, a large number of
senior cavalry officers were only too glad to have the tank controlled by the
infantry.

> The tank should be recognized as an infantry supporting and accompany-
> ing weapon, incapable of independent, decisive, strategic, and generally,
> tactical action . . . tanks can neither consolidate nor hold ground for any
> length of time . . . it is the infantry commander on the ground who must
> issue the tactical orders for the actual employment of tanks.[16]

The Tank Board itself, despite the presence of Patton, Viner, and James
E. Ware had concluded that "Tank Service should be under the general
supervision of the Chief of Infantry and should not constitute an independent service."[17] Given the board's expertise, it was difficult to argue. Brig.
Gen. S. D. Rockenbach, chief of the Tank Corps before it was disbanded,
wrote: "Tanks must be a purely offensive arm, developing and possessing
powerful means to help the infantry in its supreme mission—the attack,
penetration and occupation of ground."[18] Notwithstanding intrepid trials on
Salisbury Plain, U.S. tactical thinking was less influenced by Fuller than by
French Marshal Petain: "Infantry will in time perhaps be carried in tanks,

but for the present, the tank is an infantry arm working in the midst of the infantry."[19]

Ave Vale Atque: The U.S. Tank Corps, 1920–1930

When the National Defense Act abolished the Tank Corps and ordered it absorbed by the infantry, there was no armored Billy Mitchell to tilt against Washington. The Tank School was taken over by the chief of infantry and relocated at Fort Meade, Maryland.[20] What armor remained was substantial—over 1,000 U.S.-built tanks, some completed as recently as 1919. Most of them were the tiny two-man M1917 (copies of the French Renault), but about 100 were formidable Mk VIIIs modeled after a British series—slow (6.5 mph), rough and unreliable: "Its vibration is so great that engine bolts must be tightened after each three hours of running time."[21] Nevertheless, these were to be the only tanks available to the War Department until 1930. The British army faced the same problem; only three cadre tank battalions were saved for the postwar army, reduced from thirty-five tank battalions. However, the world's only new tank was British, the Vickers Medium, of which 100 had been produced by 1923. These, Fuller was careful to note, remained for sixteen years the sole medium tank in the British army.

Although little was initiated in Fort Meade,[22] foreign activity prompted American research. When in 1927 the British army formed the Experimental Tank Force, the postwar period's first armored formation, the U.S. secretary of war, Dwight Davis, visited Britain on an inspection tour, and promptly ordered Chief of Staff Gen. Charles P. Summeral to "organize a Mechanized Force." This decision created "jittery brass hats" of infantry and cavalry who immediately began to lobby for arms that "motors and tanks could not displace."[23]

By 1 July 1928 the "gasoline brigade" was established at Fort Eustis, Virginia. The tanks were old, few in number, and prone to regularly breaking down. The brigade was disbanded by 20 September of the same year, and so there was no tank formation available for doctrinal experimentation. The first tank produced since the war was manufactured by Cunningham and Sons at the instruction of the chief of infantry, Maj. Gen. Robert H. Allen. The T1 Light Tank was considered a drastic improvement over World War I U.S. tanks, but its performance was still far from satisfactory. A second light tank, the T1-E1 was built in 1928. The only serious competition was a private venture, a tank that was capable of 42.5 mph on tracks and 70 mph on wheels, the Christie tank. J. Walter Christie was both a brilliant maverick and a determined visionary who unfortunately produced a tank so revolutionary that it promptly alienated the entire military establishment. Even its admirers called this tank a "wildcat," and the Ordnance Corps insisted that it was structurally unsound and only good for flashy demonstrations. Nevertheless, the tank's performance at these exhibitions drew the enthusiastic attention of American and foreign tank experts alike.

Despite the stalemate in the mechanization debate, it was clear that a new armored vehicle had to be tested if the U.S. Army was to remain au courant with Europe. When Congress passed the 1929 budget, $250,000 was appropriated for the purchase of "six to eight light T1-E1 tanks for service test by the infantry." The new chief of infantry, Gen. Stephen O. Fuqua, modified the provision to permit the purchase of five to six Christie tanks instead. However, the officer responsible, Maj. Gen. Samuel Hof, opposed the Christies.[24] Hof decided that one model was sufficient, spent $62,000 for a single Christie, and returned the remaining money to the U.S. Treasury. Angry reaction to this move resulted in a congressional hearing, which concluded on 30 June 1932 that the $250,000 would be spent entirely and solely for the Christie tank. This small victory for armor advocates was diminished by news that the British Experimental Mechanized Force had been disbanded.

The independent Mechanized Force was finally re-created as the last act of the outgoing chief of staff, Gen. Charles P. Summerall, just before he handed command over to Douglas MacArthur. The formation was based at Fort Eustis and commanded by Gen. Daniel Van Voorhis ("the grandfather of U.S. armor"),[25] and it soon featured a sensible gathering of an all-arms team. The re-creation of the experimental Mechanized Force was regarded as a threat by the infantry, and its grumbling prompted the secretary of war to publicly assure the army that the employment of this force would in no way diminish the role of infantry tanks.

The actual role of tanks was still being argued. In 1929, Col. Adna Romanza Chaffee, Jr., had delivered a lecture on mechanization in the army at the Army War College but had been called "visionary and crazy."[26] Nevertheless, the impact of motor transport and the effect of mechanization on the world's military could not be ignored. In 1931, President Hoover ordered MacArthur to conduct a survey to determine whether the cavalry was obsolete. The cavalry reacted quickly and cleverly. The chief of cavalry, Maj. Gen. Guy V. Henry, inspired by Van Voorhis, persuaded MacArthur to assign the resurrected Mechanized Force to the cavalry. MacArthur declared:

> Cavalry acquired its name when soldiers mounted on horses were able to move more rapidly than any other arm. . . . Thus there has grown up a very natural conception that cavalry must include the horse. Modern firearms have eliminated the horse as a weapon, and as a means of trans-

portation he has become, next to the dismounted man, the slowest means of transportation. . . . To enable the cavalry to develop its organization and equipment so as to maintain its ability under modern conditions to perform its missions . . . the Mechanized Force will be reorganized as a reinforced cavalry regiment.[27]

Combat Cars at Fort Knox

By the end of May 1931, the Mechanized Force at Fort Eustis was disbanded and the remnants assigned to the cavalry. Armor's new home was to be Fort Knox, Kentucky. The new commander was Colonel Chaffee. Because allowing the assignment of tanks to the cavalry would have required an act of Congress, Chaffee instead adopted the term "combat car" for cavalry tanks—and was promptly considered a traitor by some cavalry officers. The old guard, led by Gen. Hamilton S. Hawkins, warned that mechanized cavalry was a rival to horse cavalry and began an *apologia pro equitati suum* (a justification for mounted warriors) that would not end until 1945. The Hawkins lobby argued the job of the Mechanized Force was to support the horse. The horse versus tank debate split the ranks of the cavalry, but there were no local philosophes to propose an American solution. Furthermore, the writings of Fuller and Liddell Hart were too extremist for all but the RTC. German and French thinking remained in a formative and experimental phase.

In hindsight, much of the 1930s debate dealt with trivia. Advocates of mechanized warfare complained that the cavalry tank was shackled to the horse; confirmed cavalrymen refused to admit that the horse was passé. In a 1933 *Cavalry Journal* article, Patton reaffirmed that "machines will always be preceded by horsemen." Meanwhile, the infantry continued to complain that its exclusive rights to tanks were being infringed upon. The Mechanized Force conducted three exercises at Fort Riley, Kansas, which included armored units and a brigade of cavalry. By the fourth exercise, the horsed cavalry was operating against the Mechanized Force using scout cars, not horses. The superior maneuverability of mechanized forces did more to annoy than inspire cavalrymen. Chaffee attacked his colleagues' reticence:

> They seemed blind to the possibilities of a mechanized cavalry. I believe that mechanization and horses will not greatly mix within the cavalry division. Those fellows at Riley ought to understand that the definition of cavalry now includes troops of any kind equipped for highly mobile combat and not just mounted on horses. The motto of the School says, "Through Mobility We Conquer." It does not say, "Through Mobility on Horses Alone We Conquer."[28]

The U.S. Cavalry was not a complete technological stick in the mud. Revised tactics included roles for aircraft and motor transport, but these were solely to augment the horse. Large "portee" trucks were used to transport cavalry regiments to save the mounts' legs. These were logistical, not tactical, answers. So, although the cavalry secured a minor triumph in seizing control of the Mechanized Force in 1931, the doctrinal infighting negated any real progress for armor.[29] Furthermore, internal debate weakened any defense against the infantry lobby, thus inducing MacArthur to state again that "the principal doctrine of the tank is to support infantry." Doctrinal mechanized development was actually split between the two branches: the Infantry School maintained its own Tank Section.

In 1933 the German Army sent liaison officers to visit Fort Knox. Van Voorhis recalled that "the Germans were less interested in equipment than our views of the proper tactical and strategic employment of mechanized forces."[30] However, the cavalry was preoccupied with internal differences, and the infantry continued to mirror French doctrine, one platoon of tanks being considered proper to support one infantry battalion. However, this was 1918 French thinking. By the 1930s the French army itself had begun to favor "breakthrough tanks" and develop new vehicles. The U.S. Army could not afford to keep pace. The 1934 budget had restricted spending, and there were not enough of the new Christies to allow any proper testing.

There was no identified doctrinal requirement simply because there was no U.S. Army tank doctrine. "Breakthrough" remained a Fulleresque concept, although bright minds on the Continent had realized that tanks had more to offer than knocking out machine gun nests. The cavalry, while it could not agree on the future of the horse, still sought a modern solution. The union with combat cars was awkward at best. As the *Infantry Journal* observed, cavalry and infantry "overlapped each other"; combined exercises served only to confuse traditionalists. The behavior of tanks was enigmatic: they were slow, noisy, and sat around in hull-down positions for suspiciously long times—and they often disappeared. The *Infantry Journal* could not help asking: "Where do they go and what do they do during these long pauses?"

By 1936, while the Americans were still debating the horse, the Germans and Russians each had raised an armored corps. Although German army delegations had toured Fort Knox, the Germans decided they had nothing to learn from the Americans.[31] But Chaffee remained determined: in 1934 he asked the chief of cavalry for self-propelled gun mounts. Mounted rifle troops were added and an observation flight not only was requested but was actually attached to the 7th Cavalry Brigade (Mechanized) by 1937. Concurrently, the Italian army was employing scores of CV 3/33 light tanks in Ethiopia while both Republicans and Fascists were deploying armored battalions in Spain. This may have prompted the British army to finally form a Mechanized Cavalry Division. The U.S. response was to mechanize another cavalry regiment (the 4th) and send it to Fort Knox.

The 1936 budget forced the U.S. Army to make a choice: more light tanks for the cavalry or new medium tanks for the infantry. The new policy dictated that infantry divisions would acquire infantry tanks for the main battle, while mechanized cavalry divisions would concentrate on its traditional mission of reconnaissance and security. This definition of the traditional mission ignored completely the historically more patriarchal role of heavy cavalry: dominating the main battle. This was not reconsidered until well after the fall of Poland.[32]

U.S. Military attaché reports from Spain were subject to close interpretation and fed both sides of the debate, giving heart to infantrymen and gunners alike. Col. A. Fuquo, the attaché in Madrid, reported that "tanks did not prove themselves." Although armored formations had done impressive things, reports began to arrive acclaiming the effects of the German 37mm antitank gun. If antitank guns could dispense with tanks, then theories put forward by armor advocates could be dismissed and the infantry would reign supreme.[33] The chief of infantry, Maj. Gen. George A. Lynch, ordered the army tank manual rewritten in 1938 because the antitank gun discredited tanks. The two arms' chiefs, Lynch and Maj. Gen. John K. Herr (chief of cavalry) were directly responsible for retarding the development of the U.S. tank force. As late as November 1940, both Herr and Lynch opposed Maj. Gen. Frank M. Andrews (G3) when he recommended to Gen. George Marshall that "the Armored Force be created as a separate combat arm." Their personal bias against mechanization hamstrung armored doctrinal thinking until 1941.[34]

Myopia was not exclusive to the infantry and cavalry. The artillery ordered the Christie tank and Holt gun carriage tested in 1923, but found them "devoid of tactical usefulness for light guns and howitzers."[35] Gunners were also loath to abandon the horse. By the mid-1930s the chief of artillery finally approved pneumatic tires for gun carriages. The gunners' self-assurance (despite Lynch's insistence that it was the infantry that gave an army its character) continued until the formation of the Army Ground Force (AGF) and the powerful influence of Gen. Leslie McNair. The belief that the antitank gun, not the tank, was the proper way of dealing with enemy armor was to dominate AGF doctrine until the end of World War II. In 1939, as Europe entered its second conflict, the U.S. Army found itself with no tank force, no effective main battle tank, and, most crucial, no clear doctrine.

North American Tank Forces:
Canadian Cavalry and Mechanization

My legs are bowed from riding on a 'orse when in the ranks.
They took away my 'orse and spurs and shoved me in the tanks.
I've spent me life with 'orses and I loved the work and toil,
But I can't stand these new fledged beasts that live on gas and oil.
                                                        —Lt. Col. C. E. Morgan[36]

The first modern Allied armored formation on the Western Front of
World War I was the Canadian Motor Machine Brigade, whose armored
cars distinguished themselves throughout 1916–1917.[37] By 1918 the
Canadian Corps, the most powerful self-contained striking force on any
battle front, had perfected the corps offensive while its fledgling armor
developed self-propelled artillery. With a foot in the doctrinal door the
Canadian army went on to order real tanks. The Canadian 1st Tank
Battalion (commanded by Lt. Col. R. L. Denison) was authorized in May
1918 (a second battalion was formed in the fall). Denison's outfit arrived in
Britain on 21 June and began training. After trials at Bovington the unit
(806, all ranks) was sent to France but did not see action. By May 1919
both battalions were disbanded.

By war's end, with little fanfare, Ottawa had developed the nucleus of
a mechanized force capable of keeping Canadian armor on a par with the
latest in European developments. But this was not to happen. Military
requirements were subordinated to British Empire needs, and the British
army preferred well-filled infantry divisions to Dominion tank units. The
Canadian military continued to define itself in British terms: drill, uniforms, weapons, and doctrine. The Canadian army of the 1930s was, as
Maurice Pope described it, "British through and through with only minor
differences imposed upon us by purely local conditions." In direct contradiction to Gen. Sir Arthur Currie's independent problem solving, and splendidly victorious staff,[38] "Canadian officers [seemed] even more dependent
on the British to do their thinking for them. . . . Reluctant to work out solutions before they saw the British answer, they were also hesitant to use their
imagination."[39] This was not altogether disadvantageous: the postwar
British Empire remained a formidable force, the British army, a first-class
fighting machine. As a part of the empire, the Canadian army was supported by a first-class staff and logistics system. The only caveat was that it
operated under the direction of Whitehall, which had its own agenda—Gen.
Sir Archibald Montgomery-Massingberd, commander of the Imperial
General Staff, 1933–1936, "insisted that the army role was not to fight in a
major war but to defend and police the Empire."[40] Meanwhile, the British
army, chuffed with victory, was enjoying the comfort of empire garrison
duty. Fuller tells of an officer who said to him on the day of the Armistice:

"Thank God we can now get back to real soldiering." By war's end, even Ottawa was anxious to rid itself of a too large and too expensive machine that was really only good for killing Germans.

The Canadian army abandoned its corps structure, dispersed its divisions, and even declined to field brigades. With the disbanding of the Motor Machine Gun Brigade there was no force left to argue on behalf of armor. The development of tank doctrine was left to the British War Office that could not make up its mind: "It must be borne in mind that the Royal Tank Corps is always experimenting; no drill or tactics are definitely laid down; all is still in process of organization and discussion."[41] Without an RTC of its own, the Canadian army resurfaced as a better model of the force that had participated in the Boer War.

The army was reduced to three infantry battalions and two cavalry regiments, and the cavalry contented itself with traditional missions. Lord Strathcona's Horse and the Royal Canadian Dragoons were divided into independent squadrons, stationed thousands of miles apart, and conducted training better suited to garrison duty in Palestine or India. Unlike the U.S. Cavalry, which had an operational task of screening the Mexican border, the Canadian cavalry simply maintained its skills as a nucleus for future wars: it remained on the periphery of tactical evolution. "We do not want our leading patrols to gallop blindly into ambush as the French cavalry so often did in 1914—but we want them to go straight for their enemy mounted whenever they have a reasonable chance of doing so and establish a moral ascendancy."[42]

If there was a doctrinal argument, it was concerned with mobility until it became patent that motorization had completely revolutionized transportation and logistics.[43] The superior mobility of a cavalry division was now best demonstrated only in rough terrain. Well into the 1930s, horsed formations could maneuver with ease in areas tanks could only advance at infantry pace, the average march rate being 5 to 8 miles per hour.[44] One solution was to share traditional cavalry roles with motorized or mechanized units. During the postwar decade several trials were conducted. The arrival of two Vickers light tanks in 1927 did little to encourage tank advocates. Worse, after the 1929 crash all permanent force training was stopped.

In 1930, a mechanized course was begun in Kingston, Ontario, based on twelve Carden Lloyd Machine Gun Carriers and evolved into post graduate tactical field training at Camp Petawawa, Ontario.[45] Experience gained resulted in the founding of the Canadian Armored Fighting Vehicle (CAFV) School in Camp Borden, Ontario, the home of Canadian armor. This was a pocket version of the Fort Knox experiment under Chaffee: a squadron of Cardon Lloyds and a squadron of cavalry (Royal Canadian Dragoons). The stakes, however, were considerably less. Fort Knox threatened the very existence of the U.S. Cavalry; the CAFV School simply provided craftsmen and technicians. Doctrinal development was secondary and demonstrated when the school refused a Christie tank.[46] However, by the late 1930s, although the requirements of empire service remained paramount, there was plenty of nationalist urging for a Canadian approach to war, as in: "We are no longer tied to the apron strings of the Motherland."[47]

More important to future battlefield operations was the domination of Canadian arms by the artillery. Between 1905 and 1939, seventy-five Canadian officers had been awarded a PSC (Passed Staff College) as graduates of Camberly or Quetta Staff Colleges. Two were from the Service Corps, eleven were from Signals, and twelve were from Engineers. The infantry corps was allotted twenty-one vacancies while the cavalry, through thirty-four years, was allowed a total of seven officers selected. Correspondingly, the artillery was awarded twenty-one positions, equal to the infantry and three times that of the cavalry. Only two cavalry Officers (C. C. Mann and H. W. Foster) were given advanced staff training between 1921 and 1939—both in the year hostilities began. The Canadian chief of staff, Gen. Andrew McNaughton "ignored infantry and cavalry officers in the 1930s. . . . The simple fact that infantry and cavalry officers were bypassed in the selection for staff college meant that they were ineligible and unready for senior commands in 1939."[48]

Canada had produced its own Leslie McNair. The gunner cabal that dominated the development of both the AGF and the Canadian army deserves examination and, likely, some criticism. The professional results achieved by McNaughton would speak for themselves.[49]

By 1939 the Canadian cavalry had passed effortlessly from horse to tank. Unlike their colleagues in the United States, there were no bitter doctrinal battles or opposing philosophies to be vanquished. There was no spiteful row between proponents of infantry tanks and cavalry tanks. This happened because the Canadian cavalry missed the interim step: partial mechanization and its accompanying baggage—the struggle for doctrinal control. The Department of National Defence (DND) estimate was simple and practical: "Tanks cost a great deal and become obsolete rapidly so we shall never have many of them."[50] Like their American counterparts, Canadian infantry and artillery generals were seduced by continental theories: "Attacking tanks will soon be rendered powerless by the surviving anti-tank weapons."[51] The senior staff seems to have spent as much energy planning an invasion of the United States as it did in producing a Dominion template for a European war.[52] But then Canada was not within a Luftflotte's or Panzer division's striking distance—not that this would have been a factor judging by Ottawa's reaction to blitzkrieg.[53] Immediately after panzers invaded Poland, DND canceled the advanced Militia Staff College course. "Incredibly, the catalyst that should have stirred an interest in staff training, i.e., the war, was the reason given to terminate the training."[54]

In contrast to the Americans and British, the Canadian mechanization debate was not a blood feud within the army and cavalry but a philosophical disagreement between an E. L. M. Burns and G. G. Simonds (an engineer and a gunner) over the best type of infantry division.[55] The Simonds-Burns debate could be dismissed as an amusing footnote to Canadian mechanization if it were not for the narrow conclusions both future generals exhibited and were to carry into battle. Burns's tanks-alone theories were somewhat disquieting: he was to command the Canadian 5th Armored Division and eventually the Canadian I Corps. However, that was in the rough terrain of Italy and under a very critical Bernard Law Montgomery, and Burns did no serious damage. Simonds, on the other hand, was by far the more dangerous. His tactical opinions and predictions about the necessity of the "holding" battle were to cost him two corps victories launched simultaneously with Bradley's breakout at St. Lô in the Norman summer of 1944.

Notes

1. Lt. Gen. G. le Q. Martel, *In the Wake of the Tank* (London: Sifton Praed, 1935), p. 37.

2. Only one U.S. cavalry regiment, the 2d, was sent to France in 1917. See James M. Merrill, *Spurs to Glory—The Story of the United States Cavalry* (New York: Rand McNally, 1966). Capt. Dale E. Wilson, *Treat 'Em Rough! The Birth of American Armor, 1917–20* (Novato, Calif.: Presidio Press, 1990), pp. 55, 173.

3. Virtually all U.S. artillery manuals and many tank manuals were translations of French manuals. Robert Allan Doughty, *The Seeds of Disaster: The Development of French Army Doctrine, 1919–1939* (Hamden: Archon, 1985), pp. 100–101. See Dennis J. Vetock, *Lessons Learned—A History of US Army Lesson Learning* (Carlisle: U.S. Army Military History Institute [hereafter MHI], 1988).

4. Col. H. B. Fiske, memorandum for chief of staff: "Training," 4 July 1918. *U.S. Army in the World War 1917–1919, Reports of the Commander in Chief, Staff Sections and Services* (Washington, D.C.: U.S. Army Center of Military History [hereafter CMH] 1991), p. 304.

5. Vetock, *Lessons Learned.*

6. Capt D. D. Eisenhower, "A Tank Discussion," *Infantry Journal* 17 (5): 454.

7. Brig. Gen. S. D. Rockenbach, "The Tank Corps," lecture delivered at the General Staff College, Washington, D.C., 3 October 1919. Int, Pt 1, Miscellaneous Lectures 1919–20, U.S. Army MHI, Carlisle Barracks.

8. Capt. Joseph W. Viner, *Tactics and Technique of Tanks,* instructional pamphlet (Fort Leavenworth: 1920).

9. S. D. Rockenback, "Tanks and Their Cooperation with Other Arms," *Infantry Journal* (January 1920).

10. Eisenhower, "A Tank Discussion."

11. Eisenhower spent World War I training a tank battalion in Maryland. Ibid., p. 453.

12. Ibid., p. 457.

13. Ibid.

14. B. G. Chynoweth, "Cavalry Tanks," *Cavalry Journal* 30 (July 1921).

15. Ibid.

16. Viner, *Tactics and Technique of Tanks.*

17. Wilson, p. 211; See also Mildred Hanson Gillie, *Forging the Thunderbolt: A History of the Development of the Armed Forces* (Harrisburg, Pa.: Military Service Publishing, 1947), p. 17.

18. *Infantry Journal* (January–February 1920).

19. Quoted in Colonel Perré, "Instruction de la troupe d'infanterie en vue du combat en liaison avec les chars," *Revue d'Infanterie* LXII (November 1925): 670–686. French maneuvers insisted that tanks remain to support infantry in any situation. Tankers breaking forward were accused of *"faire cavalier seul,"* or operating independently. Fuller's theories were dismissed as "a dangerous utopia, happily unrealizable." Colonel Alléhaut, "Motorisation," *Revue d'Infanterie* LXXII–LXXIII (February–July 1928): 425.

20. At disbandment, the American Expeditionary Force Tank Corps numbered 752 officers and 11,277 enlisted men, with an additional 483 officers and 7,700 enlisted men in tank units in Camps Colt and Polk. Here was a painful aftermath: "Rockenbach lost his star, reverting to the rank of colonel . . . Patton and Mitchell, commanders of the 304th and 305th Tank Brigades at Meade both lost their eagles and pinned on captain's bars at the end of the month." Wilson, p. 214.

21. "Intercommunication came by touch and hand signal, for a shout could not overcome the clamor of the engine and tracks: yet each change of direction was a team effort, when it required shifting of the main gears, and locking of the differential and braking action by a 'steering gearsman'—each by a different person." K. Macksey and J. H. Batchelor, *Tank—A History of the Armored Fighting Vehicle* (New York: Ballantine, 1971), p. 25.

22. The 1st Tank Regiment, "the Heavies," had a distinct Royal Tank Regiment mentality. Crittenberger recalls reporting to Fort Meade with an Olympic gold medal for marksmanship that did not impress his colonel: "Well young man, let me tell you this—we have *no* rifles, and *no* place in a Tank Regiment for a rifleman." Memoirs, Crittenberger Papers MHI.

23. Gillie, 21.

24. The problem was both Christie and his exciting machine: "mechanically unreliable . . . Christie was difficult to deal with . . . the Ordnance Department refused to deal with him." Interview, Professor George F. Hoffman. U.S. Army War College, Carlisle Barracks, August 1995.

25. U.S. armor has an extensive family tree: a grandfather of armor (Van Voorhis), a father of armor (Chaffee), a godfather of armor (Rockenbach), and a wicked stepmother of armor (Herr), who is also the patron saint of the U.S. Cavalry in that he died that the horse may live.

26. Chaffee: "I had the honor of being told by the President of the War College that my lecture was visionary and crazy." Quoted in Gillie, p. 43. See address by Col. A. R. Chaffee, "Mechanized Cavalry," Army War College, 31 September 1929, MHI.

27. Report of the Secretary of War, 1931 in Gillie, p. 48.

28. Ibid., p. 68.

29. Formed out of the 1st Cavalry Regiment ("'oldest and best-known regi-

ment of horsemen in America' . . . the surrender of their horses for tanks was cause for the deepest mourning," Gillie, p. 58), 15th Cavalry, and 68th Field Artillery ordered to Fort Knox for "training in mechanized warfare."

30. Gillie, p. 85.

31. "We believe that the German's tactics followed what Chaffee had been preaching because we had German officers coming to Fort Knox quite frequently." Col. H. H. D. Heiberg Papers, Patton Library, Fort Knox. General Grow in a 10 February 1950 letter to Lieutenant Colonel Gondek recalls a German staff visit to Fort Knox in 1934/1935: "Rommel may have been one." Hofmann Collection: Maj. Gen. Robert W. Grow's diary July 1938. Maj. Gen. R.W. Grow (hereafter Grow) papers, MHI.

32. See: Janusz Piekalkiewicz, *The Cavalry of World War II* (London: Orbis, 1979).

33. "The War Department in 1938 modified its 1931 directive for all arms and services to adopt mechanization and motorization. Thereafter, the development of mechanization was to be accomplished by two of the combat arms only—the cavalry and the infantry." Mary Lee Stubbs and Stanley Russell Connor, *Armor Cavalry* (Washington, D.C.: Office of Chief of Military History [hereafter OCMH], 1972), p. 56.

34. Their argument was that it "violated" the terms of the National Defense Act of 1920 in creating "non-infantry and non-cavalry armored units." *Cavalry Journal* (May–June, 1946): 38. For Herr's side, see: Maj. Gen. J. K. Herr and E. S. Wallace, *The Story of the US Cavalry* (Boston: Little Brown, 1953), pp. 248–262.

35. See "Report of Field Artillery Board 1923." Also *Field Artillery Journal* XIII (1923); XXVII (1937); IXXX (1939); and "Artillery and the Tank," XXX (1940). For more balance, see "Obsolescence of Horse Drawn Artillery," *Army and Navy Register* (16 May 1937).

36. Lt. Col. C. E. Morgan, "Trooper Jones Laments Transfer to the Tank Corps," *Canadian Military Gazette* 50–51 (December 1936): 22.

37. The unit was initially organized as squadrons (eight cars with sixteen Vickers heavy machine guns, two per car. The remainder was carried in specially constructed light trucks (top speed 25 mph). "The tactical armored car unit is four cars and so must not be split up." Lt. Col. W. K. Walker: "The Great German Offensive March 1918 With Some Account of the Work of the Canadian Motor Machine Gun Brigade," *CDQ* 2 (1924): 412.

38. "Most people agreed . . . that the Canadians were the best troops on the western front." James Morris, *Farewell the Trumpets: An Imperial Retreat* (Harmondsworth: Penguin, 1980), p. 213.

39. Stephen J. Harris, *Canadian Brass: The Making of a Professional Army 1860–1939* (Toronto: University of Toronto Press, 1988), pp. 203–205.

40. John A. English, *The Canadian Army and the Normandy Campaign—A Study of Failure of High Command* (New York: Praeger, 1991), p. 25.

41. Maj. T. V. Scudmore, "The Vickers Light Tank," *CDQ* 5 (1927–1928): 321.

42. Lt. Col. H. V. S. Charrington, MC, "The Employment of Cavalry," *Military Gazette* 6 (1927–1928).

43. Logistics for a cavalry division were "[for a] maneuver of 300 miles a mere twenty petrol lorries would suffice to refill the whole brigade [compared to] an ordinary division which includes 740 horse drawn vehicles [and] 360 motor vehicles needed to bring up its supplies, baggage and ammunition as it is crawling along at fifteen miles a day rate." *Army Gazette* XXII (April–July 1933): 58.

44. Maj. C. W. Devy, Lord Strathcona's Horse (Royal Canadians), "A Cavalry Trek Through Alberta." In the other great march (St. Jean, Quebec, to Petawawa, Ontario) the Royal Canadian Dragoons squadron covered 320 miles in 13 days. *CDQ* 3 (1934): 216.

45. See Lt. N. G. Duckett, "Mechanized Transport Vehicles at Petawawa Camp"; "Recent Mechanized Trials Carried out in Canada"; Maj. L. C. Goodeve, "Mechanization," *CDQ* 5 (1927–1928). The course commander was Maj. C. Foulkes, but it would be a stretch to call him "grandfather of the Royal Canadian Armoured Corps."

46. See Clara E. Worthington, *Worthy* (Toronto: Macmillan, 1961) and Brereton Greenhous, *Dragoon: The Centennial History of the Royal Canadian Dragoons, 1883–1983* (Ottawa: Guild of the Royal Canadian Dragoons, 1983).

47. Capt. A. W. Boultier, "What Price Mechanization," *CDQ* (July 1934); Maj. G. B. Soward complained that Canadians were "slavishly follow[ing] organizations that have been based upon requirements for warfare outside the [North American] continent." Harris, p. 205.

48. "From 1919–1927, when McNaughton was vice-chief of the general staff or director of staff duties, and again from 1928–1935, while he was Chief of the General Staff, fifteen artillery, ten engineer, twelve infantry two cavalry and six other branch officers went to the Staff College. Three gunners, three sappers, and only one infantry officer graduated from Imperial Defence College." Lt. Col. John A. MacDonald, "In Search of Veritable: Training The Canadian Army Staff Officer, 1899 to 1945," M.A. thesis, Royal Military College, Kingston, Ontario, 1992.

49. "Eight of the twenty-two major-generals and above who commanded divisions, corps, or the army overseas were fired for incompetence before they saw action; . . . two more were relieved after their first battle; and another survived only nine months." Harris, p. 211.

50. Maj. E. L. M. Burns, "A Step Towards Modernization," *CDQ* 12 (October 1934–July 1935): 298.

51. Chef de Battalion Baures, "The Attack Problem from an Infantry Point of View," *CDQ* 11 (October 1933).

52. "In the early 1920's, a single officer, Col. J. ("Buster") Sutherland Brown, director of military operations and intelligence was solely responsible for the formulation of strategic plans in Canada. . . . Between Dec 1920 and April 1921 . . . Brown prepared the Defence Scheme Number 1, a 200 page plan for war with the United States . . . he proposed . . . to capture key American bases at Spokane, Seattle, Minneapolis, Albany, part of Maine; as well as bridgeheads on the Great Lakes frontier from the Niagara to the St Mary's Rivers." R. A. Preston, *The Defence of the Undefended Border: Planning for War in North America 1867–1939*, (Montreal: McGill-Queens University Press, 1977), p. 217.

53. In 1936, Ottawa approved a rearmament programme with the air force and navy getting first and second priority; the DND approved four tank regiments. Preparedness for a continental war was directed by Prime Minister Mackenzie King, the only Allied leader to have actually met Hitler. See J. L. Granatstein, *Canada's War* (Toronto: Oxford University Press, 1975), pp. 55–56; Blair Neatby, *William Lyon Mackenzie King,* vol. 3 (Toronto: University of Toronto Press, 1976), pp. 279–286; James Eayrs, *In Defence of Canada—Appeasement and Rearmament,* (Toronto: University of Toronto Press, 1965), pp. 45, 197, 226.

54. MacDonald, pp. 86–87. By 1940 the year-long staff courses at Camberly and Quetta were terminated. Shorter (10to 17–week) courses were now given to empire officers at Camberly. Canadian vacancies were limited to five vacancies,

which triggered an angry protest from Gen. A. G. L. McNaughton. The DND began a Canadian staff course in the summer of 1941.

55. The opening volley was fired by Burns in his *CDQ* essay, "A Division That Can Attack," *CDQ* 14 (April 1938): 282, 297. See also E. L. M. Burns, "A Step Towards Modernization"; "Where Do Tanks Belong?" *CDQ* (March 1939): 416; G. G. Simonds, "An Army that Can Attack," *CDQ* 16 (October 1938–July 1939); "The Attack," *CDQ* (July 1939): 379–382.

Shermans of the 4th U.S. Armored Division in Lorraine. Note the mix of the under-gunned 75mm M4A3s and the much improved 76mm M4A3E8, the "Easy Eight," in the center *(U.S. Signals, U.S. Military History Institute, Carlisle, Pa.)*

CHAPTER 3

Creating a North American Armored Force: The European Influence

An American Army cannot be made by Frenchmen or Englishmen!!
—Gen. H. B. Fiske, G5, American Expeditionary Force, 1917

The development of a U.S. armored force was initially urged from within the cavalry by pioneers like Van Voorhis and Chaffee. After the 1934 Fort Riley maneuvers, new converts from the other arms embraced mechanization as the paragon future for U.S. arms.[1] This cross-fertilization created a rich professional and intellectual base that strengthened the promechanization lobby but could not overcome the political obstacles confronting their goals: the Cavalry and Infantry Departments. The infantry opposition, while unenlightened, was at least logical. Infantry tanks were better off under infantry command: the mission of the Queen of Battle was still to capture ground and hold it against counterattack. Large tank formations were of no use to staffs committed to attrition and practical, albeit limited, goals. The United States' neighbors posed no military threat, and the prospects of operational warfare against European powers was remote. Neither MacArthur, Marshall, nor succeeding chiefs of infantry were inclined to embrace tanks as an indispensable type of infantry arm.

The opposition of the cavalry hierarchy was unfortunate but should be understood as a complex process that wrestled with the quest for a practical modern doctrine. The initial opposition to tanks (1919–1933) is pardonable. Chedéville, probably unaware that he had correctly identified an operational problem, said it best: "Le char, c'est une machine très delicate." By the mid-1930s, particularly with such breakthroughs as the Christie tank and vehicles' mass production, it became clear that motorization and, therefore, mechanization would eventually dominate movement on the battlefield at the tactical, and probably the operational, level. However, like its British and French counterparts, the U.S. Cavalry remained unconvinced.

The basic argument continued that a corps of cavalry was still the only

41

arm capable of giving a field force the eyes and ears required for decisive maneuver. The horse continued to be regarded as the only dependable weapon that could accomplish the traditional missions of screening, reconnaissance, and rapid pursuit. Its commitment to the horse did not allow cavalry to resurrect the one tradition it had always been associated with: shock and the breakthrough battle. The force was prepared to accept armored cars, combat cars, and aircraft as supplementary tools, but passionately defended the role of the horse as a principle in future wars. This mixed-bag solution was to be professed at senior echelons of the cavalry as late as 1944.

The internal opposition to complete mechanization included unlikely tank veterans such as George Patton. (It must be stressed that the U.S. Cavalry did not ignore motorization and was in the vanguard of several innovations.) The question argued was whether the cavalry was to be defined as soldiers that fight on horses or was cavalry simply a generic term for mounted soldiers. One definition required hundreds of thousands of horses, the other called for equipment that would continue the cavalry spirit. The philosophical differences were inflamed by the insistence of tank purists that cavalry was dead and the tank symbolized a new era of warfare, dominated by masses of machines that attacked independently of the traditional arms and were the only key to victory in the future.

By the late 1930s this argument should have been put to rest by the experiences in Spain and at Khalkin Gol yet debate continued and opposition persisted. Worse, after-action reports from the Spanish Civil War suggesting that the antitank gun had replaced the tank were particularly well received by the Chiefs of Artillery and Infantry. MacArthur, as chief of staff, stopped the progressive mechanization movement and returned all armored fighting vehicles to the Branch Chiefs of infantry and cavalry—the very people committed to sabotaging the movement. Their reticence in accepting the inevitable is doubly confusing particularly considering the wealth of timely and accurate information provided by U.S. military attachés on developments in Europe.

Foreign Influence 1: The British Army—Excalibur Ignored

Notorious that soldiers do not read books. In fact, our own "Infantry Journal" received but failed to review FSR III. . . . Guderian read Fuller. . . . Marshall Timoshenko ordered that FSR III be made a "table book" for the Red Army.

—S. L. A. Marshall[2]

The British pioneered armored warfare and ended the Great War as the acknowledged leaders and experts. British tanks were the original breakthrough vehicles—big, menacing monsters that terrified the enemy, broke into his defenses, and overwhelmed infantry strongpoints. The British leadership in armored warfare has been extensively and exhaustively documented. The intellectual leadership demonstrated by J. F. C. Fuller[3] and Basil Liddell Hart was supported (perhaps grudgingly, but nevertheless upheld) with the result that the British army pioneered the development of the armored division during the late 1920s. Sadly, it was terminated before sufficient progress toward a true "panzer division" had been made. Converting the military masses was going to take some doing and a generous purse. Fuller's "Lectures on FSR" were a milestone in the evolution of armored doctrine. Fuller, considered by some military historians as a tank fanatic to the exclusion of combined arms, exerted influence in many of the world's armies, but failed to convince the old guard in his own patch.[4] The Fuller vision built on successful examples from medieval Mongol operations and factored in the tank. The excitement all this generated was fueled by the vision of a virtually robotic war, a technical solution to the morass of trench warfare and a promise to end wars quickly. Fuller was a maneuverist in an attritionist world, an apostle of mobility in an age where a steel and concrete defense dominated. "Lectures on FSR II" and "Lectures on FSR III" made clear sense but often bordered on science fiction.[5]

The creation of the Royal Tank Corps meant that "tank maniacs" or "military Bolshies" had a home and a pulpit in the British army. Their intent was to become a *corps d'élite*: "Cavalry can play no part in the battle between armored machines." Indeed, they flatly proposed to replace all three combat arms. This created some resistance, as in: "cavalry will never be scrapped to make room for tanks . . . we must depend on the man and horse to obtain really decisive results."[6] But as long as tanks were ghettoized into an avant-garde minority the immediate threat to cavalry was minor. Aside from rearguard actions at Whitehall, the primary difficulty lay in developing an acceptable tank that could address mechanical and logistical limitations and provide shock while emphasizing the surviving merits of cavalry. A fast breakthrough tank could reconcile major differences, but the real problem was budgetary. As Archibald Wavell wryly noted, "Speed is, unfortunately, a most expensive commodity; alike in battleships, motor cars, racehorses and women, any comparatively small increase may double the price of the article."[7]

The evolution of mechanization into full-blooded tank divisions began almost a decade after the Great War. In 1927, the British were producing an experimental mechanized force of a reconnaissance element of tankettes and armored cars, a battalion of Vickers medium tanks, a motorized machine gun battalion, and an artillery battalion composed of towed and self-propelled guns ("the first mechanized formation to be born in the world, and was the mother of all armored divisions").[8] At the same time,

the Soviets were creating an experimental tank regiment of three tank battalions. This was, in effect, emulated by the 1928 U.S. experimental tank
force. The Red Army experimented with a complete tank brigade in 1930,
and the British followed suit in 1931. The French finally fielded their own
experimental mechanized force in 1932. The U.S. reaction was to disband
the Experimental Armored Force and split tank development between the
infantry and cavalry. The British army, for all its brilliance did not create a
Mobile Division until 1938—seven years after its own tank brigade maneuvers. Even as the great European powers copied and expanded upon the
British model, the mother of armor became inattentive. Vigorous experimentation slowed and finally came to a halt; the British army would not
have an armored division until a year later. As long as the British and
French were operating under the influence of conflicting doctrines, their
experiments were debating points to either the Fuller tanks-alone school or
the infantry tanks-under-command concept.

By the mid-1930s the light no longer burned bright on Salisbury Plain.
Reports by the U.S. military attachés from Britain were received with polite
but passing interest by the cavalry. When the attaché in London reported on
the "new British Christie tank" in 1937, Col. W. D. Crittenberger, chief of
staff to the chief of cavalry, added a marginal note for his boss: "Is this
worth reading to the Officer's Class?"[9] This reflected the early opinions of
U.S. staff colleges: "In 1925 American general services schools dismissed
one of Liddell Hart's most celebrated papers as 'of negative value to the
instructors in these schools.'"[10] Studies of the British Mobile Division were
met with even less interest:

> It has always been the view of this office that the composition of the exist-
> ing British armored division is faulty. It is too big and composed of too
> many heterogeneous elements. The occasions when its use as a whole will
> be either profitable or appropriate are bound to occur but seldom . . . ill
> adapted for a defensive role and almost as ill adapted for breaking up into
> subsidiary units.[11]

The U.S. Cavalry did not officially recognize the new British organization as the final triumph for Fullerists, but it is clear that branch chiefs were
au courant and most field officers read *The Royal Tank Corps Journal.* "At
the Benning Tank Battalion mess I happened to see a copy of the Royal
Tank Corps Journal and was so fascinated with it . . . the soldiers literally
'ate it up.'"[12] Van Voorhis and Chaffee, aware of the philosophical struggles going on in the British army, also noticed that despite the efforts of
British tank pioneers, change came slowly. As late as 1938, much of the
British cavalry in Europe and India lived as it had for the past century:
"Polo was the chief distraction of the officers. . . . Almost every officer in
the Regiment played the game keenly."[13] Sir John Hackett recalled that
"you joined a cavalry regiment then largely because you liked a life with

horses. You would find out a little later on that you had, in fact, joined 'The Army,' as it were by accident."[14] In the spring of 1939, there were still four regular cavalry regiments of the line stationed in England.

Although the infantry sneered that "good grooms make bad chauffeurs," the average cavalryman was in fact not a reactionary mechanization and reluctant to accept the trend of modern invention. It was carefully pointed out that "the great majority of soldiers who joined cavalry regiments between the wars were far more mechanically minded than horse minded."[15] This was doubly true in the United States and Canada.

By early 1938 it had become accepted that "the cavalry must at last be sent to the knacker's yard. . . . The decision [was] to mechanize all but two regiments of the line, along with eight Yeomanries."[16] This action came far too late to restrain the Germans. Sir Edmund Ironside, chief of Imperial General Staff in 1939, lamented that the Royal Tank Corps "had possessed the best machines in the world and the men who knew how they should be handled in battle. By 1938 all that had gone, save for the quality of the tank crews."[17] Despite the clear need for mechanization, traditional differences lingered:

> Most of the cavalry regiments have been rounded up and pressed into tanks or armored motor cars. They have all the sensations of a saloon-bar person in public-bar circumstances. . . . The Royal Tank Regiment (the Tank men) is a creation apart: it is composed of the rude mechanicals who despise the horse.[18]

British preparedness to accommodate heretics in their midst eventually resulted, in 1939, in the the tank corps being designated the Royal Armored Corps, to have precedence in the army immediately before the Royal Regiment of Artillery. (The gunners never quite forgave that.) The 1940 campaign in France was eagerly interpreted as a vindication by both the Royal Tank Regiment and the cavalry. To the tank corps it proved that tanks win battles. To the cavalrymen it was the sudden realization that opportunity to regain past glory was not gone if they were to accept that tanks were really horses, that panzer divisions were heavy cavalry, and that maneuver and shock once again dominated tactics.

The *Cavalry Journal* regularly used Allenby's 1917 campaign in Palestine as proof that the horse continued to be decisive on the battlefield. However, in the 1930s the U.S. Army was more disposed to learn from the French than the British.[19] Crittenberger dismissed the new British armored formation with a dig at the "well known British predilection for the defensive rather than the attack."[20] For an army schooled in Grant's ideas of warfare the tradition of the thin red line had little impact, and that aloof British attitude toward American military professionalism did not help—yet continued to reappear, even when the Americans became invaluable benefactors. Maj. Gen. E. N. Harmon observed in North Africa in 1943, "I worry

greatly over the attitude of the British to split the division and fight it piecemeal ... he [General Anderson] smiled at me in a patronizing way."

Foreign Influence 2:
The Red Army—Deep Battle Misunderstood

*The tank leadership I saw at the maneuvers can only be described as bril-
liant.*
>   —Lt. Gen. G. le Q. Martel, 1936,
>   after Minsk wargames, writing for *Pravda*

*As far as tanks are concerned, I think we will have to put the Soviet Union
in first place.*
>   —Gen. Loizeau, head of French Mission,
>   Kiev maneuvers, 1936, quoted in *Pravda*

As for me, I get all I ask for.
>   —Marshal Tukhachevskii to Marshal Gamelin, Paris, 1935

Stalin's forceful style concerning armor was much like Hitler's "That's
what I need! That's what I want to have!"[21] The tank offered an impressive
solution for a Bolshevik army struggling to survive against alleged capitalist and actual Germanic threats. Tanks were relatively simple to make and
they were constructed in factories by workers. Tanks did not require elitist
bourgeois cavalry officers to direct them in battle. Whatever technical
superiority former czarist officers still held in doctrinal discussions would
be minimized by a new arm led by zealous communist leaders loyal to
Stalin. The Red Army was given all the tanks it wanted, and there was no
destructive doctrinal debate: the mechanized versus cavalry saga did not
have to play itself out in the Kremlin. In Soviet Russia there was room for
both armor and cossacks. If Stalin wanted tanks, he would be given tanks in
mass—even if, initially, they were to be outright copies of Western capitalist equipment.[22] Stalin, like Hitler, had no specific opinion on tank doctrine, his senior generals were divided over or openly hostile to Western
doctrine; however, like the führer, he had his own Guderian—Marshal
Mikhail N. Tukhachevskii.

The debates that were permitted were conducted by philosophes from
the General Staff, the Frunze Academy, and advocates of mechanization
served to outline future Red Army doctrine in specific terms: maneuver,
mass, and, the deep battle. The offense and the principle of maneuver had
to be delicately balanced against "bourgeois military theories and their
'false idealist views' of war and military organization": Fuller and Liddell
Hart had been translated into Russian and created the same doctrinal division they had instigated in Western armies. The greatest Soviet armored

thinker Tukhachevskii at first condemned Frunze and Verkhovskii's advo-cacy of Fuller; he rejected "the small mechanized armies of the type of the Fascist police." He was against an armored elite: the Royal Tank Corps would find no home in the Soviet Union. Tukhachevskii argued for mass maneuver and accused others of proposing a strategy of attrition.

The idea of an elite, professional army was discouraged from the beginning. Still, by the 1930s the Red Army consisted "of two armies in reality, the shock army—motorized and mechanized" tasked with the oper-ational breakthrough, and the "infantry-mass" which was a carry-over of the older evolution from czarist to a Bolshevik-people's army.[23] Although penetration by independent tank formations was scoffed at as "bourgeois" by the Soviet old guard, it complemented Tukhachevskii's concept of a "nonstop" offensive, or deep battle (*glubokii boi*). Eventually the "Soviet version of mechanized warfare derived from a collective effort on the part of the Operational Faculty of the Frunze Military Academy and the Operational Directorate of the General Staff under V. K. Triandafilov."[24]

The Red Army embraced mechanization with a vigor that quickly out-stripped Western experiments, fielding a mechanized corps by 1932. Stalin prevented an extended debate between the old guard army and the new, sus-piciously exclusive tank lobby. He supported operational armor: "The Red Army came about as a result of a political bargain struck between Tukhachevskii and Stalin."[25] By 1935, the Frunze reforms and Tukhachevskii's creation of a powerful mechanized army produced a Soviet tank park of nearly 10,000 armored fighting vehicles supported by an effi-cient all-arms mass. Most resembled creative variations of the Christie tank—the BT (*bystrokhodnyi tank,* "fast tank") series and its perfected final evolution, the T-34. German experiments at Kazan some years earlier inspired the Russians to develop their own breakthrough vehicle, the KV-1.

While the West was perfecting the tactical-operational breakthrough, the Soviet Union had laid the foundations for the strategic offensive of the future. The pioneering British, despite the Royal Tank Corps and Fuller and Liddell Hart's combined efforts, did not attempt an orthodox armored divi-sion until the spring of 1940. By 1936, Tukhachevskii had published the Soviet *Provisional Field Service Regulations* (PU-36) that insisted on a symbiotic relationship between the combat arms: "The employment of each arm must be governed by its particular characteristics and material capaci-ties. Infantry, supported by tanks and artillery . . . by its own decisive actions in the offensive . . . decides the outcome of the battle." But the real emphasis was on big numbers, concentration of firepower, and all-arms cooperation. "Tanks must be employed on a mass scale."[26] Although PU-36 required strategic cavalry attacks on enemy flanks and rear, the actual breakthrough was to be an overwhelming frontal assault that was quickly elevated from tactical to operational to strategic:

Mechanized armies consisting of tanks, self-propelled artillery and lorry borne infantry are able to carry out independent tasks disengaged from other types of troops, or in cooperation with them. Mechanized units possess great mobility, powerful fire capacity and great shock power. The basic form of the operation of the mechanized unity in combat consists of the tank attack, which must be secured by artillery fire. The manoeuvre and shock-blow of the mechanized unity must be supported by aviation.[27]

PU-36 introduced the first concept of what was to become the Operational Maneuver Group of 1944/1945 and, eventually, the basis of Warsaw Pact offensive doctrine. The nuance was use of mass armor striking beyond the operational battlefield both as part of an all-arms offensive and as an independent shock force committed to operational maneuver— the simultaneous destruction of the enemy's combat order throughout the whole depth of his position.

Because of the nature of the beast, Soviet technical and intellectual breakthroughs were sneered at by the West even after the Great Patriotic War (World War II). Internally, the Soviet hierarchy was infected with a deep-rooted suspicion that found treachery everywhere it looked. Further, there was that ever-present inferiority complex when facing the Germans. And the rapid progress of the Red Army's tank forces was savaged by Stalin himself during the great purges of the 1930s: most of the Soviet Union's best minds were sacrificed to the dark side. Suspicions regarding Tukhachevskii's loyalty and reports from the Spanish Civil War that argued against massed armor and lobbied for the antitank force resulted in the Red Army's dangerous step backward.[28] Its armored corps was disbanded in favor of infantry/antitank-dominated formations. The success of the panzer divisions' blitzkrieg then created more Soviet self-doubt.

Military attaché reports clearly and accurately described the Soviet theory of war: "Distant action and infantry support tanks operate uninterruptedly until the enemy is completely enveloped and destroyed."[29] Colonel Crittenberger pointed out the essence to General Herr: "Russians appear to consider the tank an all purpose weapon used independently or in combined arms operations in practically every situation."[30] Herr chose to ignore him.

Foreign Influence 3: France et l'Arme Blindé

We congratulate ourselves at not having succumbed to the lure of a cavalcade of tanks.
                                                    —*Revue d'Infanterie*, 1939

Mon Général, nous sommes toujours d'accord.
                                                    —Marshal Foch to General Pershing, May 1918

The French army's influence on American arms was considerable. French pamphlets and manuals leavened U.S. doctrine from 1917 through 1940. The U.S. Army continued to build the Renault tank even after hostilities ended. The French artillery, in both doctrine and in actual guns, formed the basis of the U.S. Army's direct and indirect fire.[31] Despite the pioneering examples of the British (there was no Royal Tank Corps equivalent in the U.S. Army), Washington chose to adopt the French solution to tank warfare and thus, as in the French army, U.S. tanks ended up with the infantry. During the mid-1930s, the French reaction to the German panzer arm was watched with interest; German trials and doctrinal concepts were reported directly as they developed.

The British tank theories ("England is the school of mechanized attack") may have inspired younger French officers but drove the French army's senior hierarchy to protect their own doctrine, forged in the bloodbaths of the Somme and Verdun. England had the Channel to protect it, but France still directly faced the Germans. Lt. Col. Charles de Gaulle's efforts (*Vers l'armée de métier—Toward a Professional Army*), which called for a return to the offensive, the abandonment of the continuous front, and the creation of a professional armored corps, caused a political uproar and were energetically opposed.[32] French doctrine evolved from offensive *à outrance* ("to the end") and a contempt for enemy fire to the 1921–1936 instructions' stress on the importance of firepower. "The attack is the fire that advances, the defense is the fire that halts." De Gaulle's theories were attacked "systematically by its top military leaders of the 1930s, and by every individual who occupied the war office from 1932 through May 1940."[33]

In 1934 Marshal Henri Pétain (as minister of war) signed off the first armor manual: *Provisional Notice on the Employment of Tanks in Liaison with the Infantry*. By 1936 the General Staff agreed that the tank program, despite Estienne's criticism, should be 75 percent light tanks. The direction accepted the concept of *chars de manoeuvre ensemble* ("tanks in massed maneuver") and defined two missions for armor: infantry cooperation and a subsequent advance well ahead of the infantry and accompanying tanks, toward successive objectives. The third mission was to "attack armored formations of the enemy."[34]

This quickly extended the debate over tank control. The French artillery argued that its mission in the advance was to ensure the protection of tanks, and therefore all artillery had to participate in the support of tanks for mass maneuver. The subsequent publication of the 1937 *Provisional Notice of Employment of Modern Tanks* and the 1939 *Regulation on the Units of Combat Tanks, 2d Part: Combat* did little to solve the issue. Rather, they hamstrung the armor and placed it under a gunner's control.

The French doctrine sought to send tanks out to reach the enemy artillery and command centers, but the French were going to do it by successive bounds instead of with Fuller's torrent. This was not the German point of view stated in *Truppenführung*: "Tanks and infantry that work together usually will be assigned the same objective, if possible—enemy artillery."[35] German doctrinal critics sniffed at French doctrine: seven minutes of attack and seventy minutes of waiting for the arrival of the infantry. The French tank battalion was given specific tactics: "Break[s] the enemy's front, begin[s] exploitation, [and] prepare[s] its completion by others."[36] American reports from the Verdun Conference suggested that basic principles corresponded to German doctrine. However, German armored doctrine recognized the tank as an independent arm, and its formations executed their own maneuver. Unlike the French, there were no planned phases. German armor was trained to exploit its own success without limit (*auftragstaktik*—"mission-directed tactics," although "directed initiative" also captures the essence). This difference, or at least its organizational result, was noted in some American circles: "French are limited to the armored division, while the Germans have created an *armored branch*."[37]

U.S. military attachés in Paris reported that France's centralized command for tanks was really a bureaucratic solution that added a layer of command without introducing a direct armored commander with authority and control over mechanized units. Doctrine specified that tanks "must always act within the cadre of a corps or of a mechanized group under the orders of a Cavalry or motorized corps commander."[38] The Gamelin solution was correct, in principle. However, without a doctrine to back it up the result was that French armor, rather than being grouped as tank divisions, was distributed as independent fire brigades stationed behind an infantry corps or the Maginot Line itself. Although the French desperately tried to form a brace of tank divisions in the spring of 1940, it was too late. They were copying the manner but not the essence of the panzer divisions' doctrine. French armor fought the war in 1940 in a compromise between Gamelin's and de Gaulle's ideas.[39] Nevertheless, this trend in French military thought was dutifully reported to Washington and again served as ammunition for the senior generals in both the infantry and cavalry to support the status quo in U.S. mechanized development: separate, equal, and, on the surface, complementary.

French Avant-Garde—Infantry Tanks and Cavalry Tanks

The army was never refused any money.

—Col. A. Goutard[40]

The French did not just debate, they also produced the vehicles to match their doctrine. By 1939 the French army had light, medium, and heavy tanks in its order of battle. The French Char B1 bis was bigger than anything the Germans had ready, and the Somua and Renault tanks were considered very advanced.[41] Despite efforts at experimentation, there was no modern U.S. tank capable of slugging it out at battle range with any European main battle tank. The influential military writer, former chief of Cavalry, Gen. Charles-Thomas Brecard, published a paper that was circulated in the U.S. Cavalry: "Decrease in number of horses [is] a danger for national defense."[42]

Before the outbreak of hostilities, the three French horse cavalry divisions had been redistributed among the five Divisions Légères de Cavalerie (DLCs). The independent Brigade de Cavalerie and three Brigades Spahis were controlled at corps level.[43] The DLCs included a mounted cavalry brigade, a mechanized brigade (with twenty-five light tanks), and a dragoon regiment of riflemen carried in trucks. In addition to the four cavalry regiments, the mounted brigade included armored cars for reconnaissance, an airplane troop, and self-propelled 75mm guns as "horse artillery" supported by a motorized battalion of 105mm guns for a total of 4,200 horses, 1,350 motor vehicles, 900 motorcycles, and 15 aircraft. The DLC was the model idealized by Herr and Hawkins.

With the introduction of the Char B and the Hotchkiss-Renault-Somua team, French armor became the avant-garde for all armies in the 1930s. Military attachés and arms chiefs flocked to Mailly-le-Camp shows with the same hunger for style that the international set exhibited at Chanel and Lanvin. These were the first true infantry and cavalry tanks designed with a specific purpose dictated by doctrine, not experimental engineering. Rather than examine the validity of the doctrine, the West copied its mode and also produced "infantry" and "cavalry" or "cruiser" tanks (the British were torn between their naval and medieval metaphors). The Char B at once became the model for future Western armor and was slavishly copied, to the point that the first British and U.S. main battle tanks to go to war were Char B spawns—big, heavy, and well armored. No existing antitank gun could stop the Char B, and its gun was capable of dispatching any foreign tank. It was the "dreadnought" of the 1930s. A hybrid of Renault and the British Mk V, it sported both a turret and a main gun in the hull. It directly influenced the British Churchill (an almost sycophantic copy) and Matilda II,[44] and the U.S. Grant, which at least sat on an intelligent suspension. All four tanks advanced proudly against German armor, but only the Grant, with its high-caliber 75mm gun and the Matilda II ("the best tank in 1940") with its impregnable armor made any impression.

Western "Infantry" Main Battle Tank

The French Influence

France 1935:
Char B1 bis

Gun: 75mm (Hull); 47mm (Turret)
Combat Weight: 32 tons
Armor (max): 60mm
Speed: 17 mph
Crew: 4
First Combat: France 1940

Hull Mounted
75mm
Main Gun

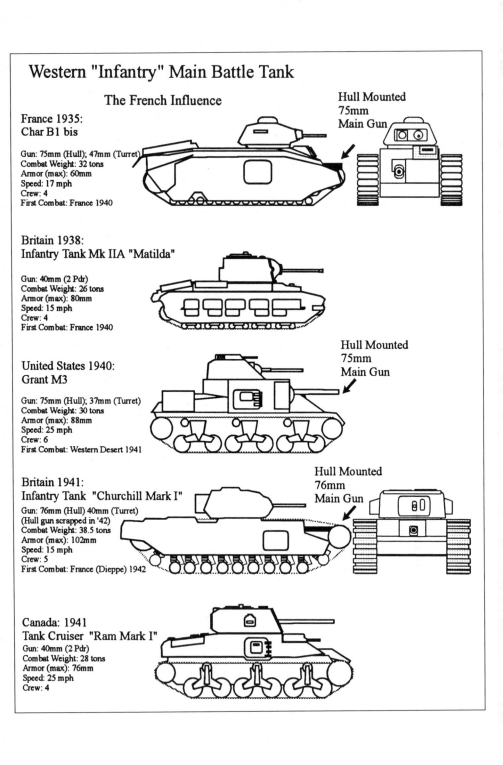

Britain 1938:
Infantry Tank Mk IIA "Matilda"

Gun: 40mm (2 Pdr)
Combat Weight: 26 tons
Armor (max): 80mm
Speed: 15 mph
Crew: 4
First Combat: France 1940

United States 1940:
Grant M3

Gun: 75mm (Hull); 37mm (Turret)
Combat Weight: 30 tons
Armor (max): 88mm
Speed: 25 mph
Crew: 6
First Combat: Western Desert 1941

Hull Mounted
75mm
Main Gun

Britain 1941:
Infantry Tank "Churchill Mark I"

Gun: 76mm (Hull) 40mm (Turret)
(Hull gun scrapped in '42)
Combat Weight: 38.5 tons
Armor (max): 102mm
Speed: 15 mph
Crew: 5
First Combat: France (Dieppe) 1942

Hull Mounted
76mm
Main Gun

Canada: 1941
Tank Cruiser "Ram Mark I"
Gun: 40mm (2 Pdr)
Combat Weight: 28 tons
Armor (max): 76mm
Speed: 25 mph
Crew: 4

La Division Cuirassée Rapide

Despite warnings by tank Colonel Charles de Gaulle that "only an armored force itself has the capability of destroying another armored force," the High Command continued to put off the formation of the Divisions Cuirassées, *the Heavy Armored Divisions . . . it was not until January 1940, on the insistance of the new Tank Inspector, General Keller . . . that Gamelin finally consented to the formation of two Heavy Armored Divisions.*
    —Jeffrey Johnstone Clark, *Military Technology in Republican France*[45]

By August 1939, the U.S. attaché in Paris reported the new French armored division, the Division Cuirassée Rapide (DCR). The French armored division's organization chart read like a Napoleonic order of battle: demi-brigades, cuirassiers, chasseurs, hussards, and dragons. Nonetheless, it had teeth: Char B1s and Hotchkiss 39s. Investigative visits by U.S. attachés noted that "French Armored Div from a stand point of armament and armor appears to have greater striking power that the German Panzer Division . . . their slogan *'Speed is not Armor'* [emphasis added] seems to have been vindicated by the fighting to date."[46]

The tank divisions' adopted maxim was designed with the Char B in mind. In January 1939, the U.S. attaché in Paris attended an attack demonstration at Verdun by the 2d North African Tanks and 6th Moroccan Tirailleurs. The attacks were conducted in careful apportionments, Char Bs in the first and Renault 35s in the second and third waves. The stress was on tactical depth: "That fast tanks, except for special uses were not necessary . . . that speed is not armor and would not give the protection so many thought. Speed is always gained at the expense of armor or armament at the expense of both."[47]

The first two "heavy" armored divisions were officially formed in January 1940[48]; a total of four DCRs were approved just before the May campaign.[49] The new divisions had three demi-brigades: two battalions of Char B and two equipped with the medium H39s or equivalents; a third *demi-brigade* composed of two battalions of *dragons portés* (infantry in towed tracked trailers); eighteen tracked personnel carriers per three companies and a fourth weapons company. The artillery regiment had twenty-four 105mm guns and a battery of 47mm antitank guns. Support troops included an engineer company and an aviation squadron.

The "shock element" of Char Bs was organized in ten companies, a total of thirty-five tanks per battalion; the H39 battalions had forty-five. Some of the more aggressive generals urged "combat between tanks" and predicted "our antitank guns will take positions to support their own tanks during combat against the enemy's armored formations."[50] All the main battle tanks for a DCR (160) were fewer than the British or German tank division totals, but French tanks were technically superior and, if properly grouped, could have scattered the Mk IIs and IIIs of the average panzer division.[51]

The DCR was not a true panzer division; its infantry tank doctrine and cautious approach—"speed is not Armor"—better suited the heavies in Fort Mead and almost convinced the U.S. chief of infantry to follow suit. The G2's report on the French 1st Armored Division enthusiastically described a unit of powerful arms and ready troops: "Keenness, enthusiasm, zip, drive . . . they're tough. . . . Messes ('popotes') plentiful, well equipped . . . rank and file live well."[52] These reports may have added to Herr's last-minute efforts to create new cavalry mechanized divisions. The fundamental difference between the mechanization of French and U.S. cavalry was the Weygand factor.[53]

General Weygand Saves the French Cavalry

General Maxime Weygand was chief of the General Staff from January 1930 until February 1931 and vice-president of the Superior Council of War from February 1931 until January 1935—the period in which the French made their major advances in the mechanization of cavalry. Weygand's support, but more important, his directives, cut short the delay of a protracted debate among the directors of cavalry, infantry and artillery. Had Douglas MacArthur instructed Herr to get on with it, instead of permitting the compromise and infighting to continue, the U.S. Cavalry may have survived as a formidable fighting force in World War II.

Weygand's vision focused on operational cavalry, not armor. He identified the traditional cavalry missions of operational reconnaissance, security, and exploitation as the ideal roles for the new mechanized divisions. A completely motorized cavalry division was formed at Reims in 1933 and became the first Division Légère Mécanisée or DLM. It fielded a reconnaissance regiment, a tank brigade, a motorized rifle brigade, an engineer battalion and a towed artillery regiment. The tank brigade comprised two tank regiments of eighty tanks each; the motorized brigade had its own company of twenty light tanks to support its dragons portés which by now were towed in tracked carriers. By 1939 the chief of French army cavalry described his divisions as "extremely elaborate . . . ultramodern" formations.[54] The three DLMs gave the French cavalry a clear doctrinal mission (strategic reconnaissance, not shock) on the battlefield. Each division had nearly 200 tanks and was completely mechanized; these were in addition to the five cavalry divisions that in themselves were a compromise between horses and tracked vehicles that would have appealed to the chiefs of the U.S. Cavalry.

The enforced compromise may have saved the French cavalry but it did not save France, and the weaknesses inherent in the compromise were officially noted by Gamelin: "France's movement toward mechanization was thus characterized more by its fragmentation and diversity than by its uniformity or clarity of purpose." The new doctrine articulated the concept of *chars de manoeuvre ensemble* but really meant that such tanks for such operations were not incorporated into units larger than a battalion. Basically, Weygand saved the French cavalry from itself. "The eagerness of the cavalry enthusiasts to form large mechanized units differed sharply from that of the infantry officers who were charged with developing tank units."[55] By the mid-1930s, cavalry was the most modern of the French army branches.

However, French cavalry doctrine was tied to the direction the rest of the army was taking. The operational strategy was defensive and anchored in the Maginot Line: the mass of French armor (1,125 tanks) was distributed throughout the infantry in twenty-five accompanying tank battalions. There was no maneuver doctrine or concept of operations for a tank corps. Nonetheless, the cavalry did have control of 1,312 armored fighting vehicles—about 700 were wasted on the eight traditional light cavalry formations—but 624 main battle tanks remained grouped in the three new armored divisions. The French cavalry had not only survived mechanization, but had it emerged numerically triumphant. This was to be a hollow victory. For example, a major shortcoming of French armor was that four-fifths of the tanks carried no radios. But Colonel Goutard remarked that "the long pauses in the advance would permit frequent refueling, and a long range wireless-set was not really necessary, as the tanks would be within sight of each other."[56] French armor was literally beyond direction.

The facts were there for any interested observer to see, but the U.S. Army branch chiefs chose to sift through the body of information to support their own agendas. The Germans, however, saw the flaws immediately. The élan of the French divisions was not debated, but the ability of the French army as a whole was in question: it was seen as too methodical and too diagrammatic. Seeming to conspire against themselves, the French did not hold large peacetime maneuvers, the feeble efforts of the 1920s were moribund in the 1930s. "The few field maneuvers that took place still concentrated on static, defensive tactics. Between September 1939 and May 1940, the French high command would make no effort to provide any large-unit training."[57]

The attempts at armored renaissance using the DCRs came too late. "The French were not ready in 1939 to refight World War I. They were ready to fight a war similar to the final phases of the western front in 1918."[58] The overcontrolled centralized approach would quickly result in chaos in 1940, when the French army lost the operational advantage to the

Wehrmacht. But until this had become apparent, French army doctrines, such as they were, exerted a powerful influence in both Europe and the United States. Before the triumph of the panzer divisions in 1939 and 1940, the preferred models for a U.S. armored force (particularly in heavy armor doctrine) were French.

Foreign Influence 4: The German Army

The fundamental basis of German strategical and tactical doctrine are the teachings of General Field Marshal Count Alfred von Schlieffen.
—Lt. Col. H. T. Kramer, U.S. military attaché, Berlin, 1939

In war only what is simple can succeed. I visited the staff of the Cavalry Corps. What I saw there was not simple.
—Field Marshal von Hindenburg, attending 1932 maneuvers

The German army has always been treated with considerable respect by the U.S. Army. In a curious love-hate relationship, U.S. arms have swung from vehement disdain to fawning esteem. It is perhaps because both militaries have so much in common. The aggressive tactical innovation and hard-edged military professionalism of both engendered mutual respect and serious study. After World War I, U.S. officers arranged exchange visits with the Wehrmacht and studied at the German Military Academy. U.S. military attachés continued their observations from Berlin well after war had broken out in 1939 and benefited from a generous series of visits to panzer training areas that even included the battlefields in Poland.[59]

The commitment of the pre-Hitler German army to Schlieffen's strategy of annihilation remained unchanged because of practical necessity. And the probability of a two-front war made a classic Cannae battle essential. The concept of blitzkrieg was both a military and economic answer. Stuka dive-bombers and tanks promised rapid operational, and thus strategic, answers. In the best tradition of objective analysis, the German General Staff studied its army's past defeats and proposed a solution for lighting destruction of continental ground forces—the *panzerwaffe,* or armored force.

> Lutz and Guderian determined the operative use of tanks in large formations . . . the growth of panzer troops in the *Führerheer* during this period was not a simple matter for many senior officers opposed the use of panzer formations in the offensive role seeing them merely as infantry support.[60]

German armor had been enthusiastically accepted and developed before Hitler's appearance. Despite the Versailles Diktat[61] German tank warfare experiments had been conducted at secret bases in the Soviet Union in the 1920s and 1930s, and, under Gen. Hans von Seeckt's masterful direction, the German army had maintained a strong professional cadre capable of rapid growth within a structure that also incorporated a modern mechanized doctrine. Hitler's enthusiastic support later facilitated brisk expansion and the rise to power of favorite generals.[62]

The German armored force was organized in October 1935. The original panzer divisions were built around two tank brigades (each of two regiments, each with two panzer battalions, for a grand total of about 550 tanks) and a motorized infantry brigade of a motorcycle battalion and two truck-carried rifle battalions.[63] Artillery assets were twenty-four towed 105mm guns and a 37mm antitank gun battalion. This organization would not appreciably change until after the campaign against France. The temperament of the *panzerwaffe* was cavalry in style. The main battle tanks that equipped its panzer battalions were designed for maneuver—Guderian did not object to the inclusion of the infantry tank concept, "a weapon adjusted to the foot soldier's scale of time and space values."[64] Wehrmacht doctrine emphasized mass and speed. By the end of the 1930s, even though panzer formations did not field the best tanks in Europe, they had marshalled a force that doctrinally and mechanically bypassed the Royal Armored Corps and, because of better communications, could outmaneuver the French DCRs.

The adoption of *auftragstaktik* (general objective–based operations) by the German army before 1914 had introduced a doctrine by which commanders were trained to tell their subordinates what to do, but not how to do it. As long as subordinates adhered to their commander's intent, they were given wide latitude to carry out orders in their own way.

> It was the responsibility of every German soldier to take whatever action was required in any military situation, without waiting for orders, and even to disobey orders if they were not consistent with the immediate situation. *Auftragstaktik* was the culmination of the military thinking and experience of Scharnhorst, Gneisenau and Moltke, and was to provide the legendary "flexibility" of the German army.[65]

Despite this, perhaps because of World War I, Wehrmacht staff officers were welcome speakers at U.S. Army schools. Captain Bechtolsheim, a German General Staff officer lectured about maneuver at the U.S. Artillery School in 1932 (well before it was realized there was a secret German tank center in the Soviet Inion). "The German Army [has] no stereotyped rules as to how it is to be done. . . . We believe that movement is the element of war and only by mobile warfare can any decisive result be obtained."[66] Another visitor, panzer expert Col. Adolph von Schell visited Fort Knox in the summer of 1937 to "study [U.S.] mechanized doctrine and equipment."

Schell appeared impressed with cavalry equipment: "I well know and have ridden in all foreign tanks. Your cavalry 'Combat Car' has more speed, more power and is easier riding than any European light tank. I consider it equal to the best in Europe."[67] U.S. military attaché reports emphasized the growing strength of the new cavalry and panzer divisions, and new maneuver doctrine was carefully reported.[68]

The Third Reich's creation of a panzer force as a separate branch was viewed with envy by mechanization converts. As in Britain and the United States, there had been as strong resistance to mechanization by the German army's old guard. Both infantry and cavalry generals were loath to create a Germanic Royal Tank Regiment equivalent. However, despite a minor success in creating their own light mechanized divisions—an unsatisfactory compromise that was quickly abandoned—blitzkrieg doctrine triumphed because the tank lobby had the führer behind it.

Further, thanks to von Seeckt, the *auftragstaktik* tradition and a sound study of the 1918 campaign's lessons learned, the German army had the advantage of beginning mechanization with a clear concept of the fundamentals of operational movement. "Our supreme tactical principle is therefore mobility. Mobility exists down to the organization of the infantry squad. The division, not the corps is the strategic unit."[69] Doctrine taught at armored warfare schools appealed to armor and cavalry officers. The Germans emphasized simplicity, aggressiveness, and common sense: "We have no great secrets at this school. The greatest factor in successful employment of armored troops is speed in obtaining initial coordination of arms and in the execution of coordinated missions by various arms."[70] Lt. Col. James C. Crockett reported on the fundamentals of German tactical principles: "1. There are no rules in tactics; 2. Mobility; 3. *Schwerpunkt*—main effort; 4. Surprise; 5. Immediate fire support for movement; 6. *Offensive Action* [emphasis added]."[71] Maj. Percy Black, after three years' experience as assistant U.S. military attaché in Berlin offered the following observations on 6 December 1939:

> The main part I would like to emphasize is that the overwhelming success of the German Army was not due to the air corps, was not due to the motorized troops alone, but was due to a balanced field army, with balanced organization and balanced equipment, executing a plan under almost perfect leadership.[72]

Interestingly, there was no comment regarding mission-directed operations and the training required to perfect this perhaps most important of German techniques. The U.S. predilection for German military style may have been natural, reflecting perhaps a cultural stratum; yet despite the eagerness to learn from Teutonic arms, *auftragstaktik* did not appear in U.S. doctrinal pamphlets. Field Manual 17-100 hints at initiative and creative maneuver by subordinates but never quite manages to break away from the influence of the Ecole de Guerre. Yet it was *within* the cavalry nucleus of armor, "the inherent flexibility of the idea fostered back in Kentucky" that Chaffee had conceived combat commands with the stern warning that they were not designed to be bureaucratic compartments but servants of ad hoc tactical creativity.[73] The spirit of the Revolutionary War and frontier independence had become a command-driven way of operation by the end of the U.S. Civil War: Grant, and then Pershing, created an army that followed orders. The German approach to battle was not beyond American military culture but it was suddenly foreign to it. After 1918 *auftragstaktik* remained hidden in plain view—the U.S. Army would not closely examine German war-fighting techniques until after Vietnam. In the 1930s, a self-confident U.S. Army was prepared to both learn from and ignore the Wehrmacht.

The Arms' Chiefs: Mechanization Denied

"Tank" was verboten in the cavalry.
—Gen. Willis D. Crittenberger, 1982 interview

Gen. John K. Herr, the last chief of cavalry particularly enjoyed attaché reports that recounted a cavalry spirit in the German army but ignored references to raising massed armor in an independent branch. Herr's chief of staff, Col. Willis D. Crittenberger, fed him attaché reports that related to horses or armored cavalry, carefully underlining any reference to mounted troops and repeatedly jotting "cavalry mission" in marginal notes to attract Herr's attention.[74] Herr liked a report by Col. Marshall Magruder (68th Field Artillery, Mechanized) based on an interview with the military attaché in Berlin, which Herr thought was an affirmation of his theories. "In general the tactics of the tank units followed that of the cavalry . . . many cavalry officers were assigned to the tanks and they try to keep alive the old traditions of the horse units . . . one outfit went fox hunting on motorcycles."[75] Herr reviewed a translation of 1940 *Das Buch vom Heer* and enjoyed what he read: "Cavalry is an independent force [and] can without excessive fatigue, negotiate larger and faster marches than foot troops, [attain] surprise, [show] greater mobility, [and] ride until hostile fire forces dismount."[76] Crittenberger's position was delicate: he was savvy enough to realize the tank held the key to cavalry's survival but had to tiptoe around his tradition-bound boss.

> As loyal cavalrymen, it would seem to be our plain duty to establish and foster a working relationship between horse and mechanized cavalry. Whether we like it or not, we have had mechanization dumped into our laps and we've got to make the best of it . . . my desire [is] to prevent the

service at large from getting the inevitable impression that there is a serious rift in the Cavalry.[77]

Crittenberger's diplomacy fell on deaf ears, and Herr's state of mind
was further illustrated by the former's observation in July 1938: "The Chief
wants to reopen the question of the saber, which was abolished in 1934."[78]
The lack of foresight displayed by both the cavalry and the infantry chiefs
was to delay the development of an armored force and open the door to
entrepreneurs who saddled the Army Ground Force with a tank destroyer
dogma and then denied it the heavy tank it needed to meet the German
army on an equal footing. As late as 1939, after blitzkrieg had savaged the
Polish army (which had more tanks than the U.S. Army)[79] into submission,
the chief of infantry, General Lynch, went on record as saying the U.S.
Infantry did not want any "*Panzer* Divisions."[80]

Notes

1. Clarke, Jacob L. Devers, Alvan Cullam Gillem, Robert W. Grow, Ernest
N. Harmon, Guy V. Henry, Bruce Magruder, Orlando Ward, and John S. Wood rose
to be division or corps commanders. Maj. Gen. Jacob L. Devers, an artilleryman,
succeeded Chaffee as chief of armor, Alvan C. Gillem Jr., an infantryman, took over
from Devers.

2. S. L. A. Marshal in 1943 Introduction to reprint of J. F. C. Fuller, *Armored
Warfare—Lectures on FSR III* (London: Sifton Praed, 1932).

3. J. F. C. Fuller, ignored and embittered, left the army. "As he grew older,
[he] seemed to withdraw from reality into a Jules Verne World [and] frightened
many staid men off the tank idea. The devil they knew was at least a familiar devil.
Had they known Fuller to be on corresponding terms with Aleister Crowley, alias
The Beast 666, they would have been more frightened still." A. J. Smithers. *A New
Excalibur—The Development of the Tank 1909–1939* (London: Grafton, 1986), p.
244.

4. When Fuller's 1920 essay was published, his immediate chief ran into his
room and burst out "Boney! Boney! What *have* you done?" Fuller's friends called
him Boney, after Napoleon.

5. "Armor can defeat the bullet; therefore a tank can replace infantry in the
attack." Maj. Gen. J. F. C. Fuller, *Lectures on F.S.R. III* (Harrisburg, Pa.: Military
Service Publishing, 1932), pp. 45, 116.

6. Field Marshal Haig in 1926: tanks' mobility was so hamstrung by logistics, and only cavalry could conduct operational pursuit. Ellis, p. 182.

7. Colonel, future Field Marshal, Wavell in 1927, quoted in Macksey, *The
Royal Armored Corps*, p. 37.

8. B. H. Liddell Hart, *The Tanks* (London: Cassell, 1952), p. 365.

9. Military attaché report, London 38985, 6 October 1937.

10. Maj. Gen. John Wood, Wood Papers, MHI.

11. Comments on military attaché, London 39856 "Report on British Armored
Division; 26 Jan 39." Gen. W. D. Crittenberger, 20 April 1938, Willis D.
Crittenberger Papers (hereafter WDC), MHI.

12. "Often the dayroom orderly would ask if it wasn't about time for another 'Limey Tank Book?'" Willis D. Crittenberger, "Memoires of the Development and Service of Armored Troops 1920–1944." Prepared by Wendell Blanchard, Lawrence R. Dewey, and Sidney R. Hinds, WDC, MHI.

13. Maj. Gen. Charles H. Miller, *History of the 13th/18th Royal Hussars (Queen Mary's Own) 1922–1947* (London: Chisman, Bradshaw, 1949), p. 19. Lord Carver, *The Apostles of Mobility* (New York: Holmes and Meier Publishers, 1979), p. 128.

14. "Cavalry generals, and they were many, denied all their recent experiences and continued to extol the power of the well-bred horse." A. J. Smithers, *Rude Mechanicals—An Account of Tank Maturity During the Second World War* (London: Leo Cooper, 1987), pp. xii, 7.

15. Miller, p. 29.

16. Smithers, p. 20.

17. Ironside noted the state of British armor: "Obsolete medium tanks, no cruiser or infantry tanks, obsolete armored cars and no light tanks apart from one unit in Egypt." Smithers, p. 266.

18. Robert Sheriff, *Salute If You Must* (London: Jenkins, 1944).

19. "American tankers attended the French Tank School [at Mailly-le-Camp]," WDC, MHI.

20. WDC, MHI, 26 January 1939. Also, H. W. Winton, *To Change an Army—General Sir John Burnett-Stuart and British Armored Doctrine, 1927–1938* (Lawrence: University Press of Kansas, 1988).

21. Hitler upon seeing tanks maneuver at 1933 wargames. *Heinz Guderian, Panzer Leader* (London: Michael Joseph, 1952), p. 30.

22. The Red Army's agent in New York, AMTORG Corp., contracted for two Christie tanks. It was eventually given the remaining test vehicles refused by the U.S. Army.

23. John Erickson, *The Soviet High Command* (London: Macmillan, 1962), p. 351; and John Erickson, *The Soviet High Command. A Military-Political History 1918–1941* (London: MacMillan, 1962), p. 412.

24. Christopher Duffy, *Red Storm on the Reich* (New York: Da Capo Press, 1993), p. 314.

25. Ibid., p. 356.

26. On September 1936, Martel and Maj. Gen. Archibald Wavell attended Red Army maneuvers: "On the fifth day over a thousand tanks marched past us on parade, and the worst we saw was a few engines missing fire a little at times." Quoted by B. H. Liddell Hart, *The Tanks* (London: Cassell, 1952), p. 370.

27. Provisional Field Service Regulations—*Vremennyi polevoi ustav RKKA* 1936 (PU-36), Moscow 1937; specifically, *Instrukstii po glubokomu boiyu, 1935—Instructions for Deep Battle.*

28. As a result of Stalin's purges the Red Army lost 3 out of 5 marshals; all 11 deputy commissars for defense; 65 out of 75 senior general staff officers; all military district commanders; 13 of 15 army commanders; 57 out of 85 corps commanders; 110 out of 195 division commanders; and 186 of 406 brigade commanders. The head of the Frunze Academy and the chief of Osoaviakhim were shot, as were 80 percent of staff officers. The highest estimate for the slaughter is about 30,000. The People's Commissariat for Internal Affairs (NKVD) was seduced by German suspicions that Tukhachevskii was sympathetic to the French. His protracted stay in Paris (a week, as guest of the French General Staff) after the funeral of King George V in January 1935 laid his enemies' groundwork.

29. "The object of simultaneously destroying the enemy throughout the whole depth of the hostile defensive position." U.S. military attaché reports from Moscow: 9341-6190; 9380-6190; 9967 dated 1936, 1937, 1940. WDC, MHI.

30. Crittenberger: Comment on G2 Report, Russian Army, April 1940, WDC, MHI.

31. Variations of the *soixante-quinze*, the French 75mm gun, and the heavy 155mm gun formed the basis of the U.S. Army's direct and indirect fire to the end of World War II and beyond. Translated French artillery doctrine was initially used in 1917 and perpetuated, albeit with modifications, up to World War II. In 1935, the U.S. chief of artillery approved French centralized control (*poste central du groupe*) and plotting techniques (circular "whiz wheels").

32. *Instruction 1936,* quoted in Doughty, p. 68.

33. Doughty, p. 11.

34. General Delestraint, *Détachement d'expériences de Sissone, Rapport de Général Delestraint commandant le détachement, Sissone, 15 May 1937.* Quoted by Doughty, pp. 152–153.

35. "When closely tied to the infantry, the tanks are deprived of their inherent speed and may be sacrificed to hostile fire." *Truppenführung.*

36. "Gamelin Note," military attaché, Berlin, secret note 4167, 18 December 1939, WDC, MHI.

37. Marginal note in WDC, MHI..

38. "Gamelin Note." See also Jeffrey Johnstone Clark, *Military Technology in Republican France: The Evolution of the French Armored Force, 1917–1940,* unpublished ms., Duke University, 1968, pp. 154, 194–196.

39. The compromise had not been without strong opposition. General Duffieux wrote to Gamelin on 3 December 1939: "In my opinion, Colonel de Gaulle's conclusions should be rejected." On 1 January 40 he added: " A new school of opinion has visions of large formations of tanks plowing up the enemy front in an irresistible onslaught and eliminating resistance in a few hours! But the example of Poland does not show this."

40. Col. A. Goutard, *The Battle of France* (London: Frederick Muller, 1958), p. 21.

41. Premier Edonard Daladier quickly approved General Gamelin's FF9,000 million four-year plan and even increased it to FF14,000 million. On 7 September 1936, the National Assembly passed the plan with an increase of 20 percent to allow for devaluation of the franc! In 1938, a further credit of FF12,000 million was allotted, and another one of FF11,000 million at the beginning of 1939. Goutard, p. 21. There was still opposition from the infantry and artillery: " One shell . . . costing 150 francs can destroy a tank which costs one million." Gen. Narcisse Chauvineau, *Une invasion, est-elle encore possible?* (Paris: Berger-Levrault, 1939).

42. "[There are] 500,000 horses fewer than in 1914 . . . [we] need 80,000 more . . . [and] 780,000 horses would be necessary." G2 Report 13 March 1939, WDC, MHI. The manpower of the French army rose gradually, in direct relation to the German threat. In 1932 it fielded 358,000 soldiers; in 1933 that fell to 320,000 (226,000 with less than six months' training). By 1938 the force increased to 438,000. More than half of the "active" formations were composed of reservists. German rearmament and actions in the Sudetenland spurred French production. In December 1938 there were only 107 Char B and 50 D2 tanks on hand. There were, however, so many cavalry tanks: 790 Renault 35s, 100 Hotchkiss 35s, and 89 FCM 36s. By 1940 the total numbers had increased by 145 percent! The French army was "unfit for beginning with a strategic offensive, but nevertheless capable of local, tactical offensives," according to Marshal Pétain. See Doughty, p. 23.

43. Colonial cavalry. The only French unit not to surrender after the fall of France was Colonel Jouffrault's Spahis brigade ("le seul invaincu de la débâcle"). Piekalkiewicz, p. 237.

44. The first attempt at a "modern" infantry tank resulted in an awkward effort that reminded everyone of a comic strip duck, and thus it became known as the Matilda. Matilda II was a much better infantry tank—only the German 88mm cannon could knock it out.

45. Clark, p. 205.

46. U.S. military attaché, Paris, G2 Report 25173, visit to 1st Armored Division, 28 August 1939, WDC, MHI.

47. U.S. military attaché, Paris, G2 Report 24728, 3 January 39, WDC, MHI.

48. Gamelin saw them as "rare and precious" weapons that could offer France "results which could not be attained in the past."

49. Only three were actually deployed when the Germans attacked, the fourth was still assembling.

50. Gen. J. Brosse, "The German Armored Divisions," *La Science et la Vie,* January 1940.

51. U.S. military attaché, G2 Report 25502, 9 February 1940, WDC, MHI.

52. U.S. military attaché, G2 Report 25517, 9 February 1940, WDC, MHI. Americans reported on the tradition of the French army mess (*popote*). The *popote,* from Revolution and Napoleonic days when officers and men gathered to eat a meal, eating out of the same pot, was an important social act in the French army— directly related to the unit's performance in combat. It was designed to quickly indoctrinate newcomers into a tribal whole: heroic acts of the unit were recounted, and toasts to patron saints were made (e.g., to St. George for the cavalry). Each table's *popotier* was expected to stand and introduce the meal: future success could be ensured by the young officer who reviewed the day's menu with cleverness and wit. "In many ways, the French system was far more 'regimental' than the British." Maj. G. M. Boire, 12e Regiment Blindé Canadien, (served with the 12e Hussards and Chasseurs de Suden, attended the Ecole de Cavalerie at Saumur, France, and graduated from the Ecole de Guerre, Paris) believes that French traditions continue to be much misunderstood in Western, particularly armies of British Empire traditions. Interview, Paris, 1992.

53. U.S. military attaché reports from Paris. For the French cavalry division type 1932: "An unsatisfactory solution . . . cannot take advantage of strategic mobility/speed of motor elements." When the French created the 1934 light mechanized division (DML), "horse units in combination with mechanized formations act only as a brake. . . . Cavalry divisions should therefore either be horse or mech." The reports were not given extensive publication by the U.S. Cavalry.

54. *Règlement de la cavalerie, Première partie: Emploi de la cavalerie* (Saumur: Imprimerie de l'Ecole militaire, 1939).

55. Doughty, p. 170.

56. Goutard, p. 28.

57. See James S. Corum, *The Roots of Blitzkrieg—Hans von Seeckt and German Military Reform* (Lawrence: University Press of Kansas, 1992), pp. 204–205. In 1929 the French army reduced conscript service to twelve months: six months' basic training and a final six with a field unit. Most were locked up in the Maginot Line. Service was lengthened in the late 1930s, but the training was inadequate.

58. During the Riom trial, held in Vichy France, April 1942, French generals attempted to defend their doctrine and tactics. Gen. Marie J. P. Keller argued that defeat "was not a question of doctrine but one of employment." Edonard Daladier

then read a letter from Keller (July 1940) about "French tank officers who were accused of indiscipline if they went beyond doctrinal constraints and charged ahead of the infantry." Doughty, p. 12, 178.

59. Report, U.S. military attaché, G2#16604, June 1938 and 16017, 23 July 1938 mention "new Panzer Division" and include photographs of PKw IV (the heaviest German tank, larger than U.S. prototypes). See U.S. Army Berlin attaché reports on organization of German Panzer units: 15596, 24 November 1937; 15827, 7 April 1938; 15957, 14 June 1938; 61425, 15 October 1939; 16955, 31 October 1939. Good relations between the U.S. and German armies resulted in the Berlin attaché's being invited to Poland. See "Visit to Polish Theatre of Operations," Maj. Percy Black, 6 December 1939, WDC, MHI.

60. Simpson, p. 131. The list of German apostles of mobility includes Oswald Lutz, Heinz Guderian, Ernst Hoeppner, Hermann Hoth, Rudolf Schmidt, Ewald von Kleist, Heinrich von Vietinghoff, Geyr von Schweppenburg, Wilhelm von Thoma, Maximilian von Weichs, and Freidrich von Paulus.

61. The Germans called the Versailles Treaty a *diktat* because it was imposed, not negotiated. A. J. P. Taylor, *The Origins of the Second World War* (London: Harmondsworth, 1964), p. 52.

62. Corum, pp. 127–141. Corum argues that western "misconceptions" have wrongly credited Guderian with the lion's share of creating a panzer force. Gen. Ernst Volckheim, Oswald Lutz, Alfred von Allard-Bockelberg, and, of course, Hans von Seeckt are particularly noted as pioneers of German armor.

63. Lessons learned from Austria and Czechoslovakia resulted in a reduction of tanks for a divisional combat strength of approximately 300 and an addition of a fourth infantry battalion.

64. Heinz Guderian, *Achtung-Panzer!* pp. 38–45. The mainstay of the Panzerwaffe were Pzkw II and IIIs and Czechoslovak Praga Pz38s.

65. Simpson, p. 82.

66. Bechtolsheim lecture, U.S. Artillery School, 1932. WDC, MHI.

67. Col. H. H. D. Heiberg, "Organize a Mechanized Force," manuscript. HHD Heiberg Papers. MHI. Crittenberger reported the visit to Herr. In 1940 Schell was named chief of motorization of the Reich. His 1937 visit "created a stir in G-2 circles."

68. Military attachés reported everything and anything about the German army. Their reports were sifted by branch chiefs of staff. Reports 15307, 26 May 1937; "6, 7, 8, 9 Pz and 10 Pz found near Prague . . . new tank regiment formed at Paderborn . . . the tank strength of the German Army must be revised upward from 1800–3200." Military attaché, Berlin, 15587, 20 November 1937, WDC, MHI.

69. Capt. Bechtolsheim, German General Staff, tactics lecture at the U.S. Artillery School, 1932, WDC, MHI.

70. Military attaché reports, AWC File 236F, bulletin 27. German Panzertruppen School, 28 November 1940, WDC, MHI.

71. Lt. Col. James C. Crockett, "Fundamental German Principles," 6 May 1941. Military attaché reports, WDC, MHI.

72. Attaché reports included interesting tidbits: "Mustard Gas used near Jaslo 12 Sept reported by Germans; 6 men killed, 20 contaminated," G2 Report D 17011, 29 November 1939; " [Polish] lack of initiative," G2 Report D 17011, 29 November 1939. Black also noted that "[German] tanks barely lasted 21 days without maintenance halts." In fact, by 24 May 1939 about half the 3,000 German tanks had been lost either through mechanical breakdown or combat. MSS G2 No.28 1940. MA Reports. WDC, MHI.

73. Lt. Col. Wayne D. Smart, "Combat Commands of the Armored Division," *Military Review* XXV, 11 (February 1946): 7.

74. "Horse cavalry reconnaissance units were used to recce the Polish Tank obstacle before the German tank attacks were launched." U.S. military attaché, Berlin, report, Maj. P. G. Black, 7 February 1940. "Poles never had a chance to reorganize or to stand." Berlin report 16882, 15 September 1939. Report for chief of armor, WDC, MHI.

75. Attaché report, Berlin: Maj. Black, 5 December 1939, and report by Col. Marshall Magruder, 68th Field Artillery, 7 February 1940, WDC, MHI.

76. Das Buch vom Herr notes the following distribution of horses throughout the German army in 1940: infantry—50 percent; artillery—36 percent, cavalry—12 percent. In a memorandum to General Herr dated 14 August 1939, Crittenberger reported the latest "Analysis of German Army" by the Berlin attaché that updated intelligence on the new Panzer Division: "The [new Panzer Division is a] nut cracker . . . under a single ground commander . . . shock troops of the German Army." (Crittenberger underlined the last phrase four times). Attaché Berlin 16805, 14 August 1939. Report for chief of armor, WDC, MHI.

77. Crittenberger, "Memorandum to the Chief of Cavalry," 1 April 1939. "1st Armored Division Official Papers 1940–1941" Crittenberger survived Herr and went on to command an armored division and a corps in France. WDC, MHI.

78. WDC, MHI. "Herr wants a mechanized division but he doesn't want to pay for it by converting any horse units." Grow's diary, July 1938. Grow, MHI. See also Maj. Gen. Robert W. Grow, Ret., "The Ten Lean Years from the Mechanized Force (1930) to the Armored Force (1940)," *Armor* (August 1987): 39. See also Lewis Sorley, *Thunderbolt—General Creighton Abrams* (New York: Simon and Schuster, 1992), p. 31. Herr, in testimony before a Congressional committee in 1939 maintaining that horse cavalry had "stood the acid test of war. . . . Pointing to this country's more than 12,000,000 horses and over 4,500,000 mules . . . as well as its predominant motor industry, he held that the United States was in a most favourable position to to develop the best cavalry forces in the world, both mechanized and horse." Mary Lee Stubbs and Stanley Russell Connor, Armor-Cavalry (Washington: Office of the Chief of Military History of the U.S. Army, 1969), p. 70.

79. "A survey of all modern tanks indicates a total of 450 in the United States today." Crittenberger, "Report to the Chief of Cavalry," 26 February 1940, WDC, MHI.

80. "Up to this date no steps whatsoever have been taken toward concentrating infantry tanks for training." Lt. Col. T. J. Camp, General Staff, Washington, D.C.. "Memo to Chief of Infantry" 26 October 1939, MHI. "General Herr met with General Lynch, the Chief of Infantry, on 17 October 1939. General Lynch stated he did not want any 'Panzer' divisions, although he was having trouble with his tank people on that point. Herr suggested that Cavalry take everything under ten tons and Infantry take everything over ten tons." Robert Grow, "Ten Lean Years," *Armor* (August 1987): 41.

A victim of German engineering. A Panther type D (note rounded mantlet and the much admired crew commander's cupola) destroyed by its crew after breaking down south of Falaise (*U.S. Air Force, U.S. Military History Institute, Carlisle, Pa.*)

CHAPTER 4

Armor's Genesis in North America: The United States and Canada Create Armored Forces

Herr had a one track mind and the horse was the only thing on it.
—Col. H. H. D. Heiberg[1]

A review of U.S. Army mechanized operations in World War II invites an obvious question: Whatever happened to the U.S. Cavalry? The U.S. Armored Force was composed of tank battalions, GHQ tank battalions, and tank destroyer battalions; the only semblance of cavalry was the occasional reconnaissance squadron attached to a division headquarters. In a war that was full of Polish lancers, British dragoons, Canadian hussars, French cuirassiers, Soviet/Russian cossacks, and even a German SS cavalry division, the complete absence of the U.S. Cavalry as a military arm is striking. In fact, although the U.S. Cavalry had been garroted, it appeared to be more self-immolation than anything else.

The creation of the armored force is a melancholy tale of misplaced devotion and cantankerous shortsightedness. The U.S. Army chose to fight World War II with tanks and decided to create a new arm to safeguard the decision. The cavalry had lost the confidence of the War Department to conduct modern operations and was savaged—reduced from an arm of influence and power to an impotent afterthought. Initially, the opportunity to create an armored force that paralleled at least some French advances or the breakthrough experimentation in Germany and the Soviet Union had been trusted to the cavalry. Its leadership, instead of embracing and defining mechanization in the spirit of its traditions chose to defend the status of the horse. Chaffee's elegant rebuttal, "The tradition of Cavalry is to fight!" was ignored. The cavalry resolutely defended its roots: "There is no such thing as Armored Cavalry—remove the horse and there is no cavalry."

The chiefs of the army branches refused the creation of their own panzer division as late as 1936 (after the Michigan maneuvers) and 1939 (Plattsburgh maneuvers). The last chief of cavalry, Maj. Gen. John K. Herr,

"staunchly refused to give up a horse unit. So he lost it all."[2] Gen. Robert
W. Grow, a lost sage in the history of U.S. armor, was one of its pioneers
and, as commander of 6th Armored Division, saw enough action to make
him one of the leading authorities in mechanized warfare. His postwar writings influenced the U.S. operational art and NATO's European strategy. He
enjoyed a brief renaissance in 1987 when his history of the U.S. armored
force was published in *Armor.*

> In March 1938, Major General John K. Herr succeeded Kromer as Chief
> of Cavalry. . . . He remained fully committed to the retention of all horse
> units, although he accepted mechanized cavalry as a significant arm and
> urged its development and expansion, as long as no horse units were sacri-
> ficed. Since expansion without conversion was impossible within budget-
> ary limitations, he effectively blocked the development of mechanized
> cavalry on the scale demanded by conditions in Europe. . . . My firm
> belief is that had General Herr, from the beginning, taken a strong stand
> for the mechanization of the Cavalry Branch, the Armored Force would
> never have been created.[3]

There was no rebuttal to this thesis. However, there is a letter in the
Grow papers written in 1945, in which General Herr, with some rancor,
takes issue with Grow and attempts to explain his position:

> I confess I was opposed to the destruction of our cavalry by absorption in
> the mechanized Cavalry, as it was robbing Peter to pay Paul, and entirely
> inadvisable and unnecessary. We needed both. . . .
>   The biggest reason is that the moment I threw the bombshell of
> October 3, 1939, demanding immediate American *Panzer* Divisions under
> Cavalry control, consternation ruled the Infantry members of the General
> Staff.
>   I had it personally from General Lynch, Chief of Infantry, that as
> soon as I threw this one Colonel Camp, executive to G3 begged . . . him to
> ask for control of this development for the Infantry. They all recognized
> that it had come and said that unless he barged in, the Cavalry would get
> it. . . .
>   What happened then? Failing in this they set up a conspiracy partici-
> pated in by recreant Cavalry officers of the General Staff to set up an
> independent Arm so that they could get promotion.[4]

The passion and the accusation are enlightening. Herr's bitterness
comes from his belief in betrayal by plotters. His counterthesis is that
although the cavalry under his leadership requested armored divisions, the
formation of the U.S. Armored Corps was caused by ambitious officers
wanting promotion in an independent arm. There is little doubt that if Herr
had had his way and the cavalry had assumed control of armored divisions,
there would have been little room for the apostles of maneuver. Herr would
have left out the sympathizers to the Alexandria proposals (sometimes

referred to as the Alexandria Recommendations) as well as their advocates: this meant Chaffee, Patton, and perhaps even Crittenberger. George Marshall could read the writing on the wall. Had the highest echelons of U.S. Cavalry embraced mechanization in the late 1930s, it may well have been John Herr, not Leslie McNair, that Marshall would choose to create the AGF in World War II.

The chief of cavalry's objection to mechanization failed to perpetuate the essential spirit of the arm: "A Cavalry general should be possessed of a strong inventive genius and be self reliant to strike out a new line and adopt reforms where he sees them necessary."[5] The development of German, Soviet, and even French armor had been ordered from the very highest level, whereas Douglas MacArthur had taken the path of least resistance. When time came for U.S. arms to answer the panzer challenge, George C. Marshall had to impose a solution that would benefit the whole army, rather than only a branch.

It would be wrong to dismiss Herr too quickly. In 1940, cavalry tactics were complex and included a sophisticated mélange of horse and machine. Cavalry included an *ordre mixte* of horses and tanks that sounded equally reasonable to the French army—but the panzers' romp through the Low Countries in 1940 forever confirmed that this was not a modern solution. The U.S. Army realized it would need dozens of tank divisions and hundreds of tank battalions; however, Herr and senior officers of the cavalry read their intelligence reports with some bias. They assumed that the German Army kept nearly 700,000 horses because of a carefully worked out operational doctrine. Of course, it is now known that German industry could not meet the demands of blitzkrieg. The Americans, however, could and did produce a totally motorized and mechanized army by 1943.

That Chaffee and Van Voorhis could rise above their natural devotion to the horse is a credit to their farsightedness. Herr's loyalty to horse cavalry is both noble and tragic. His refusal to accept reality after Munich when even the British realized that cavalry must at last be sent to the knacker's yard was unfortunate; his intractability after the fall of France was stupid.

The path to mechanization was paved by three large practice operations: the 1935 First Army maneuvers (held in northern New York State with 36,000 troops),[6] the 1938 Third Army maneuvers (Texas with 24,000 troops) and the 1939 First Army maneuvers, (held in Plattsburgh, New York, and Manassas, Virginia, with 50,000 troops).[7] The 1935 war games were initiated by Maj. Gen. Hugh A. Drum, who insisted that provisional corps staffs actually deploy and test their operational planning processes. Drum concluded that "an urgent requirement existed for the organization of an adequate field army."[8] As Hitler prepared to invade Poland, the U.S. Congress "in emergency action" increased the authorized strength of the army to 210,000 troops. After hostilities began in Europe, President

Roosevelt raised the army's strength to 227,000, and the War Department, under Gen. George Marshall, began to prepare for global conflict. Marshall appointed Maj. Gen. Leslie McNair, an artillery man with prodigious administrative skills but no combat experience, head of the AGF and made him responsible for formulating army tactical doctrine. McNair, who arrived at his job with "opinions and biases," began by reorganizing the Army's combat divisions from a square to the smaller triangular structure.[9] This set the stage for the "first genuine corps and army maneuvers in the history of the United States."[10]

The War Department planned for a preliminary period of work-up training by small units, followed by corps-level problems, and ending with corps versus corps exercises. Maneuvers in Louisiana took place in a remarkably short time. In May, 1940, the IV and IX Corps deployed in Louisiana and eastern Texas and conducted a four-phase seventeen-day series of exercises testing defensive and offensive doctrine. Some problems appeared, as the after-action report noted: "Despite the emphasis on mechanization and mobility, the commanders recommended that the corps reconnaissance regiment (horse cavalry) be retained, but that it be provided with animal transporter trailers."[11]

The official report was both deceptive and woefully incomplete. The most momentous result of the Louisiana maneuvers began in a local schoolhouse, led to Herr's office in Washington, and ended with a proposal on Marshall's desk for the creation of an autonomous tank force.

The Centurion's Revolt: The Cavalry's End

Come on Bob, I'm through with him.
        —Chaffee to his aide, Lt. Col. Robert Merrill Lee, June 1940

The Louisiana maneuvers prompted the historic gathering in the basement of an Alexandria, Virginia, public school. The meeting included all participating general officers but not the chiefs of infantry and cavalry (Lynch and Herr), although both were present at the war games. The attending officers represented a who's who of the brotherhood of armor: Chaffee, Patton, Krueger, Camp, Gillem, Andrews, Embrick, and Magruder, to name a few. They met in near secrecy to evaluate the lessons learned and quickly agreed on what the army of the future needed. The conclusions were clear: horsed cavalry had no place on a modern mechanized battlefield. The U.S. Army required a tank force—an official, independent branch devoted to the establishment of an armored doctrine, organized and equipped with the necessary weapons and supporting arms.

The "Alexandria recommendations" (a polite reference to a centurions' revolt) argued that the unified development of armored units must be initiated, separated from cavalry and infantry, and their use perfected. This required a revolutionary change and had to be presented to the chief of cavalry. Chaffee was elected to travel across the Potomac to Washington and deliver the news. His confrontation with Herr led to a momentous decision to abandon the cavalry and plead his case directly to Marshall. (Herr would have called it a betrayal.) Chaffee confronted his long-time friend Herr openly and requested that the chief of cavalry convert horsed regiments to create the first armored division, which the Alexandria meeting had recommended.

General Herr "sat there rather straight in his chair, head down—then he looked up. 'Adna, not one more horse will I give up for a tank.'" He banged his hand on the desk. Chaffee calmly stood his ground: "Johnny, if that's the way you feel about it." He saluted and turned to his aide, Lieutenant Colonel Lee, an Army Air Corps officer, and said, "Come on Bob, I'm through with him."[12] Chaffee went back to his room at the Washington Army Officers Club and wrote out a memo. They then went to see Marshall's G3, Maj. Gen. Frank M. Andrews, when Chaffee landed his bombshell: abandon the cavalry to its own ends and create an independent armored force.

It was the third time Chaffee had proposed an Armored Force but always within the cavalry. Now he was prepared to cut all ties. His recommendations had been regularly dismissed, but this was June 1940: the Germans had just crushed both the British Expeditionary Force and the French army. Chaffee now preached to interested ears. Andrews offered to take him to see General Marshall, asking, "Shouldn't we have some sort of formal proposal?" "How about this?" said Chaffee, producing his handwritten memo. "That will do fine—I'll get it typed." Within the hour George Marshall had read Chaffee's proposal and approved it. The Armored Force was born. It was the end of the U.S. Cavalry.

The creation of the U.S. Armored Force on 10 July 1940[13] was a compromise between the infantry, which had so long resisted the term "mechanized," and the cavalry, which absolutely hated the word "tank." Chaffee was appointed the first chief of the Armored Force but did not live to see the full vindication and triumph of his beliefs. The physical and intellectual strain finally overcame his Spartan spirit. He died in Boston on 22 August 1941, a martyr to the army.[14]

Fixing the Odds: Louisiana, 1941, and McNair

McNair was convinced from the start. The Armored Force was the most wasteful of the ground arms in its use of manpower and equipment, profligate, luxurious, monstrous.
—Greenfield, Palmer, and Wiley, The U.S. Army in World War II

Following the creation of the Armored Force, on 3 April 1941 the secretary for war directed "The Chief of Infantry and the Chief of Armored Force, in cooperation, will establish the tactical doctrine on the employment of GHQ tank elements as infantry support units." The force may have been created, but the concept was not fully understood; additional wargames were ordered. The Louisiana maneuvers of 1941 have been dubbed by Christopher Gabel as unprecedented in U.S. Army history and never have been duplicated in size of scope since.[15]

A preparatory period featured corps-level schemes and set the stage for an epochal contest between an armored-cavalry field force and a traditional infantry-dominated army backed by cavalry, strong artillery, and a surfeit of antitank resources.[16] The Second Army (Armored Corps, VII Infantry Corps) covered its five infantry divisions with the cavalry in its two forms: the 1st and 2nd Armored Divisions and the 2nd Cavalry Division. The Third Army (VIII, IV, and V Infantry Corps) deployed nine infantry divisions screened by the 1st Cavalry Division and the 56th Cavalry Brigade. Both armies had an Army Air Corps task force in support. The two-phase contest lasted less than a month, with 400,000 troops taking part, and ended with a convincing victory by the artillery.

The real winner was Leslie McNair, and the loser was American armored doctrine. When Patton argued for maneuver warfare rather than attrition, McNair scoffed: "This is no way to fight a war." The maneuvers were used to officially anoint the McNair solution to blitzkrieg—the tank destroyer doctrine, a determined attempt by gunners to dominate the battlefield in the two dimensions of indirect and direct fire. Louisiana, 1941, featured "the first time that armored forces figured in American battle strategy." McNair, the maneuver director, and his deputy, Brig. Gen. Mark W. Clark, controlled both the umpire evaluations and the official after-exercise critique, which was unforgiving. It was enthusiastically announced that "the maneuvers had shown that armored forces were not invincible. On the contrary, the proper use of antitank weapons, terrain, and demolitions supplied the answer to the problem of meeting what had been described as the hardest and fastest striking force in modern warfare."[17]

McNair judged that "General Griswald had used his tank strength prematurely and in piecemeal . . . First Army maneuvers were inconclusive concerning the effects of massed armor at a decisive moment in battle." Artillery patricians noted with undisguised smugness that antitank guns were rated "highly effective; umpires ruled that a total of 893 tanks on both sides had been put out of action."[18] This corresponded to about 70 percent of the German panzers that defeated the Allies in France a year before. "The umpires ruled that 1st Armored Division had been destroyed at the beginning of the attack when its Line of Communications was cut."[19] In late summer of 1941, after German panzer corps had eliminated Poland, France, and the Balkans—in fact, while the Wehrmacht, in the fury of Operation *Barbarossa,* was penetrating nearly 700 miles into the Soviet Union, surrounding and destroying armies totaling over 1,200,000 troops— General McNair decided that massed armor was passé![20] Gen. Jacob L. Devers, chief of the Armored Force, echoed the opinions of his officers: "We were licked by a set of rules."[21]

Louisiana, 1941: Lessons Learned

Patton's success in Louisiana and the Carolinas also seems to have spiked an attempt by the antitank cabal in Washington to sabotage the Armored Force by relegating it to an insignificant role. . . . McNair, who had kept his thumb firmly on Patton during the Louisiana and Carolina maneuvers . . . had exhibited evidence of a distinct bias against the Armored Force.
—Carlo D'Este[22]

Colonel D'Este's conclusion is only partly correct. In fact, the antitank cabal did rather well after the Louisiana wargames. That very December, McNair convinced the secretary for war that the Armored Force idea was flawed and that "development of antitank forces [should] be stressed."[23] The Tank Destroyer Force and its doctrine grew to a position of eminence second only to that of the Armored Force. The vast resources spent in assembling and training the Tank Destroyer Force formations plus the hundreds of millions spent on developing a series of tracked tank destroyers (M10, M18 Hellcat, and the M36 Jackson) represented the danger of powerful lobbyists pushing a wrong doctrine into an inappropriately powerful position. The essence of the tank destroyer doctrine (massed guns kill tanks) was correct. Its flaw was rooted in simple branch competition. The same sort of tribal shortsightedness that cost the cavalry a formidable place in the military history of World War II, nearly trumped the Armored Force off the tactical table. In fact, guns do kill tanks, but not as artillery—rather, as powerful, high-velocity armament mounted in well-armored, tracked main battle tanks. Nevertheless, on 7 October 1941 McNair created a new addendum to the AGF order of battle: "It was agreed that for psychological reasons that the force should be designated as a 'tank destroyer' force." This was followed by the creation of the National Tank Destroyer Training Center.

The value of an armored corps could not be dismissed, despite McNair's cynicism; the Armored Force survived but never fully prospered. In 1942 the initial U.S. Army plans called for sixty armored divisions. A much reduced total of sixteen armored divisions was actually raised, and only five were available for the Normandy breakout in 1944. It is an interesting historical speculation to imagine Operation Cobra with eight or ten armored divisions romping through the Loire Valley and into Lorraine. The Rhine may well have been crossed by the fall of 1944.[24]

The gains of the Louisiana maneuvers were complete tests of doctrine, command, and the logistic support systems. Recommendations to standardize fuel, spare parts, repair, and recovery, in addition to testing G4 movement tables, deployment, and resupply at the division, corps, and army level, enabled the U.S. Army to deploy in North Africa within a year. The question of massed armored movement was thoroughly investigated, and the raison d'être for an armored force was made clear in the minds of the tank officers who were to lead U.S. armor against the best panzer forces of the Third Reich. General McNair's exercise critique of the Louisiana maneuvers was delivered on 30 November 1941, one week before the attack on Pearl Harbor. The 1941 maneuvers were the last of the great American peacetime maneuvers, and Marshall would now be formally dealing with the business of war.

Thus the U.S. Tank Force had to survive two doctrinal challenges against the tank: the first was the cavalry's objection to mechanization, the second was an artillery attempt to wrest tactical dominance from armor. That it survived—indeed, triumphed—was due to battlefield leadership and awesome power of American industry. Despite the doctrinal squabbles, Yankee know-how and Wall Street money allowed breathing room for both points of view. By the war's end, the U.S. Army fielded nearly two dozen armored divisions and scores of GHQ tank battalions.

Creating a Canadian Armored Force

Worthington in Camp Borden

By 1939, the tank had progressed from essentially an attempt to find a way through a machine gun–swept battlefield to an aggressive arm capable of strategic decision. Canadian reaction to mechanization was a mixture of professional interest and caution—mixed with a little envy:

> The problem of armor which is a practical problem and depends for its successful solution upon a mass of mechanical detail is being largely obscured by violent propaganda and emotional appeals about "losses." The problems in staff work and leadership involved in the use of great mechanized forces are intricate and complex. A hastily improvised mechanized army will lose, at a bound, nine-tenths of its effective striking power. We must, therefore, be prepared to maintain mechanized forces in peace, and it will be impossible suddenly to expand them beyond a certain measure, without risk of a general break-down in leadership.[25]

National Defence Headquarters' Memorandum on Training clearly stated the opinion of the Canadian General Staff regarding armor: "Attack is based on manpower (the rifleman) supported by firepower (artillery and the machine gun) . . . any slender tank resources could be made use of by this method, either to lead the attacking (infantry) columns or the mopping up battalions."[26] This was the operational wisdom that would lead Canadian arms through training and onto the battlefield in the coming war. German aggression brought the government to its senses and it reacted remarkably quickly.

On 13 August 1940, after the fall of France, the minister of national defense ordered the creation of an Armoured Corps.[27] In contradistinction to the creation of the U.S. Armored Force, the Canadian army entered the tank business without a power struggle or the castration of a traditional arm. Regiments with lineages begun in the eighteenth century maintained their traditions and readied for mechanized war. Unlike the AGF, there was no pause for a Louisiana. Canadian armored doctrine would be imposed by the British Empire.

The first commandant of the Canadian Armoured School was Brevet Lt. Col. F. F. Worthington, a former machine gun officer who had distinguished himself in the Great War.[28] Worthington became commandant of the Canadian Armoured Fighting Vehicle Training Center and the 1st Armoured Brigade.

The cavalry was quickly dispatched: the Royal Canadian Dragoons "concentrated at St. Jean, held a final mounted parade and saw with heavy hearts their mounts sold or destroyed."[29] That fall Worthington visited the United States: "I then proceeded . . . to get some tanks and purchased 236 last war six ton Renaults. They were all runners and laid the foundation of armored trg in the Cdn Army."[30] These were shipped to the "Camp Borden Iron Foundry"—an expedient to allow transfer of tanks from the United States, which was still neutral. By the winter of that year, an infantry division was fully converted to armor and three units were selected for incorporation in the 1st Army Tank Brigade.[31] The most important of all principles in the regimental system—tribal identity—was waived in favor of having each unit assigned to the Armoured Corps adopt a numerical designation. "[Worthington] suggested that within the corps there must be a uniformity of training under skilled guidance, a uniformity of purpose and doctrine throughout all armored units, a uniformity and interchangeability of personnel."[32]

This followed, in essence, what the German army did but proved difficult in an army where the regimental name, tradition, and hard-won battle honors meant so much. Eventually a compromise crept in, and by the time of the Normandy campaign the units in the corps were known by lengthy designations that included both.[33]

Training the Corps

It is unlikely tanks will be used by Canadians in this war.
—DND communiqué to Lt. Col. F. F. Worthington, November 1939

Colonel Worthington ("Worthy") bristled with ideas and energy. He was Canada's answer to Van Voorhis and Chaffee—a soldier's soldier who understood war. Unfortunately he was no Patton. He understood men and the tanks but had little idea how to train a tank division or a tank force. The Canadian Armoured Corps was to grow at an amazing pace under his tireless leadership but it would not reach maturity.

Using the British example, certain designations were to mean different things in Armoured Corps parlance. "Tanks" really meant "infantry tanks," and the independent brigades with these vehicles were to serve under command of infantry brigades within the structure of an infantry corps. "Armoured" eventually referred to one of the two brigades in an "armoured division" that, in theory, would have a "cavalry tank" role. By 1944 all brigades in the Royal Canadian Armoured Corps were known as armored brigades, and the decision to adopt one type of tank—the U.S. M4 Sherman—meant that even the units that should have acted as infantry tanks did not. The Armoured Corps now began to wrestle with the doctrinal difficulties that tormented European armies in the 1930s. Not having any experimental training maneuvers and no battle experience, no one really understood the difference between assault tanks and the maneuver mass of an armored division. Doctrine was taught as pure theory but changed seasonally with each British defeat or victory in the Western Desert. By 1943, the Royal Canadian Armoured Corps would boast two armored divisions (the 4th and 5th Canadian Armoured Divisions) and two independent tank brigades (1st and 2d Canadian Armoured Brigades); including corps and divisional reconnaissance units, the corps deployed a total of nineteen combat regiments.

Although its equipment would be on a par with that of any Western ally, its leadership was in dire need of operational experience. The corps was rushed off to the lush downs of Dorset, England, where it would be schooled in the ways of desert warfare in the frustrating traffic jams that pretended to be tank training areas. Meanwhile, in Canada, bisected with efficient roads and railheads, hours from the tank assembly plants of Detroit and Montreal, lay open steppes that extended for hundreds of kilometers. It may be argued, of course, that with the gunner-infantry attitude prevailing in Ottawa, mechanized war games would not have occurred even after 1940. Certainly Worthington, who was worth his weight in gold, had neither the political clout nor the operational vision to organize exercises à la Louisiana. Camp Borden and Bovington would have to do.

The difference between the American and Canadian approach to mechanization was the vehemence of the argument. In Ottawa it was a debating point; in Washington it was a struggle for material and philosophical existence. Division and some bitterness within continued (albeit mainly from the *Cavalry Journal*) throughout the war. The Canadian move into mechanization was accomplished without bitter dispute, but also without serious experimentation. By the time real tank units were being formed, France had fallen and there was little discussion regarding the tank's usefulness. The cavalry had so little clout that its nostalgia for the horse passed mostly unnoticed. The Canadian army did not technically convert to mechanization, it was raised as a mechanized army.

Unfortunately the "new" Canadian cavalry adopted a Royal Tank Regiment style and attempted to redefine itself around the "black beret."[34] The Americans had fought through a problem and attempted to solve it first by compromise and then by substitution. "Cavalry" came to indicate a specific mission while "armor" wrote its own traditions and roles. The Canadian army evolved easily into modern mechanized warfare and then sought to define itself through ersatz traditions.

The Canadian prewar military philosophers dealt in generalities and analyses of other armies' solutions. Worse, there were no Pattons, Woods, or Grows to take command and forge the Canadian Thunderbolt. Worthington was the Canadian Chaffee, a spiritual leader, a splendid trainer of men, a cavalier romantic. The Canadian army was to become, proportionally, the most mechanized in the entire war: two armored divisions, two independent armored brigades, and three motorized infantry divisions—but without a homegrown tank doctrine. The Canadian battlefield tactical solutions were, for the most part, to be made by gunners. As stated by E. L. M. Burns: "In Canada we have no soldier trained in the operation of what responsible military opinion recognizes as the potentially most powerful arm of the service—and what is more serious, no officer trained in the command of this arm."[35]

Burns's words were prophetic. The Canadian army's failure to produce officers qualified in temperament and experience to lead an armored formation was to cost dearly. North American armor was theoretically ready to do battle in Europe, but the only active operational theatre was in North Africa where were found the best of Western tank formations. Canadian attendance at this graduate school was limited to thousands of Can-Loan officers who offered to serve with the British army to gain combat experience. No tactical formations were deployed. Canadian armor was husbanded in England awaiting the second front. Conversely, U.S. AGF armor was deployed in the desert—from an initial training base in Egypt, to a complete armored division and tank destroyer battalions in Tunisia. It was the North African desert that first educated U.S. tankers.

Notes

1. Col. Harrison H. D. Heiberg papers, Patton Museum Library.

2. Grow, *Armor* (January–February 1987, March–April 1987, May–June 1987, July–August 1987).

3. Grow, *Armor* (April–August 1987).

4. Letter from James K. Herr, President, United States Cavalry Association, to Maj. Gen. Robert W. Grow, 6th Armored Division, 7 June 1945, Special Studies, WWII OCMH Collection, MHI.

5. Col. G. T. Denison, *A History of Cavalry.* Denison (a Canadian whose work won the czar's prize "5,000 rubles" for "the best History of Cavalry" in 1877) appears to have had considerable influence in the U.S. Cavalry. His work was found in all camp libraries, and he was regularly quoted in tactical studies, particularly by General Grow. Mr. John M. Purdy, director of the Patton Museum of Cavalry and Armor, Fort Knox, suggests that Denison received more serious attention in the United States than he did in England or Canada.

6. The Louisiana maneuvers were made possible by the creation of four field armies in 1932, a general increase of the regular army, and the new triangular structure of the combat divisions. This made possible the creation of corps organization. "Training was very poorly accomplished in the Army because few officers knew much about training and there were practically no soldiers to train and no one really cared about training anyway." Gen. Hamilton Howze. Howze Papers, MHI.

7. Observed by Wehrmacht officers who "left just before the war started." Colonel Heiberg Papers. Patton Library, Fort Knox.

8. Jean R. Moenk, *A History of Large-Scale Army Maneuvers in the United States, 1935–1964* (Fort Monroe: Headquarters U.S. Continental Army Command, 1969).

9. Steven J. Zaloga, *Sherman—Medium Tank, 1942–1945* (London: Osprey, 1993), p. 3.

10. Moenk, p. 27.

11. "[There was] little attention to concealment . . . infantry and cavalry were decidedly roadbound and road discipline was extremely poor. . . . General Krueger, commander of the provisional IX Corps, pointed out that infantrymen would have to learn that trucks were not fighting vehicles. . . . Disastrous losses could be expected any time that a forward advance came within range of artillery fire." *Final Report, Third Army Maneuvers, 5–25 May 1940,* vol. III, Anx. 21, "Final Critiques." Moenk, p. 32.

12. See Gen. Robert Merrill Lee papers (a splendid firsthand account), Patton Museum Library, Fort Knox. Also see Col. H. H. D. Heiberg papers, "Report on the Alexandria Meeting."

13. Chaffee, as its first chief was promoted to brigadier general. Since there was no congressional authorization for a separate armored branch, it was established technically "for purposes of service test." The force included I Armored Corps, 1st Armored Division, the Armored Force Board, and a small Armored Force School at Fort Knox. Stubbs, Connor, *Armor Cavalry,* p. 58.

14. "Sacrificed himself for Armored Force." *Philadelphia Bulletin:* "Physical breakdown follows intense work undertaken" *City Journal.* "Creator of Army Armored Divisions . . . in 1930s predicted 'Blitz.'" *New York Times,* 23 August 1941.

15. *National Guard Maneuvers, Third Army, August 1940* proved that ad hoc corps headquarters could not function and identified the need for medical, engineer,

signals, and military police units to augment a corps organization. "National Guard peacetime training program was totally inadequate." *First Army Maneuvers, Upper New York State, August 1940:* General Drum's critique noted weaknesses in officer training, citing "inadequate reconnaissance . . . faulty signal communications; passive employment of antitank guns; improper use of horse cavalry." *Final Report, First Army Maneuvers, 1940,* reported in Moenk. *GHQ-Directed Maneuvers, 1941; Second Army Maneuvers, Tenn/Oklahoma 1941:* first to use infantry divisions at full authorized strength; Arkansas maneuvers, VII Corps, 1941: "use of terrain, obstacles and demolition in defense against armored attacks." Comments on VII Corps exercises. Moenk. Chaffee was succeeded by Devers on 1 August 1941. The third Armored Force chief, Gillem, took over from Devers on 11 May 1943.

16. "Such was the Promethean size of the new armored division that when the 2d Armored left Fort Benning for Tennessee, each of its two columns was sixty miles long." Carlo D'Este, *Patton—A Genius for War* (New York: Harper Collins, 1995), p. 394.

17. AGF Study No. 16, pp. 26–27. Also AGF Study No. 11. U.S. Army Historical Section—Army Ground Forces 1948. The maneuvers also revealed "woeful deficiencies among officers [and] low morale, slack discipline and poor performance in tactical operations." McNair ended the critique by tearing a strip off his senior officers: "I propose to have discipline and efficiency in this Army . . . men who are professionally able, who are keen and enthusiastic. . . . We must be done with shilly-shallying and indecision." Gen. Lesley J. McNair, Notes for Special Critique for General Officers only, 11 September 1941, AGF Records, MHI.

The Louisiana maneuvers' price for failure was high. McNair cleaned out the old and those he deemed untalented: thirty-two of the forty-two army, corps, and division commanders were "ruthlessly purged."

18. In the exercise 91 percent of tanks were rated destroyed by guns, 5 percent by grenades, 3 percent by mines, and 1 percent by air attack. No official results for tank kills were given. AGF Study No. 1, U.S. Army 1946, Origins of the Army Ground Forces, General Headquarters, US Army, 1940–1942, p. 33. Reported in Moenk, p. 67.

19. AGF Study No. 1, p. 33.

20. Other after-action recommendations concluded the following: "1. Standardized Fuel. 2. Simple Parts . . . Ordnance system operating through corps areas failed during maneuvers . . . to secure proper stockage at army depots it was necessary for the armored corps personnel to constantly advise army depot personnel." "Report on Supply of Armored Units based on experience in Louisiana and Carolina Maneuvers, 1941," Newton papers, MHI.

21. Devers got his revenge after World War II when he ensured that the tank destroyer program met a quiet but firm end. Carlo D'Este partly sympathizes with McNair and sees no dark artillery plot:

> Patton's tanks attempted to pry open the 2nd Armored [which] suffered heavy losses in what soon became a rout. . . . McNair mercifully ended the phase. . . . When Phase II began a week later, the roles were reversed . . . Krueger elected to launch a bold flank attack with I Armored Corps, which initiated a 350 mile end run. . . . The journey took Patton back into Texas. . . . Although McNair later denied that Patton's audacity was the underlying reason, he nevertheless decided to end the final phase of the Louisiana maneuvers prematurely after barely five days." D'Este, *Patton,* p. 396.

22. D'Este, p. 401.

23. Gabel, p. 17. See also Emory A. Dunham, *Tank Destroyer History. Army Ground Forces Study No. 29* Historical Section, Army Ground Forces, 1946, and Charles M. Bailey, *Faint Praise: American Tanks and Tank Destroyers During World War II* (Hamden: Archon, 1983).

24. The limitation to this fanciful scenario is both the shortsightedness of Supreme Headquarters Allied Expeditionary Force (SHAEF) and the problem of gasoline. A combination of Montgomery's command and fuel shortage stopped the U.S. Third Army in the fall of 1944. This problem had been predicted by Patton during the Louisiana maneuvers: "We need gas. Lots of gas. We've got a real problem here. Without gas then the war game is over. I cannot move ten miles without gas." D'Este, *Patton*, p. 398.

25. V. W. Germains, "Armored Warfare, A Plea for Common Sense," *Army Quarterly* XVI (April–July 1928): 369.

26. *CDQ* 14 (October 1936). "Memorandum on Training," NDHQ.

27. Worthington had convinced Rogers earlier, but the minister was killed in a plane crash. Ralston, the new minister of defence waited until panzer divisions had chased McNaughton's expeditionary force out of France before approving Worthington's memorandum for the creation of an armored force.

28. Worthington was born in Scotland, but was a graduate of the University of California. As a young man, he volunteered to join "Black Jack" Pershing's U.S. expeditionary force to chase Pancho Villa through Mexico. He fought as a mercenary in revolutions in Nicaragua, Mexico, and Chile. He had also been a mule skinner and a cowboy. He enlisted as a private in the Montreal Black Watch in 1914. He won both the Military Medal and the Military Cross twice. By 1944 he was a legend in the Armoured Corps: "As stern a believer in the striking power of an armored division as Martel of England [and] de Gaulle of France, Gen. Worthington is known throughout the land as the 'Father' of the Cdn Armd Corps." RG 24 17446. Camp Borden, Canadian Armoured School Journal, *The Tank,* May 1944.

29. Worthington, *The Spur and the Sprocket* (Toronto: Macmillan, 1961).

30. He examined prototypes of the Grant tank. RG 24 10455. Letter of Maj. Gen. F. F. Worthington to CMHQ, 22 March 45.

31. Canadian training attempts were frustrating: Crerar tried to get fifty men to England but the British declined. "The supply of equipment for the Canadian battalion is so doubtful that no good purpose can be served by dispatch of even a cadre." CMHQ File Policy re Armoured Troops. War Office letter to Brig. H. D. G. Crerar, CMHQ. The 1st Armoured Division later became the 5th Canadian Armoured Division.

32. Reginald Roy, *Sinews of Steel,* p. 134. "Free use of officers and other ranks capable of performing duties required irrespective of the individual units to which they belong," "Formation of Armoured Corps," memorandum from Samson to Worthington; "Organization, Training and Employment of a Canadian Armoured Corps," 19 July 1940.

33. For example, the reconnaissance regiment of the 3d Infantry Division was "7th Recce Regiment (17th Duke of York's Royal Canadian Hussars)." Maj. Gen. Sansom, commander of the armored division "would have preferred to keep original unit titles, but he bowed to the opinion of others." Roy, p. 134.

34. British military styles in uniforms were and are important in Canada and not seen as "British." The headgear of the Royal Tank Regiment was the black beret (hiding oil and grease stains, being easy to stow, fitting any head, and giving protection against bruises). The Chasseurs Alpins beret was too big and floppy, and the

Basque beret was too "skimpy," so a compromise "more akin to the Scottish 'tam-o-shanter'" was finally selected. It was universally adopted by all Empire tankers during World War II and by some NATO tankers after the war. The Wehrmacht also adopted a very large black beret for its tankers, made more awkward when fitted with a hardened leather insert—much like a bicycle helmet.

    35. *CDQ* 15 (1935). E. L. M. Burns, "A Step Towards Modernization," p. 305.

A Canadian Sherman M4A3 from the 2nd Canadian Armoured Brigade (1st Hussars) crosses an obstacle south of Caen *(Bell, National Archives of Canada, Wilfred Laurier University, Laurier Centre for Military Strategic and Disarmament Studies)*

CHAPTER 5

Creating North American Panzer Armies: Lessons from Europe and Africa

The fact is that the British had no idea at all as to the sort of war they were going to fight, nor the sort of war that it would suit them best to fight if the enemy would be so kind as to allow them to choose.
                                        —Lt. Gen. Sir Francis Tuker[1]

The Armored Division as Tactical Toolbox

The Battle of France in 1940 had been an epiphanic experience. If Poland had been dismissed as a lucky victory against a second-rate opponent, then no one could deny the triumph of panzers over both the French army and the British Expeditionary Force (BEF). The all-tanks school had triumphed. It was a double triumph in that the campaign in France at once legitimized mechanization and gave bragging rights to the Royal Tank Corps, which had been so far dismissed as made up of annoying zealots. But the U.S. War Department incorrectly interpreted the essential element of the German victory.

It was the panzer division, not the panzer, that had defeated the Allied armies in France. The German commanders had created mission-oriented, customized tactical groupings that reflected a sound doctrine backed up by an experienced organization of military craftsmen. When the task was done, the tools were put back into the box. In the Wehrmacht, there was no system of regimental fealty to overcome; loyalty was to the division. It was this ability to act as members of a larger family that permitted quick and efficient ad hoc battle organizations.

It has been suggested that the essence of the German operational art, the heart of blitzkrieg, was the natural ability to conduct audacious, creative maneuver and thwart enemy armies by getting inside their decision cycle.[2] This capacity for dynamic tactical problem solving was supposedly made possible by doctrinal commitment to *auftragstaktik* (mission-directed tactics). The opposite of *befehlstaktik* (order-directed tactics), *auftragstaktik* permits commanders at more junior levels great independence in battlefield problem solving but demands complete doctrinal competence. Despite the adoption of both maneuver and auftragstaktik by NATO armies at the end of the twentieth century, there is little evidence that the German army specifically nurtured auftragstaktik as a doctrinal goal at the tactical level. The German predilection for mission command was probably cultural rather than technical. Perhaps the best analysis of the nature of auftragstaktik was given by Field Marshal Erich von Manstein:

> It has always been the particular forte of German leadership to grant wide scope to self-dependence of subordinate commanders—to allot them tasks which leave execution to the discretion of the individual. The German method is really rooted in the German character . . . [which] finds a certain pleasure in taking risks.[3]

This readiness to roll the dice was in direct opposition to the British (and, in many cases, Canadian) tendency to respect lines and "follow the rules" in battle. Vigorous doctrine was next to impossible in an army that prided itself on obeying orders and frowned on initiative. The concept of "set piece battle" was the antithesis of auftragstaktik. The excessive comfort with befehlstaktik was eventually recognized by the British War Office itself: "The British character is naturally not inquisitive enough and individual officers and soldiers tend to shirk inquiring into matters which they consider the business of other people."[4]

This is not to suggest that individual British commanders could not demonstrate independent creativity and daring. First off, it must be recognized that the Allies had begun the war at a tactical disadvantage. For the British the 1940 campaign in France was an initial "shakeout," whereas by then the German army had already done with experimentation. Spain, Austria, Czechoslovakia and the final dress rehearsal in Poland had honed the panzer blade and produced battlewise staffs. Nevertheless, doctrinal superiority and experience could always be stopped cold by determined leadership and good equipment. The panzer forces, protected by complete air superiority, had raced through France defeating "penny packets" of Allied armor. The Germans' great fear was that a solid concentration of tanks attacking their very exposed flank could end it all. This nearly occurred when the BEF finally, albeit briefly, got its ducks in a row.

On 20 May 1940, a counterattack by British Matildas near Vimy Ridge almost succeeded in cutting off the spearhead of the panzer army—Rommel's 7th "Phantom" Panzer Division. Lt. Gen. Giffard Le Q. Martel's tanks routed the flank guard and then savaged the main body.[5] German

LESSONS FROM THE DESERT

The Tank Battle: A Gun Duel - Desert battles were compared to Naval engagements

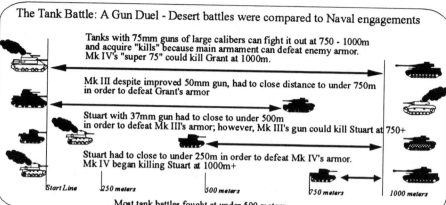

Tanks with 75mm guns of large calibers can fight it out at 750 - 1000m and acquire "kills" because main armament can defeat enemy armor. Mk IV's "super 75" could kill Grant at 1000m.

Mk III despite improved 50mm gun, had to close distance to under 750m in order to defeat Grant's armor.

Stuart with 37mm gun had to close to under 500m in order to defeat Mk III's armor; however, Mk III's gun could kill Stuart at 750+

Stuart had to close to under 250m in order to defeat Mk IV's armor. Mk IV began killing Stuart at 1000m+

Start Line   250 meters   500 meters   750 meters   1000 meters

Most tank battles fought at under 500 meters

The Tank Battle: Basic Tactics

"Hull Down":
Tank fires while vehicle hull is hidden from enemy gunfire

"Turret Down":
Tank commander observes entire vehicle (hull and turret) is hidden

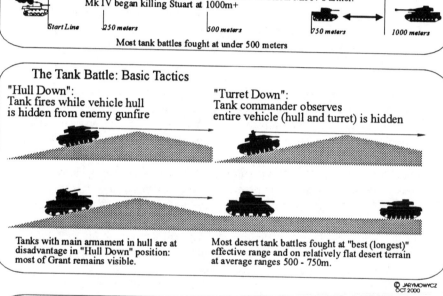

Tanks with main armament in hull are at disadvantage in "Hull Down" position: most of Grant remains visible.

Most desert tank battles fought at "best (longest)" effective range and on relatively flat desert terrain at average ranges 500 - 750m.

© JARYMOWYCZ
OCT 2000

The Tank Battle: Basic Tactics

Facing Enemy:
Frontal Armor is strongest

Tactical Maneuver:
Aim is to get a <u>flank</u> or <u>rear</u> shot while presenting own <u>front</u> to enemy

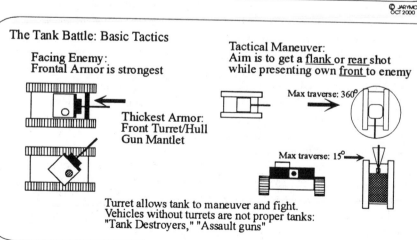

Thickest Armor:
Front Turret/Hull
Gun Mantlet

Max traverse: 360°

Max traverse: 15°

Turret allows tank to maneuver and fight.
Vehicles without turrets are not proper tanks:
"Tank Destroyers," "Assault guns"

counterattacks by Panzer IIIs and Pragas were easily beaten off;[6] the SS battlegroup *Totenkopf,* in its first campaign, broke. Martel was elated:

> His tanks were knocked out quite easily by our 2-pdr antitank gun, where-as our infantry tanks resisted the shell fire of the corresponding enemy 37-mm gun without difficulty. Some tanks were hit fifteen times without hav-ing an effect on the tank or the crew. When a tank can advance and ignore the fire of the main enemy antitank guns, a great moral effect is produced.[7]

Rommel was forced to bring up a battery of 88mm dual-purpose guns from his divisional flak battalion to finally stop the British charge: "I per-sonally gave each gun its target."[8] Martel's tanks, unsupported by infantry, were reduced to ineffective troop-sized elements and "were now practically isolated in this area,"[9] being forced to withdraw and breaking off the only menacing Allied attack in the 1940 campaign.

The lessons were clear: tanks could not attack unsupported and required both armored infantry and artillery to deal with enemy antitank gunners. Finally, mass was imperative if an armored attack was to absorb losses and still have the punch to break through. Martel was appointed commander of the Royal Armored Corps (RAC) in December 1940 and immediately began to reorganize it. His attempts at reform were resented by Royal Tank Corps (RTC) partisans, particularly Gen. Percy Hobart, who was described as "one of the rudest men in the Army, a fanatic for his own conception of armored forces, full of prejudices and especially intoler-ant."[10] Hobart was an archetype of the aggressive Fullerist advocate: "His tactical ideas are based on the invincibility and invulnerability of the tank to the exclusion of the employment of other arms in correct proportion."[11]

At one stage the British army had gone from "all-tank" forces, in which infantry, artillery, and engineers were relegated to an auxiliary role, to permanent brigade groups wherein each tank brigade was given its own infantry. British armor was organized in the French fashion: infantry tanks were grouped in independent "tank brigades," while cavalry tanks were organized into "armoured brigades." The cavalry spirit was proudly reflected: as late as 1943 the 7th Armoured Division ("Desert Rats") had a "light" and a "heavy" brigade.[12] At one stage the armored brigades became minidivisions, each with its own infantry and artillery battalions, but with-out the integral supporting arms and services (e.g., engineers, ordnance, transport, signals) to make them effective combat units. The brigade group was accused of being "a fancy name for a disastrous dissipation of effort.[13] There was the uneasy marriage of the 'tank-alone' school of the Royal Tank Corps, and the 'armour-is-cavalry' school of the cavalry. To this want of intellectual preparedness was added to want of operational experience."[14]

In August 1942, in the early desert campaigns, Gen. Claude

Auchinleck ordered armored divisions to fight in tactical concert, not as separate brigade bands. "We have always opposed the pernicious infantry brigade group system. It does for small wars but it is rubbish for modern war. It leads to confusion, dispersion, unbalancing of forces and chaotic planning."[15] Finally, the armored division was reduced to an armored brigade of three tank battalions, with its own motorized infantry battalion, and a three-battalion infantry brigade. This was the model adopted by Canada.

Because the British armored divisions fought their brigades as independent entities, they were regularly defeated in bits and pieces. For instance, "Ritchie had thrown his armor into battle piecemeal and had thus given us the chance of engaging them on each separate occasion with just enough of our own tanks."[16] The divisional organizations continued to be armor heavy; the infantry and artillery were banished to "support groups." Whereas the German Afrika Korps arrived in Tripoli in North Africa well schooled in the all-arms battle,[17] British tanks continued to attack without infantry or artillery, which were locked up in "boxes":

> There was an even more disastrous result from this failure by the British Staff to design a homogeneous battle group. The infantry in their "boxes" when in defence, would call on the tanks for support when hard pressed, for they too needed 25-pounder H.E. [high explosive] on a scale which no single battery could supply. In the result the practice grew up of requiring British tanks to run around the desert attempting to protect the "boxes" threatened with being overrun.[18]

Learning from the Desert

Tank battles stopped at night in the desert, both sides pausing to replenish and repair. The British rallied to the rear and formed protective laagers. (*Laager* is an Afrikaans word that originally meant a defensive circle of wagons.) The Germans formed laagers as well, but they did so on the battlefield, which permitted their electrical and mechanical engineers, organized into recovery and repair teams, to move forward and repair the tanks left in the battle area. The Germans had well-equipped mobile repair shops that could handle all minor and most major repairs.

> However many vehicles the Germans lost they were going to get a far greater number back in action than we could because of their efficient recovery system. Their huge tracked and wheeled tank-transporters were actually going into battle with the tanks themselves. Even while the fighting was going on, the men in the transporters were prepared to dash into the battle, hook on to damaged vehicles and drag them to a point where they could start repairs right away.[19]

Western Armored Divisions 1942 Battalion Equivalents

British Armored Division

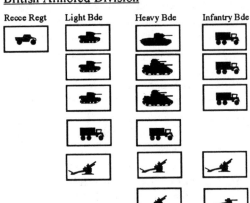

Recce Regt **Light Bde** **Heavy Bde** **Infantry Bde**

Reconnaissance Regiment

Light Brigade:
3 light tank regiments
1 motor infantry battalion
1 artillery regiment

Heavy Brigade:
3 medium tank regiments
1 motor infantry battalion
2 artillery regiments

Infantry Brigade:
3 infantry battalions
1 artillery regiment
1 anti-tank regiment

6 Tank Battalions:
Tank/Infantry/Artillery Ratio 6:5:4

Divisional troops:
anti-tank regiment, signals,
engineer, anti-aircraft units

German Panzer Division

Recon Bn **Pz Regt** **Pz Gren Regt** **Arty Regt**

Reconnaissance Battalion

Tank Regiment:
2 medium tank regiments

Panzer Grenadier Regiment:
3 Panzer Grenadier battalions

2 Tank Battalions:
Tank/Infantry/Artillery Ratio 2:3:3

Artillery Regiment:
2 medium artillery battalions
1 heavy artillery battalion

©Jarymowycz
Oct 2000

American Armored Division

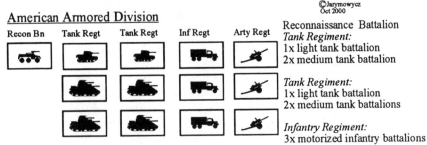

Recon Bn **Tank Regt** **Tank Regt** **Inf Regt** **Arty Regt**

Reconnaissance Battalion
Tank Regiment:
1x light tank battalion
2x medium tank battalion

Tank Regiment:
1x light tank battalion
2x medium tank battalions

Infantry Regiment:
3x motorized infantry battalions

6 Tank Battalions:
Tank/Infantry/Artillery Ratio 2:1:1

Artillery Regiments
3x artillery battalions

If they were not immediately blown up, most tanks were abandoned after one hit due to fear of fire; because both sides used solid shot, the violence of the penetration also caused "splash"—bits of molten metal bursting out internally, wounding the crew but causing minimal structural damage. By owning the battlefield, Rommel would often salvage as much as 50 percent of a day's losses. The British did not have a comparable organization: tanks were taken to corps or army rear areas to effect repairs. But by the end of the Western Desert campaign, the British army had organized its own corps of electrical and mechanical engineers.[20]

The Battle of France in 1940 had demonstrated the decisive power of massed armor in operational maneuver. The Western Desert was the tactical sweatshop, and here the debate of armor versus gun was fought to an inconclusive end as both sides scrambled to introduce better armored and armed tanks. The Germans started with one important advantage—the 88mm flak gun, that became an antitank gun. This weapon killed British armor (including Matildas) at distances of 2,000 meters or better. The "88" provided the Germans with an anvil upon which to hammer British armor or a shield with which to deflect a blow while attacking elsewhere. The British seemed incapable of effectively responding to the challenge.[21]

However, the U.S. AGF had the resources and know-how to solve the armored force problem. American industry could produce the better tank, if given the chance.

The Antitank Cabal: Armor Versus the Tank Destroyer

The tank was introduced to protect against automatic small arms fire, which was developed so greatly during and since the World War. Its answer is fire against which the tank does not protect—the antitank gun. That this answer failed was primarily due to the pitifully inadequate number and power of French and British antitank guns, as well as their incorrect organization.

—Gen. Lesley J. McNair

The tank destroyer concept, "initiated by George C. Marshall, nurtured by Lesley J. McNair, and implemented by Andrew D. Bruce, was the U.S. Army's response to the revolution in warfare known as the blitzkrieg."[22] Marshall's patience had been sorely tried by both the infantry and cavalry chiefs, and in 1940 he directed that his G3 establish a small planning and research branch, primarily to consider antitank warfare. The foxes were in the doctrinal hen house. A series of antitank conferences were called in April 1941, with representatives from all branches. It was decided to create first a "tank destroyer" (a 75mm gun mounted on a half-track) and form "divisional Antitank Battalions in each foot infantry division, motorized

DESERT SOLUTIONS
Seeking a Tactical Answer to Operational Threat

Desert Tactics: "Brigade Boxes" - The new *British square*
The "Pivot" vs Maneuver

"Brigade Boxes" act like "Waterloo squares"
- force German "cavalry" into frontal attacks.
If Germans maneuver they are pinned against minefields
by the British mass of armor.

Recce clash:
German recce defines
defensive areas;
seeks mass British armor

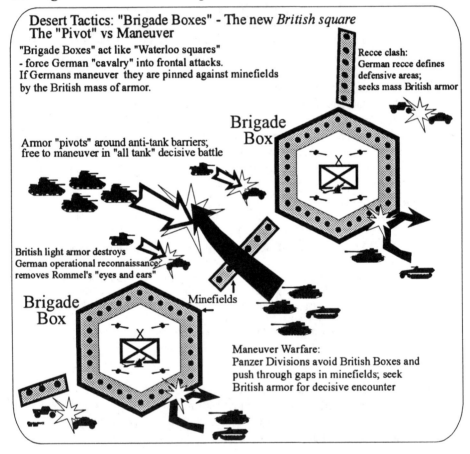

Brigade
Box

Armor "pivots" around anti-tank barriers;
free to maneuver in "all tank" decisive battle

British light armor destroys
German operational reconnaissance;
removes Rommel's "eyes and ears"

Brigade
Box

Minefields

Maneuver Warfare:
Panzer Divisions avoid British Boxes and
push through gaps in minefields; seek
British armor for decisive encounter

infantry division, and possibly, armored force division and secondly to form GHQ Antitank battalions."[23] An illustration of McNair's complete misunderstanding of operational armor is the advice he offered Marshall:

> In my view the essential element of armored action is a powerful blow delivered by surprise. While armored units may be broken up and attached to division and army corps, it is readily conceivable, and indeed probable, that the entire force, under a single command, may be thrown against a decisive point.[24]

The infantry branch, understandably, eagerly embraced McNair's doctrine:

> An increase in armor or gun power can have no purpose other than to engage in tank to tank action—which is unsound. Moreover, such a tank would be disadvantageous in carrying out the primary mission of armor— to defeat those elements of the enemy which are vulnerable to tanks. The answer to heavy tanks is the tank destroyer.[25]

The Louisiana maneuvers created an armored métier within the upper echelons of the Armored Force (Crittenberger wrote: "As we maneuver in Louisiana, so shall we fight"). Anointed graduates adjudicated tactical problems throughout the war by "quoting the Louisiana Exercise as others quoted the Bible."[26] However, proponents of Louisiana-based dogma were soon shunted to a doctrinal Avignon while the McNair group was encouraged by British experience in the Western Desert. In May 1941, the British lost over 300 tanks in two days during Operation Battleaxe. U.S. Army tank destroyer (TD) theorists noted the effect of antitank fire and crowed in vindication of their doctrine. The fact that the very deadly 88mm gun had no readily available counterpart in either the U.S. or British arsenal was overlooked.

One year later, the American Grant tank surprised the Germans in North Africa. Despite obvious shortcomings, its armor and firepower more than justified the tank's existence. The Grant's 75mm gun penetrated the new face-hardened armor on the German tanks. At long range the Grant's armor withstood the long 50mm L/60 on German Mk IIIs. Finally, when the new version of the German Mk IV, the Ausf F2 with a long 75mm Kwk L/43 gun, appeared, it defeated the Grant with ease. Nonetheless, the TD lobby continued to dismiss armor-only engagements.

U.S. Army AGF doctrine stressed that tanks were to be held in armored divisions until a breakthrough was prepared by the infantry. The tanks would then perform as the Mongol hordes and run amuck in the enemy's rear. As late as 1943, McNair insisted that the "general concept of an armored force is that it is an instrument of exploitation, not very different in principle from horse cavalry of old. . . . An armored division is of value only in pursuit and exploitation."[27]

This philosophy even crept into British doctrinal thinking, and, despite significant experience with tank conflicts in North Africa, the War Office prepared the 21st Army Group for Normandy by asserting:

> It is this fact (mobility, rapid reinforcement of threatened areas) which causes armor to attract armor. Although in theory, tanks avoid tank vs. tank battles, these frequently occur only when normal antitank measures are inadequate should tanks be used to provide a mobile reserve which can, when absolutely necessary, be used to deal with enemy armored fighting vehicles.[28]

The first test for U.S. armor would be in Tunisia. Things did not work well; predictably, the action at Kasserine Pass demonstrated that the tank destroyer doctrine was "a fundamentally flawed set of principles."[29] Marshall and McNair remained unconvinced, even after a December 1942 fact-finding tour returned from Tunisia and declared that "the Doctrine of having TDs chase tanks is absurd."[30] This program continued despite the TDs' inability to survive armed action; more serious, however, was that it diverted efforts from the race to develop an American heavy tank. The Tank Destroyer doctrine was an old artillery response to cavalry: grouping gun battalions to defeat *Cuirassiers* with a *grand batterie*. McNair's pocket battleship solution—an armored fighting vehicle that could run away from trouble—did not work because eventually, even the Graf Spee had to turn and fight.

Learning by Helping the British

The U.S. preparation for war was thorough. Tank crews were introduced to desert combat by subunits which was something the Canadian army, despite efforts by McNaughton, did not do.[31] The AGF used the Desert Training Center in Fort Irwin, California, as well as considerable maneuver areas in Texas: U.S. Armored divisions and their staffs reached North Africa ready for the desert. By 1943 American equipment had been proven, battleworthy, but the armored divisions were not. The British 8th Army command's superior attitude after the Kasserine Pass debacle enraged U.S. Army officers who had been expecting gratitude for saving Egypt with Grants and Shermans instead of getting advice on how to beat Rommel: "I do not believe we should be over exercised by the opinion of the British as to our organization and methods. I do not believe the British know any more about how to fight an armored division or how it should be organized than we do."[32]

Experienced AGF tank officers noted that El Alamein had been the one major British success, but also that it demonstrated Montgomery's inability to handle armor. The first and only time he created an armored corps of two full divisions, a *corps de chasse,* Montgomery botched the job.[33] The Western Desert had demonstrated the two approaches to armored warfare, the German integrated "tool box" versus the British two separate elements. In the British armored division the infantry was almost an annoyance: a soft-skinned target that had to be gotten out of the way or dug in so that the tanks could get on with the job of winning the main battle. This had led to the "boxes" and the "pivot" doctrine which did make some sense in the desert, but was unfortunately taught as a universal armored-infantry technique, and it found its way into Normandy.[34]

In retrospect, the Germans did most of the teaching in the Western Desert. They excelled at logistics, technology, and, most important, tactical command. And, of course, the British had no Rommel.

"The British don't know how to use armor."[35] The opinion of U.S. Army commentators about their British allies did not rise during the African and Sicilian campaigns: "The British soldier [and] his knowledge of minor tactics in general is below that of our soldiers. Between British officers, high or low, there is no comparison. Our officers are fundamentally better grounded in tactics than I have ever seen in any British officer."[36]

Allied Tank Reforms 1943–1944:
Seeking the Perfect Tank Division

The North African experience inspired both the British and the U.S. Army to reorganize their armor. By the end of 1943 the Americans had settled on the division organization they would send against the panzer forces waiting in France. It was, all in all, the perfect armored division, smaller (10,998 men) but well supported: three tank battalions(269 M4 tanks), three mechanized infantry battalions (2,994 men in 378 M3 armored half-tracks), and three self-propelled artillery battalions (54 105mm howitzers.)[37] TD battalions were brigaded in TD groups attached to infantry corps. There were two types of headquarters TD battalions, self-propelled and towed, equipped with thirty-six M10 guns on "motor carriage" or towed M1 antitank guns.[38] In an experimental measure that allowed a German-style task force, but not auftragstaktik, division command was supplemented with ready task force headquarters (combat commands A, B, and reserve) designed to control tailored groupings for specific operations. With supporting arms and attached assets it was the sort of force that would have created envy in Paderborn and Mailly-le-Camp.

The British finally settled on a two-brigade division: an armored brigade with three tank battalions (195 Sherman M4s and Model VC) with an integral mechanized infantry battalion, and a motorized infantry brigade of three truck-borne infantry battalions. The British armored division's reconnaissance regiment was equipped with sixty-five Shermans and no different (even, as operations would prove, doctrinally) from the tank regiments in the armored brigade. U.S. Army division reconnaissance was based on light armor—"Greyhounds" and a company of M3 Stuart tanks— and never had the power to chase off enemy tanks.

By the end of 1943 U.S. armor had been tested operationally and tactically. It finally won its first tank battles at Gela, Sicily, and at Salerno, where a poorly coordinated attack by 16th Panzer Division was defeated.[39] Here, the fact that naval, not tank, gunnery had dissipated this attack was recognized only in passing. The U.S. Army saw it as a vindication of the Sherman tank, and after-action reports praising the M4 were accepted at face value. The prospects of repeating this sort of success in France seemed logical, and reports from military attachés in Moscow about the new German tank, the Mk V Panther, did not cause worry.

The Canadian Armoured Corps

> Knight: "You can never guess what I did."
> Alice: "You went to war, of course"
> Knight: "Yes, but not under modern conditions."
> —Saki, *Alice in Pall Mall*

The first step in forming the Canadian Armoured Corps (CAC) was basic training, a task at which General Worthington excelled. The second, doctrinal training, was to prove elusive. By 1943, although the CAC's equipment would be as good as that of any Western ally, its leadership was in dire need of operational experience. The corps was rushed off to Britain, where training was doomed to endless repetition of squadron drills in cramped training areas and solutions to field problems were soon committed to memory by the dullest tactician. Division exercises were not held except as comprehensive movement problems that worked the division and corps staffs but frustrated the regiments and brigades because most areas, especially wheat fields, were strictly off limits to armor.

> We often fail to get the full value from our training because of restrictions that are imposed to prevent damage to crops or to property. So many orders have been issued on this subject that officers and men hesitate at times to leave the road; as a result we often see head-on collisions [tactical battles] with no attempt at quick deployment off the road, rapid manoeuvre, and flanking movements. All this is very bad . . . it leads to unreal situations; it also develops bad habits within units, and reacts adversely on the standard of minor tactics.[40]

Western Armored Divisions 1943 Battalion Equivalents

British Armored Division

Recce Regt	Armd Bde	Infantry Bde	Divisional Troops	
				Reconnaissance Battalion
				Armored Brigade: 3 medium tank regts 1 motor infantry bn
				Infantry Brigade: 3 motor infantry bns
				Div Troops: 5 artillery regiments 1 anti-tank regt 1 anti-aircraft regt signals, engineers

3 Tank Battalions:
Tank/Infantry/Artillery Ratio 3:4:6

© JARYMOWYCZ
Oct 2000

German Panzer Division

Recon Bn	Pz Regt	PzGren Regt	Arty Regt	
				Reconnaissance Battalion
				Tank Regiment: 2 medium tank bns
				Panzer-Grenadier Regt: 3 PzGren battalions
				Artillery Regiment: 2 medium artillery bns 1 heavy artillery bn

2 Tank Battalions:
Tank/Infantry/Artillery Ratio 2:3:3

American Armored Division

Recon Bn	Tank Regt	Mech Infantry	SP Arty	
				Reconnaissance Battalion
				Tank Regiment: 3 medium tank bns
				Mechanized Infantry: 3 mechanized battalions
				Artillery: 3 SP artillery battalions

3 Tank Bns: Tank/Infantry/Artillery Ratio 1:1:1

Tank crews eventually sent to Normandy were skilled in driving and communications and had an acceptable gunnery standard, but their regiment and brigade commanders had no idea what to do with them in open country.

The Canadian tank battalions prepared for the Wehrmacht in different ways. The 2d Canadian Armoured Brigade was the designated "army tank brigade" tasked with supporting the infantry battalions of 2d and 3d Infantry Divisions, as well as being the amphibious assault formation supporting General Keller's infantry on D-Day. The 2d Armoured Brigade's tank regiments spent much time practicing beach landings and waterproofing tanks. Meanwhile, the 4th Armoured Division's battalions concentrated on standard armored training, although most regiments were left queuing up for space on Salisbury Plain. The most basic standard of armored skills was covered in the initial (often the only) tank course offered. Armored crew training comprised a four-week program that covered the entire spectrum of armored skills, from driving and gunnery to tactics.[41] The final week was spent at Lullworth Ranges, where crews practiced for two days in firing 75mm antipersonnel and high-explosive rounds, coax machine guns, .50-cal. heavy machine guns, and pistols. A full five days were used up in traveling, setting up, cleaning up, maintenance, and "turning over tanks to new course."[42] A thirteenth day was set aside for rest. The remaining fifteen days were mostly spent in teaching driving skills. This was a decent introduction if supplemented by more squadron and regimental training, but the limited training areas did not permit this, except on a strictly rationed basis, and were generally limited to the troop level.

By 1943 the Canadian army had given up on its own tank, the Ram II, but decided against using the British Churchill. All Canadian armored regiments were equipped with the U.S. M4 Sherman. Division armored reconnaissance regiments were also equipped with Shermans, as were the two independent armored brigades. Infantry divisions and corps reconnaissance regiments were equipped with armored cars. The final war establishment for an armored regiment was 79 fighting vehicles divided among Regimental Headquarters and the three fighting squadrons for a total of 61 main battle tanks (MDTs) comprising 4 RHQ command Sherman V and 57 MBTs (46 Sherman V and 12 Sherman Firefly VC or IC Hybrid) in the squadrons. In addition, each regiment had a reconnaissance troop of 11 Stuart VI light tanks and an anti aircraft troop of 7 Crusader III AA Mk II. The organization called for three squadrons of M4s of four troops each. Every tank troop had four tanks: three 76mm Shermans but only one Firefly (a converted M4 with a 17-pounder, or super 76mm, main gun). Production delays had limited distribution of the Firefly, the only tank that could kill the German Panther and Tiger, to a mere 25 percent of the required establishment. This situation would not improve until 1945.

Because armored doctrine specified that tank divisions were only to be used for the breakout and pursuit phase of combat, tank support for infantry divisions came from headquarters tank battalions dedicated to this role.[43] In the British army they were tank brigades equipped with slow, well-armored infantry tanks: the Matilda, the Valentine, and eventually the Churchill. In the Canadian army, the infantry support mission was also awarded to the M4 Sherman, the wrong tank, saddled with the wrong doctrine.

The Opposition: Panzers of the Western Front

Meanwhile, in France the German army had mustered the cream of its armored force. The armored formations deployed in Normandy were the best in the Third Reich, absolutely the elite.

German panzer divisions were restructured after their defeat at Kursk. The final version, the "type 1944 panzer division," included the equivalent of three armored battalions and two panzer grenadier regiments. The tanks were grouped in the division's panzer regiment: the first consisted of a Panther tank-equipped abteilung battalion and the second was composed of Pzkw IVs, the workhorse of the German army. The panzer grenadier battalions were victims of Allied strategic bombing; production could not keep up with both losses and equipment tables. Of the six panzer grenadier units per divisions, only one was to be equipped with armored personnel carriers, the half-tracked Schützenpanzerwagen 250 series. The remainder were transported in trucks. The panzer divisions' artillery regiments had 105mm and 150mm towed guns, and there was only one self-propelled gun battalion, combining both the heavy and medium SP types, the 105mm Wespe and the 150mm Hummel.[44]

The type 1944 panzer division's total armor was divided between the panzer regiment's two battalions and the tank destroyer battalion. This latter unit was initially equipped with the Sturmgeschütz III (Stug) assault gun. The Stug had a very low silhouette (chassis of the Pzw III), was heavily armored, and was initially designed to closely support infantry assaults. Its 75mm StuK 40 L/48 gun had proven an effective tank killer in the Soviet Union, where Stugs were used both as "infantry tanks" as well as tank destroyers. The type 44 tank destroyer battalions were to be equipped with the new and very deadly Jagdpanzer (JPz) IV, the larger, sleeker evolution of the Stug based on the Pzkw IV chassis. It carried a deadly 75mm PaK 39 L/48 gun, which could kill all Western and most Soviet tanks. Again, production did not keep up with losses or Hitler's insistence that new armored formations were to be created in 1943 and 1944.

Few panzer divisions in Normandy were fully up to establishment. Units arrived in the west as skeletons with very few tanks and began to rebuild in the comparative peace of France. Within a few months the ranks were filled with recruits, transferred cadres, and veterans coming back from hospitals and home leave. Tanks trickled in from third-line repair or factory rebuilds and Pzkw IV battalions awaited their turn for conversion to Panthers. The restructured battalions were trained in the great *panzer* training centers of the Third Reich: Paderborn, Grafenwöhr, Sennelager, and the former French army tank training school at Mailly-le-Camp. Initially, the Panther battalions concentrated on their basic skills which included first-line repair and maintenance, driver training, radio operation, and gunnery. By 1943–1944 cross-training was an unaffordable luxury. New crews learned only one job of the following: driver, radio operator/loader, or gunner. The commander of the I SS Panzer Korps, Gen. Sepp Dietrich, recalled watching a Pzkw V that had to be shifted: the "crew commander drove the tank into place but [with] the greatest difficulty."[45] Once the basics were learned, troop training began and led to company maneuvers and gunnery. As soon as a graduated battalion was sent to its parent division, the second stage of training began. This consisted of concentrated gunnery and tactics based on the kampfgruppe, the all-arms team. Training ammunition was scarce: five rounds per crew per month was average. Few gunnery exercises were held, and only as stocks could be built up. Controlled gasoline rations limited large maneuvers.

The renowned efficiency of the panzer divisions was founded upon vigorous training at the subunit level and outstanding leadership. The most heavily decorated and most experienced noncommissioned and commissioned officers were placed in charge of recruit training. The battle experience of the leaders made up for the limited training opportunities available. A good example is the 12th SS Hitlerjugend Division. Made up of teenagers from the Hitler Youth, it was derided in the Western press as "the milk bottle division" or "Hitler's baby division" and used as an example of the deterioration of the German army. Within two weeks of battle it had mysteriously metamorphosed from "the kid division" to "fanatical . . . Hitler's pet crop of terrorists . . . more animal than human" to, finally, "elite."[46] Again the answer was experience. The officer and NCO cadres of the Hitlerjugend Division came from its parent unit, the 1st SS Leibstandarte Adolf Hitler Division, the absolute standard of perfection. Hitlerjugend Division officers and NCOs had a minimum of one campaign in Russia; many had two or three and members of the original cadre, like Kurt Meyer, had begun their fighting in the 1939 Polish campaign.

The Enemy Order of Battle—June 1944

German panzer divisions in Normandy sported a varied order of battle. Several had their first battalions still undergoing conversion and arrived in battle with no Panther tanks. One was partially equipped with French tanks.

The tank destroyer battalions were still primarily equipped with the Stug III and at best had one or two companies of the new JPz IVs. The Normandy panzer arm looked like this:

Table 5.1   German Panzer Formations Normandy, June–July 1944[47]

Division	1 SS	2 SS	9 SS	10 SS	12 SS	17 SS PZGR
Tank Regt.	SS Pz Regt 1	SS Pz Regt 2	SS Pz Regt 9	SS Pz Regt 10	SS Pz Regt 12	
1st Bn.	Mk V	Mk V	Mk V		Mk V	
2d Bn.	Mk IV	Mk IV	Mk IV	Mk IV	Mk IV	
Stug/Jpz Bn.	SS Stug Abt 1	SS Stug Abt 2			SS JPz Abt 12	SS Stug Abt 17

Division	2 PZ	21 PZ	116 PZ	PZ LEHR
Tank Regt.	Pz Regt 3	Pz Regt 22	Pz Regt 16	Pz Regt Lehr
1st Bn.	Mk V	Mk III/IV		Mk V
2nd Bn.	Mk IV	Mk IV	Mk IV	Mk IV
Stug/Jpz Bn.	JPz Abt 38	Stug Abt 200	JPz Abt 228	JPz Abt 130 Tiger Spz Co

Ind. Tiger Bn.	101 SS Pzabt	102SS Spzabt	503 Spzabt
Ind. Stug Bde.	PzBde 341	PzBde 394	
Ind. JgdPanther Bn.	654 Sjpzabt		
Ind. Pz Abteilung	100 Ertzpzabt	206 Ertzpzabt	

The 10th SS and 21st Panzer Division had no Panthers at all. The strongest division in France was the Panzer Lehr.[48] All of its grenadier battalions had armored personnel carriers, a ratio unmatched by any panzer formation in the West, including Leibstandarte Adolf Hitler Division. The next strongest formations were 2nd Panzer Vienna Division, and the Hitlerjugend Division. The remaining divisions averaged forty-five tanks per Pzkw IV battalion and thirty-five Panthers each. Panzer Ersatz und Ausbildungs Abteilung 100 and Panzer Abteilung 208 were equipped with obsolete French tanks that were good for chasing French resistants away from rear area headquarters but little else.[49]

Three of the panzer divisions were "born" in the West; the 9th SS Hohenstaufen, 10th SS Frundsberg, and Hitlerjugend were raised in Belgium and France and had about one year of training.[50] At the beginning of the Normandy campaign, the 9th SS and 10th SS were in Russia, sent there in April 1944 to rescue the 1st Panzer Army trapped in the Tarnopol Pocket. They returned to Normandy as the 2nd SS Panzer Korps on 26 June; by then all three Hitler Youth divisions were veterans.[51] The Panzer Lehr Division began as an elite unit simply because it was formed by grouping the staffs of the panzer training schools throughout Germany. The instructors, decorated veterans, formed a division of experts. Allied intelligence had some problem with Panzer Division 130 (Lehr) at first. Lehr meant "training," and it was assumed this was a unit composed of raw recruits. It soon became painfully evident what Panzer Lehr really was. Lavishly equipped, it fought with a determination and expertise that quickly won it genuine respect.

Only three Tiger battalions were stationed in France during the Normandy campaigns—all three fought exclusively in the Caen sector. The 101st SS and 503d Heavy Tank Battalion (*SPzAbt*) were generally east and south of Caen, and the 102d SS fought southwest of Caen in the Odon-Orne triangle. Tiger battalions were organized into three 14-tank companies for a theoretical strength of forty-five tanks. This was rarely the case, and troop strength was never maintained once combat began.[52] The Tiger battalions were originally intended to be both independent units and part of a panzer division's heavy company. In early 1944 the heavy-tank policy was changed; Tigers were no longer sent to panzer divisions, but now formed exclusive independent units under corps control to be grouped with divisions only as required. The first were Wehrmacht units and began with the 500 series; SS Tiger units were formed in the summer of 1943.[53]

The advent of the Stalin tank, the T-34/85, and to some extent the Firefly, put an end to the Tiger's virtual invincibility.[54] Tiger I production tapered off as Tiger II construction took over, stopping entirely in August 1944. This was considered a mistake by Guderian and other panzer generals. The time lost during the changeover to the more complex Tiger II deprived the Germans of several hundred Pzkw VIs. The King Tiger was the better tank, but by 1944 the question was quantity, not quality. Any super 75mm gun, let alone an 88mm, was sufficient to kill any Allied tank and most Soviet armor. In the end, only fourteen King Tigers actually fought in Normandy. The combined Tiger strength of the three *schwere* (heavy) battalions totaled only eighty-nine tanks on D-Day.[55] Technical ascendancy, however, would make up for numerical inferiority. In addition to a marked superiority in range and armor, the panzer force in France held a final ace: operational experience. The majority of NCOs and officers were veterans of at least one campaign. North Americans were about to enter a rather demanding finishing school—it was going to be a hard summer.

Notes

1. Lt. Gen. Sir Francis Tuker, *Approach to Battle* (London: Cassell, 1963), p. 384.

2. See Richard D. Hooker Jr., editor, *Maneuver Warfare* (Novato, Calif.: Presidio Press, 1993) and Robert Leonard, *The Art of Maneuver, Maneuver-Warfare Theory and AirLand Battle* (Novato, Calif.: Presidio Press, 1991). See as well British and Canadian official variations of the U.S. Army's FM (Field Manual) 100-1 and FM 100-5 *Operations.*

3. Erich von Manstein, *Verlorene Siege* (Bonn: Athenaeum-Verlag, 1955), p. 383.

4. *The Tactical Handling of the Armored Division;* "Cooperation with other Arms," War Office, February 1943.

5. Lt. Gen. Giffard Le Q. Martel, *Our Armored Forces* (London: Faber and Faber, 1945), p. 65. The tank brigade only had two battalions: 4th and 7th Royal Tank Regiment.

6. An excellent Czech tank that formed the bulk of Rommel's 7th Panzer Division as the Pz 38t. See Macksey/Batchelor, pp. 85, 104.

7. Martel, p. 69.

8. Rommel's account from B. H. Liddell Hart, *The Rommel Papers* (New York: Harcourt, Brace and Company, 1953), p. 32.

9. Martel, p. 69.

10. Hobart went into the Western Desert to take command of the 7th Armored Division and got it ready to take on the Italians, but he was soon sacked: see Martel and, J. P. Harris and F. H. Toase, eds.; *British Armor 1918–1940: Doctrine and Development. Armored Warfare* (New York: St. Martin's Press, 1990), p. 48.

11. Lt. Gen. H. M. "Jumbo" Wilson complaining to Wavell in November 1939. Kenneth Macksey, *Armored Crusader* (London: Hutchinson, 1967), p. 165.

12. This commemoration of Balaclava seems to have been intended as a victory of the cavalry spirit, not a resounding tactical defeat.

13. P. G. Griffith, "British Armored Warfare in the Western Desert 1940–43," Harris and Toase, eds., *Armored Warfare* (New York: St. Martin's Press, 1990), p. 70. See also Paddy Griffith, *Forward into Battle* (Wiltshire: The Crowood Press, 1990).

14. Correlli Barnett, *The Desert Generals* (London: Viking Press, 1983), p. 125.

15. Lt. Gen. Sir Francis Tuker, *Approach to Battle* (London: Cassell, 1963), p. 105.

16. B. H. Liddell Hart, ed., *The Rommel Papers* (New York: Harcourt, Brace and Company, 1953), p. 208.

17. Conversely, the British redesigned their formations; the 7th Armored Division went through at least four organization changes, hosted seventeen different armored regiments and nine different infantry battalions within two years. See Maj. Gen. G. L. Verney, DSO, MVO, *The Desert Rats* (London: Greenhill Books, 1990).

18. G. MacLeod Ross, in collaboration with Maj. Gen. Sir Campbell Clarke, *The Business of Tanks 1933 to 1945* (Devon: Arthur H. Stockwell, Elms Court, 1976), p. 174. "These boxes faced four-square, ready to meet attack from any direction. It was the old idea of the British square at Waterloo. . . . Each box was completely surrounded with a ring of landmines and barbed wire. Guns faced outwards. . . . The boxes were only a mile or two square at the most, and were provided with

water, food and ammunition to withstand a siege." Alan Moorehead, *African Trilogy* (London: Hamish Hamilton, 1944), p. 314.

19. Moorehead, p. 224.

20. Moorehead, p. 343. Another major problem was replenishment—the British used leaky fuel containers, easily cut with a bayonet ("flimsy square tins"). There were estimates of up to 20 percent fuel losses during transport. Their most popular use was as stoves, allowing the crew to brew up their tea. "Brew up" was a Desert term and referred *both* to meals and destroying tanks. The Afrika Korps used a steel gasoline can that was sturdy, had an effective stopper, and could carry petrol or water. The British showed ungrudging respect for these cans, dubbed "Jerry cans," and collecting them as valuable booty. They still carry this name in English-speaking armies, and the basic German design (now hard plastic) is still used.

21. "As soon as the German 88-mm. A.A./antitank gun appeared near Sollum on the Egyptian frontier in the summer of 1941, there were many calls on G.H.Q. Cairo to release some of our 3.7-inch A.A. guns for antitank work with the Desert forces, but not till the Battle of Gazela a year later were these powerful, flat-trajectory guns fitted with antitank sights and armed and converted to this ground role." Although "as many as sixty-two were so converted, only a trickle of them were in use in that battle." Tuker, p. 14. The gun was not popular with the infantry: its high silhouette was difficult to hide and its tremendous back blast kicked up great dust clouds that promptly invited enemy attention.

22. C. R. Gabel, *Seek, Strike, and Destroy: U.S. Army Tank Destroyer Doctrine in World War II* (Fort Leavenworth: Leavenworth Papers No. 12. Combat Studies Institute, U.S. Army Command and General Staff College, 1985), p. 67.

23. AGF Study No. 29., *The Tank Destroyer History,* Historical Section, AGF 1946, pp. 2–3. The McNair case rested on a sure-fire argument to convince Congress: "It is poor economy to use a $35,000 medium tank to destroy another tank when the job can be done by a gun costing a fraction as much."

24. K. R. Greenfield, *The United States Army in World War II, The Army Ground Forces, Vol. 1, The Organization of Ground Combat Troops* (Washington, D.C.: U.S. Government Printing Office, 1947), p. 66.

25. Bailey, p. 9.

26. Richard M. Ogorkiewicz, *Armor* (New York: Atlantic Books, 1960), p. 88.

27. Kent Roberts Greenfield, Robert R. Palmer, and Bell I. Wiley, *The Organization of Ground Combat Troops (United States Army in World War II: The Army Ground Forces)* (Washington, D.C.: Historical Department, U.S. Army, 1947), pp. 325, 334.

28. *The Cooperation of Tanks with Infantry Divisions,* Military Training Pamphlet No. 63 (War Office, May 1944), pp. 77, 9. "There are two main roles for armored components in an army. These are: a. in conjunction with infantry to effect the 'breakin' or breaching of main enemy defensive position. b. exploit, strike deep in enemy's rear installations either through gaps or around the flank." Pamphlet No. 63, p. 6.

29. Gabel, p. 67.

30. Devers presented interesting conclusions: "The Sherman was the best tank on the battlefield; the tank destroyer was not a practical tactical concept; the war was a war of gunpower and; American troops would have to acquire a higher standard of discipline." He was selectively ignored. Quoted by Maj. Gen. E. N. Harmon, commander, 1st U.S. Armored Division. Ernest N. Harmon Papers, MHI.

31. An advance party from the tank development center in Aberdeen established an Ordnance Training School at the Royal Armoured Corps School in

Abassia, Egypt, on 4 May 1942 under Col. George B. Jarrett. The Americans quickly proved accomplished in desert maintenance and soon established their own school, a successful rival to the Desert School. The first M4s arrived in Egypt in August 1942 ("a Great Secret") and remained hidden until the second Battle of Alamein.

32. Harmon Papers, MHI. Harmon commanded both the 1st and 2d Armored Divisions.

33. Barnett, pp. 269, 271–282; Tucker, pp. 252–257.

34. "The brigade is made up of three independent units . . . the pivot is in the form of a triangle [and the] average side for a bde will not be more than 2400 yds." RG 24 13788 HQ 4 Cdn Armd Div Trg Bulletin No. 49, "The Pivot," 12 October 1943, p. 1.

35. "I think I would be in Tunis if I had support from the artillery and infantry, or if the British had left me alone that time." Correspondence, General Orlando Ward Papers, Box 2, 1st Armored Division, 1942–1943, MHI.

36. In this letter, sent during the Salerno landings, Harmon added: "And if we should lose this bridgehead, which might happen, it will be because the German breaks through on the British side." Letter to Gen. Mark Clark, U.S. Fifth Army, 27 September 1943. Harmon Papers, MHI.

37. The U.S. 105mm self-propelled howitzer, nicknamed the "Priest" (after its pulpit-like antiaircraft machine gun mount). "The Armored Force Board early foresaw the possibilities. . . . However nothing was done in the development . . . until Col. Edward H. Brooks, the Armored Force Artillery officer, outlined to the Armored Board a program for equipping armored artillery. . . . Col. Brooks asked for the assistance of Capt. Louis Heath. . . . At an Ordnance Technical Committee meeting in November, 1941, it was decided to complete two pilot models for early test." Orlando Ward Papers. Box 2, Correspondence 1942–1943, MHI.

38. In January 1944 the War Department approved a more mobile carriage, the M18 Hellcat mounting a 76mm gun, followed by the heavier gunned 90mm M36 Jackson.

39. The Tiger tank seems to have made no serious impression during the Gela counterattack by the Herman Goering Panzer Parachute Division (ninety Pzkw IVs/seventeen Tigers), which was met by direct and naval gunfire: forty-five tanks were killed, of which ten were Tigers. Glowing reports followed: "Mighty proud of his M4 tank [he] knocked out six Tigers." Bailey, p. 53. The 1st Armored Division's performance was considered "most superior" save for "long periods of inaction. . . . See to it that all officers develop initiative." Lt. Gen. G. S. Patton, II Corps HQ to Maj. Gen. Ward, 1st Armored Division, 22 March 1943. Orlando Ward Papers, Box 2, Correspondence 1942–1943, MHI.

40. Comments by Lt. Gen. B. L. M. Montgomery as commander, South East Command. Nevertheless he went on to state: "Tracked vehicles, such as tanks and carriers, can do great damage to cultivated fields unless great care is taken. Such vehicles will keep to roads whenever they can. When moving across country they should avoid cultivated fields, root crops, hop fields etc." RG 24 14136 WD Commander Canadian Corps, December 1942: "Damage to Crops and property," issued 11 May 1942, pp. 7, 11.

41. Four hours were devoted to teaching hull down and turret down positions, the *sine qua non* of tactical survival. Two full days were devoted to troop tactics, and a further two days were set aside for squadron tactics. "Squadron tactics included "squadron in defensive posn supporting inf." One day was spent in "Tk vs. Tk action using blank, sqn against sqn, or half-sqn against half-sqn, if two sqns not

available." Canadian Armoured Corps Field Training Syllabus (Armored) 1943–1944. D Hist 141.009.

42. Almost 50 percent (twelve days) of the total 28 days were spent in movement, maintenance, and administration. Ibid.

43. FM100-5, 24 January 1941 and the original draft, FM17-10, 21 January 1941, *Doctrine and Organization of the Armored Division,* MHI.

44. Self-propelled artillery pieces were built on obsolete or readily available tank chassis: the Wespe used the Pzkw II, the Hummel the Pzkw IV. Allied self-propelled guns were put on Grant, Ram, and Sherman chassis.

45. B-155 SS Obergruppenführer Georg Keppler *I. SS Panzer-Korps 16.8–18.10 .44.* 2., and MS C-048. SS Gen. Fritz Kraemer, *Das I. SS Pz. Korps im Westen 1944* (part 2), Appendix 2, MHI. See also RG24 10 677 Interrogation Report Joseph "Sepp" Dietrich, pp. 3–6.

46. Luther, p. 58; Stacey, pp. 133–137; English, p. 212; also RG24 10811 WD II Canadian Corps, Enemy Intelligence Summaries, June 1944, and RG24 13766 WD 3 CID June 1944.

47. As of 25 July 1944, based on returns from Fifth Panzer Army Daily Reports (Abendmeldungen) and translated, Oberkommando West. See Bundesarchiv RH21-5/44, Kriegstagebuch Panzer-Armeeoberkommando 5., Abendmeldungen 23–25 July 1944. See also complete German order of battle for France, July 1944 in MS B-162, Oberkommando West war diary, translated as "The West (1 Apr–18 Dec 44)," MHI. Panther abteilungen (recently converted from Pzkw IVs) arrived at the last moment.

Table 5.2   German Divisional Strength June–July 1944 (Fifth Panzer Army Daily Returns)

Abteilung	Parent Division	Strength	Month
1./SS 12th Regt. Panzer	12th SS Panzer Div.	79	June
Panzer Lehr Regt.	Panzer Lehr Div.	89	June
1./Regt.3d Panzer	2d Panzer Div.	79	June
1./SS Regt.9th Panzer	9th SS Panzer Div.	79	June
1./SS Regt.1st Panzer	1st SS Panzer Div.	79	July
1./SS Regt.2d Panzer	2d SS Panzer Div.	79	July

The numbering of each panzer division's tank regiment varied. The SS regiments took the name of their division: 1st SS Panzer Regiment for 1st SS Leibstandarte Adolf Hitler Division, 12th SS Panzer Regiment for 12th SS Hitlerjugend Division, etc. The Wehrmacht regiments reflected a complex historical past and evolution for example, the 3d Panzer Regiment was in the 2d Panzer Division, the 22d Panzer Regiment was attached to the 21st Panzer Division. Fully equipped divisions (1st SS, 2d SS, 12th SS, 2d Panzer, and Panzer Lehr) were stabled with incomplete formations; for example, the 9th SS Panzer Division had no tank destroyer battalion, the 10th SS had neither a Jagdpanzer nor a Panther battalion. Panther abteilungs from the 116th Panzer and the 9th Panzer Divisions were sent to Normandy in late July and early August. ETHINT 67, WD 5 Pz Army 14; and Bundesarchiv RH19IX/20 Heeres Gruppe B "Meldungen & Unterlagen Ic von der zeit 1.7.44–31.8.44": 16 August 1944, MHI.

48. The 21st Panzer Division was augmented with a surprising number of

Pzkw IIIs and 94 Pzkw IVs, including outdated French tanks: 23 Somuas, 43 Hotchkisses, and 45 Lorraines converted to tank destroyers (mounting French or Soviet 75/76mm guns in open armored compartments), built in local factories on the initiative of the division staff. Lefebvre, pp. 120–123 and RG 24 10677, Interrogation Report, Lt. Gen. Feuchtinger, 25 August 1945. Panzer Lehr owned 97 Pzkw IVs and 86 Pzkw Vs, 40 Stug III/JPz IVs, and a company of Tiger IIs. Its King Tigers were cursed with a myriad of mechanical defects and only six reached Normandy.

49. **Table 5.3   Panzer Arm Strength as of 7 June 1944**

Panzer Divisions:	SS Lehr	2d	116th	21st	9th	1st SS	2d SS	9th SS	10th SS	12th SS
Pzks IVs	97	94	58	98	71	42	44	41	32	91
Pzks IVs	86	67				38	25	30		48
Tank Destroyers	40	41	21	111	5	44	36	38		44
		17th SS Panzer-grenadier	503d Heavy Panzer Abteilung		10th SS 1	10th SS 2	6th Jagdpanz 54		Pz Ersazt Batt. 100	Pz Ersazt Batt. 200
Tigers			24	37	28	12				
Tank Destroyers		32								
French Tanks									15	24
Armored Fighting Vehicles										

The independent Stug brigades were actually assault gun battalions redesignated as brigades in 1944. The 100th (Replacement) Panzer had 27 tanks (8 Hotchkisses, 18 Renaults, 1 Pzkw III); 206th Panzer Battalion had 23 tanks (14 Pzkw 38-H 735[f], or Hotchkisses; 4 Pzkw 35-S 739 [f], or Somua S-35s; and 5 Pzkw B-2, or Char Bs). See Lefebvre, pp. 122–123.

    50. R. J. Bender and H. P. Taylor, *Organization and History of the Waffen SS,* vol. 3 (San Jose: Bender, 1972), pp. 43, 57, 95. For the origins of SS division heraldry see: "A Speech made by Himmler to the 17th SS Pz Gr Division, 'Goetz von Berlichingen'" 10 April 1944, in France. Annex 2 to G2 *Periodic Report No. 32,* 12th Army Group. Chester B. Hansen Papers. Documents and Reports Folder 1–15 July, 1944, MHI.

    51. 9th and 10th SS Panzer Divisions had large cadres of Hitler Youth. Most 9th SS recruits were ethnic Germans from Hungary and German nationals from the Berlin area—70 percent were conscripts. The 10th SS was similar. The 12th SS was raised as "a new elite all-German division . . . a second *Leibstandarte.*" See Hubert Meyer, *Kriegeschichte der 12. SS-Panzerdivision "Hitlerjugend"* (Osnabrück: Munin Verlag, 1987), pp. 2–8; Luther, pp. 1–11; Bender and Taylor, pp. 44, 58, 96; also, Matthew Cooper, *The German Army 1933–1945* (London: Scarborough, 1991), pp. 502–503.

    52. The only unit to be equipped with King Tigers, besides the company in Panzer Lehr, was the 503d Heavy Panzer Battalion, which was formed in May 1942

and fought at Kursk, where it was credited with "501 tanks, 388 antitank guns." Lefebvre, p. 114.

53. They were renumbered in October 1944; the 101st SS became 501st SS Heavy Panzer Battalion, the 102d SS became 502d SS, and so on.

54. "The Tiger, for a long time regarded as a 'Life Insurance Policy', is relegated to the ranks of simply a 'heavy tank.' . . . No longer can the Tiger prance around oblivious of the laws of tank tactics." *Instructions to Tiger Abt crews fm Insp General Pz Troops.* June 1944: "This means, inter alia, that Tigers can no longer show themselves on crests 'to have a look around' but must behave like other tanks."

55. The 1st Company, 503d Heavy Panzer Battalion. King Tigers for the 3d Company "reached Paris, but not Normandy." Tiger totals were 24 for the 503d; 37 for the 101st SS; and 28 for the 102d SS. Lefebvre, p. 119, and MS 155, General Krueger, "1 SS Pz Corps (16 Aug–6 Sep 44)"; MS B-747; B-748; B-749, General der Waffen SS Bittrich, "II SS Pz Corps (14 Jun–5 Jul 44)."

CHAPTER 6

Allied Strategic Offensives in Normandy: Operation Goodwood

I do not need an American armore*d division for use on my eastern flank; we really have all the* armor *we need.*
—Montgomery to Eisenhower, 8 July 1944[1]

The Opposing Armies: 1944 Doctrine

The campaigns in Normandy and northern France present staff college students with formidable tactical and operational problem solving: breaking through a defense in depth and maneuvering against a foe that is suddenly discovered to possess armor not only vastly superior to the attackers' but virtually impregnable to direct fire. Above this hovered the political and military expectations that the Allied armored force would effect a rapid and decisive victory that would parallel, if not overshadow, German victories in 1940. Heretofore, despite effusive publicity and enthusiastic support, Western Allies' tanks had not produced the sort of results expected.

Although Allied armor had seemingly dominated the war, the reality was that save for some grand tactical maneuvering in North Africa, it had not scored a knockout punch. Had Rommel succeeded in reaching the Suez Canal and Palestine, the Afrika Korps would have scored a strategic victory and the credit would have been given to the panzer divisions. Montgomery's victory at El Alamein was an uninspired battle of attrition that finally exhausted the Germans more than the British. Its strategic conclusion at Tunisia was not caused by the spirited handling of massed armor in the pursuit phase but rather due to the U.S.-British invasions in Rommel's rear that forced a strategic withdrawal to protect his lines of communication. At a time when Soviet forces were conducting mammoth tank offensives and destroying entire German armies on the Eastern Front, British experimentation with OMGs or tank raids had been limited to "Jock columns" and Special Air Service harassment behind German lines. Montgomery, who lacked both the creativity and temperament of O'Connor, failed to exploit his victory and was content, in the best tradition of Napoleon's Marshal Grouchy, to follow a withdrawing foe. North Africa ended with a slugging match in northern Tunisia—the depleted Germans finally giving up despite the introduction of a Tiger tank battalion among last-minute Luftwaffe and infantry reinforcements.

The terrain in Italy eliminated any hope of armored warfare in the proper sense—operational maneuver in the pursuit of a strategic knockout punch. Despite the obvious limitations, the Americans committed their most experienced tank division, the 1st Armoured, and the Canadians threw away the nucleus of their tank force by agreeing to deploy both the 1st Armored Brigade and their first operational tank division, the 5th Armoured, into the Italian peninsula. These units were to fight splendidly, absorb serious losses, and eventually grind their way through Rome and into northern Italy but never participate in armored operations as defined in a blitzkrieg era. They had been sentenced to be "infantry tanks," and despite the odd gallant cavalier dash by a squadron, battalion, or regiment, moved at the pace of the slowest marching unit.

France was to be Allied armor's last chance to prove itself. The terrain favored the use of massed tanks, and, given an enlightened commander, an Allied blitz could easily duplicate Manstein's and Rundstedt's successes—indeed, overshadow the magnificent Soviet victories in the east. The sequence was straightforward: establish a beachhead, break out, and maneuver. With total air supremacy guaranteed by the summer of 1944 and the prospect of ten weak panzer divisions holding all of Western Europe, the prospects were bright.

D-Day's success was marred by American stubbornness against using duplex-drive (DD) Tanks with the assault waves and having to pay for it at Omaha Beach. Despite the failure to capture the majority of D-Day objectives, the invasion was a strategic success. In the next three months, the Allied armies would fight to break out of the Normandy beachhead. It was to prove one of the bloodiest, and to armor advocates, most frustrating periods of the war.

The Normandy campaign may be summarized as an initial success stymied by determined panzer counterattacks that created a beachhead stalemate. It was a series of failed strategic offensives orchestrated by Montgomery to break out with armored forces, followed by the double envelopment at Falaise that encircled two German armies and led to the liberation of France and Belgium.

Montgomery's attempts to break out of the beachhead featured four strategic offensives: Goodwood, Cobra-Spring, Totalize, and Tractable. The first was a British-Canadian effort, the remainder U.S.-Canadian. They are

Western Armored Divisions 1944 Battalion Equivalents

British / Canadian / Polish Armored Division

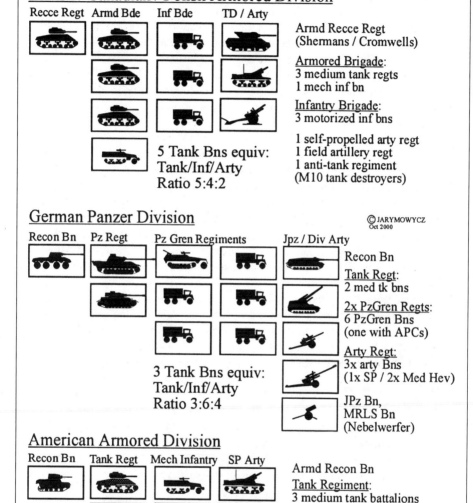

Recce Regt **Armd Bde** **Inf Bde** **TD / Arty**

Armd Recce Regt
(Shermans / Cromwells)

Armored Brigade:
3 medium tank regts
1 mech inf bn

Infantry Brigade:
3 motorized inf bns

1 self-propelled arty regt
1 field artillery regt
1 anti-tank regiment
(M10 tank destroyers)

5 Tank Bns equiv:
Tank/Inf/Arty
Ratio 5:4:2

German Panzer Division

© JARYMOWYCZ
Oct 2000

Recon Bn **Pz Regt** **Pz Gren Regiments** **Jpz / Div Arty**

Recon Bn

Tank Regt:
2 med tk bns

2x PzGren Regts:
6 PzGren Bns
(one with APCs)

Arty Regt:
3x arty Bns
(1x SP / 2x Med Hev)

JPz Bn,
MRLS Bn
(Nebelwerfer)

3 Tank Bns equiv:
Tank/Inf/Arty
Ratio 3:6:4

American Armored Division

Recon Bn **Tank Regt** **Mech Infantry** **SP Arty**

Armd Recon Bn

Tank Regiment:
3 medium tank battalions

Mechanized Infantry:
3 mechanized infantry baattalions

Artillery:
3 SP artillery battalions

3 Tank Bns equiv:Tank/Inf/Arty Ratio 1:1:1

important in that they were to conclude with the first and greatest example of Western armored competence and completely overshadowed the remaining two Allied armored operations of the war: Patton's counterstroke against the German Ardennes offensive and U.S. armored operations in Lorraine. The Battle of the Bulge (Ardennes) became a series of operational thrusts that denied Hitler a strategic victory; the Lorraine contests were tactical but with decisive operational results. Only the Normandy campaign offered tank commanders the opportunity to demonstrate the validity of armor as an arm of operational and strategic decision. Further, it pitted an inferior armored force against a technologically vastly superior force. The scandal of the European campaign was the inability of Western democracies to produce armor and, perhaps doctrine, that was at least on a par with that of their opponents.

For students of armor, among the dozen or so conflicts sufficiently documented to provide material for academic reflection, there are five important examples that ought to considered: (1) Operations Goodwood and Atlantic, July 1944; (2) Operations Cobra and Spring, July 1944; (3) Operation Totalize, August 1944; (4) Operation Tractable and Cobra's pursuit, August 1944; and (5) the Arracourt battles in Lorraine, September 1944. These operations serve to demonstrate both the status quo of Allied doctrine as well as the cultural and technical differences between the armies.

Operation Goodwood was the first Allied strategic offensive (excepting D-Day) in northwestern Europe and featured the defeat of the entire British armored force. Atlantic, Goodwood's second act, briefly captured the vital ground of Verrières (Bourguébus) Ridge, and despite the promise of a saved offensive was defeated by a series of German counterattacks.

Operations Cobra and Spring were components of the second Allied strategic offensive in Normandy. Cobra was immediately locked up in bocage attrition warfare that would not end until early August; despite this, it evolved into an armored success and featured the first German operational counterstroke of the campaign. Spring was designed to support Cobra but failed miserably; it provoked a particularly interesting corps-level counterattack by Dietrich's panzer units delivered despite total Allied air supremacy.

Operation Totalize was the third strategic offensive, designed to complement Cobra's success and destroy all German armies west of Paris. Despite initial total success, Totalize foundered in the face of spirited armored counterattacks and a repetition of Western inability to put together a breakout doctrine at the operational level. Totalize was to painfully demonstrate how far behind the Soviets the Allies stood in military art.

Operations Tractable and Cobra's pursuit are splendid examples of Allied armor at its operational best and strategic worst. Despite inspiring accomplishments by individual divisions and corps, the dynamic maneuver and total victory offered by Patton's U.S. Third Army were to be rejected by the conservative Bradley. Tractable is the only example of a non-U.S. corps acquiring operational maneuver and features the closing of the Falaise Gap by the Canadian 4th Armored Division and the Polish 1st Armored Division, then a unit in the Canadian First Army.

The Arracourt battles are admirable examples of the maturing of U.S. tactical leadership as well as the superiority of maneuver warfare in confronting a better equipped, technologically superior enemy.

Another purely armored addition for study could be the British-Canadian pursuit after Falaise, in particular the liberation of Brussels by British armor. Earlier operations, in particular, Epsom (which made Caen and Operation Spring possible) and Bluecoat (a contemporary of Cobra-Totalize), were admirable examples of tactical armored-cum-infantry actions. Bluecoat was directed into the worst of Normandy terrain with little hope of maneuver or success. Misuse of British armor doomed it to attrition warfare in the bocage until the end of the campaign. Unlike Omar Bradley, Miles Dempsey lacked the resources and Montgomery the heart to pay the butcher's bill of attrition. Bradley, in the best operational tradition of U.S. Grant, ground ahead until he broke out. Montgomery appeared torn between the strong possibility of Canadian success south of Caen and the minor chance for British success bashing up the middle. In the end he supported neither and became a meddling observer.

The Allied Strategic Commander

It is a matter of debate whether Gen. Bernard Montgomery had a strategic mind. Examination of his activities in Africa and after Normandy suggests that he liked to dabble beyond the operational art; he was just not good at it. Montgomery's great success is the set piece battle buttressed by a considerable superiority in men and material, total air supremacy, and an embarrassment of artillery. Fighting continues until one side runs out of men or equipment. This seemed to work in Africa. The breakout, often called the third El Alamein, featured an almost pathetic inability to use a *force de chasse* composed of two armored divisions designed to follow the British 8th Army *schwerpunkt* and overrun the remnants of the German-Italian army as it fled to Tripoli. Rommel, the dean of desert warfare, outfoxed Montgomery. The one "all-Monty" defensive victory over Rommel was at Medinine, where the Afrika Corps threw itself onto the British anti-tank gun line and got some of its own medicine. Montgomery arrived in Normandy experienced in the ducks-in-a-row offensive and somewhat disappointed by the stalemate of Italian operations.

The Mechanics of Strategic Offensive

Although Dwight Eisenhower was the overall of commander Supreme Headquarters Allied Expeditionary Force (SHAEF), Montgomery controlled operations and grand tactics. He was responsible for a breakout that by the end of June, with the elements of three German armies in the area, demanded organizing a strategic offensive. A strategic offensive is conducted at the army group level and uses the total resources available to create a breakthrough or strategic lodgement. D-Day was a brilliant Allied strategic offensive, whose failure could prolonged World War II by years.

The aim of a subsequent strategic offensive in Normandy was to be a breakout battle ending with the Allies' acquiring operational maneuver. Given such maneuver and the armored-mechanized corps to take advantage, the offensive was then to seek out strategic objectives: the destruction of the German army in the West or the crossing of the Seine and the capture of Paris. Either would bring about a strategic victory.

Montgomery was working against time and geography. Time was against him because every week brought in more U.S. divisions and strengthened Bradley's hand. It is not unfair to suggest that Montgomery wanted another Alamein and would have preferred a British knockout punch to an Allied or American one. Although he insisted that he had planned Normandy all along as a U.S. Army victory (draw the Germans to the east, break out in the west), his actions suggest a desperate series of attempts to crack the Germans near Caen, put them on the run, and then allow the Americans to chase them in an armored end run—an operation hamstrung by the concurrent directive to first lay siege to Brittany's ports!

Besides the panzers, Montgomery's other obstacle was the bocage. The sunken lanes, paralleled by centuries-old hedges that could and did stop tanks, reduced the Normandy battle to a series of bloody company and platoon actions fought at ranges of less than 100 yards. At least that was the obstacle in the U.S. and British sectors. The Canadian sector was wide open, and the beckoning ground beyond Caen was an armored officer's dream. The long ranges of engagement allowed for very effective use of German tank guns. This, coupled with the very determined, almost fanatic defense by the Hitlerjugend Division, created an obstacle as effective as the bocage. Nevertheless, a breakthrough near Caen meant immediate operational maneuver. A breakthrough in the British-U.S. sector meant another two weeks of fighting through bocage until open ground was reached.

If Montgomery had a strategic bent, then a generous interpretation could be that he was attempting a clever series of chess moves: Operation Epsom (reaching the Odon River), the taking of Carpiquet, dominating the Odon-Orne junction and the western Orne crossings and Caen's left flank, and, finally, Operation Windsor, the capture of Caen itself. Ignoring the thrashing of the 7th Armoured Division by the 101st SS Heavy Panzer Battalion (in effect, Wittman's two Tigers,)[2] the British had successfully pushed their way into the Odon River Valley and were doggedly fighting for the heights overlooking the Orne River Valley. It was clear that taking Caen was going to be a long, costly effort. An increasingly impatient Patton had said to Bradley on 16 July: "Monty has 3,500 tanks. . . . Hell, give me all those tanks and I'll have them in Paris in five days." Bradley's reply was: "Impossible . . . tanks need an infantry screen in bocage."[3]

Montgomery's solution was to use strategic resources to win an operational offensive—Allied bombers. Using heavy bombers to clobber Caen did marvelous service for the troops' morale but accomplished little. The city was turned into a rubble-strewn obstacle and could have become a Stalingrad had the Germans chosen to defend it. Strategic bombing in support of a ground offensive was not liked by either the Royal Air Force (RAF) or the U.S. Army Air Corps (USAAC). It put the bombers under ground force command, albeit briefly, and set a dangerous doctrinal precedent for bombers as heavy artillery. Nevertheless, Caen provided the pattern for future Allied strategic offensives, and serious attempts at a breakout would be preceded by a massive attacks by heavy bombers. It was the key difference that separated the Allied strategic mechanics of operations. The Soviets fired artillery, the Western Allies dropped bombs.

Caen initiated the pattern and Goodwood was confirmation. Montgomery had failed to break out during Windsor. There was a hurried German withdrawal but no rout, and now he had to do it all again. This time Montgomery had the benefit of being on the Orne and better able to take advantage of the British foothold on the eastern bank captured by British 6th Parachute Division on D-Day. By squeezing in his armor on the right and faced with the prospect of excellent tank country, this could well be a fourth El Alamein. This would have been a grand plan if Epsom and Windsor were the detailed part of a strategical whole. Conversely, the case may be made that the previous attacks were a series of individual attempts ending with Goodwood before Montgomery became truly strategic and ordered the double offensives of Cobra and Spring on 25 July 1944.

Operation Goodwood, 18 July 1944

The heaviest and most concentrated air attack in support of ground forces ever attempted.
        —Air Chief Marshal Leigh-Mallory, commenting on Goodwood[4]

Goodwood had the potential to break through, break out, and drive the German armies across the Seine. General O'Connor's VIII Corps, compris-

ing three British armored divisions, the 11th, 7th "Desert Rats" and the
Guards Armoured, were to crash out on the east of Caen, fan out onto the
high ground of Bourguébus-Verrières and drive toward Falaise, and perhaps
Paris. Planning on the corps level started on 13 July.

> The operation presented unusual difficulties, involving an advance for the
> first three miles through a corridor two miles wide both flanks of which
> were held by the enemy. It was therefore decided to enlist, for the first
> time on a large scale, the aid of the Strategic Air Force in the tactical role
> of neutralizing these menacing flanks.[5]

Bomber support was impressive: "Between 0545 and 0800 hours on
the 18th July, 1056 Lancasters and Halifaxes of Bomber Command, 570
Liberators of the VI 2d Air Force and 318 Mediums of the IX Air Force
operated in close support."[6] The effects of the attack were initially devastating: "70% of Prisoners of War interrogated 24 hours after Bomber
Command's attack . . . could not be interrogated because they could not
hear."[7] Montgomery's use of four-engined heavy bombers quickly convinced the German high command that any Allied offensive not preceded
by strategic bombers was not to be seriously considered.

The aims of Goodwood have been much debated. If it was part of a
grand strategic design to "write down" German armor and open the door
for Bradley in Cobra, it was not made clear to the armor commanders.
Following defeat, Montgomery portrayed Goodwood as a holding action
designed to improve Bradley's chances in Cobra (Spring's western breakout cohort) and established a pattern: future failed breakout attempts would
also be "holding actions."[8] This was not what the attacking brigadiers
understood. "Pip" Roberts relates the following:

> We had discussed in conference with Dick O'Connor what should be done
> after we were firmly established on the high ground beyond Bourguébus
> and I am quite sure that Falaise was in everyone's mind as a point to be
> aimed for. When Hobart went up to 8th Corps HQ before the battle,
> O'Connor consulted him as to "the best formation in which the three
> armored divisions should move once they had broken through into open
> country."[9]

Goodwood included a virtual "who's who" of British tank doctrine.
Besides the vast operational experience of O'Connor and the tactical background of Roberts, there was the raging bull of the Royal Tank Regiment,
General Hobart himself. It is possible that this fellowship of the British
armor decided to misinterpret Montgomery's "infantry" approach and redefine the operational aim as, in fact, a breakout. However, it is more likely
that a blitzkrieg was exactly what Montgomery wanted. Here was a bomb-
blasted schwerpunkt that made Guderian's breakthrough at the Meuse mere

child's play. Eisenhower expected "a drive across the Orne from Caen towards the south and southeast, exploiting in the direction of the Seine basin and Paris."[10]

Intelligence prior to the attack estimated elements of three panzer divisions in the area (the 21st; Leibstandarte Adolf Hitler; and Hitlerjugend), for a total of 200 tanks and thirty-five assault guns. This did not appear to include the presence of two Tiger battalions: the 101st and 503d. The 503d, a Wehrmacht unit, was equipped with one company of brand new Tiger IIs or King Tigers, the most advanced tanks in the world. The Tiger II boasted improved armor that made it impervious to any frontal and most flank attacks by any Allied gun, and carried the devastating KwK 43 L/71 88mm main gun. In the open area beyond the Orne, accurate tank fire would prove devastating, particularly at ranges in which British tanks could not reply.

The German defenses had been set by Erwin Rommel himself; Goodwood was to be the last Rommel-Montgomery battle. The defense zone began with a thin outpost belt; observation posts and machine gun nests dominated all forward approaches. This was a thin screen of listening posts, no more than a tripwire for early warning. Behind this lay the main defensive area based on a "web" defense—fortified villages with interlocking arcs of fire holding the forward zone and supported by more strongpoint hamlets and gun lines in the rear.

> On the main axis of the advance the country consisted of fairly open agricultural land, studded with a number of compact, well-built stone villages. The villages and their immediate surroundings are usually enclosed by highly fenced fields and orchards and closely growing large trees.[11]

In total, Rommel had created roughly five defense lines supported by mobile reserves and Pzkw IV, Panther, and Tiger battalions. The German armor could counterattack but, more dangerously, it could redeploy rapidly to block any British penetration with accurate long-range fire.

German Response

> AP shot 88mm was quite extraordinary—as they came across the tops of the corn you could actually see them coming—as they left a wake rather like that of a torpedo . . . and one could, in fact, take evasive action.
> —Maj. Bill Close, A Squadron, 3d Royal Tank Regiment,
> north of Cagny, 19 July 1944[12]

Resolute local commanders who had survived the savage air bombardment (most Germans were in shock or deaf, and many soldiers went mad)[13] sat tight and fought from the fortified villages that stood like rocks in an armored British sea. Decisive panzer leaders like 21st Panzer Division's

Hans von Luck arrived on the battlefield and quickly organized effective ad hoc antitank defenses.[14] Soon British armor was being shot up from the flanks and rear. Disorder began to emerge.

The British armored division still fought in two solitudes.[15] The tanks, à la old Fuller–Royal Tank Corps doctrine, went in alone. As German reserve tank battalions arrived (Panthers from the 1st SS and 12th SS Divisions, as well as Tigers from the 101st SS and King Tigers from the 503d Heavy Panzer Battalions), the British tank divisions received increasingly deadly fire. Soon the plain before Bourguébus was covered with nearly 500 burning British tanks. The Goodwood offensive failed.[16] Lieutenant General Simonds, who had just arrived to take over the Canadian II Corps, watched the disaster from the bluff on the southeast edge of Carpiquet airfield. The battle made a lasting impression and influenced his next two operations.[17]

The Canadian Phase of Goodwood: Operation Atlantic

Lt. Gen. Guy Granville Simonds activated Canadian II Corps Headquarters on 29 June 1944. The corps, fresh from four years of training in England, approached its first battle with apprehension. The Canadian 3d Infantry Division was a D-Day assault formation, and by July had seen far too much fighting. The 2d Infantry Division had just crossed the channel. Their inherent armored support, Canadian 2d Armoured Brigade (commanded by Brig. R. A. Wyman), was one of the few tank outfits to have attempted armored operations in June. By July the brigade was a group a shrewd veterans, familiar with Panthers and wary of the yet unseen Tiger. Their working doctrine was infantry tank tactics—a reasonable solution for the "dogfight" struggles of June but now out of place in open terrain.

For Operation Atlantic Simonds deployed his entire corps, including both infantry divisions, his armored brigade, and the Canadian 2d Army Group Royal Artillery (AGRA).[18] While the British armor was attacking southeast, Maj. Gen. Rod Keller's Canadian 3d Infantry Division was to cross the river, with two brigades and work its way along the east bank of the Orne driving out Germans from the industrial parks and protecting the British right flank. It would then fight toward the bridges and roads that connect Caen to the southern plains and Bourguébus Ridge. It was a slow, dirty process. Fighting in built-up areas is an infantry war. The Germans called it *rattenkrieg* ("rats war"). Bombing and artillery fire turned each house into a minifortress.

To support the 3d Infantry Division, Simonds loosed Maj. Gen. Charles Foulkes's Canadian 2d Infantry Division consisting of three fresh brigades (nine rifle battalions). Foulkes's task was to secure a supplementary crossing on the Orne River at Faubourg-de-Vaucelles and push south "prepared on orders GOC 2 Cdn Corps, to capture area Verrières 0460 by an attack."[19]

The Orne crossing was not easy. The south bank suddenly rose in steep cliffs that dominated all approaches from Caen. The German defenders were from the newly arrived 272d Infantry Division, commanded by Gen. August Schack, a mixture of regular infantry and older veterans augmented by Polish, Ukrainian, and Russian volunteers, reasonably trained and well equipped.[20]

Schack deployed his division according to Rommel's orders. The forward line was along the Orne followed by a series of strongpoints between the river and Hill 67. As more troops appeared, they were organized in a web defense and formed a third line. The fourth defense line was anchored at St. André-sur-Orne and continued west to east through St. Martin along the forward slopes of Verrières (Bourguébus) Ridge. The last defense was on the ridge itself and included May-sur-Orne on the east, Fontenay-le-Marmion, Verrières village, and Rocquancourt. Behind the ridge were Schack's artillery and Rommel's mobile reserves. These included elements of 2d (Vienna) Panzer and the elite Leibstandarte Adolf Hitler Divisions, which were in depth and part of Army Group B's attempt to build up a mobile panzer reserve.

Leibstandarte Adolf Hitler was a superb panzer formation. It traced its roots to an elite palace guard raised to protect the führer and then had earned battle honors in France in 1940 and in the Soviet Union. Its commander was SS Maj. Gen. Theodor Wisch, and he had forces of "about 100 to 120 runners." During Goodwood this division helped destroy Montgomery's armor.[21]

The First Verrières: The Plan

> *Intention: 2 Cdn Inf Div will be prepared to exploit to the SOUTH and secure areas BASSE 0163 IFS 0463 pt 72 0461 ST. ANDRE-SUR-ORNE 0261 and area VERRIERES 0560*
> —Operational Order, Canadian II Corps, Operation Atlantic, 16 July 1944

On the evening of 19 July, the British First Army commander, Gen. Miles Dempsey,[22] ordered Simonds to advance to the north spur of Verrières (which the British referred to as Bourguébus Ridge) and take over the village of Bras, relieving British armor as soon as possible. This was to prove impossible. The fields surrounding Bras, which was situated smack in the middle of the spur, were littered with tanks and covered by panzers in hull-down positions. O'Connor's VIII Corps had been stopped cold.

Keller's Canadian 3d Infantry Division had just cleared Vaucelles and managed to get a brigade into Cormelles. The Germans still held the high ground. By the next morning Dempsey issued an amended plan: VIII Corps

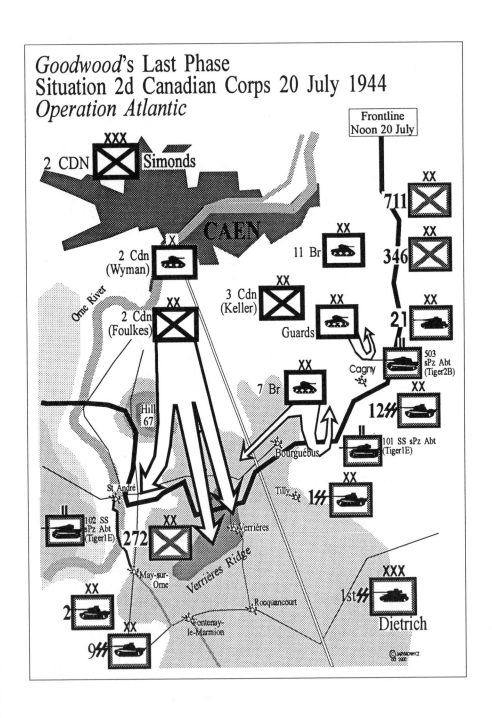

Goodwood's Last Phase
Situation 2d Canadian Corps 20 July 1944
Operation Atlantic

would hold fast, but the 7th Armored Division was to capture Bourguébus. The 3d Infantry Division would relieve the battered 11th Armored Division and the Canadian 2d Division would advance southward and establish itself on the Verrières feature.[23] Goodwood had degenerated from a strategic offensive into a tactical chess game with Dempsey shoving units about in frontal attacks hoping to wear the Germans down. Attrition triumphed as maneuver warfare proved impossible against an enemy with secure flanks and accurate long-range tank fire.

Simonds ordered Foulkes to push a brigade toward Verrières and secure the most dominating feature south of Caen. Although Goodwood failed, if the Canadians could take and hold Verrières Ridge, the operation (and Monty's reputation) might yet be saved. At the least, Rommel's main defensive area would be pierced and outflanked.

The First Verrières: The German Counterattack, 20–21 July

The final push for the ridge was made by Brig. H. A. Young's Canadian 6th Infantry Brigade.[24] The brigade was spread out across the entire Canadian 2d Infantry Division's front. The leading infantry battalions, the South Saskatchewan and Fusiliers Mont-Royal, were deployed two up and ordered to advance on a 2,000-yard front. This meant the battalions would not only be incapable of mutual support, but they would also soon be totally out of sight of each other. The forward brigades were stiffened by two squadrons of Sherman A2s. (See Appendix C for a breakdown of Sherman types used in U.S. and Canadian formations.)

Young's attack went in at 3:00 P.M. supported by RAF Typhoons and artillery concentrations. By 5:30 P.M. the Fusiliers Mont-Royal were approaching Verrières village, the center of the ridge. To the battalion's right, troops of the South Saskatchewan had pushed up onto the western crest of the ridge and were ready to swoop down on Fontenay-le-Marmion. Victory, it appeared, had been achieved. It had also begun to rain.

Behind the rain came a storm of fire that turned success into tragedy. From the area of Verrières village the Germans unleashed a fierce counterattack. The two forward companies of the fusiliers disappeared. The lead companies of the South Saskatchewan were thrown back, and the German storm then struck the depth battalion, the Essex Scottish, and threw it into rout. "Two of its companies are reported to have broken; it became disorganized and lost very heavily."[25] The German attacks were by kampfgruppen (battle groups) formed from the 272d Infantry Division, 2d Panzer (Battle Group Kohn), and the *Leibstandarte*. The latter had been brought north to deal with Goodwood on 18 July, and by 20 July had battle groups in Verrières, Tilly-la-Campagne, and La Hogue.[26] The initial Leibstandarte attack appears to have come from Verrières by 5th and 6th Companies of the 2d Battalion, 1st SS Panzer Regiment (Pzkw IVs) supported by the 9th Company, 3d Battalion, 1st Panzer Grenadier Regiment. They overran the leading Fusiliers Mont-Royal companies, turned west, and, in concert with Battle Group Kohn (2d Battalion, 3d Panzer Regiment with the Panzer Grenadier Battalion, 304th Panzer Grenadier Unit), shattered the South Saskatchewan.[27]

Atlantic Lessons Learned: Tanks Versus Infantry

Caen was briefly threatened by the German counterattack, but the line held after Simonds personally organized a corps counterattack that restored order and established new front anchored on the formidable Hill 67. The Canadians had at one point controlled Verrières Ridge—the only real obstacle between the Normandy beaches and Falaise. The German attack of 20 July was a good example of what the Royal Tank Corps ideal world was all about. If tanks could catch unsupported infantry in the open, any action would quickly become a rout. Tanks operating in pairs and troops using only machine guns can create total carnage in an infantry battalion or a brigade. In the case of the Canadian 6th Infantry Brigade, three understrength companies of Mark IVs (about twenty to thirty tanks) had routed an infantry brigade. The German counterattack demonstrated local initiative—*auftragstaktik*. The Leibstandarte Adolf Hitler accomplished two of its goals: it threw back an attack on the center of the ridge and it reestablished the forward battle area and contact with the overrun 272d Pranzer Grenadiers.

There are several questions entirely about armor raised by this battle. The first must question the grouping of armor and infantry in open terrain. The attacking brigades' armor assets amounted to about one squadron of tanks each. In previous fighting north of Caen the infantry-tank cooperation had been particularly intimate. Here in the tank country south of Caen the Shermans were content to lag behind the infantry and provide fire in front of their advance, and this created bad blood among the infantry.[28] There were legitimate reasons in both sides actions and viewpoints. First and most important was doctrinal naïveté and a serious lack of experience among commanders at all levels. Like Goodwood, Atlantic foundered on poor tactics. Second, combined operations in open country now featured mutual suspicion between infantry and armor rather than cooperation. Tank commanders, given a 2,000-yard shoot, saw no reason to physically join the infantry meandering up a ridge when they could provide an overwatch from behind and offer a steady, accurate leg on the ground. The infantry, deployed in the open and "protected" only by helmets and woolen jackets wondered, justifiably, why tankers surrounded by two inches of armor plate were not leading them in. The Shermans required distance to protect them from hidden antitank guns, *panzerfausts* (hand-held antitank rocket launchers), and, particularly, the super 75mm guns of the Pzkw IVs and Vs. Those two inches of steel were nothing to an L70 Pak 75 gun.

Armor students will quickly raise another question: Where was the armored counterattack? The immediate tank reserve, Brigadier Wyman's Canadian 2d Armoured Brigade, despite seconding three squadrons to the infantry brigades, had the better part of three tank regiments (80–120 tanks). Accepting the inequality of the short 75mm versus the German super 75mm, each troop still had the Sherman VC (Firefly) with a 17-pounder high-velocity tank gun, making this the most powerful Allied tank in Normandy. Certainly the Americans had nothing like it.

The answer was doctrinal. Current British (and therefore Canadian) doctrine held that armor was under the command of a division but in support of a brigade or battalion.[29] The Simonds plan penny-packeted the armor by squadrons and eliminated the possibility of a counterattack. Wyman did not organize a battle group ready to exploit just in case Simonds, Foulkes, Keller, or one of the brigadiers got lucky—it was simply not required in the prevailing tactical thought.

Montgomery, frustrated at his own failure, now had to take a back seat to Bradley's breakout on the western flank, Operation Cobra. To support Bradley and anchor German panzer formations east of the Orne, Montgomery ordered Simonds's Canadian II Corps to give it one more go. It was to be launched on the same day as Bradley's breakout at St. Lô on 25 July 1944. To give him the clout he needed to win, indeed, to give him the opportunity to break out toward Falaise, Monty awarded Simonds two British armored formations: the 7th Armoured and the Guards Armoured Divisions. Simonds called it Operation Spring.

Notes

1. Nigel Hamilton, *Master of the Battlefield: Monty's War Years 1942–44* (New York: McGraw-Hill, 1983), p. 720.

2. See Chester Wilmot, *The Struggle for Europe* (London: Collins, 1952), p. 309.

3. Hanson diary, 16 July 1944, MHI.

4. RG 24 10554 L215 B2.013 LD2. Secret. *The Goodwood Meeting, 18–21 July 1944.*

5. Ibid., para 1.

6. RG 24 10554 215 B2 Secret. *Tactical Bulletin No. 38.* Operations by Bomber Command in Close Support of the Army—Caen, 18 July 1944.

7. Extract from *SHAEF report on Goodwood bombing,* para 12. Diary entry from an officer of the Canadian 2d Armoured Brigade: "It was a scene of utter desolation. I have never seen such bomb craters. The trees were uprooted, the roads impassable. There were bodies in half, crumpled men. A tank lay still burning with

a row of feet sticking out from underneath. In one crater a man's head and shoulders appeared sticking out from the side. The place stank." Maj. Gen. H. Essame, *Normandy Bridgehead* (London: Ballantyne, 1970), p. 155.

8. See Field Marshal Viscount Montgomery, Memoirs (London: Collins, 1958), pp. 256–257; Hamilton, pp. 744–745,760–764. RG 24 20275 memorandum of interview with Lt. Gen. G. G. Simonds, 19 March 1946.

9. RG 24 10554 L215B2.001D2. File by C. P. Stacey, taken from draft sent to him by Liddell Hart, 9 September 1954.

10. Gen. Dwight D. Eisenhower, *Report Normandy Campaign 1944,* ETO, 1946, MHI.

11. *Goodwood* Meeting, para 5: *Terrain.* In addition, there were three railway lines that had to be crossed, two of which were elevated embankments. The entire area was dominated by Bourguébus Ridge (the northeast spur of Verrières Ridge).

12. Interview, *Operation Goodwood,* British Army Staff College documentary-training film, 1981.

13. RG 24 10554. DAT Air Ministry Tactical Bulletin No.38 (Anx 1.B). "Bombing: Colombelles 1,166 tons HE; Mondeville 1,087 tons HE; Sannerville 1,086 tons HE; Manneville 1,126 tons HE; Cagny 543 tons HE. From 0700–0745hrs US B17s dropped 100 lb and fragmentation bombs; from 0830–0900 hrs Frénouville, La Hogue and Bourguébus were bombed by 8 USAF using 1,000 lb bombs to disrupt enemy concentrations. The Commander of No. 2 Company, 503 schpzabt described Tigers thrown in the air like match sticks and soldiers driven to suicide in the midst of the bombardment."

14. Luck was shocked to see masses of British tanks heading toward Bourguébus and the Paris highway. He noticed a flak battery still engaging aircraft. "I gave clear orders to get immediately involved in this battle by fighting the British tanks." Instead, "I got a flat refusal. So I took out my little pistol and asked . . . whether he would like to be killed immediately or get a high decoration. He decided for the latter." Within minutes the 88s were destroying Montgomery's armor. See the film *Operation Goodwood* for this particular version, and Hans von Luck, *Panzer Commander: The Memoires of Colonel Hans von Luck* (New York: Praeger, 1989).

15. Brigadier Roberts, commanding British 11th Armoured Brigade, recalled the effects of antitank fire from a web defense: "Perhaps you would like to consider what you would do as commanding officer when, having not heard from your rear squadron for some time, and you look back and you find that they all seem to be knocked out . . . some of them were burning, some of the crews have bailed out—at any rate, they are not operational." *Operation Goodwood.*

16. Goodwood's failure enraged Eisenhower and fueled the desire of RAF officers, still angry after the army's failure to exploit the Caen bombing, to get rid of Montgomery: "The attempt by Tedder and the little coterie of British staff officers at SHAEF to get Montgomery sacked . . . actually got as far as Churchill." Essame, p. 157.

17. Marshal Stearns: Stearns papers. Correspondence between Prof. Reginald Roy and Stearns (Simonds's ADC) during the preparation of Reginald Roy's superb book, *1944: The Canadians in Normandy* (Toronto: Macmillan, 1984).

18. "Of no fixed composition, usually consisted of three medium and one or two heavy regiments in proportions considered most suitable to the mission [and] [o]rganized 'for the purpose of giving an army commander a wide measure of flexibility in the rapid allotment of artillery resources to the right place at the right time.'" English, p. 162.

19. RG 24 2 Cdn Corps Operational Instr No. 2, "Operation Atlantic," 16 July 1944.

20. WD 5 CIB noted PW (prisoner of war) from the German 980th Regiment, 272d Division: "Looks Jap, probably Lapland or Mongol." Ser. 68, 19 July 1944.

21. The 1st SS Panzer Division was in reserve to the rear of the 272d Infantry Division (in the area of St. Aignan, Ifs, Feugeurolles, and Bretteville-sur-Laize). ETHINT MS# B 540 Statement Gen. Schack. *272 Inf Div Normandy from 5–26 Jul 44.* Taken 19 April 1947; see also ETHINT MS # B-358 SS Gen. Theodor Wisch, "Leibstandarte Adolf Hitler—July 44"; "Battle at LaHogue," pp. 2–3.

22. Canadian First Army built up gradually. Initially the Canadian 3d Infantry Division and then, briefly, the Canadian II Corps were under command of the British First Army (Dempsey).

23. Stacey, p. 174.

24. With an extra rifle battalion (the Essex Scottish Infantry), placed under its command, the Canadian 6th Infantry Brigade had yet to taste battle. It had one of three French Canadian battalions in Normandy (there were only four in Europe), the Fusiliers Mont-Royal, a regiment led by the officers recruited from Montreal's French Canadian elite. The remaining regiments represented western Canada: the Queen's Own Cameron Highlanders of Canada and the South Saskatchewan Regiment.

25. Stacey, p. 175.

26. Bundesarchiv: RH21-5/50   *Kriegstagebuch   des   Panzer Armeeoberkommando 5.* 10.6.44–8.8.44. Reports 19–21 July 1944. The 3d Panzer Regiment and 304th Panzer Grenadier Regiment, with division HQ, did not appear in the Canadian II Corps area until 24 July. 1st SS Panzer Division was concentrated in the Forêt de Cinglais (approximately 3 kilometers south of Verrières). Rudolf Lehman und Ralf Tiemann, *Die Leibstandarte Band IV/1* (Osnabrück: Munin Verlag, 1986), pp. 178–182.

27. The Fusiliers Mont-Royal were reduced to 50 percent of effective strength. Interviews with Gen. J. J. Dextraze, Normandy, Ottawa, 1990. Also RH 21-5/50 *Kriegstagebuch des Panzer Armeeoberkommando 5.* 10.6.44–8.8.44.

28. The infantry felt abandoned, and criticized armor's tactical doctrine. See English, pp. 312–313.

29. "Tk bdes may be placed under comd of divs but regts not under comd of bdes. Regts should be placed in sp." Armd Div in Battle, p. 15.

Two CAB Shermans knocked out on Verrières Ridge during Operation Spring. The "tank country" south of Caen permitted long-range engagements, which favored the Germans *(Noble, National Archives of Canada, Wilfred Laurier University, Laurier Centre for Military Strategic and Disarmament Studies)*

CHAPTER 7

Operation Spring, 25 July 1944: The Other Cobra

It may seem ungrateful to raise criticism at this stage. We are, however, a very self-critical nation. It has been our main source of strength.
—Lt. Gen. Sir Giffard Le Q. Martel[1]

The operational problem facing General Simonds was that Montgomery had succeeded too well in "writing down" the German armor. The Canadian II Corps faced the aggregate of the German panzer force in France: complete or in part, five SS panzer divisions; three Wehrmacht panzer divisions; all three Tiger (heavy panzer) battalions; and the only Jagdpanther battalion in Western Europe.[2] Although these faced both British and Canadian divisions, they were specifically centered against Simonds's corps. The reason was simple: geography. Caen was the gateway to the best tank country in Normandy and the area that gave Montgomery the best prospects of breaking out quickly and reaching Paris. Although Bradley was about to launch Operation Cobra, the prospects of a rapid U.S. breakout appeared slim in the dense bocage and constricted road network of Normandy. Recent failures made Cobra very important. A successful attack anywhere on the Normandy front might save Montgomery's waning reputation. After the costly and inconclusive Charnwood and Epsom offensives and the disaster at Goodwood, the field marshal's ability was being questioned. Eisenhower was livid after Goodwood's failure and rumors that Churchill was about to relieve him of command abounded. "But the visit of General Marshall on 24 July must have been his worse moment—Marshall was quite prepared to unseat him because of slow progress."[3]

Across the front at St. Lô, General Bradley had two field forces ready: Gen. Courtney Hodges's U.S. First Army, with two heavy armored divisions (the 2d and 3d, each with six rather than the normal three tank battalions), and General Patton whose presence had been successfully hidden from the German high command and who was about to take over the U.S.

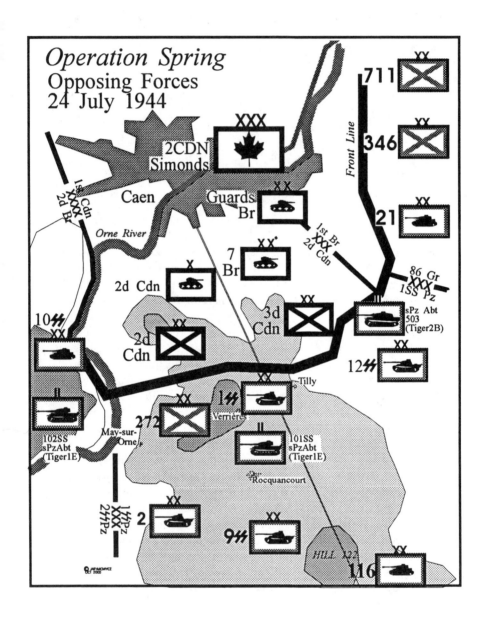

Operation Spring
Opposing Forces
24 July 1944

711
346
21
86 Gr / 1SS Pz
sPz Abt 503 (Tiger2B)
12 SS

2CDN Simonds
Caen
1st Cdn / 2d Br
Orne River
Guards Br
1st Br / 2d Cdn
7 Br
2d Cdn
3d Cdn
2d Cdn
10 SS
102SS sPz Abt (Tiger1E)
May-sur-Orne
272
Verrières
Tilly
1 SS
101SS sPz Abt (Tiger1E)
Rocquancourt
1 SS Pz / 2 SS Pz
2
9 SS
HILL 122
116

Front Line

Third Army (essentially a cavalry-tank army) and become 12th Army Group's force de chasse. Should the Eagle (code for Bradley's HQ) claw through the nest of bocage, he might take wing and soar toward the Loire River and Brittany.

Meanwhile, Montgomery had two British tank divisions (the 7th and the Guards Armoured) in the Caen area under the command of Simonds: "De Guingand phoned Ike to assure him that Monty had 'fattened up' the attack."[4] Whether through fear or prodding, the possibility of another Goodwood was real. The probability of success was minute. Nevertheless, Montgomery ordered the second attack. He pleaded strategic necessity.[5] Montgomery's confidence in Bradley and Cobra was not resolute, and he justified his scheme for Spring to Eisenhower with some optimism: "It may well be that we shall achieve our object on the western flank by a victory on the eastern flank." This was not particularly loyal to Bradley. These were, perhaps, creative tactics but not a convincing plot for a strategic offensive, which was, after all, his only job.[6] Montgomery's options were divided between a strategy of annihilation, whose sole aim was the all-consuming offensive, as was being currently demonstrated on the Eastern Front, instead of a strategy of attrition. There is little evidence that Montgomery truly understood the Normandy campaign strategically: he was no Schlieffen and certainly no Bonaparte. What there is may conclude he settled on strategy of attrition and resorted to offensives designed to exhaust the Wehrmacht.[7]

Another hypothesis is that Montgomery's vanity could not accept an all-American victory as the finale of the Normandy campaign. He must have sensed the contempt with which he was held within 12th Army Group, "strutting in with his corduroy trousers, his enormous loose fitting gabardine coat and his beret like a poorly tailored bohemian painter."[8] But this was likely secondary to his greatest ambition: he was most keen to defeat Field Marshal Erwin Rommel one more time.

The Desert Fox had held him close to the beaches for two months. Goodwood was their last test, and, unlike El Alamein, Rommel's defenses prevailed against the Montgomery set piece battle.[9] Rommel was wounded during Goodwood and was replaced by Field Marshal Günther von Kluge who did not change Rommel's defense scheme or his deployment. Similarly, Montgomery did not change his methods; he simply ordered Simonds and Bradley to launch more frontal attacks. He did not duplicate the principles demonstrated by the Red Army in the east or the western Allies in North Africa; isolated frontal attacks against an enemy whose flanks are secure invite certain disaster. Accepting that Goodwood, Cobra, Spring were the hammerblows of a strategic offensive, the distances (St. Lô and Caen are 55 miles apart), the sequence (nine days) and particularly the marshalling of resources, fall short of Soviet Stavka standards for an annihilating strategic offensive. Commanding four armies appears to have been too much for Montgomery.

Armor in Mass: Doctrine

I will never employ an armored corps.
                    —Montgomery, 21st Army Group staff conference,
                                                           13 January 1944

In his 13 January 1944 conference for the senior commanders of 21st Army Group, General Montgomery reviewed his concept of operations. There was one paragraph devoted to the use of armor, in which Montgomery insisted that tanks "must be brought through the breakthrough boldly to seize high ground."[10] Montgomery's set piece attack doctrine was force fed to Canadian corps and division commanders. Armored divisions were to be kept in reserve to be protected against casualties until after the dogfight had been won by the infantry and breakout could occur. Elevating operational success to strategic victory, as the Soviets were busy demonstrating in the east, required the active concurrent participation of a tank corps as well as an overwhelming preponderance of breakthrough artillery.[11] Montgomery preferred heavy bombers.

By 1943, the British army had officially renounced Fuller and Liddell Hart and admitted that "tanks by themselves cannot win battles."[12] The emphasis, however, remained on armored superiority. If a commander succeeds in destroying the greater part of the enemy's armor, while retaining fit for action the majority of his own tanks, he can operate freely, quickly, and boldly over wide areas. The normal roles of an armored division were defined as:

1. Cooperation with the main army and the air forces in effecting the complete destruction of the enemy, usually by envelopment, or by deep penetration through his defences after a gap has been made in his main position by other formations.
2. Pursuit.
3. Cooperation with other arms in the defence, usually by counterattack.
4. Threat the enemy to force him to alter or disclose his dispositions.[13]

The British-Canadian armored division comprised two elements: an armored brigade of three armored regiments plus mechanized battalion and an infantry brigade of three motorized rifle battalions. The new armored doctrine was explained in manly terms:

The work of a "rugger" scrum may be aptly compared with the operation of an armored division . . . infantry brigades may be considered as the "front row forwards." The armored brigade is subject to definite limitations. It requires suitable ground over which to operate and by itself is not fitted for holding ground.[14]

The basic attack doctrine required a break-in by infantry supported by armor. The squadrons made available for the dogfight were to guard the infantry against counterattacks by enemy armor or support infantry attacks against determined strongpoints. In effect, the armor used during the initial stages was infantry tanks. Armored divisions were to be used exclusively to break out and pursue. Massed tanks were to be handled with care lest the operational arm have its blade point broken.

The essence of the 1943 tank doctrine was to secure a pivot around which an armored brigade could maneuver. This worked well in the desert but was totally impractical in the bocage. It was, however, a possible option in the open ground south of Caen. Securing a pivot for maneuver was also the role of mixed divisions in the offensive. Interestingly, the infantry Division's tasks were defined as

1. Destroying the main force of the enemy;
2. Creating opportunities for the employment of the armored divisions, either around the enemy flank or through his front;
3. Seizing and holding ground as a pivot of maneuver for armored formations; and
4. Engaging and Destroying enemy armored formations.[15]

The technical inferiority of Allied tanks demonstrated inherent doctrinal problems and raised the obvious question: What was the role of armor? If the infantry's purpose was to destroy the enemy armored formations, what then were tanks supposed to do—maneuver in open terrain as cossacks? The answer, demonstrated again and again in France in 1940, Libya, and the Russian steppes was clear: the proper role of massed armor was to destroy the enemy's massed armor by combat and then to annihilate the enemy's armies by maneuver and pursuit. Operational maneuver, any maneuver, gave Allied tanks more than a fighting chance. The trick was to get past fixed defenses. In the breakin-breakout phase the Shermans bowed to the Panther-Tiger combination. The pursuit ran their tracks off.[16]

Tank Attack

We have nothing to fear from Panther and Tiger
Tanks . . . our 17 pounders will go right through them.
                                        —General Montgomery, 4 July 1944

In essence, Operation Spring was a frontal attack directly into the teeth of the strongest concentration of panzer formations in Europe and the largest number of SS units seen on either front.[17] The operation was planned in great detail by the Canadian II Corps staff and left little room for creative tactics at the brigade and battalion level. In a postwar interview, General Simonds suggested to Canadian historian C. P. Stacey that his actual mission was to conduct a "holding attack" in support of Cobra, but that the very nature of the operation prevented him from revealing his real intent at the Spring conference held on 23 July.[18]

Canadian intelligence collecting had been superb.[19] Simonds's headquarters had a complete breakdown of the enemy order of battle, and prospects of long-range tank fire raised concern. Spring was therefore planned as a corps night attack.[20] H-hour was 3:30 A.M. This allowed the brigades approximately three hours before tank light (the earliest time when tank gunsights could distinguish targets) permitted the German defenders to bring accurate fire to bear. Night attacks are complex at best; ad hoc night attacks (Spring was planned and ordered within two days of Atlantic) carry the seeds of their own destruction. Simonds ordered three phases: (1) securing the start line, (2) capturing Verrières Ridge (May, Verrières, and Tilly), and (3) pushing through second-echelon battalions to capture the reverse slope strongpoints that anchored the German defense (Fontenay-le-Marmion and Rocquancourt). Once the ridge's reverse slope had been secured, German counterattacks would be at a disadvantage. Panzers would have to advance across open terrain visible to Canadian Fireflies and forward observation officers (FOOs). Further, German mortar and artillery gun areas would be in mortal danger, some under direct Canadian fire. At this stage Simonds could release his two British armored divisions to race for the high ground and, subsequently, Falaise.

If Simonds could force SS Oberstgruppenführer Sepp Dietrich, commander of the 1st SS Panzer Korps and his opposite number, to commit the battle groups of 2d, 1st SS, 12th SS, 9th SS and 21st Panzer Divisions and if he could entice 9th SS and 116th Panzer Divisions forward, then the possibility of an armored counterstroke against Bradley's flank would be physically impossible. Besides, if Spring's aim was a holding action, the more German tanks, the merrier.[21] The composition of Kluge's "eastern" field force is shown in Table 7.1.

The importance of holding on to the western end of Verrières, with its anchor on the Orne, did not elude Army Group B Headquarters. On 23 July Schack was visited by Rundstedt and Kluge in his headquarters in Bretteville.[22] He reviewed the past days' fighting and outlined the precarious state of his division. The 272d Infantry Division was quickly reinforced. Three different divisions were ordered to support Schack for a net addition of two tank battalions, two panzer grenadier battalions, and a

Evolution of the Breakthrough Battle
Part 2: Second World War

Stage One: The Break-In
- *Infantry Tanks* and *Infantry* teams
- Penetrate the main defence

Stage Two: The Breakthrough
- *Win the "Dog Fight"*
- Conduct the *Breakthrough* and *Pursuit*

1944

Stage One (left panel)

German Depth Position:
Reverse Slope, if possible

Strong Points:
Mutually supporting
Company sized combat team
positions

Central Position:
Company Strong Pts; Mortars;
dug in AntiTank guns; Stug IIIs;
possibly Tanks

2

Brigade Level Phased Attacks:
Inf Battalions assault
individual strong points

Forward Position:
A "screen" manned by light infantry
(much like Napoleonic *Voltigeurs*) -
Machine Guns; "sniping" Tanks;
Artillery Observation Posts;
Dug-in Infantry and Snipers

1

Start Line

Stage Two (right panel)

The *"Dog Fight"*:
Counterattacks by
KampfGruppe

3

The *"Dog Fight"*:
Inf supported by
Tanks secures strong
points; Defeats
Counterattacks

The *"Dog Fight"*:
Attacker completely secures
en defence zone; attacks depth
posns sp by flanking fire

Armored Division
Grouped in anticipation
of breakthrough

All-Arms Attack:
Tanks, Infantry, Artillery,
Engineers, Electronic Warfare,
Close Air Support

Start Line

Table 7.1   Panzer Group West Armor in Caen Area, 25 July 1944

1 SS Panzer Corps		2 SS Panzer Corps			Wehrmacht
1 SS LAH	12 SS HJ	272 INF	9 SS H	10 SS F	21 Pz Div
1SS PzR (2 Bn)	12SS PzR (2 Bns)	980 GR (2 Bns)	9SS PzR (2 Bn)	10 SS PzR (1 Bn)	22 PzR (2 Bn)
1SS PGR (3 Bn)	25SS PGR (3 Bn)	981 GR (2 Bn)	PGR H (4 Bn)	21SS PGR (3 Bn)	192 PGR (2 Bn)
2SSPGR (3 Bn)	26SS PGR (3 Bn)	982 GR (2 Bn)		22SS PGR (3 Bn)	125 PGR (2 Bn)
		272 Fus Bn			
1SS Arty (3 Bty)	12SS Arty (4 Bty)	272 Arty (4 Bty)	9SS arty (3 Bty)	10SS Arty (3Bty)	Arty (3 Bty)
1SS JPz (3 Bty)	12SS JPz (3 Bty)	272 JPz (4 Bty)	9SS JPz (3 Bty)		200 JPz

Wehrmacht		Independent Battalions		Wehrmacht	
2 Pz Div	116 Pz Div	101 SS sPzAbt	102 SS sPzAbt	503 sPzAbt	654 sJPz Abt
3 PzR (2 Bn)	16 PzR (1 Bn)				
PGR (2 Bn)	PGR (2 Bn)				
PGR (2 Bn)	PGR (2 Bn)				
Arty (3 Bty)	Arty (3 Bty)				
38 JPz	228 JPz				

Notes: PzR: Divisional Panzer Regiment normally 2 tank bns.: 1x Panthers and 1x Mk IVs (10 SS, 21 Pz, 116 Pz had no Panther Bn.); sPzAbt: Tigers (503d had a co. of Tiger 2s); sJPz Abt: JagdPanthers; JPz: Tank Destroyer Bn. (Stug III / JPz IV)

PGR: Panzer Grenadier Regiment—1 SS, 12 SS, 9 SS, 10 SS and 2 Pz Divs each had 1 APC-borne Pz Gren. Bn., remainder Bns were *motor* tpt. SS Divs had 2-3 Inf Bns. per Pz Gren. Regt.

GR: Grenadier Regiment—each of 2x Inf Bns. Fus Bn: Fusilier Battalion (used as div. recon.—bicycle borne)

Arty: SS Divs had SP Battery of mixed Wespe (105mm) and Hummel (150mm) artillery on tracked chassis.

LAH: Leibstandarte Adolph Hitler   HJ: Hitlerjugend   H: Hohenstaufen   F: Frundsberg reconnaissance battalion.[23] These new troops gave Schack the depth he required to hold his sector against a corps attack. The reinforcements were not deployed within the defensive framework of 272d Division but kept in reserve to the rear of the forward regiments.[24] Schack's only dedicated armored reserve was Battle Group Sterz from 2nd Panzer Division, which comprised a weak Panther battalion, a depleted panzer grenadier battalion and a platoon of the deadly Jpz IVs.[25]

Within 1st SS Panzer Corps operational depth but only thirty minutes from May, sat two 9th SS Division panzer battle groups: Armored Group Meyer (commanded by Obersturmbannführer Otto Meyer—no relation to the Hitlerjugend's Kurt Meyer) and Battle Group Zollhöfer. This force, available to Schack but controlled by Dietrich, was the last SS reserve left in France. The remaining operational reserve in the theater, was the 116th Panzer Division deployed astride the Laison River and about forty-five minutes away from Verrières. Should Kluge be forced to use this formation, then Simonds would succeed well beyond his own expectations.

The Royal Hamilton Light Infantry and the Corps Battle

The Canadian attack began well in the center of the ridge—one of 4th Brigade's rifle battalions quickly captured a key objective. Lt. Col. J. M. "Rocky" Rockingham, the aggressive commander of the Royal Hamilton Light Infantry (RHLI), advanced boldly in the predawn, rushed Verrières village and in a fierce hand-to-hand battle threw out the SS combat team dug in among the stone houses. "Rocky" had ordered his reconnaissance platoon to creep forward and lay white mine tape to the front of the German positions. The tape, recognizable at dusk, allowed his rifle companies to charge the village. The center of Verrières Ridge was reported captured by 7:50 A.M. It was to be the only Canadian success of the operation.

The RHLI's triumph caused a stir among staff members at Panzer Group West's headquarters: listing the artificial moonlight, heavy artillery bombardment, and multiple contacts across the front, they suggested this was the follow-up attack to Goodwood. Kluge disagreed. Spring was missing the hallmark of a significant Allied effort. "Where are the heavy bombers?" he demanded. Despite Kluge's skepticism about a second Montgomery breakout attempt, the large red arrow striking across Verrières and pointing south toward Falaise could not be ignored. He drove to Dietrich's HQ.

On Verrières Ridge, the tanks of the British 22d Armoured Brigade were poking through a tree line on the crest, seemingly interested in supporting the RHLI. The British behaved timidly. With four tank regiments and four rifle battalions at hand they could have struck for May, Fontenay, or Rocquancourt.[26] They did not. Independent initiative was not in the British-Canadian doctrine. They watched patiently, ducking long-range 88mm fire from across the Orne, and waited.

Simonds, believing the initial optimistic reports from Keller and Foulkes,[27] decided to wait for his last phase to work itself out: the capture of Fontenay and Rocquancourt by the Black Watch and Royal Regiment of Canada. He postponed the armored advance and waited for his infantry to press on before armor passed through. In the interim, the 22d Armoured Brigade was ordered to continue to "support" Rockingham. Simonds had parsimoniously divided his armor, Brig. R. A. Wyman's Canadian 2d Armoured Brigade, into squadron-sized morsels, thwarting any prospect of local initiative. This is not to suggest that Wyman, who was twice checked by German armored counterattacks during June, was capable of exercising boldness. His actions at Buron and Le Mesnil-Patry demonstrated a distinct lack of feel for the situation.[28] Simonds spent a good deal of time in 2d Division's sector, conferring with both Foulkes and Maj. Gen. G. W. E. J. Erskine, commander of British 7th Armoured Division, demonstrating the Clausewitz maxim of "time which is allowed to pass unused accumulates to the credit of the defender."

Destruction of the Black Watch

> We noticed that from St. Martin area a body of infantry of considerable strength—I assume about 300–400—advanced south. This was most impressing and perplexing, the soldiers were marching holding their rifles across their breast in readiness as if on a drill square.
>
> —Lt. Peter Prein, 2d Panzer Division,
> May-sur-Orne, midmorning, 25 July 1944[29]

The Fifth Brigade's attack was poorly executed, featured no mutual support, and failed to capture May.[30] The lead battalion's companies got lost in the dark and made little progress against the 272d Division's strongpoints. By the time the Black Watch was ready to launch phase three, the advance to Fontenay-le-Marmion, the Calgary Highlanders were scattered all over the battlefield and the original start line was still not secure.

The tradition-bound Black Watch, which considered itself Canada's elite highland regiment, carried on regardless. When its commanding officer was cut down by a burst of machine gun fire, the battalion was taken over by a junior major, Philip Griffin. As Griffin attempted to clear his start line and sort out his regiment, he was continually harassed by division and brigade headquarters to press on. Griffin had a tank squadron from the 1st Hussars, Canadian 2d Armoured Brigade, in support. He decided to have the tanks skirt his advance on the right by driving south to May, deploying to cover his flank, then shooting him into Fontenay as he advanced "on a compass bearing."[31] Griffin's scouts reported that May was empty. It appeared to be, but was not. Schack had a battalion dug in; showing superior fire discipline and stealth, Schack's troops remained undetected. Griffin ordered the Black Watch to advance up the ridge, through waist-high wheat, as if on parade. They had not gone more than 600 yards when they ran into a counterattack by Battle Group Sterz.

Panzer Counterattack—KG Sterz

By 10:00 A.M. the situation for the German 272d Division was tense. Its right flank had been turned by the RHLI's capture of Verrières village, and, worse, three regiments of the British 22d Armoured Brigade (Brig. W. R. N. Hinde) had been observed on the northern slopes of the Verrières Ridge. The Shermans were supported by mechanized and motorized infantry (131st Queen's Brigade, Brig. E. C. Pepper). To his front, Schack had lost Etavaux and most of St. Martin, and parts of May-sur-Orne were in enemy hands.[32] One company of the Calgary Highlanders had worked its way south to houses just northwest of May's center. At about 10:30 A.M. reports reached Schack that a large body of men supported by tanks was moving toward Fontenay.[33] With the Canadians securing the valley, his right flank threatened and the forward battle area mostly lost, Schack ordered his armored reserve to strike against St. Martin.

Kampfgruppe Sterz[34] and the Black Watch, already under punishing fire from the 272d's machine guns and mortars, reached the crest at the same moment. "*Der Angriff gewann zunachst zugig an Boden, stiez in ein angreifendes kanadisches Bataillon hinein, das zersprengt werde.*" ("Initially the attack gained ground quickly and struck an attacking Canadian battalion, dispersing it.")[35] It was a massacre.

Sterz ordered his Panthers into May in a left hook, while the panzer grenadiers and JPz IVs crossed the open ridge to the right. As they adopted "*Hinterhangs Stellungen*" (hull-down), fire positions, Sterz's group tore into the Black Watch with cannon and automatic fire, while the Panthers engaged the 1st Hussar Squadron, now commanded by Capt. J. W. "Jake" Powell.

Powell ordered his tanks to support the Black Watch with machine guns and sent two troops up the road into May-sur-Orne. The Hussars arrived at the town center at the same time as Sterz's Panthers. A quick firefight knocked out two Shermans. B Squadron withdrew to the outskirts of May and held astride the road, giving what support it could, as the Black Watch (which by now was reduced to about sixty men) still led by Griffin, disappeared over the ridge.[36] The 2d Panzer's counterattack by fire had stopped Powell cold and destroyed the Black Watch.

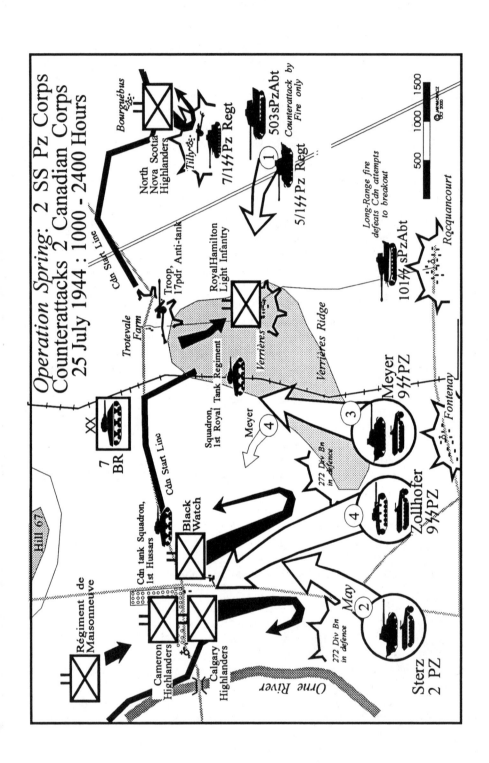

Operation Spring: 2 SS Pz Corps
Counterattacks 2 Canadian Corps
25 July 1944 : 1000 - 2400 Hours

Panzer Counterattack: 9th SS Hohenstaufen Division

> *Harzer, the Tommies have broken through in 272nd Division's sector. The axis of attack is Caen-Thury-Harcourt via Saint-Martin and May, as well as the Caen-Falaise route via Rocquancourt.*
> *The 9SS Pz Division Hohenstaufen will attack north as soon as possible and reestablish the forward battle area. Engage with two regimental battle groups.*
> *Any questions? No? Well then, move now. Speed is essential!*
> —Operational Order for divisional counterattack: SS Oberführer Kramer, chief of staff 1st SS Panzer Corps, to SS Obersturmbannführer W. Harzer, chief of staff 9th SS Panzer Division, 25 July 1944

Simonds's plans were about to be permanently disrupted by Dietrich's corps counterattack. Kluge at last gave Dietrich permission to use the 9th SS Panzer Division. The battle procedure was simple and a classic for any armored operation. Dietrich called Stadler and announced that "the Tommies have taken Verrières." The 9th SS was directed to strike north immediately, its objective, Hill 88, the high feature in the center of the ridge.[37] SS Oberführer Sylvester Stadler, commander of the 9th SS, had both of his battle groups ready.[38] Kampfgruppe Meyer was the Gepanzerte Gruppe (tank heavy battlegroup) and held most of the 9th SS armor—all available runners from the Panther battalion, the Pzkw IV battalion, and the Stug battalion. Under command were a flak troop, engineers and possibly a panzer grenadier company. Kampfgruppe Zollhöfer, composed of *Panzer Grenadier Regiment* Hohenstaufen,[39] a flak troop, and possibly a troop of JPz IVs.[40]

Stadler attacked two up. Zollhofer drove toward St. Martin, while Meyer headed for the ridge's center. Reaching the crest, Meyer was met by the concentrated fire from Canadian 17-pounder antitank guns and the tank guns of the 22d Armoured Brigade. Reporting that he had encountered a "pak front" Meyer advised his battlegroup that "Bei Höhe 88 Pak und Panzer auf 800 Meter. Wer die Höhe uberschreitet ist ein toter man" ("Who ever crosses this ridge is a dead man")[41] and sideslipped west to support Zollhöfer's attack. This was a classic example of *auftragstaktik.* Understanding his commander's intent, Meyer continued the battle in its most favorable sector. That the 9th SS arrived at Verrières, let alone continued its attack into St. Martin, a virtual *Totenritt* (death ride), is amazing given the air activity over Operation Spring. There were "1,700 sorties in order to support the attack and to limit the power of the enemy's counterattacks. Rocket firing Typhoons alone flew over fifty missions in response to the Army's calls."[42]

The Hohenstaufen Division cleared May, recaptured St. Martin, and forced the 5th Brigade back into St. André. The remainder of the evening and part of the next day was spent in fighting to keep the 9th SS from recapturing both St. André and Hill 67: Panthers had penetrated as far north as the hill's slopes and the panzer grenadiers had "reestablished the [front line]."[43] Kluge, with one eye on St. Lô, where this time there were reports of heavy bombers being used, was satisfied. Although Verrières village remained in Canadian hands, most of the ridge had been held or recaptured, and both the corps and operational armored reserves remained intact. The 9th SS counterattack had dashed all prospects of Simonds's saving Spring.

Spring—Analysis: Neither Holding Action nor Breakout

I want to write down German armor.
                              —Field Marshal Montgomery

One of the reasons for the failure of most high-risk British and American operations has been the lack of intelligence, the poor quality of what was available, and above all the refusal of many commanders even to listen to their intelligence staffs, and of those that did listen, to trust them.
                              —Brig. Richard Simpkin, Royal Tank Regiment

The classical defensive battle requires determination and aggressiveness. It demands tenacious defense, local counterattacks, and, finally, a decisive attack once the enemy offensive action has reached its culmination point.[44] When the enemy appears exhausted and has shot his bolt, the master tactician releases his own carefully protected reserve armor. The subsequent counterattack will either destroy the enemy's last echelon or, at the least, reestablish the forward edge of the battle area (the initial start line), as Stadler's 9th SS Panzer Division did.[45]

One of the techniques available is "allowable penetration." The defender invites the enemy in, beyond his direct-fire support, beyond the observation of artillery FOOs, and into a reverse-slope killing area, and then delivers the annihilating stroke. This balance of allowable penetration, blocking and counterattack on favorable ground, is the essence of the operational art in the defense. Had Simonds counterattacked the Hohenstaufen Division when Meyer and Zollhofer had reached their own culminating point, Operation Spring may have gone differently. Dietrich, given both free rein and resources by Kluge, reacted the more decisively and rewarded his boss with a "complete defensive victory." At the end of Spring, von Kluge had both hurt the Canadian II Corps "Hierbei hatte der Feind höhe bulge Verluste" ("The Enemy took high bloody casualties") and retained freedom of action for operational maneuver.[46] He could send his panzers anywhere he wished, and he had panzers to send. Lt. Gen. Fritz Bayerlein, commander of the Panzez Lehr Division, saw Spring as part of the feint at Caen: The Allied Command succeeded in completely veiling from the German Supreme Command the preparations for the break-through west of St. Lo. This was achieved by strong attacks in the British sector around Caen in the first half of July.[47]

Perhaps Spring is best recorded in military history as a determined example of a corps feint.

Bluecoat: Cobra's Unintended Holding Action

To the west, despite Bradley's determination, Cobra did not penetrate to Coutances (15.5 miles from St. Lô) until 27 July. The Americans were fighting their way through the thickest bocage and against determined rear-guards. Montgomery's new directive (M515) was issued on 27 July, and it unexpectedly ordered Dempsey to organize "a big attack with six divisions from Caumont towards Vire and hope to get it launched not later than 2 August."[48] Dempsey waited until 30 July to launch Bluecoat: "The two were complementary—Montgomery the extrovert, who loved the head-lines; Dempsey the introvert, who shunned publicity, but who got on with the job efficiently and without any fuss."[49] Preceded by 700 medium bombers, Dempsey attacked with six divisions west of the Noyers; over 3,000 vehicles struck south through the *suisse Normande* but were soon caught in an inextricable minefield where tanks, Bren gun carriers, and half-tracks became entangled and neutralized. Although it was supposed to break through to the Vire, Bluecoat was mired in heavy fighting from 30 July until 5 August when it finally fizzled. Dempsey had failed. Yet if a comparison is made between Bluecoat and Spring, one can afford to be generous to Dempsey, and say "now that was a holding action."[50]

Terry Copp, the only Canadian military historian to have produced a brigade-level study of operations in Normandy, suggests that the real prob-lem in Normandy was manpower.[51] The Canadian army, an all-volunteer force whose well was dry by August, and the conscript British army could not afford the casualties inflicted by the Germans, and this may have influ-enced Montgomery's conservative tactics. Yet sending Dempsey into the bocage in a fruitless breakout turned into a holding action cost him thou-sands of irreplaceable infantrymen regardless. ("Gave orders to Dempsey this morning that attack is to be pressed with utmost vigour and all caution thrown to the winds and any casualties accepted and that he must step on gas for Vire."[52]) Not supporting Simonds when it counted suggests that Montgomery did not recognize strategic attrition when it was most required.

Spring neither destroyed Kluge's panzer reserves nor drew them to

Simonds's sector. Since Bluecoat was attacking *away* from Simonds and toward the Allied 12th Army Group, Montgomery's directive, if anything, hastened the departure of panzer divisions toward Bradley: "[German] Armor came from Monty's front at the time of Mortain and caused trouble."[53] If Dempsey had succeeded, he could only look forward to a complex traffic jam with the U.S. First Army at Vire or to ordering a sharp left turn to face his army eastward. If this was part of Montgomery's master plan, it was awkward and launched very late and into the least favorable terrain imaginable. Dempsey ran into mined bocage and was checked by counterattacks made by the 21st Panzer,[54] 9th SS, and 10th SS Panzer Divisions, units that were supposed to have been "written down" in front of Caen.

Had Spring lasted half as long as Bluecoat, the very real threat of a push to Falaise and Paris would have taken much of Kluge's interest away from Bradley. If Spring was to be a successful holding action, it required that the panzer divisions hang around Caen for at least five days. One must seriously question Montgomery's intent. If the Canadian II Corps had achieved total success, what would Dempsey have done on 26 July? He was poised to either reinforce or, more important, exploit a Canadian breakthrough. Montgomery had not deployed British Second Army in anticipation of victory but rather in expectation of Canadian failure.

It is difficult to imagine Montgomery scheming against Crerar or Bradley, but he certainly failed to plan ahead. The best Dempsey could do was double back and move a corps east through Caen to support a Canadian penetration toward the Laison or Ante River. This would require considerable time. Montgomery's strategic overview seems vague, his concept of future operations, despite his energetic claims to the contrary, was shortsighted: "Monty looked at flat area and that of the tanks' problems in terms of the desert. Monty was never too successful except on flat ground. He didn't use terrain as we did. He liked flat country."[55]

There is another simpler possibility. In hindsight, the grand Cannae encirclement that was the Falaise pocket seems brilliant. It is everything Montgomery was not. A logical conclusion is that dull, tidy Montgomery was simply sticking to the basic strategy he laid out at St. Paul's School.[56] He wanted everyone to push south; his concept of operations was to match Bradley, not to encircle Germans. Montgomery continued to work hard to accomplish his stated goal: clear Brittany and capture a decent port. The event that followed—the armored breakout—simply overtook both Bradley and Montgomery, two conservative plodders.[57]

The Growing Importance of Cobra

After 25 July, Kluge turned his full attention to Bradley and in passing, Dempsey. Hitler's order of "Starre Verteidigung" ("unyielding defense") forced Kluge to stop everything and try to hold everywhere. Before Spring there were eight panzer divisions around Caen. Three days after Bradley launched Operation Cobra, over half of them had left. St. Lô is a half-day's drive from Falaise by convoy (approximately 37 miles by road). A tank division, moving by night through the wooded *suisse normande* could get to the U.S. battle area virtually unobserved by tactical air within twenty-four hours. Avranches (43 miles from Falaise by road), the Vire River (28 miles), and Mont Picon (19 miles) were well within the redeployment window. The Allies' only confirmation of an army-level counterstroke against Bradley was not by aerial reconnaissance but Ultra. A complete division and its trains would not take longer than three days to redeploy (the 2d SS Panzer Corps required only two weeks to move from the Brody area in the Soviet Union to Caen in June). The battle groups, the parts of a division that actually stopped Allied offensives, could move to blocking positions within a day: Schack's 272d Division left Verrières on the night of 26 July[58] and replaced the 12th SS Hitlerjugend Division on the east flank of the the Canadian First Army front. 10th SS headed west on 26 July; 9th SS Panzer,[59] 21st Panzer, and 116th Panzer Divisions withdrew on the 29th. The SS Hohenstaufen Division handed over to the 89th Infantry Division on 1 August. Finally, the 1st SS Leibstandarte Adolf Hitler advance parties left the Caen area on 3 August. On that day, eight days after Spring had ended, the Canadian II Corps was faced with but a single panzer division, the only German reserve on Kluge's front.[60] It was the old Canadian nemesis, Kurt Meyer's 12th SS Hitlerjugend.[61]

Notes

1. Lt. Gen. Sir Giffard Le Q. Martel, *In the Wake of the Tank* (London: Museum Press, 1952).

2. 1st SS, 9th SS, 10th SS, 12th SS Panzer; 2d, 21st, and 116th Panzer; 101st SS, 102d SS Heavy Panzer Battalion; and 654th JPz Battalion. All, except the 10th SS and 21st and 116th Panzer Divisions, fought the Canadian II Corps throughout Operations Atlantic, Spring, and Totalize. The 2d SS Das Reich Division's battle group was in the area shortly after Goodwood and Atlantic but was soon drawn off toward St. Lô. The panzer units facing Bradley were Das Reich, initially with only its Pzkw IV battalion, 17th SS Panzer Grenadier Division with a battalion of assault guns, and the battered but game Panzer Lehr Division. RH 21-5/44 *Kriegstagebuch Panzer-Armeeoberkommando 5.* 10.6.44–8.8.44, order of battle, 25 July 1944.

3. Montgomery's critics were having a field day at SHAEF. See Carlo D'Este, *Decision in Normandy;* Alistair Horne, *Monty, The Lonely Leader, 1944–1945* (New York: Harper, 1994). "Colonel Dawney has recorded that this was one of the few occasions when Montgomery was visibly worried," Chalfort, p. 244. Eisenhower was particularly frustrated by Montgomery's continual failure to deliver on his promise of an operational breakout in the Caen area: "Ike is like a blind dog in a meat house—he can smell it, but he can't find it." Capt. H. C. Butcher, *My Three Years With Eisenhower* (New York: Simon and Schuster, 1946), p. 619.

4. Butcher, p. 623.

5. M-514. 24 July. "Am not going to hold back and wait on western front. . . . Have ordered Dempsey to loose his forces tomorrow anyhow and the Cdn Corps attack will begin at 0330 hours 25 Jul," message to Eisenhower. The RAF's opinion was severe: "Monty was not an unusual general. He was a competent general in positional warfare. But he never exploited his victories. He wouldn't fight until he had everything . . . the breakout came because Bradley and Patton got tired of waiting around for Monty and finally Ike gave permission to Bradley to go ahead." Air Marshal Sir Arthur Coningham, MHI. Pogue Papers, interview 14 February 1947.

6. On 24 July 1944, Montgomery advised Eisenhower that his concept of future 2d Army operations included first, the Canadian attack to secure the Cramesnil spur (south of Verrières) followed by an attack by the XII Corps west of the Orne. Phase three featured an VIII Corps drive through the Canadian II Corps toward Falaise, "preliminary to a very large scale operation by possibly three or four armored divisions." Canadian control of Verrières was essential to "another Goodwood." Stacey, p. 183.

7. Hans Delbrück, *Die Strategie des Perikles erlätert durch die Strategie Friedrichs des Grossen,* (Berlin, 1890), pp. 27–28. Gordon Craig identifies this as "Delbrück's most systematic exposition of the two forms of strategy." See "Delbrück: The Military Historian," E. M. Earle, ed., *Makers of Modern Strategy* (Princeton, N.J.: Princeton University Press, 1948), p. 273.

8. Montgomery was uniformly disliked by many American soldiers. His "desert" style charmed novice British and Canadian troops, but it did not sit well with U.S. officers who had Casablanca and Kasserine Pass among their battle honors. His appearance at a pre-Cobra dinner with Eisenhower and Bradley drew particular ridicule. Chester B. Hansen Papers; Hanson Diary, "Brad Plans for Cobra," entry week of 16–25 July 1944, MHI.

9. See B. H. Liddell Hart, *The Rommel Papers* (New York: Harcourt, 1953); R. Lewin, *Rommel as Military Commander* (London: Batsford, 1968).

10. RG 24 13711. Minutes of Conference Held by General Montgomery HQ 21 Army Group, 0930 hrs 13 Jan 44.

11. See Christopher Bellamy, *Red God of War—Soviet Artillery and Rocket Forces* (London: Brassey's Defence Publications, 1986).

12. Military Training Pamphlet No. 41, *The Tactical Handling of the Armored Division and its Components* (London: War Office, July 1943).

13. Military Training Pamphlet No. 2, *The Offensive* (London: The War Office, June 1943), p. 8.

14. UK No. 41. The Tactical Handling of the Armored Division and its Components. War Office, July 1943.

15. Military Training Pamphlet No. 41.

16. Panthers were troubled with design defects: all 325 Panthers had to be withdrawn for complete rebuilding in 1943. "Many a Panther was lost because of shortage of some elementary spare part or because it could not be repaired in time." See *German Tank Maintenance in World War 2*. U.S. Army Department Pamphlet No. 20-202, June 1954, pp. 23–26.

17. Immediately available and participating were 1st SS the Leibstandarte, 9th SS Hohenstaufen, and 10th SS Fruindsberg. The 12th SS was northeast of Tilly and contributed in long-range tank/artillery fire. Its tanks were within fifteen minutes' striking distance. All three Tiger battalions were engaged, the 654th Heavy JP2 Battalion was minute march away, and two *nebelwerfer brigades* covered the area.

18. Stacey, p. 186.

19. Interrogation report, MA/239. 24 July 1944. The final days of Atlantic produced evidence, through prisoners of war and captured vehicles, of not only the presence of the 2d Pz and 9th SS Divisions (the latter a critical revelation) in the 272d Division area but a detailed listing of Shack's division. Reports MA 249, MA 238, RG 24 10677. See the Canadian II Corps intelligence summaries 45, 47, 49, 50, 54, 57, and interrogation logs for 12 July–26 July WD 5 CIB, 19–22 July.

20. "Artificial moonlight supplied by eight searchlight btys." RG 24 14,116, WD 6 CIB, 25 July 1944.

21. RG 24 14046 WD 2 CAB; intelligence summaries: "Apx A to Int Sum No.47 Dated 24 Jul 44." Allied intelligence was not quite sure where everything was: "Tank element of 1 SS Pz may have been used as the immediate counter-attack force." As shown in Table 7.2, this is what was reported.

Table 7.2   Canadian II Corps Intelligence Summary 13: Estimate of Enemy Strengths as of 23 July 1944

		Tanks			Assault Guns	Field/ Medium
Formation	Infantry Battalions	MK IV	MK V	MK VI	JPz	Guns
1 SS Pz	4.5	60	20		35	44
9 SS Pz	4	20	50		20	41
10 SS Pz	2.5	30	25		30	41
12 SS Pz	3	45	35		30	30
2 Pz	3.5	30	20		37	42
21 Pz	2	60			30	20
272 Inf	4				9	48
101 SS Pz Bn				25		
102 SS Pz Bn				30		
503 Pz Bn				30		

For an intelligence estimate, this was remarkably complete except for the 10th SS Panzer Division, which did not have its Panther battalion in Normandy. The presence of the 116th Panzer Division had not yet been discovered.

22. WD 272. Infanterie-Division. 23.7.44. RH26-272/5. Although Dietrich is not mentioned, he was probably present. He visited Schack earlier (20 July 1944) with Lt. Gen. von Luttwitz (commander, 2d Panzer Division).

23. Bundesarchiv RH26-272/5, 272. Infanterie-Division, p. 27; see also ETHINT MS #B-540 and MS #B-702: "272 Infantry Division in Normandy." Manuscript by Schack and Jenner, Die 216/272. The 9th SS Panzer was Dietrich's only corps reserve.

24. MS #B-470, Maj. Gen. Stadler, "9 SS Pz Div (20 June–31 July 44)," MHI.

25. RH19 IX/9. MS #B-257, Gen. F. v. Luttwitz, "2 Panzer Division in Normandy." Recruited in Vienna, it arrived in the Normandy battle area in early June " west of Bretteville-sur-Laize . . . 25 miles south of Caen," pp. 24–26. See also Franz von Steinzer, *Die 2. Panzer Division* (Freiburg: Podzun-Pallas Verlag, 1974), and F. J. Straas, *Kriegeschicte der 2. Weiner Panzer-Division* (Bonn: Vowinczel, 1977).

26. The County of London Yeomanry and the 1st Royal Tank Regiment were

on the ridge in the area of Beauvoir farm; the 5th Royal Tank Regiment was closer to Troteval and trading shots with German armor near Tilly. The Queen's Brigade (the 1st Battalions of the 5th and 6th Regiments, and 1st Battalion, 7th Queen's Royal Regiment) was north of Beauvoir, close to Ifs with the 8th Hussars under its command.

27. Keller and Foulkes passed on buoyant reports. At one point Simonds was led to believe that in addition to Verrières, both Tilly and May-sur-Orne had been secured.

28. See English, pp. 209–210; Roy, pp. 322–331; Stacey, p. 140.

29. Account by Lt. Peter Prein, former signals officer, 3d Panzer Regiment, 2d Panzer Division, interviewed April 1990; and Helmut Ritgen, "Kampf um May-sur-Orne am 25 Juli 1944," unpublished manuscript, 1990.

30. War Diary, Calgary Highlanders. For details, see Terry Copp, *The Brigade* (Stoney Creek, Ontario: Fortress, 1992), and David Bercuson, *Battalion of Heroes* (Calgary: Regimental Association, 1994).

31. There is considerable debate in Canadian military history over "blame." The Black Watch saw the brigade commander as the culprit. The army's investigation concluded that Griffin was at fault. At least one eyewitness account given to Stacey suggests that Griffin may have indeed been ordered to attack frontally. See Copp, pp. 77–80. Superb air photos of Verrières from July 1944 are included.

32. Etavaux is village on the Orne that protected Schack's left flank, just north of of St. André and St. Martin. Copp, pp. 60–62.

33. Prein report. Prein was part of Sterz's Battle Group and commanded the headquarters troop. Correspondence, April 1990. See also Jenner, *Die 216/272 Niedersachsische Infanterie-Div 1939–1945* (Ban Nauheim: Podzun, 1964).

34. Major Sterz commanded the 38th Panzerjäger Battalion. His battle group comprised the remaining tanks of the 1st Battalion, 3d Panzer Regiment, with twelve to fourteen Panther tanks, the remainder of the 1st Battalion 304th Panzer Grenadier Regiment (under Captain Scholing, "an outstanding one-eyed officer"), and the 75mm tank destroyers of the 38th Panzerjäger Battalion battle group. Prein, p. 2.

35. F. J. Straas, p. 168.

36. Over 300 Black Watch attacked; not more than fifteen got back to their lines. About sixty crossed the ridge, and were surrounded and taken prisoner by 272d Division troops. Griffin was killed by mortar fire. Simonds reportedly watched the action from Hill 67. War Diary, Canadian II Corps, Canadian 2d, 3d Infantry Divisions, 25 July 1944; Powis, after-action report "Spring"; Stacey, p. 192; Sterns Papers, 25 July 1944 notes.

37. MHI P Series manuscripts: SS Col. W. Harzer, "9SS Panzer Div 'Hohenstaufen,' 25 Jul–Nov 44" 162. MS #B-407. SS Gen. Sylvester Stadler, "9SS Pz Div 20 June-24 July 44." Stadler rated the 9th SS before Spring as "Troops 88%; PzGren Bn 60% (few officers); Artillery 90%; Tanks 70%; the division did not receive any reinforcements either before or after the invasion" p. 2.

38. MS #B-747and MS #B-748. 2 SS Pz Korps by SS General W. Bittrich, commander. The 9th SS reached Normandy during 14–20 June, initially without its Panther battalion.

39. The 9th SS Division's infantry strength was reduced to one regiment by 25 July. "Due to heavy losses on 18 July, 19SS and 20SS PGR amalgamated into 1 Regt of 4 bns." RG 24 13,712.

40. By 25 July, the 9th SS Panzer Division's strength was reported as eleven JPz IVs, eighteen Pz IVs, and eighteen Panthers. Herbert Fürbringer, *9.SS-Panzer-*

Division Hohenstaufen: 1944 Normandie (Osnabrück: Munin Verlag, 1987), p. 342.

41. Ibid., p. 340.

42. Ellis, *British Official History: Normandy*, p. 379. See also MS #B-470: Stadler feared the Canadian II Corps guns more than RAF Typhoons. "The use of artillery by the British was definitely much more powerful and oppressive than enemy air superiority" MHI.

43. The 9th SS bumped into Canadian Régiment de Maisonneuve (also counterattacking) and forced it back to St. André. See Jacques Gouin, *Bon Coeur et Bon Bras—Histoire du Régiment de Maisonneuve* (Montreal: Regimental Association, 1980), p. 103. Canadian 2d Armoured Brigade radio logs confirm a knocked-out Panther at GR 023615, the southern slope of Hill 67. See also RG 24 10677: interrogation report, Oberstgruppenführer Sepp Dietrich.

44. "The point of culmination will necessarily be reached when the defended must make up his mind and act." Clausewitz, *On War,* books 6, 7.

45. Army Group B credited the 9th SS Panzer and the 272d Infantry Divisions with this effective counterattack: *Den Gegenangriff der 9.SS Pz.Div. und der 272.I.D.* WD Armeegruppe B, Tegesmeldung, 26 July 1944.

46. WD Heeresgruppe B, Morenmeldung, 26 July 1944, RH19 IX/M.

47. ETHINT #67, 15 August 1945. "An Interview with GenLt Fritz Bayerlein: Critique of Normandy Breakthrough," MHI.

48. Letters of instruction, M515, 27 July 1944, Heiberg Papers.

49. Sir Brian Horrocks, *Corps Commander* (New York: Charles Scribner's Sons, 1977), p. 23.

50. Fuller defined a holding action as "[a] holding attack to force [the enemy] to [the defensive]; in other words to pin him to the locality. Once this was accomplished [would come] the true attack form of a flank or rear maneuver." *Armored Warfare,* p. 113. For camparison, see English, p. 260: "Too much has been made of whether or not "Spring" was a holding attack."

51. Copp's understanding of the Canadian II Corps makes him particularly competent to discuss whether the corps was close to breaking by August. T. Copp and Bill McAndrew, *Battle Exhaustion* (Montreal: McGill-Queen's University Press, 1990. Copp contends that the situation was as bad, if not far worse, in Dempsey's army. Interview with T. Copp, Waterloo, Ontario, May 1997.

52. Montgomery to War Office 30 July 1944, quoted in Stacey, p. 200.

53. Gen. Omar C. Bradley, 14 October 1946, Interview, Pogue Papers, MHI.

54. "21st Panzer Division, being brought up from the east bank of the Orne . . . the enemy break-through to Vire was prevented for the time being." MS B-748, 2d SS Panzer Corps, pp. 3–5.

55. Hansen Papers. 37-B. S-27, MHI.

56. A review of Overlord strategic plans will show an ever widening bridgehead that eventually reached the Loire and Seine rivers and Paris only after Brittany was secure. See Letters of Instruction, HQ 12 Army Group 6 June–31 August 1944; Heiberg Papers, Patton Museum, Fort Knox; and Crerar Papers, Eisenhower, Hamilton, D'Este, and others.

57. A Montgomery apologist argues that "if the Germans could have shifted even a single battered panzer division toward Bradley . . . it would have made his breakout infinitely more difficult and costly—perhaps even impossible before August." Alistair Horne "In Defense of Montgomery," *Quarterly Journal of Military History* 1 (Autumn 1995): 67. In fact four, and eventually six, panzer divisions shifted over.

58. RH21-5/44 *Kriegstagebuch Panzer-Armeeoberkommando 5.* WD 10.6.44–

8.8.44.

59. The 9th SS Panzer Division, initially with only one tank battalion arrived in Falaise after Operation Spring, and continued west toward Mortain.

60. Remaining panzer divisions thinned out after Operation Spring in direct reaction to Cobra: RG 24 14046 WD 2 CAB. Intelligence summary 4 August 1944. The 9th SS was at Caumont; "10SS has during past three days gone west"; "28 July . . . 116th Pz Div requested to St. Lo ... 2 Aug, 9 SS launched an attack [against Bluecoat]." See MS #155, General Krueger, "1 SS Pz Corps (16 Aug–6 Sep 44)"; MS #B-358 SS Gen. Theodor Wisch, "Leibstandarte Adolf Hitler in Aug 44"; MS #B-034 and B-358, and MS #B-470 Maj. Gen. Stadler, "9 SS Pz Div (20 June–31 Jul 44)." Also, MS #B034 *OKW War Dairy,* "The West (1 Apr–18 Dec 44)," MHI.

61. The Canadians had met the 12th SS on the morning of 7 June in one of the first armored battle group actions on the beachhead. Savage fighting continued throughout June and July as the 12th SS Panzer Division dug in opposite the Canadian 3d Division and blocked the road to Caen. See Stacey, pp. 121–158, and Roy, pp. 25–50.

CHAPTER 8

Operation Cobra: Bradley Acquires Operational Maneuver

On the other hand you may be restricted to roads and have no freedom of maneuver but there is also a limit to what the enemy can put on the road to stop you—once you're through him—you're through.
—General George S. Patton[1]

The battle of annihilation in Normandy—the breakthrough at St. Lô, resulting in the envelopment, encirclement, and annihilation of the German defenders (Fifth Pz and Seventh Armies)—appears to me to be the greatest strategical and tactical achievement of this war, as well as the most decisive.
—Lt. Gen. Fritz Bayerlein, commander, Panzer Division Lehr[2]

The troops sure like to see you up front.
—Unidentified staff officer to Gen. Leslie J. McNair,
Normandy, 24 July 1944[3]

Omar Bradley had looked forward to Cobra with the greatest enthusiasm and anticipation: "I've wanted to do this now since we landed. When we pull it, I want it to be the biggest thing in the world. We want to smash right through."[4] Operation Cobra began with the now standard Allied signature for a major offensive—strategic bombers ("Brad wants . . . craters 16 feet in every direction.") Despite the carefully chosen bomb line, an approach error resulted in bombs falling short; the heavy bombers established an unfortunate pattern that would be repeated in Totalize and Tractable and created serious U.S. casualties at the outset.

> It was horrible. Ground belched, shook and spewed dirt into the sky. Scores of our troops were hit, their bodies flying from slit trenches. Huebner, an old front line campaigner, said it was the most terrifying thing he had ever seen. . . . Doughboys are still quivering in their holes.[5]

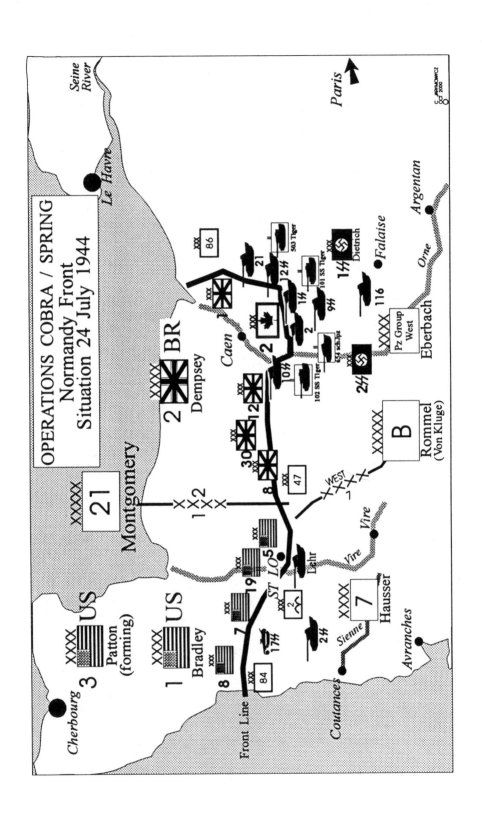

OPERATIONS COBRA / SPRING
Normandy Front
Situation 24 July 1944

Nevertheless, the shock and destruction created in the German front lines was everything Bradley hoped for.[6] In a horrid irony, the advent of Cobra and the triumph of U.S. armor brought about the death of armor's nemesis, Leslie McNair.[7] Perhaps because of his complete absence of operational experience, McNair had gone to great lengths to demonstrate his personal courage by visiting front-line troops. Wounded once in Tunisia, he again tempted fate at Cobra's launch, where, had he given Devers the support requested, there would have been ten U.S. armored divisions breaking out instead of five. However, there were forty-five tank destroyer battalions available to Bradley—a force equivalent to fifteen armored divisions except for the drawback of their being incapable of offensive operations.[8]

After the Army Air Corps had blasted a hole at St. Lô, the U.S. First Army broke in. General Collins's VII Corps (three infantry, two armored, and one motorized division) drove into Hauser's forward defenses and began to battle through the hedgerows. Despite the horrific Allied "carpet bombing," they were soon under fire as survivors from Panzer Division Lehr recovered.[9] As the dogfight continued, Collins released the 2d and 3d Armored Divisions. By 26 July, four combat commands from the 2d Armored had advanced 6 miles, having first to recover the initial forward edge of the battle area by recapturing abandoned ground.

> Results of bombing were devastating but certain shortcomings reduced its effectiveness considerably. The necessity to withdraw our troops from the front lines caused initial loss of 1500 yards which had to be regained by fighting because the enemy followed our retrograde movement closely.[10]

By the end of 27 July, the 2d Armored Division drove south another 7 miles. Their progress, although slow, was spectacular given normal bocage conditions.[11] An enterprising soldier, Sgt. Curtis G. Culin of the 102d Cavalry Reconnaissance Squadron, had invented a simple solution. This consisted of welding iron prongs (cut to create Rhinoceros-tusk-like prows) to the front of tanks, permitting them to pierce the banks of obstructing hedgerows and rip them out—thus allowing easy passage without exposing their bottom hull to pak or panzerfaust fire. This new tactical freedom to maneuver upset Hauser's plan for delaying the advance with roadblocks and craters. Rhino-Shermans could now cut a bypass and continue to exploit while engineers dealt with the obstacles.

As the infantry battered to the south, Bradley permitted Middleton to unleash what were to become the two best tank divisions in the U.S. arsenal, Gen. Robert W. Grow's 6th Armored Division and Maj. Gen. John S. Wood's 4th Armored Division. The U.S. VIII Corps advanced 8 miles, and by the end of July the Americans created the first Normandy encirclement, the trap at Roncey.

The Roncey Pocket

General Wood's Combat Command B entered Coutances on 28 July and inadvertently drove the Germans south, denying Maj. Gen. J. Lawton Collins a quick bag; however, Gen. Maurice Rose's resourcefulness created an even bigger encirclement and Cobra's first "pocket." Two combat commands from the 2d Armored Division were spurred southwest until they had outflanked the retreating units of the German LXXXIV Corps. By 29 July a third U.S. combat command, 3d Armored's Combat Command B, had reached St. Denis-le-Gast. Along the western coast of the peninsula, Wood and Grow raced two combat commands abreast toward Bréhal and slammed the door.

The trapped group comprised three infantry divisions and the remaining western Panzers Divisions, the 2d SS Das Reich and 17th SS Panzer Grenadier. As the Germans attempted to extricate themselves, they were struck in the flank by Combat Command A from the 3d Armored Division, and their columns were surprised on the roads by Maj. Gen. Elwood R. "Pete" Quesada's U.S. IX Tactical Air Force. The combined efforts of 3d Armored's tanks and P-47 air strikes shot the German units to pieces.[12] This decisive attack was the first of two successful Cobra assaults mounted by the IX Tactical Air Force. The Thunderbolt-Typhoon airplane team was to make a name for itself during the Falaise campaign.

By 30 July, Middleton's armor (combat commands from the U.S. 4th Armored Division advancing 18 miles) had captured the bridges at Avranches.[13] Cobra was, like Goodwood, a strategic offensive. It may have not met Soviet standards, however. With two armies at his back and a tactical air force overhead, Bradley had enough to chase Kluge out of France. Bradley was less colorful than Montgomery, but by the summer of 1944 he surpassed the victor of El Alamein in determination. Once he got his teeth into Kluge he would not let go.

Cobra's spectacular beginning almost bogged down in dirty close-quarters fighting: "Between July 26th and August 12th, for example, one of 2nd Armored's Tank battalions had lost to German tanks and assault guns 70 per cent of its tanks."[14] The intensity of this combat cruelly tested the armored divisions. General Harmon's post-Cobra evaluation concluded that the "outstanding weakness of the Armored Division has been its lack of infantry."[15]

Although Bradley finally cleared the bocage by the end of July, Montgomery, lacking confidence in the Americans but aware that Bluecoat was a bloody disappointment, ordered Crerar to launch Operation Totalize. The situation still fit Montgomery's master plan—in its most elementary definition. Despite subsequent pleading, the original strategic development from the beachhead had nothing in it that suggested a bold encirclement:

General de Guingand didn't tell the truth about that. It is true there was a plan which showed the Americans coming up on the right towards the Seine. . . . But that is far different from the decision to strike out on the right and pull quickly around. Monty undoubtedly wanted to start the breakout on his front and then let the Americans come around as they could. He intended at first for Patton to spend his time cleaning up the few Germans in Brittany.[16]

Once Bradley got past Avranches, he was to busy himself with Brittany and the Loire River flank. Forward progress toward the east was to be symmetrical: both army groups would reach the Seine at the same time. Montgomery's initial plan called for pushing the German army out of Normandy, not destroying it in a modern Battle of Cannae.[17] The prospects for this battle of annihilation presented themselves when Patton's U.S. Third Army began to race through the rear areas of U.S. Seventh Army and the bold cavalier decided to push west: "General Bradley simply wants a bridgehead over the Sélune River [10 miles south of Avranches]. What I want and I intend is Brest and Angers."[18] Angers was 100 miles south of Avranches. Rather than busying himself with cleaning up the east, Patton wanted to expand his horizons. He was promptly reined in by Bradley, who was progressively more worried about Operation *Lüttich* after Ultra intelligence made it clear that Eberbach's Fifth Panzer Army had been ordered to chop Patton's neck at Mortain. Bradley's reaction was considered "one of the colossally stupid decisions of the war."[19] A defiant Patton ordered the XXth corps to carry on and capture Angers: "I'm doing this without consulting Gen Bradley as I am sure he thinks the operation is risky. It is slightly risky—but so is war."[20] Despite the strategical evolution of Cobra, Bradley was allowed to do as he wished. Although Bradley now commanded two operational armies (Hodges's First and Patton's Third), Montgomery was still controlling grand operations.[21]

Montgomery's 4 August directive ordered Crerar to attack toward Falaise, while Dempsey abandoned the drive for Vire and pushed toward Argentan. Hodges was to continue an advance to the west, and Patton, delegating the U.S. VII Corps to secure Brittany, was to advance toward Le Mans.[22] The aim was still to reach the Seine River eventually, but now Montgomery toyed with the idea of using his airborne troops to take the river's bridges and block the escape routes. Kluge's offensive at Mortain (6–8 August) forced him to reconsider.[23]

Tactical Air at Mortain

By 7 August 1944 Kluge finally launched Operation *Lüttich*. It was a sound operational plan: an armored strike at the flank of the breakout aimed at a short drive toward the coast. Any panzer division that reached Avranches or

Granville would cut off at least four U.S. Army corps—Patton's romping armor and Collins's forces holding the hinge at Avranches. A spectacular operational victory could destroy both U.S. armies; a tactical victory would, at the minimum, force a halt to Patton's advance, and perhaps even cause a full retreat. The plan did not count on the Allied tactical air situation.

A counterattack against Mortain had several advantages for Kluge: the ground was unfamiliar to the Americans and defenses would be light, the mass of U.S. artillery had not been deployed south, and no obstacles or mines would hamper the attackers. Mortain was vital ground because it was the center of a height that dominated the approach to Avranches and reasonably good tank country in the south, with enough closed areas to allow for effective infantry advance to infiltrate U.S. defenses. The Germans had learned that although open space favored their tank guns, their infantry performed best when it could close with and penetrate Allied defenses. A further bonus was the habitual fog in the area that would screen panzer concentrations and allow initial surprise. If the Panzers got into Bradley's rear, the cautious general was sure to withdraw.

Von Kluge had assembled three of his best divisions: 1st SS Leibstandarte, 2d SS Das Reich, and 2d Panzer—approximately 177 armored fighting vehicles (70 Panthers, 75 PzIVs, and 32 Stugs and JPz IVs.)[24] It worked out to 30 tanks per battalion, with two 15-tank companies each. Given the armor and firepower assembled, few Allied armored forces could stand up to this type of concentrated assault. However, the Germans were attacking. All German victories in Normandy had been defensive. Their offensive successes had been limited to battle group–sized counterattacks.

Even though most of Eberbach's panzers were tied up with Dempsey and Crerar, he still had a second-echelon tank force comprising the 116th Panzer and 10th SS Panzer Divisions (the Frundsberg Division had been tasked to exploit the breakthrough). The 17th SS Panzer Grenadier and Lehr Divisions, reduced to weak battle groups, were "holding the shoulders" of the bulge. None of the Tiger battalions were available. The 503d Heavy Tank Battalion was still with the 21st Panzer Division engaged in the last throes of Bluecoat, and both the 101st SS and 102d SS Heavy Tank Battalions were near the Orne, soon to be placed under command of the 12th SS Panzer Division in a successful attempt to stop Simonds's Operation Totalize. Eberbach's attack was to be supported by 300 Luftwaffe fighters and fighter-bombers to ensure that Allied tactical air would not interfere. The ground plan had merit. The air plan was unrealistic.

Bradley turned to IX Tactical Air Force and had his staff develop a plan for defense: the U.S. 30th Infantry Division would hold fast and the

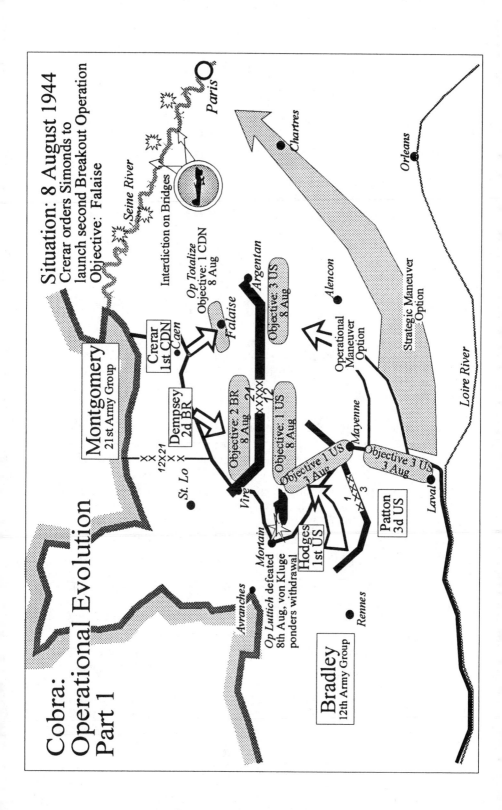

Cobra:
Operational Evolution
Part 1

Situation: 8 August 1944
Crerar orders Simonds to
launch second Breakout Operation
Objective: Falaise

Interdiction on Bridges

Seine River

Paris

Chartres

Orleans

Montgomery
21st Army Group

Crerar
1st CDN

Caen

Op Totalize
Objective: 1 CDN
8 Aug

Falaise

Argentan

Objective: 3 US
8 Aug

Alencon

Operational Maneuver
Option

Strategic Maneuver
Option

Loire River

Dempsey
2d BR

Objective: 2 BR
8 Aug

XXXX
21
XXXX
12

Objective: 1 US
8 Aug

Mayenne

Objective: 1 US
3 Aug

XXX
3

XXX
1

Objective: 1 US
3 Aug

Laval

Patton
3d US

St. Lo

X 12×21
X
X
X

Vire

Mortain

Op Luttich defeated
8th Aug, von Kluge
ponders withdrawal

Hodges
1st US

Avranches

Rennes

Bradley
12th Army Group

fighter ground attack (FGA) squadrons would help take care of the panzers. General Quesada had organized a deadly air cover.[25] First he established a defensive umbrella to prevent Luftwaffe interference: IX Air Force P-51 Mustangs and P-47D Thunderbolts would patrol overhead to provide an impenetrable radius against the Luftwaffe. Within the perimeter, P-47s and RAF 83d Group Typhoons would rake the attacking German columns with rockets and cannon.

As Operation *Lüttich* began, the ground fog began to lift. "Von Kluge arrived in person at LXXXVII combat post to spur the now fully assembled corps to the attack."[26] At noon the first Typhoons took off from their forward landing fields. Just before 1:00 P.M.

> a concentration of some 60 tanks and 200 vehicles [was] observed along a hedge-lined road near Mortain. The tanks, some heavily camouflaged, were closely bunched together as if unprepared for the rapid lifting fog. After overflying at low level to confirm them as German, the Typhoons commenced dive attacks upon the front and rear of the column, which was immediately brought to a halt. The pilots observed their attacks caused great confusion, and saw German tank crews baling out and running for cover regardless of whether or not their tanks were left blocking the road. Also at this time the first American fighter-bombers arrived in the area, with P-47s, including the squadron equipped with rockets, attacking the German transport.[27]

Between them, the 83d Group and IX Air Force flew 494 sorties into the area. German flak was slow to respond.[28] Eventually defensive antiaircraft "boxes" were set up, but the damage had been done. Although the Allied pilots' claims for 252 tanks and 228 transport vehicles destroyed were rather optimistic, the aircraft did knock out forty-six panzers and fifty transport vehicles, enough to wreck *Lüttich*. The attack continued but sputtered out around 30 July. "Despite the warning (Ultra intercepts), tank destroyers were not massed. Instead, the 30th Infantry Division and its single attached tank destroyer unit, the 823rd TD Battalion with thirty-six towed guns, met the brunt of the German attack."[29]

With no Fireflies in the cupboard, Bradley relied on infantry antitank defenses to stop von Kluge: "The heavy towed tank destroyer guns were sitting ducks when they revealed their locations by firing . . . with a heavy onion breath that day the Germans could have achieved their objectives."[30] Some impressive die-hard gains were made by panzer grenadiers at the company level, but chances for an operational victory had been quashed. By their own admission, the Germans' attack had failed because of the Allied fighter-bombers: "They came in hundreds, firing their rockets."[31] As *Lüttich* petered out, Allied dash returned, and Patton was redirected toward Argentan. The prospects of the Americans' (not Simonds) reaching Falaise were very real. The problem was that the boundary between the Twelfth and Twenty-First Army Groups that Montgomery had drawn *through* Argentan. To his disgust, Patton was forced to bide his time. Meanwhile, John Wood's division was an operational yo-yo. On 4 August Wood was, to his disgust, ordered to besiege Lorient and St. Nazaire, 75 miles southwest of Rennes. By 19 August the 4th Armored Division, now under Patton's command, was in Orléans, 180 miles east of Rennes. Patton concentrated his armor near Le Mans, threatening von Kluge's escape from the pocket, but had his eyes were on Paris.

Bradley's halt order has been much criticized: "[Bradley] was not a man that was going to do anything different than what was taught at Infantry School in the 1930's. He didn't understand these crazy Armor people."[32] Bradley's decision to sanctify drawn boundaries and protocol appears overzealous, perhaps vindictive. Stubborn insistence on adhering to a clearly outdated control measure both needlessly complicated an already confusing situation and served to highlight Montgomery's inability to control the battle.[33] As divisions struggled to complete the Falaise encirclement, Bradley actually refused direct liaison between the Canadian First Army and the U.S. Third Army headquarters.

> A British Liaison Officer by the name of [name not given in entry] reported as Liaison Officer from the Canadian Army. He was told that unfortunately the Army Commander could not accept Liaison Officers from the Canadian Army, but that the liaison between the two would have to be through Commanding General, Twelfth US Army Group; that he, the Army Commander, was very sorry that this was true, but it was the policy of the Army Group Commander, therefore would have to be carried out.[34]

This is an extraordinary example of an army group commander failing to understand his own commander's intent—a high-level failure of *auftragstaktik*. Maneuver warfare flouts conventions when they interfere with the mission: "Boundaries are not impenetrable barriers. Quite the contrary such a line constitutes an invitation to a commander to seek out his neighbour across the boundary and arrange with him their adjoining operations to ensure mutual advantages."[35]

Crerar's failure in reaching Falaise on schedule may have convinced Bradley that the Canadians were not going to meet him in Argentan: "Like all the Allied Commanders, Bradley was then far too optimistic about the pace of the Canadian advance."[36] The prospects of an encirclement at Falaise seemed to be slipping away. Von Kluge, hounded by Hitler to resume the offensive, was preparing a second attack against Bradley's exposed flank between Argentan and Mayenne. The attack never took place because the U.S. VII Corps deployed to block the exposed gap. Later,

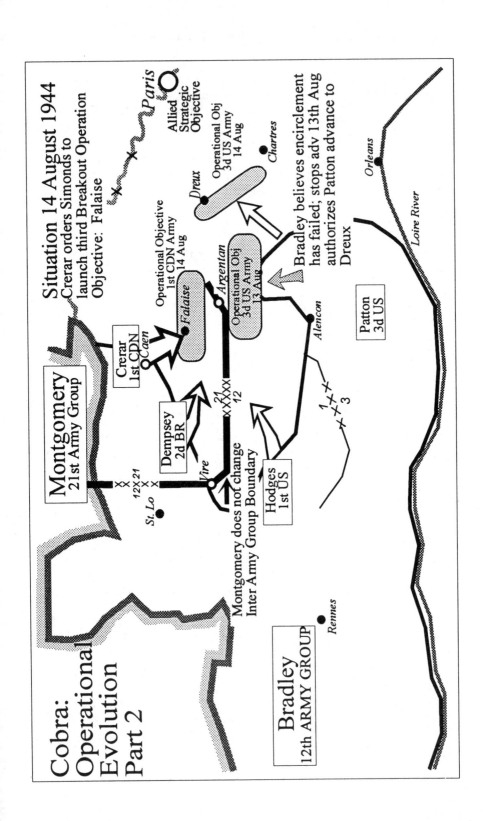

Cobra:
Operational
Evolution
Part 2

Situation 14 August 1944
Crerar orders Simonds to
launch third Breakout Operation
Objective: Falaise

Paris

Allied
Strategic
Objective

Montgomery
21st Army Group

Bradley
12th ARMY GROUP

Rennes

St. Lo

12 X 21
X   X
X X

Vire

Dempsey
2d BR

21 XXXXX
12

Montgomery does not change
Inter Army Group Boundary

Hodges
1st US

Caen

Crerar
1st CDN

Falaise

Operational Objective
1st CDN Army
14 Aug

Argentan

Operational Obj
3d US Army
13 Aug

Alencon

1
3

Patton
3d US

Dreux

Operational Obj
3d US Army
14 Aug

Chartres

Bradley believes encirclement
has failed; stops adv 13th Aug
authorizes Patton advance to
Dreux

Orleans

Loire River

German resistance at Argentan stiffened when Field Marshal Walter Model, who replaced von Kluge, reconfirmed his predecessor's order for a withdrawal of all divisions within the forming pocket.[37]

The situation further changed when Gen. Stanislaw Maczek's 1st Polish Armored Division blew past the Dives River and appeared north of Trun: Allied hope for an encirclement returned. Montgomery ordered both Crerar (specifically, the Poles) and Bradley to take Chambois.[38] The pocket was finally closed on 21 August but only after over 150,000 Germans escaped.

Patton had initially ordered General Haislip's XV Corps to drive west toward Dreux. "Neither the Third Army nor the XV Corps had anything to do with the actual breakthrough. We merely poured through the hole. When my Corps hit the Mayenne River, I had two infantry divisions abreast and an armored division [2d French] was delivered to me southwest of Laval."[39]

On 14 August, Patton pushed the XX and XII Corps east after Wood's armor. When Chartres fell on 18 August, given the reality of the situation, Bradley at last removed all restrictions to a continued eastern advance. Results were spectacular. A U.S. bridgehead was established across the Seine by the XV Corps on 19 August, Leclerc's French 2d Armored Division entered Paris on 25 August, and what was left of the Panzer Group Eberbach scampered across the Seine at Elbeuf and Rouen. Finally, a joint drive by Canadian, British, and U.S. divisions sealed all German escape by reaching Elbeuf on 26 August. By then, Model had crossed the Seine with a total of 165,800 men and a surprising amount of tanks and artillery.[40]

The operational sense Patton showed—driving east to secure the Seine crossings—was not initially mirrored by Bradley or Crerar: "Well, Bradley was a good basic Infantry soldier, a lovable character, a man that you could admire as a being a great soldier. He didn't have too much imagination."[41] Both Bradley and Crerar had relatively light forces blocking the eastern routes to the heart of France, and both persistently directed their subordinates to concentrate on the Falaise gap rather than the Seine or Paris. Patton, to his credit, kept trying to convert his boss.[42]

Notes

1. File 37-B, Col. Chester B. Hansen Papers, U.S. Army Military History Institute (hereafter MHI).

2. ETHINT 67, Lt. Gen. Fritz Bayerlein, "Normandy Critique," ETO, 15 August 1945, MHI.

3. Entry in personal diary, Col. Chester B. Hansen, 26 July 1944, Col. Chester B. Hansen Papers (Hereafter Hansen Diary). MHI.

4. Hanson Diary, "Brad Plans for Cobra" 12 July 1944. The bombing zone was 2,500 by 6,000 yards and received 4,200 tons of bombs. MHI.

5. Hanson Diary, 25 July 1944. See also Dr. Michael D. Pearlman, "Close Air Support in World War Two: The Roots of the Tragedy in Operation Cobra," in R.J. Spiller, ed., *Combined Arms in Battle Since 1939* (Fort Leavenworth: U.S. Army Command and General Staff College Press, 1992): "The US Army Air Corps entered World War II without doctrine" p. 154. Bradley was furious: "The planes flew a course perpendicular to our lines rather than parallel to it as I had been assured they would. I have seldom been so angry. It was duplicity—a shocking breach of good faith."

6. "My front lines looked like a landscape on the moon, and at least seventy percent of my men were out of action—dead, wounded, crazed or numbed. . . . All communications were practically broken on 25, 26, 27, and 28 July 44. Messages and signal communications were replaced by motorcyclists." ETHINT 67, 15 August 1945: An Interview with GenLt Fritz Bayerlein, "Critique of Normandy Breakthrough—Pz *Lehr* Div from St Lo to the Ruhr," p. 12.

7. McNair's death caused a colossal flap: Marshall was furious. As part of the Bodyguard deception McNair had been appointed to "replace" Patton as commander of a "First U.S. Army Group." He had observed the bombing from a slit trench with the forward battalion of 30th Infantry Division. "Some person had said: 'The troops sure like to see you up front.'" Bombs landed right on top of him "[and] threw his body 60 feet and mangled it beyond recognition except for the three stars on his collar." Initial entries in the 12th Army Group war diary referred to "General X. . . . Strict secrecy on the X death." Secrecy was not kept; visiting officers returned to Washington and broke the news. Hansen Diary, 25 July 1944, MHI.

8. McNair envisioned 222 tank destroyer battalions, but by April 1943 the activation of new units was halted. Only the M36, available late in the war, could penetrate Panther and Tiger armor. The M36 and M18 began to reach Europe in August 1944 and began replacing M10s. "By the end of hostilities, 12th Army Group had 45 tank destroyer battalions of which 27 contained M36s, 13 had M18s, 6 were equipped with M10s and only 4 were towed." Shelby L. Stanton, *Order of Battle US Army, World War II* (Novato, Calif.: Presidio Press, 1984), p. 26.

9. The Panzer Lehr Division put together a battle group composed of "eight Mark V tanks and elements of the Reconnaissance Battalion." The 2d and 116th Panzer Divisions were ordered into the area by Kluge but both were "worn out." Bayerlein, p. 8.

10. Report of the 2d Armored Division, Appendix A to Operational Memorandum No. 34, 30 August 1944. Col. S. E. Edwards Papers, G3 Air, 12th Army Group, MHI.

11. "The bocage [was] . . . a mass of roots, great huge roots, great huge trees. No tank was able to get through . . . they'd put booby traps along the front of the hedgerows, and then they'd have the gaps marked." Gen. W. E. Depuy, lecture, Senior Officers Debriefing Program, 19 March 1979, USAWC, Carlisle Barracks, MHI.

12. Ground forces found "122 tanks and 259 vehicles . . . destroyed or damaged," victims of air and ground attack. The ground support strikes were to be a precursor to the Mortain operations. Eventually, small battle groups of the SS divisions managed to break out and rejoin the Panzer Lehr Division outside the bulge. See Ian Gooderson, "Allied Fighter-Bombers versus German Armor in North-West Europe 1944–45: Myths and Realities," *The Journal of Strategic Studies* 14, 2 (June 1991): 217.

13. The bridges at Avranches were essential to Bradley's success. They were attacked by everything von Kluge could muster, including frogmen and radio-guided missiles.

14. 2d Armored Division Staff, *Hell on Wheels in the Drive to the Roer* (Fort Knox, 1949). Also, William S. Biddle Papers (113th Cavalry Regiment), HMI: "One English speaking kraut bawled out sneeringly, "You're not in Brooklyn now, Joe!" One tank battalion from the 2d Armored Division had 51 percent casualties and 70 percent of its tanks knocked out. The 4th Armored Division reported "bitter and intense hedgerow fighting . . . 60 killed, 290 wounded, 11 MIA" in the bocage (17–27 July) as compared to 52 killed, 87 wounded in action, 28 missing in action in the pursuit period 14–31 August. "After Action Report 17 July–31 Aug 44. 4th Armored Div" *FUSA Monthly Ordnance Report Aug 44,* Armored School Research Report, MHI.

15. Despite U.S. readiness to pay a heavy price for victory, German intelligence produced contemptuous evaluations: "The English and even more so the Americans, have been afraid of and avoided any large sacrifices of men during the entire course of the war . . . they still shrank from the all-out, the true soldierly sacrifice." "G2 Periodic Report No. 130. 1st US Army" October 1944, and G2 Periodic Report No. 229. Translated from a 1st SS Leibstandarte Adolf Hilter Panzer Division intelligence bulletin based on fighting in Normandy. U.S. leadership was also evaluated: "Resumption of known methodical, exceedingly cautious advance . . . close combat usually avoided . . . coord attacks generally only to Bn strength. . . . Breakthroughs are speedily and capably supported from the rear, and the attacks continually reinforced." Martin M. Philipsborn Papers; Ernest Nason Harmon Papers, MHI.

16. Wing Commander Leslie Scarman. Aide to Air Marshal Lord Tedder; also Capt. J. Hughes Hallet, naval chief of staff, COSSAC: "Monty's talk of his original plan to hinge on Caen is absolutely balls." Pogue Papers, 12 February 1947, MHI.

17. The "Monty touch" appears less certain given his series of directives M502, M504, M505, M510, M512, M515, and 516, which constantly revised or changed his operational vision of the unfolding battle. M518 redirected Dempsey and ordered Crerar to plan for Operation Tractable, a "second Totalize." On 19 August, Bradley returned from a meeting with Montgomery and Eisenhower and wrote in his diary: "He now has a new plan."

18. When Wood realized that his division was as close to Paris as it was to Brest, he immediately ordered his units to advance southwest to Angers. Initially "Patton exploded" and forced Wood back. See Caleb Carr, MHQ 14 No. 4. 1992.

19. Wood to Liddell Hart, quoted in B. H. Liddel Hart, *History of the Second World War* (New York: Putnam, 1970), p. 557.

20. Ladislas Farago, *Patton—Ordeal and Triumph* (New York: Obolensky, Inc., 1963).

21. "Monty had always planned his big battles from direct penetration . . . he wins his battles by envelopments he never planned." Lt.Gen. W. Bedell Smith.

22. Patton to Grow (6th Armored Division): "Listen Bob, I've bet Monty five pounds that we would be in Brest by Saturday night." Grow was instructed to "bypass resistance." He had "received a cavalry mission from a real cavalryman!" Charles Whiting, *Patton* (New York: Ballantine, 1970), p. 51.

23. Interestingly, Bradley denied this later: "Ultra was of little or no value [re Mortain]. Ultra alerted us to the attack only a few hours before it came." Omar Bradley and Clay Blair, *A General's Life* (New York: Simon and Schuster, 1983), p. 291. However, Ultra reports and intelligence summaries describing western move-

ment of key panzer units must have been instrumental in his caution about Patton's drive east.

24. The initial attack was to be based on the 116th and 2d Panzer Divisions: "116 Pz . . . 60 to 70 tanks; 2 Pz . . . 40–50 tanks . . . one third of the infantry lost at Caumont . . . 1SSPz . . . 60 tanks . . . one infantry regiment beaten up but artillery was complete, Regimental Commander Joachem Peiper was ill." SSGenMaj Fritz Kraemer, "Counterattack on Avranches" ETHINT 24. ML 2148. The Leibstandarte Division had "22–25 Panthers left . . . arrived at Mortain with between 70 and 80 tanks." Wisch, p. 3.

25. *Report IX Tactical Air Force:* "Mortain Operations. August; No. 2 Operational Research Unit Report #4: Air Attacks on Enemy tanks and Motor Transport in the Mortain Area, August 1944," and RAF Report: "The Liberation of Northwest Europe, Vol. III, The Landings in Normandy," pp. 84–86.

26. MS#B-723 Breakthrough to Avranches, p. 13.

27. Gooderson, p. 220.

28. Kraemer lamented later that "if Peiper had been there, this would not have happened." ETHINT 24. ML 2148.

29. Charles M. Bailly, *Faint Praise: American Tanks and Tank Destroyers during World War II* (Hamden: Archon, 1983), p. 111. Norman bocage had not permitted the battle-testing of doctrine required by U.S. tank destroyer and armored battalions.

30. Offrs Adv Course, Comm 24 Study, The Armored School, "Employment of Four Tank Destroyer Battalions in the ETO" (Fort Knox: 1950), p. 95. For some unit historians Mortain was a "near run thing."

31. Milton Shulman, *Defeat in the West* (London: 1948), p. 148. The 2d Panzer Divisionhad actually advanced some 10 miles before the air attack. Lt. Gen. Gerhard Graf von Schwerin, commander of the 116th Panzer Division, felt there were six reasons for the "failure of the Avranches Counterattack: a. Recognition too late of the weaknesses and critical condition of LXXXIV Corps . . . b. Incorrect choice of the point of main effort . . . c. The premature attack of XLVII Pz Korps . . . d. The 116 and 2 Pz Divs already were too exhausted . . . e. The strong enemy artillery . . . f. The superior enemy air force." ETHINT 17 ML-863 116 Pz Div in Normandy, 1 Sep 45, 19–21. Hitler did not agree: "The attack failed because Field Marshal von Kluge wanted it to fail." Warlimont, p. 449.

32. "He [Bradley] relied on his G-2, who let him down in the Battle of the Bulge." Gen. Bruce C. Clarke Papers.

33. Senior RAF officers were critical: "Monty is supposed to have done a great job at Falaise. Really helped the Germans get away . . . he brought in his damned Inter-Army Group division again. Jealous of Patton—little man." Air Marshal Sir Arthur Coningham, 14 February 1947, Interview, Pogue Papers, MHI, p. 3.

34. Extract from war diary, HQ U.S. Third Army, 17 August 1944; Hobart R. Gay Papers, MHI.

35. Gen. R. W. Grow Grow designates boundary lines as "stop, look, and listen lines . . . when properly employed they become aids not barriers." HIS 314.7 Special Study, MHI.

36. Sir Brian Horrocks, *Corps Commander* (New York: Charles Scribner's Sons, 1977), p. 39.

37. Von Kluge, visiting a forward unit, lost contact with the German High Command. In the suspicion that prevailed in Hitler's HQ after the July 1944 assassination attempt, this gave immediate rise to panicky scenarios. What if von Kluge

was attempting to surrender the West to Bradley? See Correli Barnett, ed., *Hitler's Generals* (London: Weidenfeld and Nicolson, 1989), pp. 406–408.

38. Dempsey, who was also ordered to take Falaise and later to strike southeast into the pocket toward Bradley, later complained: "I was forced to hold back our British forces while the Americans, who had swung around the right flank, withdrew from my boundaries. . . . Eventually the Americans withdrew two divisions which had crossed my front before I could advance further. That delay cost me 48 hours." *Daily Telegraph,* 5 September 1944. This enraged Bradley. He sent off a letter to Eisenhower: "I consider General Dempsey's statement to be a direct criticism of American forces and unfair." Omar N. Bradley Papers, correspondence. 10 September 1944, MHI.

39. "The Corps in Combat—XV Corps closes Falaise Gap from South" Wade H. Haislip Papers, p. 11, MHI.

40. Estimates vary from 250 tanks (No. 2 ORS) to 72 tanks (report of Army Group B, 22 August) rescued. The Germans also gathered stranded elements (Tigers and/or Panthers) onto flatcars where tactical air strikes had destroyed rails or engines), as well as training cadres from the Panzer school at Mailly (south of Paris).

41. Bruce Clarke Papers.

42. Patton to Bradley: "You and I make a hell of a good team. I come out bursting with ideas. You pick out the right ones." Patton was toadying—he managed to ignore most of Bradley's orders. Hansen Diary 22-A, pp. 5–6, MHI.

Sherman tanks from the 1st Polish Armored Division advance through an area recently bombed by B17s and swept by AGRA fire during Operation Totalize. Note the savaged trees and countryside *(Bell, National Archives of Canada, Laurier Centre for Military Strategic and Disarmament Studies)*

CHAPTER 9

Breaking Out: Operation Totalize, 8 August 1944

Monty's trouble was that he never rose to Army Group Commander level. He liked to go off by himself and fight the Corps or the Army.
—Lt. Gen. Walter Bedell Smith, chief of staff, SHAEF[1]

The enemy's first objective, while continuing frontal breakthrough attacks, is to outflank and encircle the bulk of the 5th Panzer Army and the 7th Army on two sides.
—Secret intelligence report, Army Group B, 7 August 1944[2]

Although immature and sluggish by Stavka standards, the summer offensive of Supreme Headquarters Allied Expeditionary Force (SHAEF) was making some impressive progress. Montgomery and Bradley, presented with the rare creative opportunity of an operational problem crying for an elegant resolution, fell back on the by now rather dated master plan and answered with stodgy grand tactics. Operation Bluecoat was conceived while Collins was still stuck in the bocage. The Americans were fighting their way through the thickest hedgerows, against determined rearguard actions—tough going for armor. As General Martel liked to say: "The tank is not afraid of the gun; it is afraid of the concealed gun."[3] By midnight of 29 July, Drew Middleton's vanguards reached the Avranches bridges. Spring's failure and Cobra's steady progress was creating operational asymmetry on the Normandy front. As Bluecoat produced scant results, an irritable Montgomery[4] hedged his bets and ordered the Canadian First Army to launch another armored breakout attack on the Caen front.

Crerar, the antithesis of Patton, left everything to his key corps commander, Guy Simonds. Simonds controlled the first grand Canadian armored force with the aggregate equivalent of four Allied tank divisions—a weapon capable of giving Montgomery operational maneuver on the east flank to allow him to outrace Bradley. Simonds arguably could have become the Canadian Patton by breaking through and maneuvering to reach

Haislip, thus trapping all German forces and liberating Paris, the Allied strategic objective. This would have required a successful tactical penetration elevated to an operational breakthrough, the stuff that strategic victories are made of. The Soviet High Command (Stavka) would have been interested in the state of the Western Allied operational art: on the western wing in France, as Bradley managed two complete armies, the next major Allied offensive on the eastern flank would be planned and executed by a corps commander. On the plus side, Montgomery did provide the Canadians with heavy bombers—the West's answer to Soviet breakthrough artillery.

In contrast to the disappointments around Caen, the U.S. sector became an armored fest. Collins had sealed the Roncey pocket just as Middleton's tank corps—the 4th and 6th Armored Divisions—were unleashed toward Avranches. Grow's Combat Command B drove 18 miles to grab the first bridge leading out of Normandy. On 1 August, as the U.S. Third Army became operational, Patton pushed seven divisions into Brittany. That afternoon, he had ordered Grow to capture Brest and launched Wood toward Rennes. As the Avranches corner was turned, the classic Cannae battle suddenly became a very real possibility. Cobra had graduated from breakthrough to full-sized operational breakout: Bradley had gained maneuver in Kluge's operational depth.

By 3 August, Grow was halfway to Brest and Wood appeared in Rennes to the absolute shock of Kluge's senior staff. Patton had penetrated 80 miles beyond Normandy. That evening Montgomery telephoned Crerar and instructed him to launch a heavy attack from the Caen sector in the direction of Falaise. But Crerar would not get Operation Totalize going until 8 August, the day after the Mortain counteroffensive.

Totalize, unlike Cobra and Bluecoat would attack into tank country. The open plains south of Caen were ideal for armored maneuver and excellent for long-range target acquisition by Tigers and Panthers. Fear of German armor forced Simonds into his second successive night attack. Totalize would be launched a full two weeks after Cobra, and one day after von Kluge scheduled Operation *Lüttich*. By then Bradley had encompassed Normandy, Brittany, and the Loire, and the war in France appeared about over. But Bradley suddenly became ultraconservative. Intelligence reports of Hitler's directives for counterattack, as well as the seven panzer divisions motoring toward Mortain, inspired caution. These were the same panzer divisions that Simonds failed to pin to the Caen front during Spring and Dempsey failed to make any impression upon during Bluecoat. The 21st Panzer Division, and the 9th SS Panzer and 10th SS Panzer Divisions (with only one Panther battalion) continued to look after Bluecoat. The four remaining panzer divisions (with three Panther battalions) continued west toward Bradley. Their movement was enough to make the U.S. commander balk at granting the Third Army the carte blanche Patton so strongly

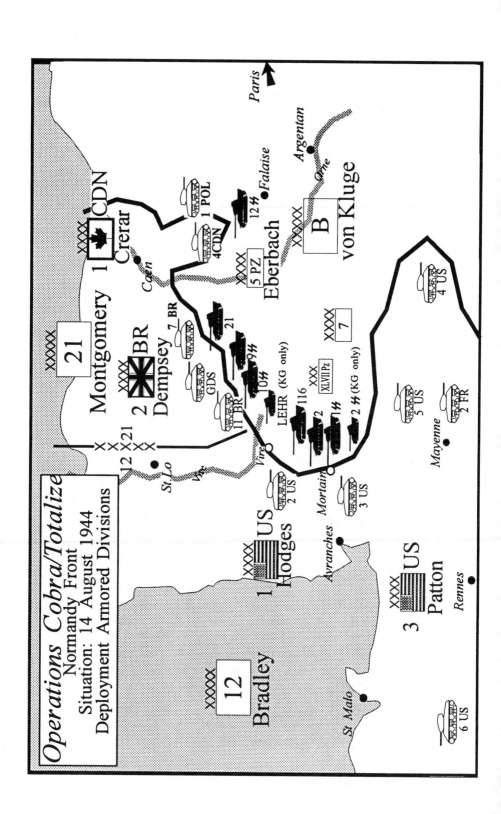

Operations Cobra/Totalize
Normandy Front
Situation: 14 August 1944
Deployment Armored Divisions

desired. Given Bradley's reticence to allowing Patton to run loose, the operational pendulum swung back to the east.

Totalize should have been easy: certainly the odds had changed. During Goodwood-Spring the combat ratio was seriously in the Germans' favor. Now Simonds had the resources of three infantry divisions (Canadian 2d and 3d, British 51st), two armored brigades (Canadian 2d, British 33d), plus his *pièce de résistance,* two fresh armored divisions (Canadian 4th Armored and Polish 1st). Facing him was the recently arrived 89th Infantry Division, just out of garrison duty in Norway.[5] Behind lay but one panzer division, the remaining German operational reserve on the Normandy front, SS Oberfhhrer Kurt Meyer's 12th SS Hitlerjugend Division.[6]

Totalize was to be the last great offensive in the Normandy campaign. No longer a second cousin to Cobra, it enjoyed the vital component of classic SHAEF offensives—strategic air power. The presence of the heavy bombers had sealed the contract, and it was all or nothing. Because there was little option for maneuver before breakout, Simonds decided on technique to give piquancy to his frontal attack.[7] The changes were doctrinally astounding. Armor was to lead at night: the spearhead of this night attack was not going to be infantry but a meat grinder of armored columns as a breakthrough force.

Totalize was an intricate parade: a medley of navigation tanks, mine clearing flail tanks, armored bulldozers, flame-throwing Churchills ("Crocodiles") and main battle tanks followed by Kangaroos, which were armored personnel carriers converted to infantry use from Priest self-propelled guns at Simonds's request.[8] Each armored group was packed closer than Piccadilly Circus at rush hour: "I left my tank and walked back to the end of the regimental column, we were closed so tight that my feet never touched the ground, I just stepped from tank to tank."[9] The attack was to advance on compass bearing, while flails and dozers cleared the ground of mines. To ensure that direction was maintained, Bofors guns were deployed on either side of the columns to fire tracers down the axis of advance. Batteries of giant searchlights provided both artificial moonlight and powerful beams fixed over the distant objective—a surreal guide. While tanks had been used in small groups during Spring and Atlantic, this time there would be a surfeit of armor. Two tank brigades were to lead in phase 1, and two entire armored divisions would attack in phase 2, "[in] a mass, a 'phalanx,' of tanks on a narrow front. What hope have the defenders got?"[10]

Armored Blow

Look, the Russians have broken through to St. Lô!
                                                        —Chester Hansen, July 1944[11]

*When we told them that we were going to attack they were greatly sur-
prised.*
                                    —Simonds, on his Soviet visitors; 27 July 1944[12]

The solution to Simonds's problem, indeed to the 21st Army Group's
inability to break through German defenses, was found on the Eastern
Front: overwhelming artillery fire and echelons of mechanized corps tearing gashes that could not be plugged by tank reserves. German armor
attempting to block the advance of second-echelon tank armies would be
forced to fight with open flanks, becoming easy prey to operational maneuver groups (OMGs). Allied generals did not study Soviet techniques,
although, ironically, just before Totalize, a delegation from Stalin visited
Simonds on 27 July.[13] They asked "what the enemy strength opposite us
was compared to our own. When we told them and that we were going to
attack they were greatly surprised. They stated that they would not attack
unless they outnumbered the enemy by at least 5 or 6 to 1."[14]

Simonds and his staff smiled politely and ignored the Russians: they
lacked style and (it was decided) they also lacked credibility. This assessment was lamentable, for the Soviet operational art was "echelons above"
that of the western allies. The Stavka solution had been noted with impreci-
sion in attaché reports and ignored in Western staff colleges. The Soviets'
use of mass was dismissed as the only method available to a technically
crude and doctrinally unsophisticated army. In fact, the opposite was true.
Although the Soviets were the poor tactical cousins of the allied armies at
the platoon, battalion, and division level, they totally outdistanced the
British and Americans and general staffs at the army group and theater level.

Simonds was convinced that he faced not one but two heavily mined
defensive lines and that the SS Hitlerjugend Panzer Division had been clan-
destinely reinforced by the SS Leibstandarte Panzer Division.[15] Had he
redone estimates he might have considered a few significant items. It is
likely that Simonds was the only corps commander in Normandy with
access to Ultra information,[16] which could have informed him that with
Hitler's directive, the last of the forward SS divisions had left Simonds's
front on 3 August. Second, the only German mobile reserve in the Canadian
corridor was the 12th SS Panzer Division—well back in the Falaise area.
Third, the front line was held by the inexperienced 89th Infantry Division.
So, Simonds's II Corps assault forces exceeded the minimum of the Soviet
formula. In fact, if actual infantry strengths and tank-artillery superiority
were compared, Simonds was close to the ideal Soviet attack ratio of 10:1.
Here was a golden opportunity for mass armor in the blitzkrieg traditions of
1940 and 1941.

Totalize has been misrepresented as a masterpiece of creative planning,
but the simple fact remains that the operation was essentially a slower,
overcontrolled version of Spring. While Spring gave the brigades and

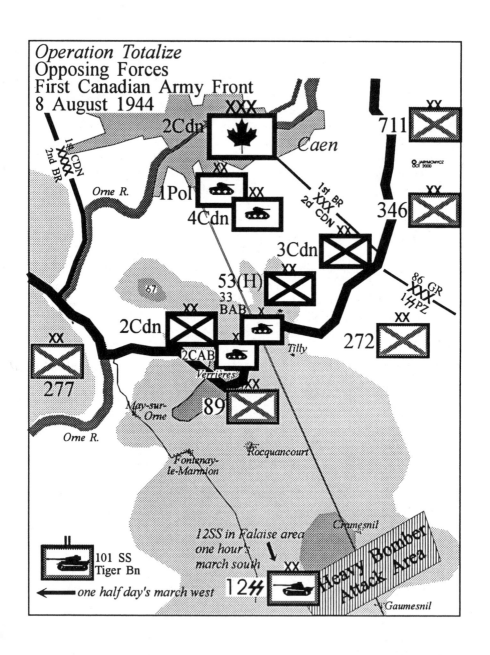

Operation Totalize
Opposing Forces
First Canadian Army Front
8 August 1944

2Cdn

Caen

711

1st CDN
2nd BR

Orne R.

1Pol

4Cdn

1st BR
2d CDN

346

3Cdn

86 GR
1st PZ

53(H)

67

33
BAB

2Cdn

272

2CAB

Tilly

Verrières

277

89

May-sur-Orne

Orne R.

Rocquancourt

Fontenay-le-Marmion

Cramesnil

Heavy Bomber Attack Area

101 SS
Tiger Bn

12SS in Falaise area
one hour
march south

one half day's march west   12SS

Gaumesnil

divisions little room for creative maneuver, Totalize ensured there was none. Further, once breakthrough had occurred, the entire offensive would stop and wait for U.S. Army Air Corps B-17s to blast Norman villages out of the ground.

A passage of lines operation is always difficult, and was bound to be chaotic with two untried armored divisions entering their first battle. To make it even tougher, Simonds deployed his armor two up—he squeezed the Polish 1st Armored Division beside the Canadian 4th Armoured Division and gave each a "frontage of only one thousand yards." This reduced each division's frontage to an area normally given to a regiment. Maj. Gen. George Kitching, commander 4th Canadian Armoured, recalled that "both General Maczek and I asked General Simonds to extend our frontage to give us room for maneuver, but he would not agree as it would mean changing the objectives of one of the assaulting divisions."[17] There were, unfortunately, traffic control difficulties: "Soon visibility literally nil . . . hampered by large bomb craters . . . tanks fell in . . . recovery impossible." Regiments lost direction and became involved in "friendly" firefights. "[The] head of column became split in individual parties led by officers who were attempting through the thick haze to pick up landmarks . . . officers were leading tanks on foot . . . one party . . . had gone so far off its line to get involved with a Canadian column on the right."[18]

Morning found them anything but a force in place, but rather a congested tank park deployed near the bomb line for phase 2. Before them lay empty fields. The Canadian II Corps had broken through.

All Revved Up and No Place to Go

We have to risk everything. A breakthrough has occurred near Caen the like of which we have never seen.
> —Kluge to Hausser, evening of 8 August 1944[19]

The II corps battle plan called for a halt to allow artillery to move forward while heavy bombers pulverized what Simonds was convinced was Kluge's in-depth, main defense line behind Verrières. This was a pity, for there was no secondary zone of defense. Every passing minute allowed the 12th SS Panzer Division commander, Kurt Meyer, and the I SS Panzer Corps Sepp Dietrich to bring in more reserves to plug the breach. But it was too late to call off the bombers: Crerar would probably have been reluctant to tell Harris "no thanks after all" following the difficult staff work required to arrange for them in the first place. At first light, all forward advance stopped as the Canadian II Corps waited on its start lines for the B-17s' arrival, which would not happen for another six hours.[20]

The first German to reach the area was Kurt Meyer, who immediately organized an ad hoc defense around Cintheaux by ordering stragglers from routed formations into new blocking positions. The bombing pause also gave Lt. Gen. Wolfgang Pickert (commander of the III Flak Corps) time to deploy his 88mm guns to complement the antitank gun line the 12th SS Panzer had formed with its own antitank guns and divisional flak in the Quesnay wood area. Individual initiative, unity in command, and tight discipline again saved the German army. Although this scene could have happened in the Canadian, British, or U.S. armies, it was more normal in the German. The British-Canadian regimental system, tribal identity, "our officers" versus "their officers," the mentality of "Look, the other regiment broke" often made ad lib regrouping difficult.

German senior headquarters reacted immediately to Totalize. Sepp Dietrich ordered his 12th SS Panzer to stop the enemy breakthrough in a counterattack; at the same time General of Panzer Troops Heinrich Eberbach, supreme commander of the Fifth Panzer Army, drove up to meet Kurt Meyer in Urville. He agreed with Meyer's assessment of the situation and supported his decisions for a counterattack. Meyer decided to strike with two battle groups, KG Waldmüller and KG Wünsche. He then sent for the remainder of his division.[21] The counterattacks ordered by Meyer were to be a who's who of tank warfare in Normandy. The Hitlerjugend Division brought up the great warriors of the SS: Krause, Waldmüller, Wünsche, and the Black Knight himself: Michael Wittmann.

Waldmüller and Wittmann arrived first, quickly deployed, and smartly went into the counterattack. As they shook out in the open fields leading to Point 122 (the center of the Canadian start line), Waldmüller left his panzer grenadiers and JPz IVs at Cintheaux, creating a block on the main road. His Pzkw IVs maneuvered northeast, while Wittmann's Tigers rumbled due north beside Route 158. Meanwhile Meyer had motored forward to peek at the Canadian front line. When he saw the massed armor, he was astounded: "Seeing these concentrations of tanks almost took our breath away. We could not comprehend the behavior of the Canadians. Why did these overwhelming tank forces not push on their attack?"[22] As Meyer surveyed the inert phalanx he noticed the single B-17 overhead. It was a Pathfinder, the FOO of the heavy bombers, an airborne forward air controller leading the heavy-bomber stream and marking the target. Meyer had seen it before during the bombing of Caen and before Goodwood. Safety lay near the Canadian start line. He ordered Waldmüller and Wittmann to attack.[23]

As the Canadian 2d and 4th Armoured Brigades jockeyed for fire positions north of Gaumesnil they were attacked by Waldmüller's battle group: thirty-nine Pzkw IVs and ten Tigers. The odds were laughable: forty-nine tanks against 600. However, thanks to the narrow frontage allotted, the best Simonds's armored brigades could do was move one regiment up and deploy two squadrons forward. That reduced Meyer's attack ratio to 1:2—

poor odds, but given the advantage of high morale in the attack, Waldmüller had a fighting chance. He used the scattered farmhouses for cover and closed the distance, firing as his troops moved forward bound by bound. Wittmann, alone with a handful of Tigers, simply charged up the center.[24]

Panzer Counterattack

Tigers always attacked if the opportunity presented itself. The benefit of creating elite panzer battalions was that they were well trained and highly motivated and exhibited a faith in the superiority of their machines that often ignored tactical reality. "Tigers sometimes were used almost recklessly; their crews taking risks to a degree which indicates they have the utmost confidence in the vehicle."[25] This time there was little choice. Wittmann shook hands with Meyer, adjusted his throat mike and ordered "Panzer marsch!" His four Tigers advanced in a V formation, stopping briefly near the hedgerow at Gaumesnil, then rolled across the open fields, pausing now and then to knock out a Sherman at long range: "The attention of the attacking Tigers was concentrated on the Canadian tanks of the 2nd Canadian Armored Brigade which were advancing on both sides of the Route Nationale."[26] As the distance closed, 75mm and 17-pounder guns of the 2d Canadian and 33d British Armoured Brigades replied. Suddenly, Wittmann's Tiger exploded, the flash temporarily blinding Allied tank gunners. The turret was lifted into the air and slammed into the ground behind tank 007. The ace of aces was dead. The debate over who scored this most spectacular of tank kills still continues.[27]

The attack by Wittmann's Tigers and Waldmüller's tanks rattled the entire Canadian front. Directly above droned 492 Flying Fortresses of the U.S. VIII Air Force.[28] A couple of lead bombers dropped their bomb loads short, and the following squadrons did the same, bombing Simonds's forward troops. The Poles were badly hit as were elements of Canadian 3d Division, the main headquarters of the Canadian 2d Armoured Brigade, Canadian 2d Army Group Royal Artillery (AGRA), and 9th AGRA. Shock and confusion followed. At 1:30 P.M. Simonds's HQ demanded that Crerar "stop all bombing." One of the Canadian casualties was the commander of 3d Infantry Division, Rod Keller, who was last seen being carried into an ambulance shouting to his batman, "Roberts, bring me my revolver! I'm going to shoot the first goddam American I see!"[29]

Kitching's Battle Groups

> *The enemy seems to be reorganizing his units. He carried out all his attacks with tanks and without infantry.*
> —General Eberbach reporting to Marshal Kluge,
> 10:30 P.M., 8 August 1944

As the Polish 1st Armored and Canadian 4th Armoured Divisions were trying to sort themselves out, they were attacked by Battle Group Waldmüller; grim duels were fought by the Canadian 2d Armoured Brigade Shermans and Wittmann's Tigers. Waldmüller pivoted around Wittmann and assaulted Simonds's front line. The ferocity of the 12th SS Panzer Division set the Canadian 4th and Polish 1st Divisions back on their heels. The attack disrupted H-hour.[30] Totalize's second phase did not get going until 3:30 P.M., almost two hours late and nine hours after the initial rupture of the German 89th Infantry Division.

Finally, the Canadian 4th's armor advanced and promptly began taking long-range antitank fire. The attack by Halpenny Force—an armored battle group commanded by Lt. Col. Bill Halpenny, composed of his own armored regiment, the Canadian Grenadier Guards, and the Lake Superior Regiment (a mechanized infantry battalion)—bogged down a kilometer (about one-half mile) south of Cintheaux, which was still held by the ad hoc rear guard thrown together by Meyer. Maczek's lead brigade, attacking two regiments up (Polish 2d Pulk Pancerna [Armored Regiment] and 24th Lancers), had forced Waldmüller's Pzkw IVs back but now ran into another counterattack from the east by the German Divisional Escort Company, which had JPz IVs under its command. The well-armored, low-silhouetted tank destroyers brewed up twenty-six Shermans. The Poles no longer dared to leave Cramesnil forest. Simonds, trying to control the battle by radio, was not pleased: "Why don't the Poles get on?"[31] Maczek tried to explain: "Les Allemandes avaient caché des cannons anti-tank et quelques 'Tigres' dans deux bosquets . . . Mais on effectua aussitôt un regroupement de blindés et dans un bruit infernal l'avance continua lente et inexorable. ("The Germans had hidden antitank guns and a few Tigers in two groves . . . But we immediately regrouped our tanks and continued the slow, relentless attack through the infernal noise.")[32] Although it faced mostly Pzkw IVs, the Polish 1st Armored Division attack against Meyer's elastic defense could not make progress on the narrow front.

The Canadian attacks went in unsupported and piecemeal. Meyer noted that the Germans were unbelievably lucky in that the opposite side failed to carry out one single concentrated attack. As battle groups took turns charging Bretteville-le-Rabet, they were engaged by fire from Meyer's antitank battalion and 88mm guns of Pickert's antitank gun line in Quesnay Wood[33] that were "well camouflaged and offered excellent targets . . . in less than forty-eight hours the hulks of over 150 Sherman tanks dotted the rolling wheat fields north of the Laison River."[34] Kitching's armored assault was over; for all intents and purposes, so was Totalize. Kurt Meyer's analysis bears repeating:

> Every opening phase of a Canadian Operation was a complete success and the staff work a mathematical masterpiece . . . every Canadian operation

bore the mark of intensive planning and was built on sound principles. Canadians never followed up their opening success to reach a complete victory. Every one of the Canadian attacks lost its push and determination after a few miles.

Armored warfare is a matter of using opportunities on the battlefield, therefore the Divisional Commander belongs with the leading combat group.[35]

Command and Control

What is hold up? . . . Put Sunray on set! . . . If you have no opposition you must push on. Outflank and push on! No opposition in front yet the going is very slow. I'm not waiting any longer—I want you to move fast!
—Orders from General Kitching, 8 August 1944

Despite exhortations throughout the day by Kitching, his armored regiments could not get properly stuck in. Inexperienced, rattled by Waldmüller's counterattack, and shaken by the friendly bombing, the Canadian 4th Armoured Brigade moved gingerly past the bomb craters and reacted with undue tactical intent to any enemy salvo. Actually, "tanks alone," that is, a tank-heavy battlegroup with little or no infantry but accompanied by FOOs, forward air controllers, and engineers, could have accomplished wondrous things against a maneuvering counterattack force. The 4th Armoured Brigade's armored regiments were overwhelmed by their first action: they either forgot about the supporting arms or were "not wholly aware of the capabilities of the gunners; we were never asked for smoke."[36] The tactical situation required both: balanced infantry battle groups supported by artillery to clear out defended localities and armor-heavy combat commands to maneuver against Waldmüller's panzers. Most important, dynamic leadership from the saddle was imperative. The answer was operational maneuver, not tactics at the squadron level. Maneuver required a brigadier or general staff officer to point regiments and brigades in the right direction and bring up second-echelon units to exploit.

Simonds's panzer leaders, the Polish Brigade's Maciejewski, Canadian 2d Armoured Brigade's Booth and 4th Armoured Brigade's Wyman, imposed no influence or direction on the battle. Simonds's armored division commanders never rose above the immediate demands of headquarters and resorted to management rather than leadership. Kitching quite rightly wanted the breakout to keep going: every hour lost meant more Tigers, more Panthers, and more panzer grenadiers on the battlefield. To Kitching's fury and exasperation the regimental commanders went back to a "rear rally."[37] Ordered to press on through the night, the armored regiments did exactly what all armored regiments had been doing in England, Italy, the desert, and Italy since 1939. It was night so they stopped and laagered.

General Crerar watched patiently and left things to Simonds. His opposite number, Heinrich Eberbach, face badly scarred from battle burns, wearing a cloth cap and the black armored troops' uniform, a Knight's Cross at his throat, personally drove forward to see Totalize and then reported directly to Kluge. This was Eberbach's somber evaluation: "I have no other forces left. If this keeps going the same way tomorrow, we shall be unable to stop it."[38] It convinced Field Marshal Kluge to release the Panther unit of the 9th Panzer Division and 102d SS Heavy Tank Battalion (Tigers) as reinforcements for Meyer.

Totalize: The Second Night Attack

Simonds was still determined to make something of Totalize. He would again attack at night and again would use searchlights to create "movement light." Two tank battlegroups were given objectives astride Route 158, the road to Falaise. The Hitlerjugend Division would not be able to cover a breakthrough 6 miles wide, particularly if the Polish 1st Armored Division swung boldly east and drove south.

Totalize deserves study because it was the first series of attacks by a Canadian armored corps. The combat ratio finally favored the attackers: the Canadian 4th Armoured Brigade alone had 240 tanks against about 100 tanks available to Kurt Meyer. Furthermore, Meyer's tanks, which were still arriving in the area, had to cover the entire front. The only additional reinforcements expected were the Panther battalion from the 9th SS Panzer Division, which were seconded to Meyer on Kluge's orders, and the grenadiers of 85th Infantry Division arriving on bicycles via Vimoutiers and Trun. With luck, at best fifty German tanks would be in 4th Armoured Brigade's area confronting more than 200 tanks. Factoring in Wyman's 2d Armoured Brigade, the II Corps enjoyed an overall attack ratio of roughly 685 Canadian/Polish tanks against about 100 scattered panzers. In terms of Fireflies alone, the Canadian attackers held a decisive numerical advantage.

Table 9.1   Armor Available to Simonds for Phase 2 of Totalize

Canadian 4th Armoured Division	1st Polish Armored Division	Independent Brigades	
4 Cdn Armd Bde	10 Pol Armd Bde	2 Cdn Armd Bde	33 British Armd Bde
29 Armd Recce Regt	10 Chasseurs[a]		
21 CAR (GG)	1 PAR	6 CAR (1 Hussars)	144 Bn Royal Armd Corps
22 CAR (GGFG)	2 PAR	10 CAR (FGH)	1 East Riding Yeomanry
28 CAR (BCR)	24 Lancers	27 CAR (SherFus)	Northamptonshire Yeomanry

Total: 14 armored regiments (840 tanks)

Notes: a. 29 Recce was equipped with Sherman M4s; 10 Chasseurs used the British Cromwell cruiser tank.

CAR/PAR: Canadian/Polish Armored Regt (approx. 60 main battle tanks)

In the early hours of 9 August, a now frustrated and angry Kitching finally got his regiments going. His assault included Worthington Force, an armored battle group based on the Canadian 28th Armoured Regiment (the British Columbia Regiment) grouped with three companies of the Algonquin Regiment mounted in M3 half-track armored personnel carriers. One military historian suggested that "the subsequent performance of this force in contrast with that of Halpenny's illustrated the depth of the tactical schizophrenia that gripped the armored corps of the British and Canadian armies."[39]

Armored Breakthrough:
The Death of Worthington Force, 9 August

The wild dash they had to make did not lend itself to calm ground appreciation.

                                                                —Maj. L.C. Monk[40]

Lt. Col. Don Worthington (no relation to Gen. F. F. Worthington) planned to head south parallel to Route 158, cross the highway, and then head southeast toward the highest piece of ground, Hill 195, his given objective. However, a night approach through what had now become a German defensive zone was a risky challenge for a regiment in its first battle. The atmosphere, already electric with the excitement of the bombing and first enemy contact, was heightened by the befuddled pace of the advance. "It was so dark I could only see the red back lights of the tank in front. Sometimes we crawled along. . . . There were breakdowns. My troop pulled out around a broken down Sherman and promptly got lost—there were too many tank tracks."[41]

The main body of Worthington Force turned southeast. It may have been confused by the hard-surfaced road that ran east from Bretteville-le-Rabet and mistaken it for Highway 158. At dusk, high ground was sighted and the tanks headed for it. They arrived in the area of Point 140, bluffs overlooking the Laison River and stopped. Unknowingly, Worthington had captured one of the Polish 1st Armored Division's objectives: "They were four miles northeast of their objective and well inside the boundary assigned to the Polish Division."[42] Nevertheless, the British Columbia Regiment battle group had broken through. The tragedy was that they and Simonds's headquarters did not know it. Morning found Worthington north, not south, of 158. If the British Columbians and the II Corps HQs were somewhat perplexed, the Hitlerjugend Division was not.

Worthington's force set off a real panic in the 12th SS Panzer Division. An armored battle group and, it was supposed, two Canadian tank brigades were about to descend on Falaise. The only thing that stood between the British Columbia Regiment and Falaise was Meyer's own HQ, less than

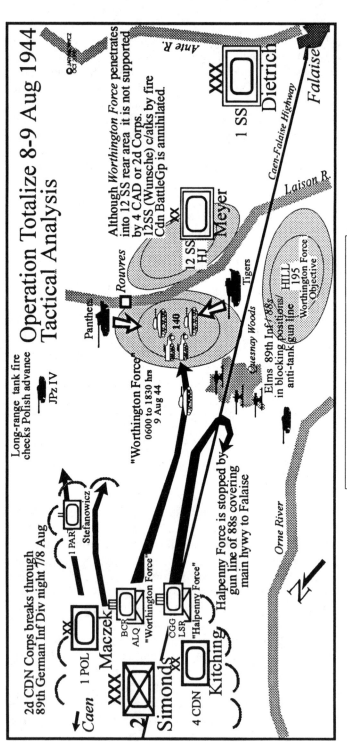

Operation Totalize 8-9 Aug 1944
Tactical Analysis

Long-range tank fire checks Polish advance

JPz IV

Although *Worthington Force* penetrates into 12 SS rear area it is not supported by fire by 4 CAD or 2d Corps. 12SS (Wunsche) c/atks by fire Cdn BattleGp is annihilated.

Ante R.

Rouvres

Panthers

"Worthington Force"
0600 to 1830 hrs
9 Aug 44

2d CDN Corps breaks through 89th German Inf Div night 7/8 Aug

1 PAR
Stefanowicz

Caen

1 POL

XXX

Maczek

XX

BCR
ALQ
"Worthington Force"

CGG
LSR
"Halpenny Force"

XXX

2

Simonds

XX

4 CDN

Kitching

Halpenny Force is stopped by gun line of 88s covering main hywy to Falaise

Tigers

Laison R.

12 SS
HJ

XX

Meyer

1 SS

XXX

Dietrich

Falaise

Caen-Falaise Highway

HILL
195
Worthington Force Objective

Quesnay Woods

Elms 89th Inf / 88s in blocking positions/ anti-tank gun line

Orne River

N

Cdn Tk Squadron
(12 - 19 MBT)

Cdn Mech Inf Coy
12 - 15 M3 APCS

Anti Tank Battery
(4 - 8 88mm ATK Guns)

German Tiger Company
(12 - 13 Tanks)

German Tk Company
(12 - 15 MkV or IV MBT)

12 - 15 MkIII Stugs / JPz IV

2 miles away. He ordered Battle Group Wünsche to counterattack immediately. Using a Panther company from the 1st Battalion, 12th SS Panzer Regiment, and a handful of recently arrived Tigers from the the 102d SS Heavy Tank Battalion, Wünsche ordered a double envelopment of the British Columbians' position. The southern hook of Tigers would engage Worthington's Shermans at long range, but was also capable of covering against a supporting approach along Route 158. The northern hook effectively blocked an advance by Polish 1st Armored Division, whose regiments were right behind Worthington.

However, the Poles' performance was not discernibly better on 9 August. Although they faced considerably fewer antitank positions, their advance was halted as quickly as the Grenadier Guards' attack on Quesnay Wood. The real tragedy was the Poles' inability to close the distance to Worthington's British Columbia Regiment battle group as it was being steadily decimated on Hill 140, directly to their front. A determined brigade attack would have not only rescued the Canadian 28th Armoured Regiment but completely turned Dietrich's flank. Whenever Maczek pushed a regiment forward, it was savagely engaged by Wünsche: "They have tanks Mk IV and VI estimate 10–20 strong. Enemy inf defending St. Sylvain. En making good use of mortars."[43] German aggressiveness and the ever-present fear of Tigers of inexperienced crews saved Meyer and slew Worthington: "Les Allemandes lancerent de fortes contre-attaques appuyées par des Tigres" ("The Germans launched a strong counterattack supported by Tigers.")[44] Some squadrons gave it a determined try. The Polish 10th Chasseurs reached St. Sylvain but were forced back by a handful of Panthers thrown in by Wünsche.[45]

A second regiment, the Polish 1st Armored, commanded by Major Stefanowicz, attacked from the northeast and claimed to have reached the Laison River near Rouvres (somewhat over 1 mile from the British Columbia Regiment) where they shot up a bicycle company from German 85th Infantry Division. They were at once engaged by Wünsche's panzers: "Die 12.SSPzDiv HJ (Meyer) ... brachte die Polen bei St. Sylvain zum stehen ("Meyer's 12SS Pz Div stopped the Poles at St. Sylvain.")[46] Stefanowicz, without infantry or FOOs, decided to retreat. Maczek's armored regiments were being attacked by a weak company of Panthers supported by a few Pzkw IVs and JPz IVs left over from Waldmüller's 8 August attack. These tanks were again mistakenly reported as Tigers by the overcautious Polish regiments, which stopped short and withdrew from the disadvantage of a long-range gun duel.[47]

Despite support from RAF Typhoons and the presence of the Polish vanguard only 2 miles away, Worthington Force was left unsupported the entire day as Wünsche's tanks picked off the force's tanks one by one. By evening the BCR's tanks were destroyed and most of the Algonquin

Regiment's armored infantry had been destroyed, killed, or wounded.[48] Hill 140 was a tank graveyard abandoned to the Germans as survivors fought their way back to Canadian lines. Among the dead was the gallant Lieutenant Colonel Worthington.

Much has been made about the British Columbia Regiment's arrival at the wrong objective as an "episode, with its tragic mixture of gallantry and ineptitude."[49] The regiment's attack has been seen as the glass half empty, but the fact remains that an armored battle group had broken through and penetrated into Dietrich's rear area. What the British Columbians required was the reinforcement of success. In the full scope of an armored break-through, particularly at the division and corps level, a matter of 4 miles is a mere bagatelle. Maneuver warfare is not a battle for position but a mobile action that encompasses enemy positions. Had Worthington been reinforced immediately by a second regiment and then flanked by a second armored brigade, the British Columbia Regiment's breakthrough would have been the tale of Rommel's 7th Panzer Division on the Meuse in 1940. Worthington did not know where he was, but conversely neither did Kitching or Simonds, although they had between them five reconnaissance regiments. To paraphrase Wilde, losing one's regiment in the dark is unfortunate, but losing an entire battle group in clear daylight is sheer carelessness.[50] The British Columbia Regiment may have been lost, but the Canadian II Corps had also lost the regiment.[51]

Simonds sent the Canadian Grenadier Guards armored regiment south to look at Hill 195. It was savagely turned back by Pickert's 88mm guns. The rest of the day was spent in frustrating radio calls. In essence, the Canadian II Corps (thirteen armored regiments) simply stopped and waited for the British Columbians to find themselves. Neither the Poles nor the Canadian 4th Armoured Brigade seemed capable of maneuvering past the handful of tanks Wünsche had holding the flanks. The determination of Maczek's division is in question here. The presence of a Canadian regiment on the division's objective seems to have made little impression on the Poles' tactics: "Some seemed to turn away in face of comparatively minor opposition."[52]

Regrettably, neither Kitching nor Simonds had exercised their commands in England before Normandy. Their late arrival in February 1944 made corps or divisional wargames unrealistic as Montgomery's armies were busy practicing for D-Day's amphibious operations. The Canadian 4th Armoured and Polish 1st Armored Divisions had arrived in Normandy just in time to shake out for Operation Totalize.[53] Simonds committed an armored corps to his greatest battle without fully testing the corps's standard of tactics or communications. In anticipation of gasps from the "lessons-learned" clique, it must be pointed out he was not given sufficient opportunity. He was in mid-campaign against a very pesky enemy and an unforgiving timetable. Although the 4th Armoured Division's regiments had conducted a trial "raid" before Totalize and participated in two unsuccessful attacks against Tilly-la-Campagne, the two armored brigades proved not ready for division and corps operations.

Any Totalize post mortem must find inexperience as the probable cause of death. This is a particularly harsh criticism given the Canadian Armoured Corps's four years of preparatory training. Tactically, the Canadian and British independent armored brigades had easily defeated the initial counterattack by Waldmüller. The Firefly had the Tiger's number. Old hands were capable of taking Tiger on; new crews still feared the Tiger bogeyman. A German critique could, quite correctly, reflect upon self-imposed Canadian delays. Kurt Meyer was unforgiving in his evaluation of Totalize:

> British and Cdn planning was absolutely without risk; neither army employed its armd strength for (the job for) which it was created. In both armies, the tk was used, more or less, as an inf sp weapon. . . . Armd warfare is a matter of using given opportunities on the battlefield, therefore the Div Comd belongs on the leading combat gp, to see for himself, to save precious time, and to make lightning decisions from his moving tank. He, and no one else must be the driving force of his div. . . . The Brit and Cdn forces executed the ops in an inflexible, time wasting, method. Never once did "Speed" as the most powerful weapon of Armd Warfare, appear.[54]

Meyer's comments have been sniffed at by both veterans and historians, but this may be sour grapes. His qualifications to criticize Totalize are the best imaginable. He won the battle.

There is little to suggest that a U.S. tank division would have fared any better than Canadian 4th Armoured or Polish 1st Armored. On the other hand, given their combat record, the combination of Patton's chutzpa and the collective *Fingerspitzengefühl* of Grow and Wood was more apt to order bold maneuver as soon as it was required. Tactically, Clarke and Abrams would have met the same fate as Halpenny or Worthington, but it is more likely that Wood would have found a more elegant solution than Kitching. Rated beside the uninspired numbness shown by Crerar's armored brigadiers, Patton's generals demonstrated the greater creativity and drive.

Simonds briefly tasted operational maneuver, then lost it. The operational results of Totalize were a gain of over 8 miles, the virtual destruction of one German infantry division, and the savaging of another. It was the deepest penetration made by either the Canadian First or British Second Army thus far in the campaign. The German forces were stretched to the breaking point and Crerar was poised on an excellent jump-off place to attack Falaise. Strategically the Western Front, to quote Kluge, "had burst."[55] Patton entered Le Mans, 80 miles due south of the British Columbian Regiment's last stand. A "Falaise pocket" could now be formed.

Notes

1. Interview Lt. Gen. Walter Bedell Smith, 8 May 1947, Pogue Manuscripts, Dr. Forrest C. Pogue, Patton Museum Library.
2. *Kriegstagebuch oberkommando der Heeresgruppe B Ia III H 15450* August 1944, RH19 IX/8.
3. Gen. Sir Giffard Le Q. Martel, *Our Armored Forces* (London: Faber and Faber, 1943), p. 216.
4. Eisenhower, bitterly disappointed with Goodwood, Spring and Bluecoat, sternly ordered Montgomery to "be bold."
5. RG 24. composed of 1055, 1056 Grenadier Regiments, Fusilier Company, 189th Artillery Regiment "Fighting total inf: 3000 men." Canadian First Army intelligence summary No. 38, 6 August 1944, and *Kriegstagebuch Panzer Armeeoberkommando* 10.6.44–8.8.44. RH21-5/44. This unit did, however, have a respectable complement of artillery and antitank guns.
6. Meyer took over the 12th SS Panzer on 14 June, when SS Brigadeführer Fritz Witt was killed by naval gunfire.
7. Canadian II Corps war diary. August 1944. Instruction No. 4, Operation Totalize. "Intention: To Breakthrough the enemy positions astride the Caen Falaise Road. Method: 3 Phases: I. Breakthrough the Fontenay (0358)—La Hogue (0960) posn. II. Breakthrough the Hautmesnil (0852)—St. Sylvain (1354) position. III. Exploit as ordered by Comd 2 Cdn Corps."
8. The self-propelled M7 Priest regiments attached to the Canadian 3d Division (12th, 13th, 14th, and 19th Field Regiments, Royal Canadian Artillery (RCA)) were initially armed with 105mm guns but were outranged by the 25-pounder gun (equivalent to 88mm), the standard gun found in the RCA. Self-propelled Sextons (found in the Canadian 4th and 5th Armoured and Polish 1st Armored Divisions) carried 25-pounder guns. The decision to create "defrocked Priests" did not come about (as it is often suggested) because self-propelled guns were no longer required by the Canadian II Corps. The infantry was served by towed 25-pounders; the armored brigades were supported by Sextons.
9. Interview, Gen. R. V. Radley Walters, Caen, 1991.
10. "Current Reports from Overseas" (CRFO) 6 (26 July 1943), pp. 17–18. Quoted by English, p. 267.
11. Hansen Diary, 13–26 July 1944, MHI.
12. Stearns Papers, correspondence to Dr. Roy, 27 April 1981.
13. They had just visited Bradley's HQ (13–26 July), where wags cracked: "Look, the Russians have broken through to St. Lô!" The officers were Maj. Gen. I. Skliarov, Maj. Gen. V. A. Vasiliev, Col. V. Gorbatov, and Rear Adm. N. Kharlamov. Hansen Diary, MHI and RG 24 10808 WD. Canadian II Corps, 27 July 1944. The group that visited Quesada and Simonds were "young men in baggy trousers with tunics tightly belted and high leather boots, peaked hats. Shy and unsmiling. They greeted the general with few halting words of English in heavy boyish accent." See Hansen Diary, Stearns Papers, and RG 24, Canadian II Corps war diary.
14. Stearns Papers, 27 April 1981.
15. The Leibstandarte Division had redeployed for the Mortain counterattack.

The date for the road march was 6 August 1944. MS #358 LAH in Aug 44. SS Gen. Theodore Wisch, MHI.

16. G2 SHAEF Internal Memo, "List of Recipients of Ultra." Richard Collins Papers (G2 SHAEF) August 1944. MHI and, SRH-023, "Reports by US Army ULTRA Representatives with Army Field Commands in the ETO," MHI.

17. Maj. Gen. George Kitching, *Mud and Green Fields. The Memoirs of Maj. Gen. George Kitching* (St. Catherine's, Ontario: Vanwell Publishing, 1993), p. 193.

18. RG 24 10455 Armor: *Totalize Report:* 2 CAB and 144 RAC, with 51st Highland Div.

19. SS Gen. Paul Hausser, ETHINT B-179 "Seventh Army in Normandy 25 July–20 Aug 44" ETO, 1946.

20. The armored vanguards were almost in position by 6:00 A.M., the two armored divisions would be in place by 1:100 A.M. The time for bombs on target was 12:55 P.M.

21. An interesting example of *Auftragstaktik*, maneuver warfare, feeling for operations, and luck. See Meyer's complete order for the divisional counterattack in H. Meyer, p. 172.

22. Meyer's account, given to Canadian interrogators, is exaggerated. At this time elements of the Canadian 2d and British 33d Armoured Brigades were shaking out near the start line. The Canadian 4th Armoured and Polish 1st Armoured Divisions were only beginning to reach the battle area.

23. "I shook Michael Wittmann's hand and mentioned the extremely critical situation. Our good Michael laughed his boyish laughter and climbed into his Tiger. Until that moment, 138 enemy tanks had become his victims." K. Meyer, p. 173. See also RG 24, Interrogation Report, Kurt Meyer, pp. 7–8.

24. "One of the simplest methods of sealing off a break-through or eliminating a penetration is the frontal counterattack." *German Defense Tactics against Russian Break-Throughs* (Department of Army Pamphlet No. 20-233. Oct 1951), p. 63.

25. RG 24 14186 BRAC, 1st Cdn Army 15 Oct 44 from: 2 NZ Div Int Sum 334 "Experience with Tiger Tanks."

26. Pamphlet No. 20-233, p. 336.

27. Both the Canadian and the British armored brigades were in the area. Their forward squadrons were covering the Canadian 4th Armoured Brigade's deployment. For a while it was assumed that Wittmann had been hit by Typhoons (his body was not discovered until 1982). A Study of photographs in the Canadian archives is inconclusive. One article in a military history journal (see Les Taylor, "Michael Wittmannn's Last Battle," *After the Battle* 48) suggests that the credit goes to Trooper Joe Ekins, Firefly gunner in A Squadron, 1st Northhamptonshire Yeomanry. The unit war diary records, "Three Tigers reported moving towards A Sqn and were brewed at 1240, 1247, and 1252 hours." Another possible claim may be awarded to Gen. Radley Walters, who recalls that his squadron had also engaged the same Tigers from the northwest and that his own gunner knocked out a Tiger. Max Hastings notes that Wittmann "met his end in the thick of concentrated fire from a clutch of Canadian Shermans." Max Hastings, *Overlord* (New York: Simon and Schuster, 1984), p. 299. Simpson states that "Wittmann spotted a number of Allied Shermans advancing towards Cintheaux and began firing at these machines . . . these tanks were from a Canadian armored unit trying to take the high ground in the vicinity of Pt 112 from the west." Gary L. Simpson, *Tiger Ace: The Story of Panzer Commander Michael Wittmann* (Atglen: Schiffer, 1994), p. 304.

28. Bombers were rescheduled for 12:26 P.M. Records show that marker shells were fired by the 23d Field Regiment at 12:55 P.M. Surprisingly, there was laughter from the 12th SS Panzer. The tension was broken by a young Panzer grenadier who

shouted: "What an honour. Churchill is sending one bomber for each of us!" K. Meyer, p. 173.

29. Maj. Gen. W. J. Megill, interview, Kingston, Ontario, 15 January 1990, also see Tony Foster, *Meeting of Generals* (Toronto: Methuen, 1986), p. 360.

30. "At 1425 hrs, 2 Tk Regt was stopped in attack by twenty German tks, probably of German Tiger type and Mk IV" RG 23 WD, 1 Pol Armd Div MajGen S. Maczek "Operational Report C.O. 1 Polish Armd Div"—*Fighting During the Period From 7–12 August 1944 Normandy,* 13 August 1944, p. 2.

31. RG 24 10635. WD; Ops Message Log. 2 Cdn Corps HQ. 1705 hrs, 8 August 1944.

32. Historically, the Poles have been more comfortable with French than English as a second language. *La Première Division blindée polonaise* (Brussels: Welfare Section of Polish 1st Armored Division, 1945), p. 11. Maczek continued to argue: "It was, one must admit, the first battle of the division. Up to this time, no one had any combat experience." Gen. Stanislaw Maczek, *Avec mes Blindés* (Paris: Presse de la Cité, 1961), pp. 187, 188. See also RG 24 10942 Polish Armored Division: "Operational orders for attack in *Totalize.* 1 Dyvisia Pancerna, Rozkoz Dnia 7 Serpnia 1944."

33. By the evening of 8 August 3d Flak Corps reported: "South of Langannerie an 8.8-cm tank trap has been constructed." *Kriegstagebuch Panzer Armeeoberkommando* 10.6.44–8.8.44. RH21-5/44.

34. Shulman, p. 151.

35. DHIST 81/104: Interview Kurt Meyer; Cdn Chaplain's Report. 3 September 1950.

36. Lt. Col. R. S. Lucas, Forward Observation Officer, 23d Regiment (SP) supporting Canadian 4th Armoured Brigade during Totalize. Letter to Lt. Col. J. A. English, 12 March 1990.

37. Training by British/Canadian officers fresh from the desert and Italian campaigns resulted in a "tanks fight only during the day" mentality: "Unless there is some final objective there is no limit to the advance which must be pressed from first light until the light fails. As a matter of routine approximately one hour before dark commanders automatically begin their night dispositions and if possible get themselves disengaged, secure and capable of being replenished. If this is done well a good start can be made at first light the next day." DHIST. Royal Armoured Corps. Operational Circular No. 1. 7th Armd Div Ops. 26 Nov North Africa to Nov 43, Volturno River Italy. RG 24 BRAC files and TRG Files 4 CAD.

38. Kluge to Hausser, German Seventh Army telephone log, August 8, 1845 hrs.

39. English, p. 280.

40. Maj. L. C. Monk quoted in Maj. G. L. Cassidy, *Warpath: The Story of the Algonquin Regiment, 1939–1945* (Toronto: Ryerson, 1948), p. 80.

41. "The Regiment was being led by Lt. 'Wing Ding' Wilson—he made a right turn but everyone else turned left—didn't believe 'Wing Ding' could navigate . . . that's how we got lost." Account by Lt. Harvey McDermot, troop leader, British Columbia Regiment, 9 August. Regiment historical file, provided by Lt. Col. P. A. Philcox, 1994.

42. Roy, *1944,* p. 214.

43. RG 24 13712. WD 2 Cdn Corps. Msgs fm 1 Pol AD, 1800 and 2345 hrs 9 Aug 44.

44. *Le Première Division blindée polonaise* 12, 13. There were no Tigers facing the Polish 1st Armored Division.

45. Maczek insisted that "ST SYLAIN was occupied by a strong enemy force with the sp of hy mortars and arty . . . several times tks of Tiger type numbering 10–15 against which the regts were fighting suffering losses. . . . By 2200 hrs ST SYLVAIN was occupied." *Operational Report* 1 PAD, 13 Aug 44, p. 3. Maczek's final explanation was that rescuing the British Columbians was not accomplished "because it was beyond our capability." Maczek, p. 188.

46. See K. Meyer, p. 178 and Maczek. *Avec mes Blindés.* Pickert's 88s were reinforced by mobile tank destroyers (Stug IIIs), which may account for Stefanowicz's and Halpenny's inability to maneuver their squadrons past the Quesnay and St. Sylvain: "Meyer's 12SS Pz Div, reinforced by 80 assault guns and 88 Flak guns brought the Poles to a standstill at St. Sylvain and prevented the Canadians from getting out of Bretteville." Eddy Bauer, *Der Panzerkrieg* (Bonn: Verlag Worteverlegar Bodo Zimmermann, 1965), p. 135.

47. The 12th SS Panzer Division history credits Maczek's attack with destroying two German combat teams. H. Meyer, p. 178.

48. Forty-seven tanks, 250 men of the British Columbians and Algonquins, plus an undetermined number of half-tracks.

49. Stacey, p. 229.

50. Brigadier Booth, in a less than controlled manner, ordered the Canadian 21st Armoured Regiment "to make a mad dash forward to relieve sit!" RG 24 14052 WD 4 CAB. 10 Aug 44.

51. There were determined attempts made to find them. The Canadian 4th Division artillery commander, Brig. "Herm" Lane, frustrated at his guns' seeming inability to support the British Columbians, flew his Moth spotter aircraft south along Route 158 searching for Worthington Force. His eyes fixed on Hill 195, he reported no contact as he determinedly flew past that feature until he could actually see Falaise. Had he glanced left, he would have quickly spotted a regiment of Sherman tanks on high ground, mixed with M3 half-tracks and infantry, with scores of vehicles burning black smoke. That he failed to see them is a mystery. The simplest explanation is that he did look, and, because they were not supposed to be there, he did not see them. What he did see, he decided, were the Shermans of Maczek's Polish division.

52. Stearns Papers, 23 March 1981. Simonds's displeasure soon reached Montgomery's ears. Monty to Brooke, 9 August 1944, as in Hamilton, p. 782.

53. The training in England lacked vision. In Exercise Frost (4 December 1943), the aim was to "practice harbouring by day and night"; the emphasis was on "leaving harbours scrupulously clean." Subsequent exercises (Flash; Sodamint) did not emphasize maneuver: they were "restricted by use of roads." In hindsight, the Royal Canadian Armoured Corps rush to get to England, where realistic training was impossible, was most unfortunate.

54. See Kurt Meyer, "Analysis of Totalize." Meyer suggested how a determined Soviet commander would have conducted the attack for the benefit of Canadian officers interested in predicting future NATO conflicts. He would not stop for tactical air strikes and would emphasize a wide front that would enable the attacker to bypass strongpoints. He did not indicate whether the attacking Shermans were to be replaced by Stalins and T-34/85s. DHIST DHD 3–4: Interview Kurt Meyer; Cdn Chaplain's Report. 3 September 1950.

55. Hitler, upon seeing Kluge's worried report, snapped at Warlimont: "You tell Field Marshal von Kluge to keep on looking to his front, to keep his eyes on the enemy and not to look over his shoulder." Walter Warlimont, *Inside Hitler's Headquarters 1939–45* (New York: Praeger, 1962), p. 446.

A self-propelled 17-pounder attack gun (converted M10 tank destroyer) of the 5th Canadian Antitank Regiment, during Operation Tractable *(National Archives of Canada, Wilfred Laurier University, Laurier Centre for Military Strategic and Disarmament Studies)*

CHAPTER 10

Strategic Breakout: Operation Tractable

Tractable was certainly one of the strangest attack formations anyone ever dreamed up and without a hope of succeeding as planned.
—Brig. Harry Foster

He formed deep, massive columns, and put them in motion toward the point of attack. Not one of the horsemen in these masses would have been able to give his horse another direction had he wished to do so. Besides, Murat attacked at the trot to preserve the close formation.
—Hohenlohe: *Conversations Upon Cavalry*

General Simonds's commitment to the Montgomery set piece battle remained undaunted. In fact, although Operation Tractable was a day operation, it had borrowed heavily from Totalize. The operation still carried the SHAEF seal of approval: a heavy-bomber attack. By now the Allied offensive had been totally subverted by a dangerous dependence on air power. Air Chief Marshal Trafford Leigh-Mallory "became the primary advocate of carpet bombing, a tactic rarely used before Cobra."[1] Conversely, a lukewarm Air Marshal Arthur "Bomber" Harris now found himself a major part of the ground offensive. The operations were planned by the army, and the air force filled in. It was almost like being "under command." He did not like it but grudgingly accepted the taskings. Harris reviewed Operation Charnwood (the first use of heavy bombers) and offered an acid critique: "The army unfortunately did not exploit its opportunities."[2] A subsequent failure of Goodwood and Totalize created and fed an angry anti-Montgomery lobby in the RAF that became determined to get him sacked.[3] Air Marshal Harris may have said, "Don't be shy of asking," but there is reasonable doubt that he actually meant it. Besides being used improperly as superheavy artillery, bombers were, despite exaggerated claims, an area weapon. Bombing radii could vary from 2 to 15 miles. Going after Rocquancourt or the start line at Cobra was not the same thing as slamming

Berlin or Cologne. Mistakes were made, and the air force got the bad press. Bombs were always landing in wrong places. Harris, aware of the problems, had already grumbled that he did not enjoy bombing between the army's legs. During Cobra, Totalize, and Tractable, the USAAC and RAF killed or wounded an impressive number of senior officers and hundreds of Allied troops. It was big-scale, big-time fratricide.

At any rate, thanks to Montgomery's support and Crerar's diplomatic skills, the bombers were back again for Tractable. This time it was the RAF.[4] The aim, again, was to drive south and harass German lines of communication to the Seine. Montgomery's instructions issued in his 11August directive included:

> 10. Canadian Army will capture Falaise. This is a first priority, and it is vital it should be done quickly.
> 11. The Army will then operate with strong armoured and mobile forces to secure Argentan.
> 12. A secure front must be held between Falaise and the sea, facing eastwards.[5]

Then Montgomery revised the mission and decided the British Second Army would capture Falaise. The object of Tractable was to dominate Falaise "in order that no enemy may escape by the roads which pass through or near it." What Montgomery meant is not clear, but quick capture of Falaise might trap Kluge's armies and give Dempsey some much deserved recognition.[6] Meanwhile, Bradley had won a spectacular victory at Mortain and the attention of the world's press as U.S. armor ran unchecked into Brittany and the Loire Valley.

The 21st Army Group, specifically the Canadian First Army, ignored its eastern flank, stretched thin as an inflated balloon, and held by tired, unsupported Wehrmacht divisions. A viable operational option was to look beyond Falaise-Argentan and strike directly for the Seine and Rouen or Paris. That was what Patton wanted. However, both Montgomery and Bradley seemed content with nearer, more conservative objectives.

Assigned by Crerar to dominate Falaise, the Canadian II Corps was committed to another frontal set piece attack. Still smarting from Totalize's failure, Simonds laid down the law to his tank commanders. He sternly "stressed the necessity for pushing armour to the very limits of its endurance and that any thought of the armour requiring infantry protection for harbouring at night or not being able to move at night was to be dismissed immediately."[7] The van of the attack paraded flail tanks, heavy reconnaissance units, and then massed armor followed by the mechanized infantry.[8] Marching brigades brought up the rear. The corps flank was secured by the Canadian 18th Armoured Regiment (12th Manitoba Dragoons) operating Staghounds, the most powerful armored cars on the

Allied front. Medium bombers would make rubble of the villages, artillery smoke would close in on the flanks, and flail tanks would take the lead sweeping for mines. Despite the extensive preparation, first-class staff work, and creative planning, it was a cheesy solution for mass armor: "The result was a scheme few coffee-table strategists would use—even in desperation."[9]

Simonds's armored commanders dutifully deployed two up using as much ground as they could squeeze out of their allotted boundaries. It was all very classic heavy-cavalry stuff. The problem was that this was Normandy, not Wagram. Kitching's deployment has been criticized by J. A. English for countermanding Simonds's own operational policy.[10] The fault was doctrinal: specifically, there was no efficient Allied breakthrough formula. It is easy to fault Simonds's and Kitching's deployment, and probably unfair, because army-level breakthroughs are not the responsibility of corps or division commanders. Kitching may not have had much armored experience but he had learned his Totalize lessons—having been frustrated by the repeatedly narrow frontages, he demanded room to maneuver. The battle for ground would have been solved had the breakout problem been given an effective operational solution—second-echelon Soviet-style tank armies, OMGs, and breakthrough artillery—but no one appeared to be familiar with the "alchemy" for the armored offensive (in Russian: *tankovi-iudar*). Having given them a bit more room, Simonds promptly drew them up as straight lines in tight boxes.

The RAF and Smoke

Like Totalize, Tractable began with a bombing attack. Like Totalize, the air force again practiced fratricide and pounded Simonds's troops waiting on the start line. Simonds watched the attack accompanied by Air Marshal Sir Arthur Coningham, who had come forward assuring everyone that the RAF would get it right. "Then on looking up, there could be no mistake. The bombers were very low (less than 100 feet) and we could see the bomb bay doors open and the bombs drop out."[11] It was another short bombing. After the dust had settled, the order was given to move and the phalanxes surged forward.

The armored battle did not go according to plan. The Canadian 2d Armoured Brigade's tanks led into the smoke and dust, aiming for a hazy-sun. "In certain areas the tks were completely blinded by the smoke, in others they were forced to advance across extremely open ground without any supporting cover from the smoke at all."[12] The van of the attack was an armored heavy battle group comprising the tank regiments of the Canadian 2d Armoured Brigade (less the Canadian 27th Canadian Armoured

Regiment), Canadian 7th Reconnaissance Regiment, two squadrons of Dragoons (Sherman flail) tanks plus the 80th Assault Squadron (of AVREs [Armoured Vehicle Royal Engineers]) British Armoured Engineers, and a detachment of Royal Canadian Engineers (two Bulldozers)—the makings of an armored offensive. German outposts were overrun,[13] and the lead tanks quickly reached the Laison River, a narrow stream declared easy going for armor by Royal Canadian Air Force (RCAF) air photo interpreters but whose banks proved steep enough to ditch a Sherman or make a tank throw a track. Operation Tractable had encountered a tank obstacle Simonds did not predict, and the advance paused.[14]

Immediately behind the tanks and infantry battalions were the reconnaissance squadrons of the 17th Duke of York's Royal Canadian Hussars. While the armor waited for the Churchills to come up with fascines, armored cars searched for a crossing. Eventually two were found,[15] and the Hussars surged out of the smoke onto the high ground dominating the river, the last feature before Falaise. They immediately took direct fire as hidden tanks and antitank guns unmasked. The advance stalled and broke up into troop-sized actions.

> Both squadrons now found themselves, instead of in a mopping-up role, taking the bridgehead over the river and coming under heavy anti-tank and machine-gun fire. Col Lewis, realizing that his two squadrons were now in front of the armor, crossed the river and found them digging in on the south bank.[16]

Finally, Canadian armor crossed the Laison and took the lead. Squadron sized *Goums* galloped up the high ground. As bold troop leaders pushed forward, they were knocked out by Kurt Meyer's antitank guns and panzers. "In several places 88mm were encountered sited in hedges or woods . . . these were the FLAK guns sited in A/TK role. More tk loses were sustained."[17] The advance sputtered, then stopped. Tractable appeared over.

Simonds would not accept that. After a month of frustration, he had finally caught the scent and began to move like an armored corps commander rather than a gunner. He quickly appreciated that his frontals were going into the only area that the 12th SS Panzer Division could defend; then he began to use ground. Simonds shifted the Canadian 4th Armoured and Polish 1st Armored Divisions southeast and ordered them to cross the Dives River. It was the beginning of Maczek's and Simonds's golden hour.

Division Commander Maczek and Operational Maneuver

Pija piwa pelne dzbanki Kochaja ich Lublinianski
Lance gubi malo warty To jest pulk dwacziesty czwarty
                                                    —24th Polish Lancers[18]

Table 10.1   Simonds's Armored Corps, August 1944

4th Canadian Armored Division	1st Polish Armored Division
Maj.-Gen. G. Kitching	Maj.-Gen. S. Maczek
Recce Regiment (Shermans) 29 Recce Regt (The South Alberta Regt)	Recce Regiment (Cromwells) 10 Pulk Strzelcow Konnych (10 Chasseurs)

4th Cdn Armored Brigade
 21 CAR (Governor General's
   Foot Guards)
 22 CAR (The Cdn Grenadier Guards)
 28 CAR (The British Columbia Regt)
	10 Pol Armored Cavalry Brigade
	 1 Pulk Pancernego (1st Polish Armd
	   Regt—1 PAR)[a]
	 2 Pulk Pancernego (2nd PAR)
	 24 Pulk Ulanow (24th Lancers)

Mech Inf Battalion The Lake Superior Regiment	Mech Inf Battalion 10 Pulk Dragonow (10th Dragoons)[b]
10th Infantry Brigade The Lincoln and Welland Regiment The Algonquin Regiment The Argyll and Sutherland Highlanders	3 Pol Rifle Brigade Podhale Rifles 8th Rifles 9th Rifles
Divisional Artillery 23rd Field Regiment (SP 15th Field Regiment (Towed)	Divisional Artillery Pancerna Artilleria Pulk (Armd Arty Regt—SP) 2 Pancerna Artilleria Pulk (Towed)
Antitank Regt 5th Anti Tank regiment (SP)	Antitank Regt 1 Pancerna Artilleria Proti Pancer (1st A/Tank Regt (SP)
Total: 240 Main Battle Tanks	Total: 240 Main Battle Tanks
Simonds Corps Total: 480 Main Battle Tanks; 72 Tank Destroyers—552 AFVs	

a. Pulk: Regiment; Pancerna: Armored, *Ulanow:* Lancers (as in German Uhlans); *Strzelcow:* Marksmen, musketeers—combine with *Konnych* (horses) to make Chasseurs a Cheval. The Napoleonic influence on the Polish army is considerable, for example *10 Chasseurs a Cheval* for "mounted rifles" since they were a recce in the tradition of French Chasseurs.

b. *Dragoons* in the traditional Napoleonic sense of "mounted infantry."

An intriguing study of the effects of equipment, doctrine, and senior leadership versus military culture at the operational level is the Polish 1st Armored Division: commanded by Canadians, fitted out with U.S./British equipment, and forced to conform to British doctrine, it becomes de facto the only available operational laboratory study of Allied armor during the Normandy campaign (Le Clerc's French 2d Armored Division is another option). Save for their regimental badges, they wore the same uniforms as the British and Canadians and had surprisingly similar traditions. By the time the 10th Polish Dragoons arrived in Normandy, they even had a regimental tartan and *dudziarz* (pipers).[19]

Although some of the senior Poles (including Maczek himself) had seen action in the early wars against the Soviets as well as the 1939 and 1940 French campaigns, the bulk of the officers and men were as new to combat as their Canadian counterparts.[20] Their initial performance, much like the Canadian 4th Armoured Division's, was disappointing; their tank units were criticized for showing little aggressiveness, and their commanders little drive or tactical skill. During both Totalize and Tractable, the Poles had found themselves victims of friendly fire. Simonds was not very impressed with Maczek after Totalize. He considered disbanding the division altogether, but was persuaded by Crerar and Stuart to give Maczek another chance. By 16 August his faith was finally rewarded—Maczek and his crews seemed to find their pace. The armored advance of the division from the Dives River to Chambois and Coudehard, despite decidedly poor tank country, is a textbook example of an armored division in action: the Polish 1st Division became the antithesis of its former self. In the next five days it was to conduct a series of admirable operations that were to close the Falaise gap and allow Crerar (Montgomery would eventually take the credit) to trap two German armies.

By the time Tractable-Falaise ended, Simonds had been jerked around like a puppet on a string. Crerar's operational directives changed almost daily, but Crerar himself was a victim of Montgomery's indecision. Torn between the covert desire to achieve some kind of flashy grand finale that would give him credit for the greatest victory of the war, and his main job, to direct the operations of both 21st and 12th Army Groups, Montgomery fell short. He did not know what to do with Bradley: at first he let him range far and wide, well away from the Falaise front, but when Dempsey and Crerar failed to deliver, he called Bradley back. There were no fewer than five different operational instructions regarding the technical procedure to capture Falaise and close the pocket: "On August 4, he assigned the place to Crerar, on August 6 to Dempsey, on August 11 to Crerar or Dempsey, on August 13, to Dempsey, and finally on August 14, to Crerar. His inconsistency on Falaise paralleled his lack of firm decision on how to trap the Germans in Normandy."[21]

Montgomery interfered regularly, reset corps objectives, and practically hounded the Canadian II Army commander until he got his personal goal: that someone, anyone (anyone from *his* armies), close the gap. The lucky fellow turned out to be Maczek.[22]

The Polish 1st Armored Division began Tractable as the depth armored division, the II Corps, turned Maczek loose after Kitching had crossed the Laison but became bogged down on the high ground. General Maczek found himself with both room to maneuver and a mission that seemed tailored to his division's heretofore frustrated élan. The Polish commander took off like a bat out of hell. Maczek broke out as the left forward armored division of the Canadian II Corps, and he soon reached the Dives River.[23] As Tractable butted against Falaise, it finally became clear to Montgomery that waiting for Crerar to take William the Conqueror's keep while Dempsey and Hodges bashed forward through the bocage was simply squeezing German toothpaste out of the tube. The center of the gap was Trun.

After having agreed upon Argentan as the interarmy group boundary on 13 August, Montgomery now ordered Bradley and Crerar to strike for Trun and Chambois. Simonds's corps was to use its two armored divisions to capture Trun. The Poles were in the right place, but Simonds had to order Kitching to sidestep along his front and reposition his division to strike toward Trun. This was no easy feat for a new division, but Kitching was in position by 16 August.

Maczek organized his force into two combat commands: the Polish 10th Armored Brigade, followed in turn by the Polish 3d Infantry Brigade (two mechanized battalions grouped with the 24th Lancers); a smaller battlegroup based on 10th Mounted Rifle Regiment with an infantry battalion formed the vanguard.[24] Maczek quickly pushed past his Dives bridgehead and penetrated deeply into I SS Panzer Corps rear areas. He advanced his battle groups like the bull's horns of a Zulu *impi,* with preliminary thrusts on the flanks while the head drove for Chambois. Meanwhile, the Canadian 4th Armoured Division fought its way past traffic jams and minor but stubborn German rear guards. Both armored divisions were running out of tank country: Maczek, flanking wide, pushed past Meyer's rear guards; Kitching, bashing into the Dives River Valley, soon got bogged down.

Outside in the vast plains of the Loire Valley, the U.S. Third Army's tanks ran virtually unopposed, but Patton had been forbidden to cross the interarmy group boundary by the careful Bradley. This was more petty bitterness than caution; it was certainly not maneuver warfare. By 16 August the frustrated Patton had ordered his forces to advance toward Paris; the XV Corps armored cavalry had reached the Seine on 15 August. Meanwhile, Haislip had three divisions available at Argentan: 80th and 90th Infantry supported by the French 2d Armored Division. Bradley had previously forbidden Haislip to advance north when the latter could have easily reached Falaise, and he abruptly ordered Patton to capture Trun. The earliest U.S. Army H-hour would be 6:30 A.M., 18 August.

If Montgomery was to close the gap, he would have to do it with Crerar's troops.[25] He had to hurry: that same day (16 August) von Kluge had ordered a general withdrawal of German forces from the Falaise pocket hours before he was sacked by a suspicious führer: "[von Kluge] was a good leader of troops, but he was no armored general, and was a rather petty type of Junker."[26] Fritz Bayerlein's description of "der Kluge Hans" (clever Hans) could easily have described Montgomery, as well.

Pursuit and Operational Maneuver: Closing the Gap

*The best news I can give you tonight is that the gap has now been closed
and the Polish* Armored *Division has reached TRUN and is pushing on to
CHAMBOIS.*

—Montgomery to Brooke, 17 August 1944[27]

By midday of 17 August, the Canadian 4th Armoured Division was
ordered across the River Dives at Couliboeuf. By now Maczek was well
beyond the Dives. He had outflanked Meyer and reached not only
Kitching's objective but created an expanded bridgehead that allowed for
Corps maneuver.[28] In the next series of Maczek's chess moves one
armored battlegroup struck southwest to cut off Trun and established itself
on the high ground dominating the town and the Dives Valley. The important thing was Maczek continuing the advance, relentlessly playing the
center game towards Chambois and the Americans. His second armored
battlegroup maneuvered southeast and captured Champeaux, anchoring
the envelopment and establishing a six mile front, the center of which was
four miles from Chambois. This was pursuit and Operational Maneuver.
Montgomery was both pleased and excited. He ordered that it was "essential" that the Polish 1st Armored Division struck "past Trun to
Chambois."[29]

**Table 10.2   Polish 1st Armored Division, Divided into Combat Commands,
18 August 1944**

Maciejewski	Kostzutski	Zgorzelski	Reserve
10th Mounted Rifle Regiment	2d Armored Regiment	24th Lancer Regiment	1st Armored Regiment
10th Dragoon Regiment Company	8th Rifle Regiment Battalion	10th Dragoon Regiment	9th Rifle Regiment, Battalion
1st Armored Antitank Squadron	1st Armored Antitank Squadron	1st Armored Antitank Squadron	1st Armored Antitank Squadron

Maczek's organization for the final phase was simple—four *groupment
tactiques*. Each was built around an armored regiment. Battlegroup
Maciejewski comprised the reconnaissance regiment, the 10th Mounted
Rifles (or as Maczek preferred, "10e régiment de chasseurs à cheval,"
equipped with Cromwells) and a company of the 10th Dragoon Regiment
mechanized infantry battalion, mounted in M3 half-tracks; the remaining
three Polish infantry battalions carried their riflemen in Bren-gun carriers.
Battlegroup Koszutski grouped the 2d Armored Regiment with the 8th
Mounted Rifles; Battlegroup Zgorzelski grouped the 24th Lancers with the

10th Dragoons. The reserve was based on the 1st Armored Regiment and the 9th Mounted Rifles. Each attacking battle group had an attached squadron of tank destroyers—a standard Normandy grouping as practiced by the Germans.

This was not the sort of matrix or maneuver the British-trained Canadian staffs may have felt comfortable with. O'Connor would have recognized the old desert style, and certainly Grow and Wood would have approved. Maczek was not to be denied as long as he produced results and brought Montgomery's blessings on the Canadian First Army. At 10:15 A.M. on 17 August, Simonds issued orders from main headquarters of the Canadian 4th Armored Division: "Link up with US Forces and hold the line of the River Dives."[30] By 9:00 A.M. of 18 August, the Canadian Grenadier Guards were in Trun, which they found abandoned. Kitching had closed the northern part of the gap. "[Here is] country which has not been ravaged by war. Houses are intact, fields are greener and not littered with wrecked enemy eqpt. Even the air smells fresh."[31]

At 11:00 A.M. on 19 August, Simonds held yet another conference with his four division commanders. His almost daily conferences were hardly *auftragstaktik,* but part of the blame was in Montgomery's changing directives, and part was doctrinal. The Poles were to leave the Trun area to the Canadian 4th Armoured Division and concentrate on securing Chambois. The 4th Armoured would then hand Trun over to The Canadian 3d Division and advance southeast to capture Vimoutiers.[32] Somewhere behind them, and from the southwest, would appear the vanguards of Dempsey's army, driving the Germans before them onto the Canadian gun line on the Dives. It was to be like shooting grouse.

Despite the air attacks and increasingly stubborn German rear guards, by the evening of 18 August Maczek's leading elements had cut the German line of escape. He had a battlegroup outside Chambois, another on the ground of tactical dominance northeast of Coudehard, near Vimoutiers, and two battlegroups in his hip pocket. By 19 August he had closed the gap: "La Première Division avait atteint tout ses objectifs" ("The first Division has reached its objectives.")[33]

The presence of the Polish 1st Armored Division at Chambois alerted the new German theater commander, "square-jawed, square-built" Field Marshal Walter Model.[34] He had assumed command on 17 August; by the next day, he was planning both a continued fighting withdrawal out of the pocket and a rescuing counterattack. Maczek forced the Germans into a desperate reaction: the 2d SS Panzer Corps (now composed of 2d SS Das Reich, 9th SS Hohenstaufen, 9th Panzer Divisions and elements of the 116th Panzer) were ordered to stop, regroup, turn around, and attack back into the pocket.[35]

Simonds now had to make fast the Polish cork with Canadian glue.

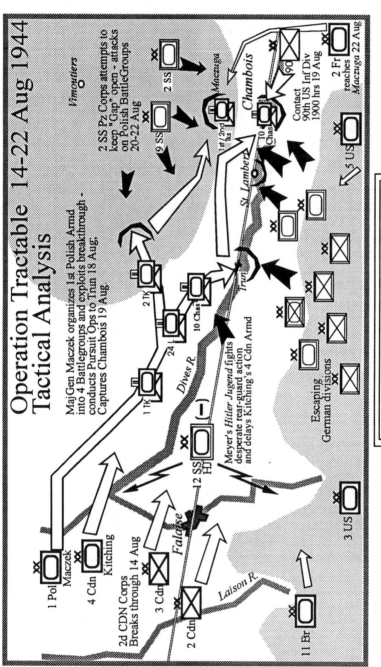

Operation Tractable 14-22 Aug 1944
Tactical Analysis

MajGen Maczek organizes 1st Polish Armd into 4 Battlegroups and exploits breakthrough - conducts Pursuit Ops to Trun 18 Aug; Captures Chambois 19 Aug

2 SS Pz Corps attempts to keep "Gap" open - attacks on Polish BattleGroups 20-22 Aug

Contact 90th US Inf Div 1900 hrs 19 Aug

2 Fr reaches Maczuga 22 Aug

Meyer's *Hitler Jugend* fights desperate rear-guard action and delays Kitching's 4 Cdn Armd

2d CDN Corps Breaks through 14 Aug

Escaping German divisions

Vimoutiers

Maczuga

Chambois

St Lambert

Trun

Dives R.

Falaise

Laison R.

1 Pol — Maczek
4 Cdn — Kitching
3 Cdn
2 Cdn
11 Br
3 US
1 TK
24
2 TK
10 Chas
12 SS HJ (-)
9 SS
2 SS
1st / 2nd Tks
90
3 US
2 Fr

Legend

ALLIED ARMD DIV	GERMAN PZ DIV
ALLIED INF DIV	GERMAN INF DIV
POLISH BATTLEGROUP (1 TK)	

JAPROWICZ OCT 2000

Kitching's regiments were advancing cautiously, while Maczek's units were taking the bulk of Canadian II Corp casualties.[36] Montgomery did not adjust the boundaries to conform to the changing situation, and Bradley refused to exercise any initiative despite Patton's alleged offer to "drive the British into the sea for another Dunkirk."[37] With Bradley's stubborn inactivity and Montgomery's indecisiveness, the gate was shut but not bolted. The Americans stayed put at Argentan. Direct liaison with the Canadian First Army was refused: Bradley would only deal with Montgomery.[38]

Maczuga: A Polish Battlefield

> La providence nous offre ainsi la joie d'une revanche sur cette unité combattue en Pologne en 1939, mais cette fois, les roles en sont inversés.[39]
> —General Maczek, when attacked by 2d SS Panzer Das Reich, 19 August

Model ordered the 2d Panzer Corps to begin its counterattack on the afternoon of 19 August. It soon pushed the Polish 1st Armored Regiment's patrols away from Vimoutiers. Maczek's northern battlegroup fell back onto his center and the highest terrain in the gap, Hills 262, 252, and 240. In the valley below, the 10th Mounted Rifles penetrated into Chambois and met the vanguard of Task Force Weaver, U.S. 90th Infantry Division.[40] Soon it too was under attack. The Polish 1st Armored Division had closed the gap, but it was an armored division in the pursuit—divided into maneuver elements and securing ground of tactical, indeed, strategical importance. It now had to hold ground in closed terrain. This was not the accepted operational doctrine for armor, and it would have been understandable if it withdrew.

With one battlegroup linked up with the the 90th Infantry's "Tough Hombres" at Chambois,[41] Maczek had operationally plugged the gap. Tactically, his armored division was now a series of strongpoints with practically no mutual support. His troops isolated islands trying to stem the tide of withdrawing Germans, and Maczek organized his force into two strongpoints. Chambois would be held by the 10th Mounted Rifle Regiment, reinforced with the 24th Lancers battlegroup. The Coudehard-Bojois feature, dominating the Dives River Valley, would be held by the Polish 1st and 2d Armored Regiments' battlegroups. The battle position resembled a club or, better, a battle mace, and that was what Maczek (who hated using grid references) christened it: *Maczuga,* a symbol of sovereign power for Poles.[42]

The Polish commander was alone: his regiments had outrun Kitching and his Canadian 4th Armoured . There is some reluctance in Canadian military history to heap praise on Maczek. Terry Copp argues that Kitching may have been cheated of his just rewards, because the 4th Armoured had captured Trun,[43] Crerar's first objective, and went on to St. Lambert-en-

Dives. This is technically correct, although there is some evidence that the Poles were there first.[44] An operational analysis of this battle would argue that at the corps-army level, terrain expands to include operational objectives. Therefore Simonds had two goals (Trun and Chambois), and correctly sent his two mobile formations to secure both. Maczek grabbed one, Kitching finally grabbed the other. Since the gap was not hermetically sealed until after 21 August, some argue that to single out Maczek for this praise is excessive. However, the Poles did take the last operational objective for the 21st Army Group. It may not have been tidy, but it did the job. Montgomery's boundary line finally merged with the 12th Army Group's blue line. Maczek's accomplishment was enthusiastically noted by both Bradley and Montgomery. That they chose to overlook Kitching is unfortunate, but it is not totally unfair.

The Polish presence on the heights above Chambois was not appreciated by the Germans until Friday, 18 August: "The Germans, to their stupefaction and fright, discovered that their retreat is henceforth cut off."[45] Hill 262 above Chambois was immediately subjected to mortar fire, and this constantly increasing bombardment was to last four full days. Meanwhile, a battle group of the South Alberta Light Horse (Canadian 4th Armoured's heavy reconnaissance regiment equipped with Shermans) commanded by Maj. D. V. Currie, determinedly attacked into St. Lambert-en-Dives from the north in attempting to close the last fissure in the Falaise gap, "a real valve through which the whole pocket was deflated."[46]

The key to the puzzle was *Maczuga*. Maczek's men were surrounded and running low on food, medicine, and ammunition. By now, the pocket had become a nightmare filled with retreating German units. Model's troops were under the harassing fire of over 3,000 U.S., British, and Canadian guns. The sky was filled with Allied aircraft whose constant attacks savaged the withdrawing columns as they approached the gap.[47] Allied air did not, however, attack Germans inside the gap. The real fear of hitting their own troops—which they had been doing throughout Tractable and Falaise operations, resulted in the imposition of a no-fire line for artillery and air. German columns quickly realized that as they approached the St. Lambert-Chambois area they were granted a respite from rocket-firing Typhoons and Thunderbolts.[48] The slaughter inside the gap, from St. Lambert to *Maczuga,* was caused by direct fire from Polish and Canadian infantry and armor, as well as battalion mortars and regimental artillery batteries firing over open sights.

Kitching Relieved

Maczek's fiercest day was on 20th August. Hammered from all sides, the Polish 1st Armored Division was near to being overrun.[49] The heaviest fighting continued around Currie's block in St. Lambert and Maczuga. The

Germans hammered the position with mortars, artillery, nebelwerfers (multiple rocket launchers), and direct tank fire. Battle group–sized attacks from the II SS Panzer Corps (basically, Das Reich and 9th Panzer Divisions) began to penetrate the outer perimeters of Maczuga.[50] At first the Canadian II Corps did not accept the seriousness of the Poles' situation: "Sont accueillis avec une certaine incredulité a l'état-major canadien." ("We were greeted with a certain incredulity by Canadian headquarters.")[51] Finally the corps commander decided to see for himself: "L'arrivée à mon P.C. du commandant de corps canadien, le general Simonds, fait finalement changer d'opinion l'état-major canadien" ("The arrival of the commander of the Canadian corps, General Simonds, finally changed the opinion of the Canadian high command.")[52] Simonds ordered Kitching to save the Poles.[53] To Simonds's rage, Kitching dragged his feet.[54] On the morning of 21 August, the Simonds relieved Kitching of command and personally "ordered 4th Armored Brigade to rescue the Poles immediately."[55] Two tank regiments, the Canadian Grenadier Guards followed by the Governor General's Foot Guards, attacked with determination and bashed through to Maczuga. They were much welcomed: "The Poles cried with joy when we arrived."[56]

The Victory Numbers

The Allied Intelligence had seriously underestimated the ability of the German leaders to form effective battlegroups out of the more fanatical of their men who were determined to escape or die in the attempt.
— Lt. Gen. Sir Brian Horrocks, British XXX Corps

The Normandy campaign was over. The Germans eventually withdrew 157,800 men from the Falaise pocket itself as well as the bulk of their rear-echelon troops, with equipment, for a total of 165,800 troops safely evacuated north of the Seine.[57] Although the divisions were shattered[58] and the panzer force all but destroyed, there were enough left over to wreck Operation Market Garden, cause the Americans serious worry in Lorraine, hold Calais, defend the Scheldt River, and form the bases of another strategic offensive in December. The order of battle for German forces in France and Belgium still totaled well over 250,000 troops (165,800 escaping from Normandy, 72,000 of the German Fifteenth Army north of the Seine, plus training and support cadres).

Historically, Falaise has produced a minor statistics kampf. Recent studies suggest that 44,800 troops got out of the pocket.[59] A good example is the 12th SS Hitlerjugend Armored Division, whose alleged reduction from 20,000 men to a battle group of 500 is often cited as evidence of the Normandy bloodbath. The Hitlerjugend Division did suffer, and many of its commanders and panzer grenadiers died in Normandy. The bulk of division headquarters and most of the B echelon escaped despite the supposedly tight net created by Allied armor and tactical air. Records show that 12,000 Hitlerjugend troops and ten tanks were assembled at Verneuil-sur-Avre after the battle. It was enough that the division remained a formidable force for the Ardennes offensive three months later.

The SS divisions in general seem to have gotten out of the Falaise pocket surprisingly well.[60] The real losses were in the infantry battalions, experienced units that were overrun during Cobra or that could not quickly road-march out of the pocket (the German army was still 65 percent horse drawn). Although there was no surrender and the bulk of the trapped forces escaped, the battle has been dubbed the "Stalingrad of the West." The entire campaign was a long, slow bloodletting for the best formations in the Reich that ended with a spectacular feat of Allied arms.[61]

The U.S. performance in the Normandy breakout has been both praised and criticized. The argument may be made that Bradley was not perfect. But to deny the U.S. 12th Army Group's accomplishments would be unfair and petty. Achieving operational maneuver, the Americans performed in a grand style that was as creative and effective as Manstein's 1940 campaign in France. Montgomery was presented with the opportunity for a battle of annihilation—his own Cannae—but finally settled for a battle of exhaustion. And Model's determination had salvaged much from the debacle.

The Canadian army did its job, albeit at great, perhaps too great, a cost. Canadian losses per capita of their male population were the heaviest of the Western Allies. Crerar appeared content to follow orders rather than to read the battle and exhibit tactical initiative. At a time when Patton was both taking Brittany and stretching the envelope east toward Dreux, Crerar continued to smash south toward Argentan.[62]

The performance of Canadian armor is another story. Normandy was a learning experience, *and* it turned out to be the only experience. After the Cobra-Tractable breakout and pursuit to the Scheldt, the Canadian armored divisions were never to be given the opportunity vis-à-vis terrain or mission to perform in the style in which they were now prepared to fight. The early Normandy actions demonstrated that armored divisions were ill prepared at the operational or brigade level. Conversely, the exploits of individual regiments, troops, and squadrons were in the finest traditions of any army. The difficulties lay in command and control. It should be noted Simonds had had two months to perfect his art, Kitching and Maczek had three weeks.

Notes

1. Pearlman, "Close Air Support in World War Two," p. 150.
2. Turraine, p. 651.

3. Tedder stated the RAF felt it had been "had for suckers. I do not believe there is the slightest indication of a clean breakthrough." Pogue Papers, MHI. See Turraine, Hamilton, and D'Este.

4. A peculiar choice. The RAF itself was committed to "area bombing." The USAAC, with all its faults, was most practiced at daylight bombing and committed to putting all the bombs "in the pickle barrel." The RAF bombed at night, and any-thing within 10 miles of the bombing point appears to have been "a wizard prang" judging by Berlin, Nuremberg, and Dresden.

5. Letters of Instruction 12 August 44, Richard Collins Papers (SHAEF G2) August 1944. MHI.

6. The 30 July British offensive, Operation Bluecoat, was a costly disap-pointment. The fighting had been absolutely savage; the operational results were unspectacular and costly in morale and commanders. Lt. Gen. Bucknall, command-er of the British II Corps, had failed to perform after being ordered by Monty to "get on or get out" and paid the price. He was followed by a virtual hemorrhage of senior officers: "Bullen-Smith (51st Highland Div) . . . had to go. . . . I removed Bobbie Erskine (7th Armd Div). . . . I also had to remove Loony Hinde (23 Armd Bde)."

7. RG 24 13789 WD HQ 4 Armd Div. 13 August 1944.

8. These were accompanied by Wasp flame throwers mounted on Bren gun carriers, used for the first time. They were a terrifying weapon—Wasp crews, like the Churchill-Crocodile crews were generally shot if captured.

9. J. L. Granatstein and Desmond Morton, *Bloody Victory* (Toronto: Lester & Orpen Dennys, 1984), p. 173.

10. English, p. 290.

11. Stearns Papers, 5 October 1981. Stacey confirmed that "disciplinary action was taken against individuals whose responsibility could be established. Two Pathfinder crews were re-posted to ordinary crew duties, squadron and flight com-manders personally involved relinquished their commands and acting ranks were re-posted to ordinary crew duty."

12. RG 24 WD 2 CAB *Op Tractable* "An Account of Ops by 2 Cdn Armd Bde in France 14 to 16 Aug," p. 4.

13. Although pieces of the 271st and 85th Wehrmacht Infantry Divisions were in the area, the principal burden of defense rested on the remaining battle groups of the Hitlerjugend Division.

14. A serious oversight, for he had written an exhaustive appreciation, or com-bat estimate, of the problem, including terrain. His photo interpreters and G2 let him down here. See RG 24 WD 2 Cdn Corps, Aug 44.

15. Reconnaissance regiment tasks were to "mop up area between river line and 2 CAB, then join 2 CAB on OBJ." Lt. D. Ayer found a crossing that could accommodate tanks. Meanwhile Sgt. G. Routley, found that Rouvres had another usable crossing. Interviews with Col. G. W. Routley and J. Domville, Montreal, 1988. See W. G. Pavey, *An Historical Account of the 7th Canadian Reconnaissance Regiment (17th DYRCH) in the World War 1939–1945* (Montreal: The Regimental Association, 1948), pp. 47–48, 53–54.

16. Pavey, p. 53.

17. RG 24 WD 2 CAB *Op Tractable* "An Account of Ops by 2 Cdn Armd Bde in France 14 to 16 Aug," p. 5.

18. "We drink from full tankards, the girls from Lublin love us, We've lost our lances but not to worry—we're the 24th."

19. The Polish 1st Armored Division symbol was the famed polish "winged hussar," a warrior's symbols that traced their origins to the great Polish kingdoms of the Middle Ages. The 10th Dragoon Regiment adopted the Lord Hamilton tartan

and trained its pipers in the Scottish tradition. See Henryk Smaczny, *Ksiega Kawalerii Polskiej 1914–1947* (Warsaw: Tesco, Przedsiebiorstwo Zpgraniczne, 1989); Stanislaw Komornicki, *Wojsko Polskie 1939–1945* (Warsaw: Wypawnictwo Interprises, 1990). Marian Zebrowski, *Polska Bron Pancerna* (London: White Eagle Press, 1971).

20. The Polish 1st Armored Division was built from veterans of the 1939 campaign, the 1939 Bzura encirclement who arrived in Britain via the Baltic, the Balkans, and France. They were joined by volunteers from North America, Latin America, and even Africa. The division was largely built through General Sikorski's energy and political contacts in the United States.

21. Martin Blumenson, *The Battle of the Generals: The Untold Story of the Falaise Pocket—The Campaign That Should Have Won World War II* (New York: William Morrow and Company, Inc., 1993), p. 217.

22. Maczek was Austro-Hungarian by birth and had been a kaiserjäger in the Hapsburg cavalry. He commanded one of Poland's two armored brigades in 1938. He was a "modern tank officer," one of the few Polish divisions to counterattack in 1939 and succeed. He raised the the Polish 10th Armored Brigade not as a British legion but as a constituent element of the army of the Republic of Poland. See Keegan, Maczek.

23. RG 24 13712 WD 2 Cdn Corps. 15 August 1944: "Pol Mtd Rifles Regt crosses R. Dives apx 1530." See also RG 24 10942 Polish Armd Div: "Tractable: Rozkaz Nr. 1."

24. RG 24 10942: *Polish Armored Division. Rozkoz do Natarcia Nr.1.* Confirmatory orders issued 16 August 1944, and *Operational Report C.O. 1 Polish Armd Div* "Fighting During the Period From 12 Aug to 22 Aug 44," pp. 8, 10.

25. Bradley later argued that his decision was actually a beau geste to support a faltering Crerar: "If Patton's patrols grabbed Falaise, it would be an arrogant slap in the face at a time when we clearly need to build confidence in the Canadian Army."

26. ETHINT 67 Lt.Gen Fritz Bayerlein, "Normandy Critique" ETO, 15 August 1945, MHI.

27. Hamilton, p. 796.

28. RG 24 13712. 2 Cdn Corps WD and Ops Log. Aug 44. Also, RG 24 10942, Polish Armd Div: Confirmatory Orders of S Maczek Maj Gen of Gen Verbal Orders issued on 16 Aug 44 "Rozkaz Nr. 4." Cdn Corps WD/Ops Log: "10 Pol Mtd Rifles on wide front . . . en resistance weak. Chief hindrance rd blocked by retreating south civilians." RG 24 13712. 2 Cdn Corps WD and Ops Log. 16 Aug 44.

29. RG 24 13712 WD 2 Cdn Corps. 17 Aug 44. See also RG 24 10942 Polish Armd Div, 17 Aug 44.

30. RG 24 13789 WD 4 CAD 17 Aug 44.

31. RG 24 13789 WD 4 CAD 17 Aug 44. Particularly hated were the mosquitoes: "They are definitely organized . . . fly at low level and never miss," and "Dysentery. We all have it now."

32. RG 24 13 712. WD 2 Cdn Corps. 19 Aug 44.

33. See also *La Première Division blindée polonaise* and *1st Polish Armored Regiment 1939–1946.* Both published privately by the Divisional Association.

34. Shulman, p. 170, and D'Este in Correlli Barnett, *Hitler's Generals* (London: Weidenfeld and Nicolson, 1989), p. 319.

35. 116th acquitted itself well, fighting despite the bad reputation it appears to have gained during August. See MS #B-162 116th Pz Div (11–24 Aug 44) and MS #B-058 116 Pz Div, Falaise: GenMaj H. Voigtsberger, Comd, 60 PzGren Regt.

36. By last light of 18 August, the Polish 1st Armored made up 50 percent of

Canadian II Corps entire casualties (263 compared with 286 for the remaining three divisions and two brigades). On 17 August U.S., British, and Canadian air squadrons flew 2,029 sorties into the Falaise pocket, on 18 August it was 2,057, and on the next day, they would fly an additional 3,856 sorties.

37. There is debate over whether Patton actually said this. See Blumenson and Weigley.

38. The exception was for artillery. Bradley permitted communication between corps artillery headquarters.

39. "Providence offered us the pleasure of revenge against this unit which we had fought in Poland in 1939, but this time, the results were reversed."

40. Maj. Gen. W. G. Weaver, *Yankee Doodle Went to Town* (Ann Arbor, Mich.: Edwards Brothers, 1959), pp. 95–98. Simonds advised Crerar, who responded with undisguised delight: Crerar to Simonds, 19 August 1944, 9:40 P.M.: "Desire you transmit to GOC Pol Armd Div my congratulations concerning the important and gallant part all under his command have played in recent fighting. The First Cdn Army is very proud to count the Polish Armd Div amongst its formations." RG 24 13712.

41. The 90th Infantry Division was formed from Texans and Oklahomans, hence the stylized "TO" shoulder patch and nickname of "tough hombres." John Colby, *War From the Ground Up* (Austin, Tex.: Nortex, 1975).

42. Maczek, p. 218. The position was based on two heights that dominated the Dives Valley: Bosjois and Coudehard (which was just northeast of Mont Ormel, often confused with Maczuga). The third element was a point just north of Coudehard. It was against this flank that the II SS Panzer Corps attack struck first.

43. Conference with Terry Copp, Waterloo, Ontario, May 1996.

44. Maczek certainly thought so and apparently so did the British: "Freddie (de Guingand) thought Bradley should have joined the Poles at Trun." Pogue Papers, MHI; interview with Brig. Sir Edgar Williams. John Keegan agrees: "The 10th Cavalry Brigade departed from its start line near Trun in early afternoon (17th August)." *Six Armies in Normandy,* pp. 272, 274. "The 24th Polish Lancers crossed Louvières-en-Auge; the Poles could have descended on Trun which they could see as if from a balcony, three kilometers lower down the slope." Eddy Florentin, *Battle of the Falaise Gap* (London: Elek Books, 1965), p. 177.

45. Bernage, p. 490.

46. RG24 13712. 2 Cdn Corps Ops log: 19 Aug 44, 1145 hrs, fm 18 CACR: "En breaking through at St. Lambert sur Dives 3326."

47. The effect of the air attacks was considerable, although the effective kill ratio against armor was much exaggerated. See *No. 2 Operational Research Unit Report #4:* "Air Attacks on Enemy tanks and Motor Transport in the Mortain Area, August 1944."

48. See Gen. Richard Rhomer: *Patton's Gap.* This air force opinion is both supported and attacked by military historians.

49. RG 24 13712. WD 2 Cdn Corps. 1 Pol Armd Div to Corps: "Amn sit grave." 1830 20 Aug 44.

50. "9th SS Panzer was able to push . . . to the Les Cosniers area. . . . 2d SS Pz Div at first gained ground unhindered until it ran into a heavy tank engagement north of Coudehard." MHI MS # B-748. II SS Pz Corps (15 Jul–21 Aug) by Wilhelm Bittrich.

51. Maczek, p. 218.

52. Ibid.

53. The Polish situation was bleak: "Gentlemen, all is lost. I do not think the Canadians can come to our rescue. We have . . . no food and very little ammunition.

. . . There is no question of surrender. . . . Tonight we shall die." See Keegan and Florentin for different versions of this speech.

54. "I said to General Simonds words to this effect: 'To hell with them. They have run out of food and ammunition because of the inefficiency of their organization; our people have been fighting just as hard but we have managed to keep up our supply system.'" Kitching, p. 205.

55. "Avant de repartir il ajoute en passant que depuis ce matin la 4e division blindée canadienne est placée sous les ordres du colonel T., chef d'état-major du corps." [Before leaving, he added in passing that as of this morning, the Canadian 4th Armored Division had been placed under the command of Col. T., corps chief of staff]." Maczek now knew that Simonds had made Kitching pay the price for failure. Maczek, p. 219.

56. Duguid, p. 282; RG 24: WD 22 CAR August 1944: "The picture at Point 262 was the grimmest the regiment had so far come up against . . . unburied dead and parts of them were strewn about by the score."

57. See Meyer, *Kriegsgeschichte der 12.SS Panzer Division,* p. 354. Georges Bernage, *La Retraite allemande* (Bayeux: Editions Heimdal, 1988), pp. 36, 87. Michel Dufresne, "Normandie: Août 1944," *Revue historique des armées* 3, 114–115.

58. Some units managed to soldier through with heads high. The 2d SS Das Reich Division was "greatly impressed" when Meidel's 3d Airborne Division paratroopers marched out of the gap "in cadence" and singing their march.

59. Dufresne claims "un effectif nominal de 371,000 hommes," p. 119. Over 150,000 combat troops appear to have left the pocket: "44,800 hommes sortis de la Poche, 60,000 hommes entre la mer et Gace, 15,500 hommes entre Gace et Nonancourt, 25,500 hommes entre Nonancourt et la Seine, 12,000 hommes a l'est de Vimoutiers." Bernage, p. 114.

60. The panzer divisions 1st SS Leibstandarte Adolf Hitler: 10,000 all ranks; 2d SS Das Reich: 12,000; 9th SS Hohenstaufen Panzer: 15,000; 10th SS H Pz Div: 10,000; 12th SS Hitlerjugend: 12,000; 17th SS Panzer Grenadier: 6,000; Lehr: 8,000; 2d: 8,000; 9th: 1,000; and 116th: 8,300; the 3d Airborne Division: 5,000; 2,000 each for the 276th, 277th and 353d Infantry Divisions; 1,000 each for the 84th, 326th, and 363d Infantry Divisions. See MS #B-631 Feuchtinger: *21 Pz Div,* Meyer, Bayerlein (who detailed "20 tanks and tank destroyers . . . four batteries of artillery . . . one and one half batteries of antiaircraft . . . about 100 half-tracks, and about 100 motor vehicles." These are impressive totals for a division that endured the initial bombing at St. Lô on 25 July). Bernage, and Dufresne, pp. 114, 119.

61. Estimates have include a grand total of 460,900 German casualties (including naval and air forces) for the entire campaign, but since military historians habitually quote one another ("et cette erreur est devenue un cliché reproduit à l'infini," Dufresne) the actual numbers for Normandy, particularly German withdrawal totals, have been only recently corrected. Allied losses were high as well; a total of 206,703, of which 124,394 were U.S. and 82,309 were British and Canadian. The Canadian First Army suffered 18,444 casualties by 23 August (5021 were fatal).

62. Nevertheless, Crerar was highly regarded by at least one of his British corps commanders: "General Crerar, who in my opinion, has always been underrated, largely because he was the exact opposite of Montgomery. He hated publicity, but was full of common sense and always prepared to listen to the views of his subordinate commanders." Sir Brian Horrocks, Everslet Belfield, and Maj. Gen. H. Essame, *Corps Commander* (New York: Charles Scribner's Sons, 1977), pp. 182.

CHAPTER 11

Armor in Its "Proper Role": The Pursuit Doctrine

The classic US armored encirclement of German forces: During the passage through the corridor, Gen Patton's feint westward with a combat command toward Brittany and Brest misled the German command with the false view that Gen Patton would first capture Brittany. . . . As the American armor suddenly appeared in front of Vitre, Mayenne, Laval, and Le Mans, the greatest astonishment and consternation reigned.
—Gen. Günther Blumentritt[1]

The first objective of any exploitation is to deny the enemy the power of maneuver.
—Gen. Robert W. Grow, U.S. 6th Armored Division[2]

The U.S. Third Army's pursuit into the Mayenne, Sarthe, and Loire valleys was a masterful operation. Bradley, despite unfortunate delays for which he has been bitterly called to task, succeeded in capturing both Brittany and Paris and destroying the better parts of three armies. The U.S. armored advance was a learning experience—tactically and operationally. U.S. doctrine had attempted to predict the conduct of armor in this phase of war but it was a doctrine based on no practical experience. U.S. division commanders were now forced to create impromptu solutions to a series of logistics problems. The issue was operational maneuver. There was no clear plan from SHAEF, Eisenhower, or Montgomery. Having achieved deep battle, the Allies were offered the opportunity to secure either political (Paris) or military (complete entrapment of Model's armies) goals. Both Eisenhower and Montgomery could not make up their minds. The U.S. armored divisions were the first Allied formations to conduct deep battle in Europe. The mechanics of the art were to be based on control and logistical support as the bulk of the German army, thanks to Hitler's orders, was neatly wrapped in the Falaise pocket.

Initial attempts by armored commanders (Wood and eventually Patton)

to dash for the Seine and secure a strategic objective were forbidden by
Bradley. The Cobra pursuit would test corps-level armored operations. The
missions of the armored division were defined in FM 17-100, but these
were general and, once the pursuit was launched, proved vague. The conduct of pursuit operations required the use of reconnaissance, armor, mechanized infantry, and tactical air. Communications were constantly at risk.
The eastward progress of U.S. armored divisions during Cobra proved significant—this was the first time that the American armor was given the
opportunity to conduct operations of this scale.

The U.S. Armored Force began Normandy in the middle of doctrinal
controversy. The North African campaign had clearly indicated that
McNair's tank destroyer philosophy was defective. Experience showed that
tank destroyer battalions were rarely grouped as complete units, and enemy
armored superiority made them incapable of offensive action.[3] As it
became clear that the Germans were not going to attack in large formations
and that future fighting would consist of offensive actions on the part of the
Allies, the doctrine had to be amended. U.S. armor was divided into three
distinct types: cavalry (reduced entirely to regimental reconnaissance missions), GHQ armored battalions (used in the same manner as British and
Canadian infantry tanks grouped in armored brigades), and, finally, the
armored regiments of the pure tank division. One experienced cavalry officer noted a manifest difference between tank division units and GHQ tank
battalions: "Quality of GHQ tk bn in training for battle, aggressiveness and
general all round efficiency was far below the standard of the tank battalion
in the Armored Division . . . the tank/infantry/artillery team is little understood outside the Armored Divisions."[4]

Despite the dash of commanders like George S. Patton, Sicily had
given U.S. armor little opportunity to strut its stuff. Italy was poor tank
country as was the U.S. sector of Normandy. The bocage limited actions to
groupings of, at most, a tank platoon (from the GHQ tank battalion) and an
infantry company.[5] Successful small-unit actions required a delicate balance of all arms. Fighting for each section of bocage (about the size of an
American football field) required infantry units' close assaults supported by
their own heavy machine guns and mortars. Attacks were supported by
FOOs capable of bringing down extremely accurate artillery fire, an FAC,
where possible, to coordinate ground attack by P-47s, and, finally, combat
engineers to clear the obstacles and mines that abounded in the Norman
hedgerow country.[6] By the time Cobra was launched, the modern U.S.
combat team—really a pocket version of the Kampfgruppe—had been perfected. The GHQ battalions did not have Tigers[7] to contend with, but in the
bocage a Panther, Pzkw IV, Stug, or JPz IV was formidable enough because
most engagements took place at ranges of under 100 yards.

Combat Commands: Auftragstaktik Unrealized

The U.S. armored division underwent six separate reorganizations; the most significant occurred on 1 March 1942, when the armored brigade was eliminated in favor of two combat commands and artillery was reorganized into three separate battalions. The second revision took place on 15 September 1943 creating three combat commands and eliminating the regimental organization, substituting separate battalions in its place. The reorganizations followed four continuous trends: decrease in light-tank strength; increase in medium-tank strength; an increase in the relative strength of the infantry element; and the elimination of needless command echelons and the lightening of the service elements. By 15 January 1944, FM 17-100 *The Armored Division* stated the role of the division to be primarily to perform missions that require great mobility and firepower.

The doctrinal reorganization prepared the division for combined-arms operations, albeit at the brigade group level. Each division commander owned three fighting headquarters in addition to his main headquarters. The combat commands (A, B, and Reserve) were manned command centers and ready to accept specific mission-directed tasks using allotted resources from the divisional "tool box." This procedure appeared tailored to emulate the German doctrine of forming *Kampfgruppen*.

The approach was somewhat superior to the British and Canadian organization, which continued the brigade system and was culturally uncomfortable with battle groups of mixed arms. In this system, infantry battalions attached to armor assumed that they would eventually go home to their parent formation.[8] The formality of established combat commands permitted the U.S. Army to go beyond the natural prewar traditions that separated the combat arms.[9] On the other hand, the combat commands were criticized by senior U.S. armored commanders because the commands were a too rigid interpretation of a simple and adaptable system initially proposed by Edna Chaffee. The 2d Armored Division's Nason Harmon recorded that "Combat Commands tend to encourage the breaking up of the division by higher command."[10]

Chaffee's reservations proved correct. Combat commands soon became de facto brigade groups and lost their flexibility. Assigned units tended to stay. General Harmon, who had commanded 2d Armored Division in the Battle of Aachen, argued for complete freedom for the division commander to "create his own *kampfgruppen* as he wills it."[11] Much like Canadian brigades, a tribal relationship appeared within those divisions where commanders who did not understand the essence of the philosophy (simply put, larger battle groups) permitted a permanent bureaucracy to develop. In some divisions, the combat command organization mutated into semipermanent task forces. The army appeared to prefer bureaucracy to the ad hoc philosophy of *Auftragstaktik*. This may have been the essential cultural difference between the two armies and perhaps one reason why modern American fondness for Germanic principles is unrealistic. Harmon felt that combat commands were "a step forward but a half measure . . . the correct step was not organizational change but a mental change."[12] On the other hand, the frontier heritage of the U.S. Army should have given it a natural understanding of the system: "I told him I was working under superiors who were accustomed to two miles an hour advance and I often ran out of orders by 1000 in the morning. I said, 'What will I do in such cases?' Patton said: 'Go East.' I went several hundred miles on that short mission type order."[13]

Mission-type orders were given, but subordinates were not always encouraged to demonstrate the spirit behind the term. Bradley's short leash on Patton and shorter leash on Grow and Wood illustrates the 12th Army Group's comfort level with mission orders or maneuver warfare:

> I was still under First Army, and it could not react fast enough. When it did react its orders consisted of sending its two flank armored divisions back, 180 degrees away from the main enemy, to engage in siege operations against Lorient and Brest. August 4 was that black day. I protested long, loud and violently—and pushed my tank columns into Châteaubriant (without orders) and my armored cavalry to the outskirts of Angers and along the Loire, and ready to advance (east) on Chartres. I could have been there, in the enemy vitals, in two days. But no! We were forced to adhere to the original plan.[14]

The U.S. armored division was supported by the U.S. infantry division. "infantry division" is misleading, "panzer grenadier" or even "panzer" would be more accurate. Given the normal attachments of GHQ tank or tank destroyer battalions, the average U.S. infantry division held more armored fighting vehicles than the average German armored division. The abundance of GHQ battalions again resulted in semipermanent groupings available to a resourceful division commander for creative battle groups or combat teams. Canadian and British infantry formations enjoyed no such luxury.

Armored Pursuit

Tanks are weapons of terror and when they get behind German lines they create chaos.
            —Col. Bruce C. Clarke, HQ CC A, U.S. 4th Armored Division

They should be launched boldly against vital areas deep in the hostile rear. There must be no relaxing of pressure on the shaken or beaten enemy.
—FM 17-10 *Armored Force Field Manual,* 1942

In a command in the field which does not have a professional reconnaissance, the movement in a given direction is habitually a blind groping, or halting at a given place because of ignorance of the tactical situation.
—Lt. Col. Charles J. Hoy, U.S. 1st Armored Division

To be accurate, Bradley did not break into Kluge's operational rear, he penetrated the strategic flank of a German army group. There were no headquarters, gun lines, or reserves to destroy, but there were logistic areas, communication centers, and propaganda prizes. Isolating the U-boat ports in Brittany and Biscay was more a psychological victory: the bases were simply invested, yet their operations continued while tying down Allied besieging troops. There were few purely military prizes available, because the preponderance of German troops were at the Normandy front and were either initially overrun by Cobra or about to be trapped in the Falaise Pocket.

Cobra did not scatter German divisions before it, nor did it intercept operational reserves; again, these were already at the front or headed to Chambois. There were no tank battles of note other than in the immediate pocket area.[15] However, seeking out enemy operational reserves is not the only goal of an armored force. Montgomery had been presented two strategic objectives, but now it was Bradley's, and particularly Patton's, show: "Georgie was a character that would take chances. He would command by mission-type orders. The people that he had confidence in—he just told them what he wanted to do, and then he left them alone . . . he was the smartest general that we had there."[16]

Pursuit relies on three major aspects. The first is armored reconnaissance (supported by air) to find the enemy armored force, to determine the suitability of routes or crossing sites, and, especially, to maintain the panic by overrunning headquarters or centers of communication. The second is the armored battle group (also supported by tactical air) composed of armored infantry, armored engineers, and self-propelled artillery. These *groupements tactiques* are the heart of the pursuit. However, it is armor that creates and maintains the real momentum and panic. The presence of an armored force on vital ground will make the enemy's operational position untenable. Key terrain continually changes as the advance, like a riptide, floods the enemy rear. The third and final aspect consists of the signals and supply columns vital to any armored advance.

The pursuit is, in the main, problem solving at all levels and requires

American Armored Divisions during Operation Cobra: 25 July-25 August 44

2d Armored Div "Hell on Wheels"
MajGen E.N. Harmon

1/41
2/41
3/41

1/66
2/66
3/66

1/67
2/67
3/67

4x SP/Hev Arty Bns

Corps Affiliations
V Corps 12 June
VII Corps 18 July
XIX Corps 2 August
VII Corps 7 August
XIX Corps 13 August
V Corps 18 August
XIX Corps 19 August
XV Corps 21 August
XIX Corps 29 August

3d Armored Div "Spearhead"
MajGen L.H. Watson
MajGen M. Rose

1/32 1/36
2/32 2/36
3/32 3/36

1/33
2/33
3/33

4x SP/Hev Arty Bns

Corps Affiliations
VII Corps July - August

4th Armored Div "Breakthrough"
MajGen J.S. Wood

8 10
35 51
37 50

3x SP Arty Bns

Corps Affiliations
VII Corps 15 July
XII Corps 13 August

5th Armored Div "V for Victory"
MajGen L.E. Oliver

10 15
34 46
81 47

3x SP Arty Bns

Corps Affiliations
XV Corps 31 July
V Corps 29 August

6th Armored Div "Super Sixth"
MajGen R.W. Grow

15 9
68 44
69 50

3x SP Arty Bns

Corps Affiliations
VII Corps July - August

7th Armored Div "Lucky Seventh"
MajGen L.McD. Silvester

17 23
31 38
40 48

3x SP Arty Bns

Corps Affiliations
XX Corps July - August

2e Div Blinde Française
MajGen J.P. Leclerc

12e Cuirassiers
12e Chas d'Afrique
501e RCC

3x SP Arty Bns

Corps Affiliations
XV Corps August

2d and 3d US Armd were "Heavy Armored Divisions", each with 2x Armored Regiments (6x Armored Battalions); 1 Armd Inf Regt. Regular Armd Divs had 3x self-propelled Artillery Battalions. 2d and 3d had 4x Artillery Battalions. LeClerc's 2d Fr Armd was equipped/organised as a US Armd Div.

Paris
2 Fr
4
German Armies
Falaise
1 Pol
4 Cdn
Vernian
3
5
2
7
2 Fr
5
3
7
2
4
6
6
6

competent, quick-thinking staff work. The best contingency planners are regularly overtaken by events. A typical example was Combat Command A in the 4th Armored Division. Colonel Clarke organized

> two mutually supporting Armd columns, each consisting of tank and armored infantry companies, engineers and artillery support. . . . Do not mop up as you go! . . . By noon I was 40 km down the road . . . I was to by pass Rennes and move on to Lorient . . . very low on gasoline. Almost two days elapsed before POL [petrol, oil, and lubrication] arrived from the rear. . . . If we could not defeat any opposition we might run into, we could at least out-maneuver, if not out run them. . . . No instructions or SOPs had been formulated. My solution came about when we were confronted with numbers greater than I had anticipated. Although it was obvious to me that unarmed German soldiers were being turned loose in the French country side, I had assumed that other divisions and corps troops would follow up my advance closely enough to apprehend and care for them. This apparently was not the case. The speed of the advance of my Combat Command was apparently not considered possible by my commanders.[17]

Reconnaissance

The aim of reconnaissance—information—provided at times an embarrassment of riches for Allied commanders. SHAEF's G2 section was blessed with a cornucopia of data flooding in from air reconnaissance, an enthusiastic French Resistance, eager deserters, and acme intelligence gathering, Ultra. Eavesdropping on German High Command communications and battlefield orders was an awkward blessing because Ultra intelligence recipients could not let on to the Germans how much they really knew: "To protect the Ultra source, Bradley and Patton, like their colleagues, used the full spectrum of their intelligence assets. Patton required his reconnaissance forces not only to secure information aggressively but also to protect the intelligence information secured."[18]

As the U.S. Third Army broke into Model's rear areas it entered the domain of Gen. Kurt von der Chevallerie, commander of the German First Army who was tasked by commander in chief, West, to defend the Orléans gap, 60 miles of open tank country.[19] Chevallerie could not conduct a proper covering-force battle, indeed he could barely manage an effective screen. Nevertheless, he displayed remarkable resourcefulness in the face of four armored divisions, a sky full of Thunderbolts, Typhoons, and Mustangs, and spunky cavalry scouts on the ground.

> The Third Army's indigenous cavalry groups and squadrons (mechanized) scoured the front, identifying von der Chevallerie's second delaying position . . . aggressive reconnaissance was in the finest traditions of the cavalry and air corps. . . . Von der Chevallerie's security screen based on

strong points held up the U.S. Army for two days. On the afternoon of 22
August, von der Chevallerie instructed his garrisons to withdraw behind
the Seine . . . each German combat group crossed the river, German engineers blew up the bridges.[20]

Chevallerie's success, while commendable, was aided by Bradley's
conservative tactics and the operational magnet of the Falaise pocket. The
actual armor pursuit from Avranches to Rennes to Chartres and, finally, the
Seine and Paris was initially conducted by the U.S. 6th and 4th Armored
Divisions; although they were augmented by U.S. 7th and French 2d
Armored Divisions for the home stretch to the Ile-de-France, the main tasks
fell to bold division and task force commanders. Before them were a handful of reconnaissance troops.

Forward reconnaissance was particularly dangerous in a U.S. armored
division. Unlike their British and Canadian counterparts, the cavalry reconnaissance squadrons (the size of a Canadian armored regiment) were mainly equipped with armored cars, not main battle tanks. The armor they did
have (Stuart light tanks) were not capable of fighting for information
against a rear guard supported by even one Stug or Jagdpanzer: "Recon was
constantly sniped, bridge recon tasks were particularly difficult . . . [there
were] seriously wounded troopers . . . [and] fire fights with small rear
guards while searching."[21]

Reconnaissance tactics were generally dismounted in order to use best
cover. German rear guards were routinely small, "less than a company, with
an inordinately high proportion of bazookas . . . covered by a single 88 or
single tank approx. 1000m rear or flank rear."[22] The "recon" units were
often not pleased with the supporting mechanized infantry either: "Co of
50th Armd Inf Bn which was with the adv guard was slow to dismount
from their half-tracks and still slower to bring up their mortars."

U.S. armored doctrine permitted two types of reconnaissance, close
and battle.[23] Distant reconnaissance was best performed by aircraft. Close
reconnaissance was conducted well in front of a division's advance axis.
Battle reconnaissance was performed in front of the vanguard or flank
guard. The job was demanding, requiring detailed reports on bridges and
road conditions, as well as locations of enemy rear guards that could delay
the advancing tank columns: "Obtain all possible information concerning
routes and hostile dispositions within a specified area, necessary for the
Divisional Commander to formulate a plan of action and issue necessary
preliminary orders."[24]

When battle reconnaissance encounters enemy rear guards, it is
required to *piquet* the enemy and bypass him to provide timely and accurate
information of what is ahead with "detailed reconnaissance of terrain and
hostile dispositions—frequently dismounted."[25] The first lesson learned by

cavalry reconnaissance troops attached to vanguards was that it was "important for [supporting] infantry to dismount right away, [and] bring up mortars, otherwise the delay is twice as long."[26] The composition of forward reconnaissance was most hotly debated in the units. There were two schools of thought: "sneak and peek" versus "fight for information."[27] Doctrinal opinion held that it was better to be wily: "The armored cavalry regiment (light) is the most mobile of armored units. It lacks the heavy gun firepower of tanks or the armored division."[28]

All U.S. nondivisional mechanized cavalry regiments were restructured in 1944 to form separate reconnaissance groups and squadrons. Each cavalry group comprised a headquarters and headquarters troop and two or more attached mechanized cavalry reconnaissance squadrons. If they were part of an armored division, cavalry reconnaissance squadrons were equipped with fifty-two M8 armored cars, seventeen M3 Stuart light tanks and thirty-two M3A1 half-tracks, augmented by eight 75mm self-propelled howitzers on M3 "motorized gun carriages."[29]

The tactical mix for a reconnaissance squadron in the pursuit varied according to the tactical commander's *Fingerspitzengefühl* and personal style:

> Beware of that misused word "firepower." Don't tie a reconnaissance unit down with tanks, 81mm mortars, SP guns, because it makes the unit too unwieldy. . . . Understand me, I am in complete accord with General Scott's statement that "Reconnaissance capable only of observation is not worth the road space it takes." The recon unit should have sufficient firepower, but too much is as bad as too little.[30]

Aggressive reconnaissance was in the U.S. Cavalry's blood but brought best results when correctly grouped for conditions: "We felt much more confident after the replacement of the M5 (Stuart) light tank by the M24 (Chaffee)."[31]

The correct employment of reconnaissance must, above all, reflect the intent of the commander. Since the Allied leadership did not exhibit a forte for maneuver warfare, the operational evolution of the strategic offensive was very much uncontrolled and left to dynamic division commanders. Unless their bosses had cavalry experience, too many reconnaissance units were regularly assigned liaison and rear-area security duties or relegated to the flanks.[32] But once the Falaise pocket was closed, the Allied squadrons were set loose like a pack of fox hounds. "Good squadron leaders are a Master of the Hunt—must also lead from the front—you can't control things by sitting in an HQ looking at a map."[33] They crossed the Seine and raced across northern France running down withdrawing German columns.

Mad, sunny days, tearing down the *route nationales*—as we came to the end of a map, we flung it out over our shoulders—they were British overprints of rather dated French *cartes rouges*. Most enemy contacts were small rearguards near bridges or some sort of mine or tank ambush—normally from the rear. Single tanks—assault guns or Mark IVs, rarely Tigers or Panthers—they'd allow the lead cars to go by then engage the troop leader or main body. We always sent the heavy car[s] first in case of mines—they could withstand the explosion. We were instructed by division not to fire MGs as much as we did—burned up too much ammunition, the A echelons could not keep up.[34]

U.S., British, and Canadian reconnaissance was given but one opportunity in World War II to conduct traditional cavalry operations and this was the post-Cobra "mad dash across France."[35]

Armor-Infantry Cooperation in Pursuit

The armored division should be given and should use mission type orders.
It is unrealistic for the corps commander to assume that he can visualize
the circumstances in which the armored division will find itself three days
hence and one hundred miles behind enemy lines.
               —Lt. Col. Creighton W. Abrams, 4th Armored Division[36]

During the pursuit the U.S. armored infantry, in the manner of panzer grenadiers, remained mounted as long as it could and relied on the firepower of its half-tracks' .50-caliber heavy machine guns to clear away rear guards or overwhelm strongpoints. This made sense since their armored personnel carriers gave them protection, but this technique was not popular with the tanks they supported who lived in dread of the Panzerfaust: "Mech infantry often refused to dismount when ordered by local OC if their own officer was not in the half-track—they preferred to stay instead of searching hedgerows . . . instead they crouched in their track and sprayed the hedges with MG."[37]

Vanguards reported constant German rear-guard action, but this mostly meant snipers. Church steeples were immediately engaged and destroyed to prevent their use by German artillery spotters. This was known as speculative fire in the British and Canadian armored regiments and sometimes referred to as prophylactic fire by U.S. tankers. "Brassing up the area" became a normal procedure as vanguards approached villages or areas of likely ambush. The tank's complaints about the mechanized infantry were returned in kind:

Martin, company commander, never had any contact with Capt Mead, commanding the medium tank company and his efforts to get individual tank commanders to support his men moving against the enemy were all failures. The tank commanders said they were waiting for orders from their platoon leader.[38]

U.S. infantry battalions experienced much the same problems in getting infantry tanks to lead as did Canadian units. Once armor was grouped under the command of reconnaissance or infantry, it tended to behave more conservatively:

> At Lananneyen the tanks wouldn't move until the inf knocked out the [antitank] guns. Inf were constantly ahead of tanks; tks didn't do much firing . . . said they were getting fire. Inf was widely deployed and after they'd cleared out resistance on flanks tanks just rolled up road. Tankers kept all the liquor captured—5 cases of it; they got it first.[39]

The combat command system permitted quick custom-tailoring for the advance. On 1 August, the U.S. 6th Armored Division was divided into three pursuit combat commands. General Grow's tactical matrix ensured that each combat command had a specific balance of tanks, mechanized infantry, tank destroyers, armored engineers, air defense artillery, and self-propelled artillery to reflect his maneuver requirements as shown in Table 11.1.

Table 11.1   6th Armored Division Organized for the Pursuit, 1 August 1944

Leading Reserve Command	CC A	CC B	Artillery Command
86th Cav. Sqdn.			
9th Inf. Bn. Recon.	44th Inf. Bn.	50th Inf. Bn.	C Btry. 965th Fld. Arty.
15th Tank Bn.	68th Tank Bn.	69th Tank Bn.	Bn. (155)
B Co., 603d TD Bn.	603d TD Bn.	C Co., 603d TD Bn.	174th Fld. Arty. Bn. (155)
C Co., 25th Eng. Bn.	B Co., 25th Eng. Bn.	25th Eng. Bn.	83d Fld. Arty. Bn. (105)
C Bty, 777th AA Bn.	B Bty 777th AA Bn.		
234th Fld. Arty. Bn. (105)	212d Fld. Arty. Bn. (105)	128th Fld. Arty. Bn. (105)	
83d Fld. Arty. Bn.			

Note: Two Cub aircraft were assigned to each combat command and an additional two to division artillery command.

Grow adopted two columns because he was given two good roads. Grow could further divide his combat commands into "task forces," the equivalent of heavy infantry or heavy armor battle groups (see Table 11.2). Grow's cavalry background prepared him well to quickly adjust to a situation much different from previous Cobra operations: "The Brittany cam-

paign of the 6th was unique in that it was an extensive exploitation by a
single unsupported armored division."[40]

Cobra's "mailed fist" was the heavy 2d and 3d Armored Divisions
(Maj. Gen. Edward H. Brooks and Leroy H. Watson) with six tank battalions apiece.[41] They conducted the bulk of the dogfight that allowed Bradley
to batter through German rear guards and loose Grow and Wood into the
green fields beyond. Their tactical grouping varied considerably. Heavy
combat commands were subdivided into task forces permitting attacks
along as many as four axes and still keeping a considerable reserve for
maneuver:

> The successful application of the principle of teamwork to the employ-
> ment of armor in the ground team requires the assignment of objectives
> and missions which will utilize to the maximum the distinguishing char-
> acteristic of armor. This applies with equal importance to tank units
> organic or attached to infantry divisions, the armored cavalry regiment
> (light) and the armored division.[42]

Table 11.2   Heavy Armored Division Groupings, Circa August 1944

CC A		CC B		CC R		Artillery Command
TF 1	*TF 2*	*TF 1*	*TF 2*	*TF 1*	*TF 2*	
Tank Bn.	Tank Bn.	Tank Bn.	Tank Co.	Tank Bn.	Tk Bn.	Fld. Arty. Bn. (155)
Tank Bn.						Fld. Arty. Bn. (155)
TD Co.	TD Co.	TD Co.	TD Co.	TD Co.	TD Co.	
Inf. Bn.	Inf. Co.	Inf. Co.	Inf. Bn.	Inf. Co.	Inf. Bn.	
Eng. Pl.	Eng. Pl.	Eng. Pl.	Eng. Pl.	Eng. Pl.	Eng. Pl.	
AAA Pl.	AAA Pl.	AAA Pl.	AAA Pl.	AAA Pl.	AAA Pl.	
Fld. Arty.		Fld. Arty.		Fld. Arty.		Fld. Arty.
Bn.		Bn.		Bn.		Bn.

Two Cub aircraft were assigned to each combat command and an additional two to division artillery command.

Command and Control: Signals

Pursuit operations move quickly and totally depend on communications.
The division pursuit commander directs operations by radio and must be
able to control both forward arms and rear services. Cobra soon unveiled
interesting problems. The mechanized infantry battalions began to demand
trailers for radios: "299s [radio model] won't go into half-tracks and armor
protection is very valuable for armored sigs."[43] The U.S. 6th Armored
Division reversed the prescribed system of laying wire: "at each C Comd
was a track 299 to keep in touch with Div and speed wire, the construction
teams travelled with the C Comds . . . wire was started to the rear—a place
they knew—while the 299 radio kept interim contact."[44]

Maintaining contact with Corps and Army was a challenge: "Corps told 6 AD to 'wait' incessantly due to jam up . . . acceptance of urgent traffic only."[45] Since often both corps and division headquarters were on the move, armored division HQs absorbed little of corps radio communication.[46] Because conservative-operation directives increasingly frustrated Patton, he took advantage of communication difficulties and demonstrated a duplicitous creativity: when the 6th Armored Division was held back by General Middleton and ordered to remain near Brest and Lorient, Patton visited Grow and told him to "slip a combat command west along the Loire. . . . Patton directed the operation, not VII Corps."[47]

Security was precarious, resulting in adventurous solutions: radio silence was lifted during the breakout even though increasingly less wire was used: "Corps teletype was avail—operated on VHF and high power radio." Armored signals were required well forward and regularly engaged in firefights with German rear guards, and risked being overrun by determined counterattacks. This would create serious problems if an Ultra unit was forward. "Several signal men stayed with the electric code machines to destroy them with self contained thermite canisters. Msg sent: 'CP under attack; codes in danger—may destroy' sent in clear to Corps via 299."[48] The pace of advance forced signal units to use captured German equipment, particularly cable and switchboards that could be integrated into U.S. radio nets: "We never used German radios—[they were] usually damaged, low powered and had bad antennas."[49]

Tactical Air Force and Artillery

As the armored divisions advanced, normally on parallel routes, each column was protected by a standing patrol of three to four P-47s flying CAP, or combat air patrol. (Patton's tanks carried fluorescent marking panels on their back decks to identify their forward units.) Each combat command had air controllers in constant communication with the fighters and fighter-bombers. It required about two hours to order a complete air strike on a stubborn German rear guard or threatening column.

> So swift was the pace of the Patton advance that most of the emphasis during this period was on Tactical [air] Reconnaissance. Aerial photographs became out of date almost as soon as they were made, with the result that there was comparatively little need for photo recce . . . 432 tactical recce missions versus 81 photo recce.[50]

Self-propelled artillery moved with the vanguard. At minimum, a battery was always deployed well forward ready to engage and the last to leave because requests for fire continued until last the moment: "Tanks aren't much at indirect fire and Germans would pick places where they couldn't be got at with direct fire."[51] The pursuit taught that artillery could not fight effectively unless it used its airborne observers. Artillery officers leapfrogged ahead in Cub L-40 liaison aircraft; each battalion had two L-40s, headquarters also had two. The aircraft were jealously guarded: "When the arty bn changes from one CC [combat command] to another, the planes go with it."[52] Although the demise of the Luftwaffe was regularly reported, U.S. Third Army columns moving south of Mortain were frequently attacked: "GAF [German air force] FGA sorties, pilots were shot down, captured. Ln pilot for 212 FA shot down 5 Aug by 6 ME 210s."[53] As the distances increased, army-air cooperation achieved high standards:

> I particularly noticed the cooperation of armor, especially tank spear-heads, with the air force. . . . The tanks were guided by aircraft over the Soulles brook. . . . On 27 and 28 Jul 44, artillery fire ceased completely and was replaced by bombing and strafing attacks. . . . The fighter-bombers were in action over the main attack sector without a minute's interruption.[54]

Forward air controllers (FACs) complained they could not keep up with the tanks' cross-country maneuver, and when the FACs did arrive they were exposed to enemy fire and not able to go forward to coordinate effective strikes. When General Quesada was offered Shermans for his FACs, he accepted readily: "I told Medaris [Bradley's G4] to deliver two tanks at once."[55] Army artillery spotters, USAAC reconnaissance, and P-47 pilots on continuous fighter ground attack (FGA) overwatch, provided the most intimate support of ground operations yet seen.[56] Wood's 4th Armored Division immediately took full advantage of their armored FACs and sent them forward with each vanguard to call down all the support strikes requested. After reaching the Seine, Wood sent the U.S. XIX Tactical Air Force two cases of cognac.[57]

Logistics

We learned the best way to handle control was by means of a large chart. Top was divided into 24 hours of day (showing minutes). On the left side we listed names of important crossroads on principal traffic routes. Convoys had to report the time length of the column, rate of speed and time to reach the crossroads . . . using different colored pencils for each day, it was possible to plot clearance for several days in advance. But we also learned we needed a close fast working arrangement with the Provost Marshal's office so that MP's were at key points.
—Lt. Gen. A. C. Gillem, commander, U.S. XIII Corps

The armored division lived on oil and gasoline.[58] Fighting divisions were supported by their supply "trains." Perhaps the real hero of the encir-clement at Falaise was the 2.5-ton M32 "6x6" truck. Standard procedures that worked in the battle of the Normandy bridgehead had to be revised in the battle of the pursuit. The divisional staffs struggled with two major logistics headaches: resupply and security problems. The first schools for the ordnance system in support of U.S. armor were the Louisiana and Carolina maneuvers of 1941; the next major series of armored support "lessons learned" took place in France after 27 July 1944. Staffs were taught that existing tables of organization and equipment had to be augmented with extra men and twice the number of vehicles:

a. Div dumps must be established when Army installations are not in close support.
b. All avail pers must be used regardless of T/O assignments to accomplish successful resupply.
c. Armd Div requires a minimum of twice the number of Quarter Master Truck Cos and Gas Supply Cos for extended operations.
d. Time must be allotted for efficient installation of Div dumps.[59]

Flexibility and invention was the cardinal requirement for the service echelon of an armored division attempting to exploit a breakthrough. The U.S. Third Army introduced a "rolling ammunition depot on 5 truck companies." Eventually the ammunition resupply problem grew so acute that "Bradley ordered all 8 inch and 240mm artillery battalions grounded."[60] The movement and support of armor demanded experienced armored officers, particularly at the corps staff levels, as the Canadians had already discovered.[61]

Grouping is vital to the successful formula for rapid exploitation. The Americans' experience in Cobra demonstrated that reconnaissance units require main battle tanks and close air support (at least air reconnaissance) and should be grouped with mechanized infantry with which they have developed a common operational doctrine. Ad hoc grouping proved a failure in Allied formations. Units, even from the same division, that had not developed a mutual trust were not as effective as units that were friends. The answer of course was an effective, tried, and well-understood common doctrine.[62] German success with *Kampfgruppen* could not rely on the regular grouping of units yet worked splendidly in battle. Perhaps the real difference between Allied and German doctrine was more cultural than technical.

Notes

1. ETHINT 67, p. 4.
2. CMH 319.7 Special Studies—The Lorraine Campaign by General R. W. Grow, MHI.
3. "Much to the dismay of the TD Bn Comd these weapons were just farmed out indiscriminately to combat commands and the integrity of the battalion was

completely destroyed." NAC. Maj. Gen. White Papers. Maj. Gen. Isaac D. White was commander, 2d Armored Division.

4. Harmon Papers. Maj. Gen. Ernest N. Harmon was commander, 1st Armored (April 1943–July 1944) and 2nd Armored Division (July 1942–May 1943).

5. "The regiment is a buzz saw and the combat platoons are the teeth along its outer edge." Sidney T. Mathews Collection. "Small Unit Actions." MHI. See also FM 17-36 *Employment of Tanks with Infantry,* U.S. Armor School, 7 February 1944, pp. 46–49, and FM 17-33 *The Tank Battalion.* U.S. armor was not respected: "The enemy tanks are timid," 2SS Das Reich report Combat in Bocage Country. RG14186: Apx G to Armored Bulletin No. 5. Feb 45.

6. German attacks comprised "small assault groups, close cooperation between tanks, pz grenadiers, Pz Engineers and artillery . . . 2 PzGren Regiments leading, 2 tank companies to support the infantry . . . in an assault gun role." 2SS Das Reich.

7. Although Panzer Lehr did have a company of King Tigers, they were beset with so many mechanical problems that they were simply abandoned or destroyed in the retreat to Falaise.

8. The French 2d Armored Division was organized the same as U.S. Armored Divisions. Report on French 2d Armored Division, 1 July 1944. Philipsborn Papers, MHI.

9. "All of them were used in the 4th Armored Division in the same way. They had basically been taught to fight as Combined Arms Combat teams, and it always had a Reserve Command." BCC Diary, interview by Francis B. Kish, vol. II, MHI.

10. Harmon Papers, MHI. Harmon also noted: "I have often divided my division into three, sometimes four columns."

11. Major General Harmon, quoted by Lt. Col. W. D. Smart: "Armored Divisions' Combat Commands," *Cavalry Journal* LV (January–February 1946).

12. Ibid.

13. "The Liberation of Orleans," Clarke Papers, MHI.

14. Wood to Liddel Hart, p. 557.

15. Although most German units in Brittany were low-level infantry formations, spirited actions were fought, particularly with Grow's 6th Armored, but never enough to give Bradley pause.

16. BCC Papers.

17. Gen. Bruce C. Clarke: "Handling of Prisoners during a Deep Penetration into Enemy Territory by Armor," BCC Diary, MHI. The German army reported to the Red Cross in Geneva that Clarke had refused to accept surrender of German prisoners of war. Bradley was instructed to investigate.

18. Samuel J. Lewis, "Reconnaissance—Fighting on the Upper Seine River, August 1944," in R. J. Spiller, ed., *Combined Arms in Battle Since 1939* (Fort Leavenworth: U.S. Army Command and General Staff College Press, 1992), p. 214.

19. Chevallerie's command comprised "two badly battered divisions from Norway . . . still west of Paris . . . two weak SS replacement brigades . . . and the 48th Infantry Division." None of these units was in the area save for 1010 Security Regiment and the German First Army's reconnaissance company "consisting of twelve obsolete and road bound French armored cars." Lewis, p. 215.

20. Lewis, pp. 216–218.

21. Lt. Col. A. E. Harris, 86th Reconnaissance Squadron, MHI.

22. Company-size rear guards occurred more regularly as U.S. armor approached Lorraine and Germany. Reconnaissance missions approaching the

Falaise gap would often meet small decoy rear guards. If any of these was attacked, the supporting battle group would unmask and engage the reconnaissance unit.

23. There were three types of U.S. reconnaissance: "*Distant Reconnaissance . . . [that]* depends largely on the efficacy of air observation . . . *Close Recon . . .* concern[ed with] terrain, routes and hostile dispositions within a specified area . . . *Battle Recon . . .* when a division is committed to combat . . . it prepares plans to initiate pursuit, generally by encircling maneuver." Maj. I. D. White, "Reconnaissance Battalion, Armored Division," *Armored Cavalry Journal,* reprinted in *Armor* (June 1985): 24. The British/Canadian version reconnaissance is: "Distant," "medium," and "close" recce. The missions included (1) locating hostile flanks and rear; (2) maintaining observation; (3) performing harassing operations against hostile command and supply installations; and (4) preparing plans to initiate pursuit, generally by encircling maneuver.

24. White, "Reconnaissance Battalion, Armored Division."

25. Ibid.

26. 86th Recon After Action Report, August 1944, MHI.

27. Lt. Col. B. P. Palmer Jr.: "New Battle Lessons on Reconnaissance," *Armor* (1944).

28. Abrams, BCC Papers, MHI.

29. Nondivisional squadrons held forty M8s, seventeen light tanks, twenty-six half-tracks, and six 75mm self-propelled howitzers. Stanton, p. 23.

30. Lt. Col. Hoy, quoted in Palmer Jr.: "New Battle Lessons on Reconnaissance."

31. Gillem Papers, MHI.

32. General Grow refused to task his "Cavalry Squadron . . . with liaison duties." Grow Papers, MHI.

33. Interviews with Lt. Col. W. C. Bowen, Huntingdon QC, 1990, p. 92.

34. Bowen 1990. See also Pavey, pp. 45–48.

35. Maj. William "Bill" Bowen's A Squadron, 17th Duke of York's Royal Canadian Hussars, invested the fortress of Calais days before the Canadian 3d Infantry Division arrived. Bowen tried to bluff a surrender from the German garrison commander, who advised Bowen to get out before he turned his heavy guns on him. Bowen's reply was: "I've been thrown out of better places than this." Interviews with Lt. Col. W. C. Bowen. See Pavey, p. 48, and Stacey, p. 345.

36. Lt. Col. Creighton W. Abrams. "Armor in the Team," *Armor* (1944).

37. 6th Armored Division Files. "After Action Reports 44–45." Hofmann Collection.

38. B Company, 9th Armored Infantry Battalion. Action at Lananneyen, MHI.

39. Report Maj. Godfrey, commander, 9th Armored Infantry Battalion, 27 August, MHI.

40. George F. Hofmann, *The Super Sixth* (Louisville: Sixth Armored Division Association, 1975), p. 98.

41. Replaced by Maj. Gen. Maurice Rose on 12 August 1944.

42. Abrams, "Armor in the Team."

43. Grow Papers. Correspondence with Lt. Col. William Given, 6th Armored Signals Division officer. 12 January 1952.

44. Given. Correspondence with Grow, 12 January 1952.

45. "Corps didn't know our location . . . radios failed on 3 Aug . . . the 3rd Aug '*stop*' order was a hand written note." Hofmann Collection. Grow Papers: unit history correspondence Grow-D.F. McCormack. 10 January 1949 (hereafter McCormack).

46. "About 20 messages were lost . . . imp messages were sent by two separate

message vehicles . . . we used Cubs as far as possible. . . . I sent Gen Spang (German PW) back with an armored car platoon." McCormack, 10 January 1949.

47. Ibid.

48. Ibid., 12 January 1952.

49. Forward unit headquarters quickly ran out of essentials to fight the paper war. "By mid August many 6th Armd Div messages and reports were written on the back of German HQ files: After Action reports are being written on captured German HQ documents and Leave passes!" Maj. C. E. Rousek Jr. Papers, MHI.

50. "Reconnaissance in a Tactical Air Command," XIX Tactical Air Force, 13 February 1945. Edwards Papers.

51. McCormack.

52. The Cub's maximum range was 120 miles with three and a half hours' endurance. During the Cobra pursuit the 6th Armored Division artillery lost six Cubs ("3 crack ups, 3 lost to enemy action"). Two pilots were killed. *6 Armd Div Report* G3 Div Arty. Maj. Crawford and Div Arty Air Officer, Capt. Peck. Grow Papers, MHI.

53. The 6th Armored Division way diary records three forward ground attacks on artillery reconnaissance aircraft between 29 July and 31 August 1944. A penciled note was added to the report of the downed artillery liaison pilot, Lieutenant Bloomberg: "Bloomberg thinks it was Mosquitos chasing Me 109s." 6 Armd Div After Action Reports: 6th AD Bty, Grow Papers, MHI.

54. ETHINT 67. Bayerlein, p. 12.

55. Bradley Papers, MHI.

56. "Pilot called the column and told them there were tanks up ahead. Fellow on the ground said, 'Hell, they're ours.' Pilot: 'No, they're Tigers.' Ground: 'Hell they are.' Pause. 'Goddamit, they're Tigers.' And they were." Hanson Papers. 23-b, MHI.

57. Gen. O. P. Weyland, commander, Tactical Air Force, quoted in Carr.

58. "Because of a lack of gasoline supply in sufficient quantity for offensive operations, the division was restrained to holding bridgeheads on the Meuse. . . . During the period 1 September through 10 Sept the 25th Cavalry was permitted to continue its patrolling by the expedient of draining gasoline from other vehicles of the division." AG 319.1. After Action Report Sept/Oct 1944. 4th Armored Division Papers. MHI.

59. NAC Report C1-279: "Operations of 6th Armd Div Trains During the Brittany Campaign. 26 Aug 44." Some staff officers felt there were too many small and medium "utility" and liaison vehicles in the armored division that consumed gasoline better left to tanks and trucks: "We have what I call too many '*road lice*' in various elements of the division." Gillem Papers. MHI.

60. Hansen Diary. 37-B, S-1.

61. "Ridgeway was an Airborne fellow. Airborne had no equipment except what they carried themselves, so they didn't have to maintain their equipment. And, when he issued a silly order . . . at St. Vith, I said to him, 'General, I've been fighting for five days now and I have very little gasoline, ammunition or rations. I'm just about out so I can't last much longer.' He said, 'That's a problem for you damn Armored people,' and just walked away and left me. Now, there was the Corps Commander. He had no concept of logistics at all." BCC Papers, MHI.

62. "The revolution [was] wrought by Abrams and others in the field when they made up what was to become the armored forces that rolled across Europe. They had not been taught this, they invented it." BCC Papers, MHI.

CHAPTER 12

Patton's Lieutenants in Lorraine: A Maturation of Maneuver Warfare

Only the 4th Armored Division met German armor in a situation that could be termed a tank vs. tank battle. This happened in September 44 when the Fifth Panzer Armee attempted a major counterattack.
—Maj. Gen. R. W. Grow[1]

The accomplishments of this Division have never been equaled . . . and by this statement I do not mean this war, I mean in the history of warfare.
—Gen. George S. Patton[2]

If the pursuit from Avranches confirmed the U.S. Army Air Corps operational skills, the Lorraine campaign was U.S. armor's tactical test. After Cobra's finale, the ensuing advance was no less spectacular than the dynamic breakout that resulted in victory at Falaise and the capture of Paris. Nonetheless, Montgomery's 21st Army Group collected the greater laurels as British and Canadian armored divisions raced across France netting V-1 rocket launching sites, investing the fortresses at Calais, and liberating Flanders. General Horrocks's XXX Corps charged into Brussels and then captured the greatest prize of all, the port of Antwerp. Despite Horrocks's splendid pursuit, the British Second Army was brought to a halt facing the Nijmegen and Rhine obstacles in Holland. Montgomery had convinced Eisenhower to divert a lion's share of Allied fuel resources to the British lion. He bamboozled Eisenhower into accepting his argument for a Canadian clearing of terror weapon launching sites and a gathering of a mighty British scrum to ruck into the Ruhr, the industrial heartland of the Reich. The supreme commander caved into British political pressure and committed "the most momentous error of the war."[3] London was being attacked by the "buzz bombs," but Eisenhower ignored the hard facts that by late August the British had nullified the threat with radar directed anti-aircraft fire and fast interceptors. The odds of a V-1 reaching London dropped to virtually nil; whatever got through was strictly of nuisance value. The Allies' greatest strategic enemies were supply and time. Although landings in southern France opened up more ports, the supply situation remained critical. The issue was petrol, and Eisenhower gave it to 21st Army Group.[4] Montgomery responded by not opening the port facilities of Antwerp, not crossing the Rhine and doing his best to annihilate SHAEF's strategic airborne force by dumping three parachute divisions into Arnhem in the disastrous Operation Market Garden. Given Montgomery's catalog of operational foul-ups, pompous self-patronage, and snippy attitude, the Eisenhower's sustained faith and forgiveness were both saintly and militarily naive. His careful nurturing of British political sensitivities delayed both operational and strategic victory. Eisenhower's sudden flirtation with the strategy of annihilation would not come to fruition:

> If with such a share of the available support, any general could have dealt the Germans a knockout blow, the man to do it was not Montgomery. He squandered Eisenhower's logistic generosity in listless failure and then he blamed Eisenhower for the failures implicit in the whole logistical situation and aggravated by his own insufficiently aggressive generalship.[5]

The Siegfried Line and the mighty Rhine remained in German hands. Hodges's army was directed into the Ardennes, encountering slow going despite the absence of major German tank formations: a couple of optimistic thrusts into the Schnee Eiffel and the Wallendorf area were met with defiance. Patton, however, inherited the route with the most potential. He promptly took up the pursuit with Maj. Gen. Manton Eddy's XII Corps and Maj. Gen. Walton H. Walker's XX Corps: "One quarter of the [Third] Army was not available due to casualties and maintenance."[6] The province of Lorraine, the Paris-Metz-Frankfurt corridor, was the best approach to the industrial core of Germany. Patton soon made impressive gains, threatening to cross the Rhine before Dempsey could. Montgomery then decided he would steal no more headlines: Patton's tanks were placed on starvation diets.[7]

Nonetheless, after a dizzying pursuit of 500 miles in twenty-six days, Walker's XX Corps found itself on the Moselle River facing the fortress of Metz. First constructed during the seventeenth century by Vauban, it had been progressively modernized by Napoleon, Napoleon III, and, after 1870, Kaiser Wilhelm I. The French called Metz "La Pucelle" (the nickname for Joan of Arc) for it had never been defiled by an attacker. The most recent additions had been part of an attempt to integrate it with the Maginot Line. Confronted with twenty-six forts, many of them equivalent to two-level underground shopping malls capable of withstanding direct hits from the heaviest artillery, Patton was suddenly faced with the terrible alternative all cavalry officers dread—fixed fortifications and attrition warfare. "Metz was important to our strategical, tactical and logistic operations. Its importance lay in the road and rail net, and from a psychological viewpoint, its historical and political significance."[8] Patton did a rather uncavalry-like thing: he ordered Walker to attack. Although the best maps available were prewar Michelins maps, he was armed with current data from the Deuxième Bureau (the French Secret Service) and his own personal experience from the Great War. He was quite familiar with the area, and he ought to have known better than to attack the fortress complex. Patton was diverted from his aim of the Rhine to a prestigious but secondary objective.

Patton had shelved his own maneuver plan even though a wider envelopment would have trapped large numbers of enemy infantry as well as panzer formations that were reorganizing.[9] Dutifully, Walker assaulted Fort Driant, the keystone of the Metz defenses. Walker's own G2 anticipated a minor delaying action from the German troops present, who were reckoned to be third rate. U.S. XX Corps faced a number of impediments. The first, terrain, decisively favored the defender. The second was a last-minute reinforcement of the garrison by near-elite formations (the Unterführers School Unit formed from noncommissioned officer candidates and the Cadet School Regiment of officer candidates). The last obstacle was the attacker's uninspired plan.

Walker gamely gave it his best. On 6 September, he sent Maj. Gen. Lindsay Silvester's 7th Armored Division forward to scout the ground. Cavalry squadrons fanned out, sniffing for crossings. By 7 September, Silvester had three combat commands up against Metz's outer ramparts. Within three days Brig. Gen. John B. Thompson's Combat Command (CC) B had forged a crossing at Dornot, while Maj. Gen. S. LeRoy Irwin's 5th Infantry Division seized a second at Aranville. German reaction set the tone for the remainder of the Metz operation. Their attacks against the Dornot bridgehead soon forced its abandonment; the Aranville bridgehead cowered under deadly indirect fire and savage close-quarter fighting. The welcoming committee now included an old friend, the 17th SS Panzer Grenadier Division, supported by two more mechanized infantry formations brought up from Italy (some still in tropical uniform): the 3d and 15th Panzer Grenadier Divisions.

By 11 September prospects had become grim—fighting had almost destroyed the U.S. 2d Infantry Regiment and disheartened its commander. Walker brought up Maj. Gen. R. S. McLain's 90th Infantry Division. The the "tough hombres" had no sooner arrived when they were struck by an intrepid counterattack from the 106th Panzer Brigade, which managed to overrun flank guards and penetrate as far as division headquarters. The Germans chanced upon the boundary between the 358th and 359th Regimental Combat Teams and blitzed up the seam. This was a daring venture and could have humiliated the entire XX Corps, but the U.S. 90th held firm and 106th's battle group was decisively defeated. With reinforced confidence, McLain sent his troops against Metz on 16 September, but the 359th Infantry Regiment was soon "stopped and cut up" astride the Verdun-Metz highway.

The Metz front was an operational shambles. "This is to inform you that those low bastards, the Germans, gave me my first bloody nose when they compelled us to abandon our attack on Fort Driant."[10] A contemporary commented: "It is not clear why Patton chose to butt his head against Metz fortifications when he had the opportunity of penetrating the German line much more easily around an open flank."[11] Lorraine appeared destined to become a black mark on Patton's record: "The encirclement of Metz absorbed the full effort of XX Corps for ten days and six more days elapsed before troops could be oriented to NE and the drive to the Saar. The enemy conducted a tenacious elastic defense."[12] The Third Army would continue to fight for the fortress until 18 November, and some forts held out until mid-December 1944.

However, if Patton would lift his operational spirits then he had only to look toward the Lorraine gate (Metz-Saarbrücken corridor) where, about the time Walker's XX Corps began to stagger, U.S. armor approached the dawn of a golden day. General Haislip's XV Corps had reached the Troyes area (south of Nancy) by 11 September. Left with two divisions, Gen. Jacques Philippe Leclerc's French 2d Armored Division (which had to be browbeaten out of Paris) and the U.S. 79th Infantry Division (the "Cross of Lorraine"), Haislip secured Third Army's southern flank by taking Charmes after a hard fight for a bridgehead across the Moselle. With General Wyche's 79th Infantry Division now south of Nancy, Patton, should he choose, had the option of striking northeast up the Charmes gap and into the heartland of the Reich. But as Haislip extended his bridgehead by resolutely pushing east to Dompaire, his armor was met by a sharp counterattack.

A column led by Lt. Col. Jacques Massu, who had been the first U.S. Third Army tank commander to make contact with Maczek at Maczuga in the Falaise operation, was bumped by a new outfit—the 112th Panzer Brigade.[13] The ensuing fight was well supported by the U.S. 406th Fighter Bomber Group's P-47 Thunderbolts. The panzers' attempt to outflank the French column resulted in heavy German casualties—leaving "thirty-four of their forty-eight Panthers and twenty-six of forty-eight Mark IVs rusting at Dompaire,"—and heady optimism in the U.S. XV Corps.[14] Back at SHAEF headquarters, a more somber G2 section quickly realized that the war had taken another turn—German withdrawal operations were being bolstered by panzer units heretofore undetected in the enemy order of battle. "The accumulation of German armor surely suggested that something was in the wind."[15]

In early September, Field Marshal von Rundstedt was reappointed as commander in chief, West; Model took over Army Group B in Holland and Belgium; and only Col. Gen. Johannes Blaskowitz was spared and continued as commander of Army Group G.[16] Blaskowitz's First Army, under General von Knobelsdorff and responsible for the Lorraine gate (the Metz-Saarbrücken corridor), stood deployed in the Metz–Nancy–Château-Salins region awaiting the arrival of Patton's divisions.

The German defensive victory at Fort Driant staggered the Third Army and spurred Hitler into renewed aggressiveness. "[He] severely criticized the way in which Blaskowitz had commanded his forces, and reproached him with timidity and lack of offensive spirit. In fact he seems to have thought that Blaskowitz could have taken Patton's Third Army in flank and flung it back on Reims."[17] Hitler was not happy: his orders for a defense to the last had been quietly circumvented by field commanders who saved the situation by withdrawing all mobile troops from Metz and leaving a potpourri of static units in cement fortifications. This exemplary implementation of one of the principles of war—maintaining the aim and economy of force—allowed the panzer force to rebuild itself. Blaskowitz's aim was to have a "highly mobile armored mass in general reserve" maneuvering against Patton while Metz remained an impregnable strongpoint held by well-fortified infantry.[18] The continued success of Blaskowitz's prudent strategy was at the mercy of Hitler's schemes, one of which was an army-level counterstroke toward Reims with a wish list of six panzer divisions and six panzer brigades. This precursor to the Battle of the Bulge was impossible to realize after the strategic disasters on the Eastern Front and in Normandy. The reality of Allied air superiority, paucity of German mechanized forces, and, finally, an even greater dearth of gasoline soon made it clear, even to Hitler, that a strategic effort was temporarily beyond German resources. The führer eventually settled for a shorter operational stab toward Metz based on Manteuffel's Fifth Panzer Army. But this was forestalled by Patton's advance across the Moselle in the week of 14 September. The insatiable Hitler ordered Manteuffel to plan an offensive to relieve Nancy.

Nancy Bridgehead: 5–10 September

The campaign for the Nancy bridgehead was fought in two phases. The initial stage was a U.S. armored exploitation across the Moselle, Meurthe, and Seille rivers that disrupted German Army Group G rear areas and delivered the fortified city of Nancy to Patton without a fight. The second phase featured a U.S. mobile ("elastic") defense against two panzer corps that thwarted Manteuffel's efforts and presented lessons in maneuver warfare to some of Germany's finest panzer generals. The opening move was by Patton, frustrated at Metz, who ordered an offensive against Nancy by Eddy's XII Corps. "Don't stop us now Brad. . . . If I don't secure a couple of good bridgeheads east of the Moselle by the night of the 14th, I'll shut up and assume the mournful role of defender."[19]

Charged with devising a corps attack, Manton Eddy decided to cross near Dieulouard, halfway between Nancy and Metz, where a bridgehead could threaten either city, and then establish a second bridgehead below Nancy at Flavigny. John Wood warned Eddy against crossing a major obstacle in two unsupported areas with divided resources, and was proven correct when, on 5 September, Maj. Gen. Horace McBride's 80th Infantry Division was repulsed in an attempted river crossing. Frustrated at Dieulouard, Eddy now decided to make the area south of Nancy his main effort and ordered Maj. Gen. Paul W. Baade's 35th Infantry Division (Mechanized) and 4th Armored Division to cross the Moselle in the area of Pont St.-Vincent–Flavigny.

Wood considered this impractical. The southern axis required bridging the major obstacles of rivers, their tributaries, and the Marne-Rhin Canal. The 4th Armored's engineering resources were limited, and a single bridgehead afforded the enemy a tempting target in excellent tank country. Wood, reconsidering his previous estimate at Dieulouard, now convinced his corps commander to attempt *two* simultaneous crossings—a northern and southern pincer. The 80th Infantry Division would try again near Dieulouard, while the 35th Infantry's assault would be supported by two armored combat commands. Bruce Clarke's CC A, with a large slice of the division's resources, stood ready to exploit either crossing. Under pressure, Eddy concurred and issued the new corps attack order.[20]

While Walker's XX Corps (which still included the 7th Armored Division) assaulted Metz, the southern front (Nancy-Strasbourg, or Nancy-Mannheim) should have been Patton's main area of concern. But here he briefly neglected his very own sermon: "The record of all history shows that the unchanging end has been, is, and probably will be this: predominant force of the right sort, at the right place, at the right time; or as [Nathan Bedford] Forrest is credited with putting it, 'Getting there fust with the mostest men.'"[21] Specifically, the Third Army required an army-level grouping of the three available armored divisions. In a situation that appeared written for maneuver warfare:

[Patton] could well have used 4th and 7th Armd Divisions on the right, adding the 6th Armd Division upon its arrival, thereby forming an armored corps [Leclerc's French 2d Armored would have made it four armored divisions strong] and exploited both mass and mobility for a thrust through the West Wall, at that time all but naked.[22]

Certainly Patton, Grow, and Wood had the *Fingerspitzengefühl* to maneuver the Germans out of Lorraine. Instead, Patton watched Eddy shuffle three divisions around, while Wood experimented with operational maneuver groups (OMGs) alone.

Battle of Penetration—Exploitation by the Book

My God, are we under the command of a madman?
                    —Armored recovery crew, 14 September 1944[23]

Both of the XII Corps crossings of the Moselle River succeeded. On 11 September, the 35th Infantry Division (Mechanized) secured its bridgehead, easily defeating a battalion-sized counterattack. Opposition from the 553d Volks Grenadier Division (assigned as the Nancy garrison) and 15th Panzer Grenadier Division was sporadic; armored German battle groups were held in reserve, which was unwise against aggressive armor. Wood ordered the 4th Armored Division across: CC B and CC Reserve advanced along two axes, followed by the division trains, artillery, and Wood's own headquarters. His cavalry found gaps in the 15th Panzer Grenadier defense and penetrated into German rear areas, quickly reaching the Meurthe.[24] Crossing the two rivers used up the bulk of the 4th Armored's bridging resources, and the Marne-Rhin Canal still lay ahead: the division staff recommended waiting for corps engineer resources.

Wood decided not to wait forty-eight hours for corps assets. He launched Clarke's CC A across the northern bridgehead and continued the attack, seeking a double envelopment. This left Maj. Gen. Holmes Dager's CC B and Blanchard's CC Reserve to push the southern pincer toward Lunéville and then try to bounce the Marne-Rhine Canal. Reports from reconnaissance patrols indicated that the 15th Panzer Grenadier Division had fallen back, giving up Lunéville (and exposing the 553d Volks Grenadier's left flank) to defend the Marainviller gap, 5 miles to the west. CC B struck north, driving a wedge between the 553d Volks Grenadier and the 15th Panzer Grenadier Divisions. U.S. Cavalry reconnaissance discovered that the Marne-Rhin Canal was fordable in several places, and Dager's combat command crossed without having to bring up bridging units.

North of Nancy, the U.S. 80th Infantry Division crossed the Moselle at Dieulouard before last light of 12 September, and was promptly met by a strong counterattack delivered by the 3d Panzer Grenadier Division. Clarke sent his cavalry troop across to help; it was held up by the corps control officer, who insisted on waiting until "all friendly artillery could be notified American armor was entering the bridgehead."[25] When the Germans closed to small-arms range, he gave "reluctant consent" for Capt. R. Trover's D Troop, 25th Cavalry Regiment, to cross the canal. The Stuarts' 37mm cannon scattered the panzer grenadiers, but the tanks were forced to take cover when supporting Stug III assault guns entered the fray. Clarke ordered Abrams's tanks across: the first M4 tank company chased off the Stugs and swept the enemy infantry from the field. The bridgehead was temporarily secured but not a safe place, because artillery bombarded the bridges. The XII Corps headquarters feared a second, and stronger, counterattack.

At 7:00 A.M. Eddy held a conference with Wood, Clarke, and Abrams. Clarke, "the Syracuse Sparkplug," was keen to continue the bold, almost reckless, pursuit he had practiced from Rennes to Chartres. Already famed as the tank commander "who taught his tank crews to shoot from the hip,"[26] his best battalion was commanded by the audacious Lt. Col. Creighton Abrams, "an incisive fellow . . . [who] could make up his mind in a hurry and he was usually right—a down to earth, practical soldier."[27] In the meeting it was agreed that both bridgeheads were now known to the enemy: the southern one presented logistic concerns, and the northern crossing was under attack. There was some temptation to abandon the Dieulouard bridgehead. Abrams ended the debate pointing toward the Moselle's east shore and saying, "Colonel, that is the shortest way home." Clarke agreed with a: "Get going!"[28]

By 8:00 A.M., under artillery fire, Abrams was leading his 37th Tank Battalion across the Moselle. Clarke, adding a page to armored doctrine, controlled his troops by radio from an airborne artillery L-40.[29] Clarke's force comprised the elements shown in Table 12.1.

Table 12.1   Combat Command A—Col. C. B. Clarke, 13 September 1944

2 Companies medium tanks, 37th Tank Battalion
1 Battalion armored Infantry (borrowed from 80th Infantry Division)
1 Company light tanks
1 Company tank destroyers
1 Battalion armored engineers
3 Battalions self-propelled artillery

Combat Command A attacked as one armored column, a cavalry troop providing security on each flank parallel to the axis of advance, which was the national highway to Château-Salins.

The column was now "rolling!" It stormed through Aulnois-sur-Seilles, scattering the personnel of a German regimental supply installation and

> seizing intact a valuable bridge over the Seille River. . . . As the column neared Lemoncourt, German infantry, in considerable numbers, were surprised in a close formation. The tanks ran through and over them without stopping and with all guns firing.[30]

By the evening of 13 September, Clarke's force had penetrated 35 miles beyond the Moselle, right on the edge of the German First Army's rear areas and with a window toward the Rhine—and stopping only to establish a "360-degree defense perimeter" near Château-Salins. The next afternoon, Wood ordered Clarke to bypass Château-Salins and drive south to Arracourt and link up with CC B, thus cutting the German supply lines from Nancy to the Reich. Clarke's tanks tore through enemy supply columns and marching reinforcements. By 7:00 P.M. on 14 September CC A seized its objective: at Arracourt and Valhey, the headquarters of the German 15th Panzer Grenadier Division was overrun and most of its personnel captured or killed.[31]

Clarke sent out his cavalry to make contact with CC B at the Marne-Rhin Canal while the 35th Mechanized Infantry Division's tanks continued their sweeps. Abrams, high in his turret, chewing on a cigar, directed his tanks with a maestro's aplomb, their being "fanned out to begin a four day campaign of destruction behind German lines."[32] Mechanized "raiding parties" were sent to the limit of artillery range, while armored infantry secured key crossroads. "Its [CC A's] ride around Nancy is comparable on a modern scale to Stuart's ride around Richmond."[33] Clarke established a wide perimeter around Arracourt, then dispatched a battalion-sized task force to help Blanchard cross the Marne-Rhin Canal. CC Reserve remained south of the canal at Lunéville.

Clarke's raid rattled the 553d Volks Grenadier Division enough to abandon Nancy on 15 September, allowing the 35th Infantry to occupy the city. With Nancy, Lunéville, and Arracourt in U.S. Army hands, "the road to Germany was open." Clarke urged Wood to continue the advance and grab Saarbrücken, but General Eddy rejected the proposal. "Eddy diverted this weapon of exploitation to assist infantry in consolidating ground."[34]

Stopping Wood's deep battle was unfortunate, since he was Patton's, indeed, Eisenhower's, only Operational Maneuver Group equivalent threatening Blaskowitz's operational depth. On 17 September 1944, CC A was ordered to return the infantry battalion borrowed from the 80th Infantry Division. The 4th Armored Division ground to a halt. Wood's delay at the Lunéville-Arracourt bulge proved serendipitous: it was the area where Manteuffel would commit his new panzer brigades and a pack of worn panzer divisions to test the U.S. Third Army's mettle and to drive toward Nancy.

Eddy's caution was based on an anticipated debacle at the Dieulouard bridgehead where the 3d Panzer Grenadier Division attacks continued, indeed increased in strength, threatening CC A's communications. Even though the Germans had evacuated Nancy, the 553d Volks Grenadier Division had simply pulled out to the east to high ground and become a pocket in the U.S. XII Corps center. Meanwhile, the severe diminution of supplies convinced Eddy, and eventually Wood, that continued mechanized operations were unrealistic for the time being. The overall solution required the introduction of a second-echelon corps to free Eddy's infantry to concentrate on bridgeheads and follow Wood's momentum into Germany, and this was the Third Army commander's job. Patton finally announced a plan to resume the advance into the Reich: corps objectives were assigned on 16 September.

The Third Army would advance two up: the XX Corps was to seize Frankfurt, the XII Corps was tasked "with a bridgehead across the Rhine." Haislip's division, in army reserve, stood ready to either capture Mannheim or become the second echelon for a successful breaching operation. Patton put Eddy's corps "in the center—to lead off in the initial deep penetration by further use of the line plunging tactics of the 4th Armored Division."[35] Eddy's own maneuver plan was a "one up" assault: Wood was tasked with breaching the German West Wall between Sarreguemines and Saarbrücken. Baade's 35th Infantry followed, with instructions to reinforce the 4th Armored with an infantry regiment while the main force extended the breach. The 80th Infantry Division, still fighting in the Dieulouard bridgehead, was to mop up. Operational exploitation was assigned to Grow's 6th Armored Division: Patton promised Eddy that when Grow finally reached Lorraine, the 6th Armored would be his. But the ambitious plans were about two weeks late. While Dieulouard and Nancy were made safe and Patton made ready, the initiative had passed to Manteuffel.

Wood gave orders for the drive against Saarbrücken at 12:30 A.M. on 18 September, warning Eddy that "this job of getting supplies across the river [the Moselle] and on the roads is getting to be a major problem. This will not be a very fast operation—no blitz."[36] Wood waited for Blanchard, still at Lunéville but about to be relieved by the 6th Armored's CC B. On the afternoon of 19 August Patton visited the Arracourt area to supervise the Rhineland offensive personally. Clarke's CC A was Wood's lead battlegroup and de facto Third Army vanguard. "General Patton gave the combat commander [Clarke] authority to make battlefield promotions to include the rank of lieutenant colonel and to give battlefield commissions to deserving non-commissioned officers."[37] The tank columns had just crossed their start lines when reports reached Wood of enemy action on his southern flank, against Lunéville. Although it was not yet apparent to Wood, Eddy, or Patton, Manteuffel's Fifth Panzer Army had launched its own offensive, a counterstroke ordered by Blaskowitz in response to Hitler's angry prodding.[38]

On 18 and 19 September our Fifth Panzerarmee was again drawn into fighting around Lunéville; it had been assembling for a deliberate counterattack into the rear of the Americans, but the situation on the Moselle was so critical that von Manteuffel was ordered to join the battle.[39]

The Fifth Panzer Army's mission was to destroy the U.S. bridgeheads on the Moselle and relieve Nancy and Metz. "Hitler's great error was to insist on the counterattack being delivered before all available forces were assembled."[40]

The designated forces were the 111th, 112th, and 113th Panzer Brigades, the 15th Panzer Grenadier Division, and the 11th and 21st Panzer Divisions.[41] The new panzer brigades had been raised at Hitler's specific instruction, and had been given priority over veteran units attempting to rebuild. New tanks went direct from the factory to these brigades. Numbered 101 to 113, they were designed as self-contained battle groups— minipanzer divisions. Their organization was one panzer battalion of four tank companies each ("17 Panzer IV or V or 14 Panzer VI")[42] for a total of about seventy tanks. These were supported by two reconnaissance platoons (tracked and wheeled), three mechanized infantry companies (carried in armored personnel carriers), a heavy weapons company, a signals platoon, and an armored engineer company.

The Americans were to be forced to either maneuver or withdraw—the odds for a tank fight in open terrain still favored the Germans. Operation Cobra had proved that U.S. armor could boldly secure operational objectives; the question now remained, as a British Eighth Army veteran put it: "Yes, they can drive, but can they fight?" Manteuffel ordered an attack against Lunéville and a second spearhead against the center of the U.S. salient at Arracourt.

On paper, Manteuffel had all the troops he needed to break through Eddy's flank and penetrate the 4th Armored Division, separate it into isolated commands, and crush each as he had done with Soviet tank armies. The Führer had given him two new panzer brigades and the 11th Panzer Division. He could attack through the excellent tank country between the Seille and Moselle rivers where the armor and superior firepower of his Panthers should easily rout any U.S. force before it could get close enough to defeat Krupp steel. Manteuffel had only one man to beat, "Professor" Wood.

Tiger Jack Versus the Baron

Wood is the Rommel of the American Armored Force.
—B. H. Liddell Hart[43]

Patton was arguably at his operational worst in Lorraine, abandoning the sacred tenets of Yankee armored doctrine forged in Louisiana. Worse, having himself suffered under Bradley's whip, he permitted an uninspired corps commander to rein in his best horse. Manton Eddy meant well, but his vague grasp of armored operations was made further insecure because he commanded a general who not only dwarfed him tactically but, unfortunately, pointed out Eddy's shortfalls at every appropriate opportunity. John Shirley Wood[44] may have inspired Eddy's controlling attitude, but it is curious why Patton permitted the drama to continue—particularly when it was clear Wood had a superior grasp of what was going on and what had to be done.

Wood was a natural panzer leader. More accurately, he was a master of maneuver—tactically imaginative and "personally irresistible and out-spoken." He insisted that his division support, not compete with, its components and trained his commanders to use initiative and bold maneuver. "He was a big blustery sort of fellow that the men liked."[45] Captain of the football team at West Point, the "Professor" (he had tutored slower cadets) was technically minded and had a command of French, a background in Fuller's theories, and repeated success in battle. A perceptive man who did not suffer fools gladly, no matter what their station, he was

> openly contemptuous of men he considered to be of lesser competence and had, for example, tangled publicly with General Ben Lear in Tennessee and General [Walton] Walker when he thought they were grossly in error. On the other hand he was a matchless leader who inspired trust, confidence and love in his subordinates down to the last private in the Division.[46]

Wood quickly became one of Patton's most fascinating and irksome commanders; the 4th Armored Division was a "headstrong crew that became rambunctious in Brittany." Liddell Hart called Wood "the Rommel of American Armored forces. . . . [Wood] was more conscious of the possibilities of a deep exploitation and the importance of speed than anyone else."[47] He was popular with the ranks, and the troops called him "Tiger Jack" as, eventually, did his German counterparts: "He is outstanding among generals of American Divisions."[48]

Wood faced two German corps in Lorraine: to the west the LVIII Panzer Corps commanded by General of Panzer Troops Walter Kruger; southeast lay the XLVII Panzer Corps, led by General von Luttwitz, whose old division, the 2d (Vienna) Panzer Division had battered the Allies during Operation Spring and then conducted determined rear guards throughout Bluecoat and Cobra. The parent formation, the Fifth Panzer Army, was commanded by General of Panzer Troops, Baron Hasso von Manteuffel, marginally taller than Napoleon and unquestionably as energetic. A cavalry

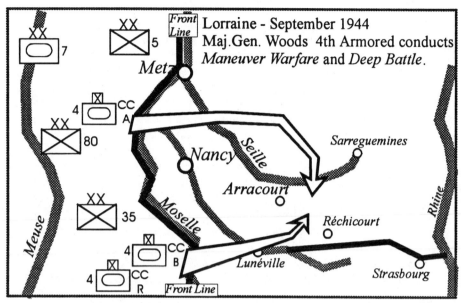

Lorraine - September 1944
Maj.Gen. Woods 4th Armored conducts *Maneuver Warfare* and *Deep Battle*.

Front Line

7

XX
5

Metz

XI
4 CC
A

XX
80

Seille

Sarreguemines

Nancy

Arracourt

XX
35

Moselle

Réchicourt

Meuse

Rhine

XI
4 CC
B

Lunéville

XI
4 CC
R

Strasbourg

Front Line

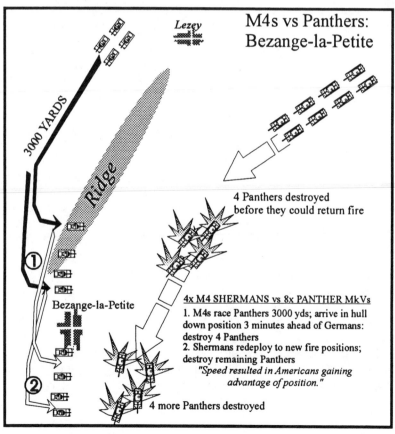

M4s vs Panthers:
Bezange-la-Petite

Lezey

3000 YARDS

Ridge

4 Panthers destroyed
before they could return fire

①

Bezange-la-Petite

②

4x M4 SHERMANS vs 8x PANTHER MkVs

1. M4s race Panthers 3000 yds; arrive in hull
down position 3 minutes ahead of Germans:
destroy 4 Panthers
2. Shermans redeploy to new fire positions;
destroy remaining Panthers
   *"Speed resulted in Americans gaining
   advantage of position."*

4 more Panthers destroyed

officer with a sterling record on the Eastern Front, the baron's past successes were to mock him in Lorraine. With neither trained troops nor complete
formations, Manteuffel ordered his staff to prepare the final map overlays
for a breakthrough to Nancy. Although this was not quite the Brody pocket
of the Eastern Front, success here would buy time.

The XLVII Panzer Corps struck first. "On the 18th September the 15th
PGD [Panzer Grenadier Division] and the 111th Panzer Brigade broke into
Lunéville after hard fighting"[49] and set the CC Reserve back on its heels.
The battle soon drew away all of Wood's reserves and prompted Eddy to
request immediate reinforcements from Patton. In the end Blanchard, aided
by a task force dispatched by Clarke, and the timely arrival of Combat
Command B (Col. George W. Read)[50] from the 6th Armored Division held
firm. The appearance of fresh armor turned the tide: "[The XLVII Panzer
Corps] was not able to capture the city core after the enemy brought up a
fresh armored force, according to the 18 September night report of 15th
Panzer Division. When darkness fell, the city had to be surrendered to the
enemy after a bitter fight."[51] With Lunéville secure, Patton and Wood saw
"no reason for worrying further about a German threat in the Arracourt sector, since CC A reported that forty-three enemy tanks, mostly Panthers, had
been destroyed and that its own losses had been only "6 killed and 13
wounded with 2 TDs and 6 M-4 tanks destroyed."[52] The Rhine push was
back on.

The Arracourt Battles

Arracourt was the greatest tank battle of the war on the Allied Front.
                                                      —Maj. Gen. John S. Wood[53]

Wood was being pulled in two directions at once. Patton wanted him to
drive north toward the Siegfried and Maginot lines, but his secondary task
was to screen Nancy. This forced him to expose a long right flank. Any
major threat against this sector would compromise the Rhine offensive. The
4th Armored Division held a thin crescent, three combat commands in line,
north to south: General Dager's CC B was near Fresnes-en-Saulnois, about
20 miles north of Arracourt. Wendell Blanchard's CC Reserve was behind
Lunéville, and, in the center, CC A held 25 miles of open terrain that led
directly to Manteuffel's start line.

Clarke was about to conduct a covering force battle against a force
three times his own. The tank battles of the Nancy bridgehead, sometimes
called the "Battle of Arracourt," began with a probe along the Metz-
Strasbourg highway. A division-sized battle group composed of the 113th
Panzer Brigade (forty-two Pzkw Vs) and 2113th Panzer Grenadier
Regiment, entered the Arracourt bulge.[54]

Clarke had deployed simply, with a battalion of armored infantry grouped with a company of medium tanks between Chamberly and Arracourt. His own command headquarters, field artillery with one troop of tank destroyers, held Arracourt, and the engineer battalion covered his right facing the canal. The forward screen was composed of "combat outposts" held by Stuarts and Shermans from Abrams's task force.

Lezey

The 113th Panzer Brigade's battle group was organized into armor-heavy combat teams: one tank company grouped with a panzer grenadier platoon. Just after dawn of 19 September, a tank column emerged from the thick fog surrounding Lezey, bumping C Company, U.S. 37th Tank Battalion: "Neither side saw the other until leading Panther broke out of the fog at 75 yards."[55] The column, factory-new Pzkw Vs moving down a road in chain-of-ducks formation, was surprised by concentrated fire from a Sherman M4 section on standing patrol. At ranges of over 500 yards the Shermans' 75mm guns were all but useless; however, at point-blank range the M4s' guns quickly dispatched three leading Panthers. The remaining German tanks retreated into the fog. The Germans turned south toward Bezange-la-Petite (a little over a mile southwest of Lezey) and were again engaged by a platoon of the 704th Tank Destroyer Battalion.[56] This was the only armored reserve available to CC A; it was ordered into action to "prevent the encirclement of Co. 'C' 37 Tk Bn. . . . The approach march was made through fog and the first encounter was at a range of 50 yards. The leading TD accounted for 2 tanks before being disabled. The remaining TDs withdrew to high ground 350 yards to the rear."[57]

The M18 tank destroyers, vehicles hopelessly outclassed by the Pzkw Vs, advanced to the edge of the first decent kill zone, deployed in hull-down positions, and opened fire at 150 yards. "The Americans had the advantage of surprise on the first round, thereafter [the battle was] even."[58] Even at this range, the advantage should have quickly shifted to the attackers, but there was no German maneuver. The Panthers simply poked their snouts through the fog and fired at gun flashes. During the long gun duel, the tank destroyer platoon took out eight Panthers but was reduced to one vehicle. The tenacity of the crews and platoon leader was notable. After losing the better part of a company, the Germans withdrew. To have M18s winning frontal fire fights against Panthers, even at 150 yards, was unusual.

Bezange-la-Petite

The 113th Panzer Brigade's continued effort dissolved into a series of uncoordinated attacks across a 5-mile front, the poor visibility making

Wood's 4th Armored vs von Manteuffel's 4th Pz Armee

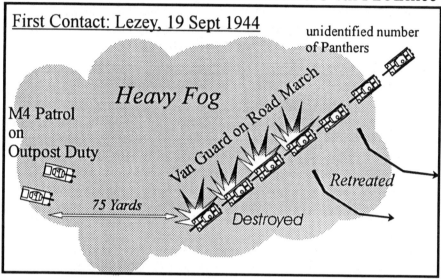

First Contact: Lezey, 19 Sept 1944

unidentified number of Panthers

Heavy Fog

Van Guard on Road March

M4 Patrol
on
Outpost Duty

75 Yards

Destroyed

Retreated

Heavy Fog: *"Neither side saw the other until leading Panther broke out of the fog at 75 yds.
"Advantage with American force which was halted and hull down:
laid on the road and waiting for the Germans as they came out of the fog."*

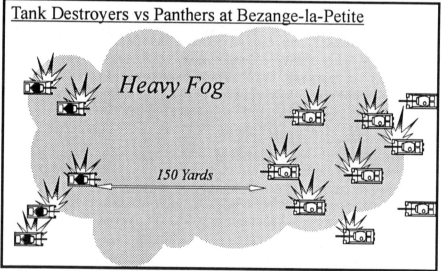

Tank Destroyers vs Panthers at Bezange-la-Petite

Heavy Fog

150 Yards

*"Americans have advantage of surprise on first round, thereafter even."
Number of German tanks unknown due to fog: 5x TDs and 7x Panthers destroyed.*

mutual support impossible, with the fog lifting briefly only now and then. After the abortive attack against Lezey, a German column attempted to outflank C Company and cut the road to Arracourt, but this maneuver was spotted by four Shermans stationed south of Lezey. Using the small ridge as cover, the M4s raced 3,000 yards to head off the Panther column as it headed for Bezange-la-Petite. They arrived in position "3 minutes ahead," topped the crest, and engaged the German van at 500 yards, firing hull down from the flank. "Four Panthers [were] destroyed before they could return fire." The M4s then withdrew and circled to the south of Bezange-la-Petite: "speed resulted in Americans gaining advantage of position."[59] The second engagement knocked out another four Panthers—the column turned back.

Réchicourt-la-Petite

The fog persisted and German piecemeal probes continued. Clarke reorganized his center force, grouping A Company, 37th Tank Battalion, which had just arrived from Lunéville, with B Company and put them under the command of the 37th's G3. Task Force Hunter rumbled south to assist the M18s at Arracourt. Captain Hunter, seeing a Panther column, quickly turned and withdrew to the southwest, away from the Germans. In fact, he executed a maneuver that demonstrated auftragstaktik at its finest: "'A' and 'B' Companies . . . circled to the rear and around to the right to strike the enemy from the flank."[60] In the ensuing fire fight the Sherman's traded three tanks for nine Panthers. The enemy broke again. Given the firepower of the panzer brigades, the Shermans should have been at a serious disadvantage, particularly in a maneuver battle where the Panthers' wider tracks and superior cross-country speed again held the trump. Task Force Hunter was ordered to mop up any panzers left behind and conducted a final sweep, "guided through the night by burning German tanks."[61]

Patton visited Wood that evening; both believed that the recent German attacks were nothing to worry about. It certainly did not look like a corps push, and the results of three tank destroyers and five M4s lost for forty-three new Panthers, spoke for themselves. Indeed, the attackers themselves did not think much of the effort. "On the 19th the 113th Panzer Brigade made a determined attack on CCA of the 4th Armored Brigade at Arracourt . . . [the] attack cost nearly fifty tanks and achieved nothing."[62] Wood had been fortunate: "Had it not been for a timid employment of the enemy, the attack would probably have resulted in a breakthrough to Nancy."[63] It was not yet apparent how fortunate. The XII Corps ordered the resumption of the advance into Germany. CC Reserve, relieved by the 6th Armored's CC B, had left Lunéville and assembled west of Arracourt. With three combat commands available, Wood focused on Sarreguemines. Arracourt would be

covered by a tank company from the the 35th Tank Battalion, while the
320th Infantry, CC Reserve, and the 602d Tank Destroyer Battalion
deployed to shield the 4th Armored's right flank.

Mannecourt Hill: 20 September

The following day, 20 September, the battle area was again shrouded in
fog. At 8:00 A.M., the 4th Armored Division began the drive to Saarbrücken
with CC A (reinforced by two companies of the 35th Tank Battalion and
remainder of 10th Armored Infantry Battalion) in the van. Clarke advanced
two columns up, each lead by an armored task force. At 11:30 A.M., as Task
Force Oden approached Hampont (10 miles north of Arracourt) and Task
Force Abe secured Dieuze (15 miles northeast of Arracourt),[64] General
Wood received a situation report confirming enemy tank columns were
behind him and approaching Arracourt.

Manteuffel, smarting from Blaskowitz's reproach about his lack of
offensive spirit, attacked Wood's flank, a panzer brigade in each fist. The
111th Panzer Brigade, bruised from the Lunéville battle, circled north using
the Forêt-de-Parroy for cover, crossed the National Canal and reached
Coincourt, southeast of Arracourt, without being detected by Wood's reconnaissance units. The 113th Panzer Brigade's Kampfgruppe reassembled
east of Ley and headed toward Réchicourt-Arracourt.

Near midday, both outfits got lucky. The Americans were reporting that
"enemy tank forces had penetrated . . . through Bures, Coincourt, and
Rechicourt to the outskirts of Arracourt."[65] A persistent group of Panthers
had padded through the fog and slipped past the tank destroyer guard (1st
and 2d platoons of C Company, 704th Tank Destroyer Battalion) and were
soon threatening Wood's command post. One Panther company surprised a
limbered battalion of 155mm howitzers from the 191st Field Artillery
Battalion: it was a tanker's dream of overrunning a gun line. The American
gunners were not routed but fought back with point-blank fire, destroyed
two tanks, and drove the rest away. Nevertheless, Wood was livid. Clarke
was ordered to come back and sweep the entire Arracourt area once and for
all.

Notified that CC A was turning south, Col. Heinrich Bronsart von
Schellendorf, commanding officer of 111th Panzer Brigade, dispatched a
battle group toward the high ground south of Lezey to protect his right
flank. The area included Mannecourt Hill, a long lazy ridge dominated by
two higher features, Hills 260 and 241. The latter were seized by
Kampfgruppe Junghannis, comprising Pzkw IVs and heavy tank destroyers,
perhaps JPzs.[66] Captain Junghannis first blitzed through Ley, driving C
Company, 37th Tank Battalion, before him. He then deployed on Hills 260
and 241 dominating Route 55 (the Strasbourg highway) and the roads to

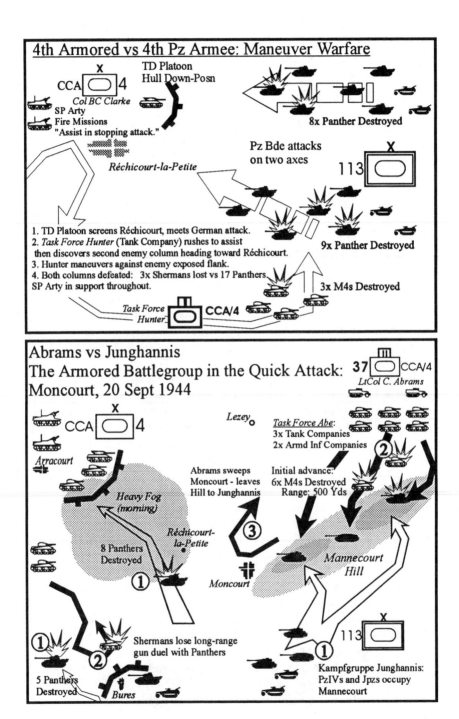

4th Armored vs 4th Pz Armee: Maneuver Warfare

X
CCA [ ] 4
Col BC Clarke
SP Arty
Fire Missions
"Assist in stopping attack."

TD Platoon
Hull Down-Posn

8x Panther Destroyed

Pz Bde attacks
on two axes

X
113 [ ]

Réchicourt-la-Petite

9x Panther Destroyed

1. TD Platoon screens Réchicourt, meets German attack.
2. *Task Force Hunter* (Tank Company) rushes to assist
   then discovers second enemy column heading toward Réchicourt.
3. Hunter maneuvers against enemy exposed flank.
4. Both columns defeated: 3x Shermans lost vs 17 Panthers.
   SP Arty in support throughout.

3x M4s Destroyed

Task Force Hunter [ ] CCA/4

Abrams vs Junghannis
The Armored Battlegroup in the Quick Attack:
Moncourt, 20 Sept 1944

37 [ ] CCA/4
LtCol C. Abrams

X
CCA [ ] 4

Arracourt

Lezey

Task Force Abe:
3x Tank Companies
2x Armd Inf Companies

Abrams sweeps
Moncourt - leaves
Hill to Junghannis

Initial advance:
6x M4s Destroyed
Range: 500 Yds

Heavy Fog
(morning)

Réchicourt-la-Petite

8 Panthers
Destroyed

①

Mannecourt
Hill

Moncourt

X
113 [ ]

Shermans lose long-range
gun duel with Panthers

①

②

5 Panthers
Destroyed

Bures

Kampfgruppe Junghannis:
PzIVs and Jpzs occupy
Mannecourt

Moncourt, Ley, and Ommeray. As the Germans set up a defensive perimeter, C Company doubled back and attempted to establish a fire base on Mannecourt Hill: it was immediately engaged by Junghannis's armor. After a brief firefight the Shermans drew back to await Abrams's arrival.

As soon as Clarke understood the tactical situation he ordered 37th Tank Battalion to counterattack immediately. Task Force Abe, with two M4 companies, two armored infantry companies, and a self-propelled artillery battalion, drove southeast astride Route 55, using Ley and Mannecourt to cover its approach. Abrams appeared on Junghannis's right flank and conducted a quick attack from the line of march.

The Shermans advanced boldly, rapidly closing the distance. The Pzkw IVH was always a fair match for the Sherman M4—its frontal armor could not defeat U.S. tank guns, but its L/48 gun was more effective than the U.S. 76mm. Abrams lost six tanks in the initial charge. U.S. forces' ability for rapid maneuver evened the odds, and "subsequent fighting resulted in about 12 losses each."[67] The fight ended in a draw: Abrams left Junghannis king of the hill, and the Germans logically claimed victory. As darkness approached, Abrams broke off to continue his sweep through Schellendorf's flank and into the village of Moncourt, which he cleared in a well-coordinated night attack. Abrams then reassembled his forces in the vicinity of Lezey, leaving the Mannecourt hills to von Schellendorf: "Der Feind bei Avricourt war zurueckgegangen." ("The enemy at Avricourt retreated.")[68] This was an interesting armored battle and an unusually fair fight for France in 1944; it featured aggressive use of fire and maneuver, demonstrating Abrams's subsequent postwar "mobility multiplies weaponpower" thesis for maneuver warfare.[69] "The operations of 20 September again showed American superiority in maneuver. The German tanks outranged the American but this was compensated for by fog plus American maneuverability and marksmanship."[70]

In fact, even though Abrams lost the firefight, he dominated the maneuver and left Junghannis in a static role holding a virtually useless bit of real estate. Operationally, the open Mannecourt Hill area was absolute trifle to an armored division: the moment a force was committed to hold it, it became an albatross around its neck. Clarke's tanks were now free to fight another day. Wood reviewed the tally (about twenty-five panzers for fourteen Shermans) and, deciding the Germans had been defeated, let his division stand down and replenish itself.

To illustrate the technical norms of the Western Front, about the same time that Abrams advanced toward Mannecourt, a U.S. tank company was sent south toward the Marne-Rhine Canal to scout and mop up. To the west of the village of Bures, they bumped into a patrol of five Panthers doing the same thing. The firefight quickly claimed all five Panthers. The U.S. commander, chuffed with victory, continued toward Bures. The subsequent engagement was far more traditional. As the Americans advanced through the lifting mist they were taken under long-range fire by a German platoon. The Panther's armor made it impregnable in a frontal engagement and its L/70 super 75mm gun killed anything it could see. After watching their rounds ricochet off Panthers' glacis and losing a pair of Shermans, the Americans withdrew to their lines. There was no further German advance, and Blaskowitz soon blasted Manteuffel about losing his operational freedom.

The setback cost General Blaskowitz his job. On 21 September, determined to sort out Army Group G, Hitler ordered in fresh *panzer* leaders: Gen. Hermann Balck, an armored legend from the Eastern Front and, as his chief of staff, General von Mellenthin. These two men were masters of the operational art and had successfully practiced their craft in a most unforgiving environment. However, their experience on the Eastern Front was to be of little consequence.

Combined Arms in Battle: Lezey-Juvelize, 22 September

I'm supposed to be the best tank commander in the Army, but I have one peer—Abe Abrams.
—attributed to General Patton[71]

While 4th Armored Division rested, Eddy and Wood prepared to resume their northern thrust toward the Rhine. Eddy reinforced Wood with the 9th Tank Destroyer Group and the 42nd Cavalry Squadron, which was tasked to establish a guard from Ley to Lunéville. The 25th Cavalry Squadron screened CC A's left flank from Moyenic to Dieuze. Nevertheless, German attacks would again disrupt Wood's plans.

Although Balck took a day to regroup, he did not produce a better tactical solution; he simply ordered Manteuffel to capture Lezey and Juvelize. Despite augmentation by a competent formation (the 111th and 113th Panzer Brigades were joined by a Kampfgruppe from the 11th Panzer Division), it was a sloppy operation.[72] H-hour was missed because the panzer grenadiers arrived at the start line three hours late. German armored infantry, without armored personnel carriers, were forced to ride their tanks into battle, the antithesis of panzer grenadier tactics.

The attack went in at midmorning, covered by the now familiar mist. Taking a page from Rockingham's attack on Verrières, German patrols laid white mine field tape from their start lines to within 75 yards of Sherman M3s standing watch on the Lezey-Juvelize road. A German company-sized combat group suddenly appeared and quickly took out seven Stuart tanks, scattering the rest. "More Panthers crept under cover of fog to the 25th's bivouac near Juvelize."[73] The potential rout was contained by C Company, 704th Tank Destroyer Battalion, positioned hull down behind the screen of cavalry. Three Panthers were destroyed; the tank destroyer's sudden fire surprised Schellendorf, and the panzers pulled back, leaving their infantry stranded. Things then went from bad to worse for the 111th Panzer Brigade when the sun came out and burned off the fog, exposing the battle area to the Thunderbolts of U.S. XIX Tactical Air Force. Air strikes decimated Schellendorf's formations.

Clarke now ordered Abrams to counterattack. After a quick combat estimate, Abrams directed flanking to the left, driving northwest with two tank companies, while the 10th Armored Infantry, supported by C Company M4s and D Company Stuarts, held the ground east of Lezey, providing both a hard shoulder and flank defense against any threat moving up Highway 55.

A Company circled Juvelize and secured Hill 257, a feature known as les Trois Croix. With Juvelize outflanked and his tanks holding ground of tactical importance, Abrams took on 111th Panzer Brigade's next assault—a second battle group moving south from le Bois-du-Sorbier. Controlling a near-perfect killing zone Abrams devastated the enemy with tank, air, and artillery fire. Both Sherman companies maneuvered forward, systematically engaging targets at 2,000 yards and finally closing to ranges of 200 yards. The 111th staggered, then, hit by a second P-47 attack, it was routed.[74] Fourteen Panthers were destroyed and Schellendorf was killed. The 405th Fighter-Bomber Group destroyed the remaining forces "with the help of armored field artillery and cut them to pieces as they straggled back to the northeast."[75]

Balck ordered Manteuffel to keep attacking, ignoring the baron's situation reports and bitter complaints over the Luftwaffe's lack of support. Manteuffel sent in his last reserve, a battle group from 113th Panzer Brigade in an uninspired effort along Route 55 toward Lezey. German attempts to relieve Nancy had been soundly rebuffed. The operation lasted four days; Manteuffel's panzer force was defeated at a cost of twenty-two German tanks and approximately 113 American casualties. Manteuffel conceded defeat but hinted that the issue was less Wood's aggressive tactics than a more serious threat from Leclerc's French 2d Armored Division against his (Manteuffel's) southern flank:

> In the following days another attempt from the north and east failed to capture Lunéville or at least secure the crossings. Moreover, enemy pressure along the Meurthe increased and the Corps had to fall back to the east bank on 22nd September and finally withdraw behind the Vezouse by September 23rd. Particularly heavy, embittered fighting against the 2nd French Armored Division occurred in the area of the Mondon Forest. The forest was lost.[76]

Heavy fighting continued around the Lunéville,[77] Château-Salins, and Réchicourt areas until 29 September, when the back of the Fifth Panzer army was broken. Despite valiant attempts by panzer grenadiers, U.S. superiority in artillery and tactical air proved insurmountable obstacles.[78] German attacks did succeed in forcing Clarke back from the Arracourt-Mannecourt Hill salient, and, by Eddy's own admission, after 16 August, his corps was entirely on the defensive; but Wood's combat commands had taught the Germans a lesson in maneuver warfare. Although the Cobra encirclement and Falaise pocket showed the armored force at its operational best, U.S. armor came of age in Lorraine.[79] "[The] 4th and 6th Armored carried out several independent or semi independent operations as did 10th Armored for a short point near the close of the campaign. Only 4th Armored met German armor in a situation that could be termed as a tank vs. tank battle."[80]

The majority of the 4th Armored's pure tank battles were fought by CC A. The battles featured two key armored counterattacks, both conducted by Lt. Col. Creighton Abrams's 37th Tank Battalion. The conflicts are doctrinally interesting because they put U.S. armor into situations comparable to those in Normandy in which British and Canadian tanks had been forced back or soundly trounced. Arracourt is a good example of what aggressively led tanks, given the opportunity to maneuver, can accomplish despite technological inferiority. Whatever the problems facing the German army (and Hitler's interference cannot be discounted), there were enough panzer leaders left in the Reich to make the armored battles in Lorraine a valid test of U.S. armor. The use of untried units such as the 111st and 113th Panzer Brigades was imprudent. "[They had been] activated July 1944 by direct order of the Führer against the will of the Inspector General of Armored Forces who would have preferred to supply the tanks and sundry weapons to those Panzer Divisions which had lost their vehicles."[81] Hindsight might argue that Manteuffel would have been better off with a collection of battle groups from the seasoned I and II SS Panzer Corps, but these veteran units were still rebuilding from the effects of the fighting in the Falaise gap and the withdrawal from Normandy.[82] The Arracourt battles featured the type of mobile action that was predicted for the open plains beyond Caen. The tactical difference was that the Germans were doing the attacking.

Lorraine mirrored the German offensive record in Normandy, which was generally mediocre: most armored attacks were broken up before they began.[83] Although counterattacks by fire worked well during Goodwood and Totalize, the assault by the 9th SS Panzer Division during Operation Spring succeeded only because Meyer's battle group abandoned its initial objective in the face of determined antitank fire and sideslipped to join Battle Group Zollver in the attack on St. André. The tank battles of Totalize may be compared with the Lorraine battles in two aspects: open tank country (the battles being fought beyond prepared defenses) and near-equal combat ratios. Although the odds had favored Simonds operationally, things were fairly close on the tactical level. His preference for narrow fronts and suffocating phase lines ensured that Canadian armor was denied both maneuver and numerical superiority. Wood was permitted an extensive maneuver area by Eddy, and the former allowed his tank commanders the tactical freedom that Kitching or Maczek continually requested. Both Lorraine and Operation Totalize featured "meeting engagements"—the sort of contests that experienced tank commanders favor: lots of ground for maneuver and emphasis on tactical initiative at all levels.

American Armor in Normandy and Lorraine

Montgomery, the master of the tactical battle realized this only too well; . . . to be quite honest, it was because of their lack of battle experience that he had little confidence in the U.S. Commanders.
—Lt. Gen. Sir Brian Horrocks, XXX British Corps[84]

It has been suggested earlier that the American breakout was fortunate that it did not run into the formations that faced Crerar and Dempsey. U.S. armored success during Cobra was spectacular but relatively easy once the corner was turned. Fighting Tigers and Panthers in hull-down positions is not the same as chasing rear guards through the Loire Valley. It makes for interesting debate whether a U.S. armored corps in Goodwood would have fared better than O'Connor's brigades. A U.S. armored corps in Operation Spring or Totalize as a second-echelon breakthrough force invites intriguing speculation. It is quite possible that it would have succeeded for two reasons: overwhelming numbers and command. Patton, a cavalry officer with considerable experience and an intuitive understanding of armor, presumably would not have conducted operations in the same confusing manner that Crerar or Simonds did, whose deficiencies were not that they were artillery officers or that they had little practical armored experience but, most vital, that they lacked *Fingerspitzengefühl*—a sense of maneuver warfare. Conversely, a critical look at Patton floundering around Metz one month after Cobra gives Crerar and Simonds more room to maneuver in Canadian military history.

Patton's Cobra romps have been both criticized and praised. The science of war decries him for dissipation of strength, taking mad risks, and seeking to break Bradley's and Middleton's nerve. It is also true that save for Ramcke's paratroops, the forces opposing Patton's pursuit to the Loire were a second-rate lot, and his columns did not have to contend with a serious German battle group until Haislip reached Falaise. But this was not Patton's failing—this was his moment of glory. The art of war has room for those who dare. If not in the pursuit, then where does the armored commander ignore his flanks and strike for the political, the psychological prize? Wood's arrival at Rennes destroyed what was left of the vaunted composure of the German General Staff: "The news that an American armored Division was in Rennes had a shattering effect, like a bomb burst, upon us."[85]

Patton's decision to have Haislip strike for Argentan instead of reaching for Le Mans rattled them again. The decision to head east and attempt the great battle of annihilation is the stuff of Schlieffen. Montgomery's short stabs at Falaise, Argentan, and Trun were nothing more than corps tactics.[86] Operational maneuver, without a strategic plan, is wasted. All Patton wanted to do was send an Operational Maneuver Group to Paris and another to Brest.[87] The Stavka would not have thought twice about it. Bradley was irate.

Simonds aficionados will note with some satisfaction that some of U.S. armor's great captains did not spring from cavalry backgrounds. Wood was a gunner: his tank savvy had come from prewar cross-fertilization during the 1930s and in the Louisiana maneuvers, where he commanded Patton's artillery in the 2d Armored Division. However, most of Wood's technique appears to be intuitive—he just naturally understood armor. This was not just rustic cunning. Wood, like Patton, was as near to a military intellectual as any regular officer would dare aspire. A linguist and well read in military philosophy, Wood had studied Fuller and Liddell Hart before the war and was well aware of the indirect approach, although he did not buy into it. Wood's determined rejection of British military *philosophes* ("Fuller and Hart are contrary to the US Army tradition set by Grant: attrition—wear the enemy down") was an interesting reaction.[88] His right to objective analysis may have transcended military historians; perhaps Wood understood the American culture within doctrine with more detached practicality than his peers.

The American way of war, synopsized by Liddell Hart and explained by Russell Weigley, entrenched the "Grant tradition."[89] However, Weigley was closer to the crux of the U.S. military culture than Liddell Hart, who saw Grant as the antithesis of the indirect approach, the classic attritionist: "How did he [Grant] seek to gain the required early victory? By reverting to the strategy which good orthodox soldiers always adopt—that of using his immensely superior weight to smash the opposing army."[90] A better interpretation of Grant's strategy is that he used both the opposite "poles" of attrition and maneuver. "Unlike Lee, Grant entertained no illusions about being able to destroy enemy armies in a single battle."[91] In fact, Grant's distinction is that while he sought annihilation, he accepted that there was need for both attrition and maneuver. Grant sought to annihilate the South, not simply to exhaust Lee. The American way of war accepts the operational strands of the battle of annihilation—these include both attrition and maneuver, as demonstrated in Grant's encouragement of deep war against the Confederacy. "You I propose to move against Johnston's army, to break it up and get into the interior of the enemy's country as far as you can, inflicting all the damage you can."[92]

By August 1944, both Patton and Wood had realized the opportunity Cobra would have afforded Grant, and immediately aspired for a Sherman-like march to the Seine and Paris. By September, Wood well understood that the Rhine was as attainable as the Seine had been in August and again sought operational freedom. But divisions are tactical units; operations require entire corps, and Wood had become small change to SHAEF. Allied Headquarters may have hamstrung the two armored generals the Germans really feared, but the Montgomery lobby was quick to point out that neither was a sure bet. Patton's record suggested that he was all too human, some might argue irrational, and guilty of "poor generalship, lack of imagination."[93] Patton's dark side had been observed earlier by Maj. Gen. Orlando Ward, commander of the 1st Armored Division, during the Tunisian campaign. Patton, as corps commander, asked about the casualties suffered by the 1st Armored after repeated attempts to capture Maknassy Heights on 30 March 1943:

> Patton: "How many officers did you lose today?"
> Ward: "We were fortunate today, we didn't lose any officers."
> Patton: "Godammit Ward, that's not fortunate. That's bad for the morale of the enlisted men. I want you to get more officers killed."
> Ward: "You're not serious, are you?"
> Patton: "Yes, godammit, I'm serious. I want you to put some officers out as observers, keep them well up front until a couple get killed. It's good for enlisted morale."[94]

If the 21st Army Group's operational inexperience was a poor excuse in July, then by September 1944 the U.S. Third Army had no excuse. Despite the dullness of his superiors, Patton had within his own grasp the opportunity to create a great armored host. The Lorraine campaign required an organized echeloned mass of tanks as desperately as the battles south of Caen. Patton uncharacteristically divided his armor and dabbled with attrition warfare, but Wood's tactical talents made him look good in the end. While Clarke embarrassed an entire panzer corps, Wood humbled von Manteuffel's army. At his best (Cobra and Battle of the Bulge), Patton took Western armored doctrine to a level where it began to approach Soviet operational art. Validation of U.S. armored doctrine did not hinge on Patton's success or failure: U.S. tank divisions had become finely honed sabers during Cobra, and after Lorraine they were veteran *beau sabreurs*.

The German conduct throughout the Arracourt battles was an example of mediocre tactical planning and execution; however, the Germans fared better at the operational level: "The important point is that the German commanders (except Hitler) never permitted fixed defenses to become prisons for their forces, but utilized them as firm anchors to maintain the solidarity of the front while counterattacks and withdrawals were executed."[95] Manteuffel's staff faltered, though. The battle groups of the 111st and 113th Panzer Brigades were committed piecemeal in lumbering offensives. In many cases attacking brigades broke off action as soon as the vanguard was defeated, often by screening forces. Manteuffel's Fifth Panzer Army was further handicapped by an "inability to mass armor in the face of US air supremacy . . . there was never enough to punch through." Weather was a significant factor; at least four of the six engagements began in thick fog that closed the range to under 100 yards and favored U.S. tank turrets' electric traverse—the single advantage the Sherman had over Panther.

The Arracourt engagements featured bold, creative maneuver on the part of U.S. Army platoon, company, and battalion commanders. Previous battles in the bocage had forced the Americans and British to rely on infantry if they were to advance through the bracken to tank country. After Lorraine and the Ardennes, U.S. tank commanders led from the front. Sadly, Wood was not present; he had been fired by Patton at the request of the XII Corps:

> 4th Armored's triumph sowed seeds of severe dissension between Wood and Eddy over the conduct of the battle . . . a serious clash of both personalities and perspectives between Wood and the stolid, humorless Eddy. . . . If ever there was an example of the philosophical and personal disparities between the aggressive armor generals and the Fort Benning-trained infantrymen, it was the appalling relations between these two men.[96]

Wood had dared to question tactical decisions he disagreed with: "There was no conception of far-reaching directions for armor in the minds of our top people."[97] In other words, he behaved just like his Third Army boss. Perhaps Wood was too good for his own corporate well-being. With Patton's failures at Metz and Wood's successes against Manteuffel, there were now too many chefs in the Third Army tactical kitchen. Wood was sent away, and Patton added glitter to his faded stars when Abrams reached Bastogne to save the Bulge. Lucky Forward's tanks were victorious again.[98]

Notes

1. CMH 319.7 Special Studies, Grow Papers, MHI.
2. "The Establishment and Defense of the Nancy Bridgehead," prepared by

subordinate commanders and the staff of Combat Command A, 4th Armored Division (ETO 1945). (Hereafter Nancy Bridgehead), MHI.

3. Liddell Hart, *History of the Second World War* (New York: Putnam, 1970), p. 562.

4. During a meeting with Eisenhower at Chartres on 2 September Patton pleaded that "my men can eat their belts but my tanks gotta have gas." Shortages were severe enough to affect combat support. Twelfth Army HQ ordered that "armies will not move their 240mm howitzers or 3" howitzers *east* of the Seine." Sheffield Edwards Papers, G3 Air, Headquarters 12 Army Group. 22 August 1944. MHI.

5. Weigley, p. 350. Patton hedged: "[T]his talking cooperation [by Eisenhower] is for the purpose of covering up probable criticism of strategical blunders. . . . Whether or not these were his own or due to too much cooperation with the British, I don't know. I am inclined to think he over-cooperated." Patton, quoted by Martin Blumenson, *The Battle of the Generals* (New York: William Morrow, 1993), p. 272.

6. CMH 319.7 Special Studies—The Lorraine Campaign by General R. W. Grow, "Broad Front vs. Narrow Front" (hereafter Lorraine Study—Grow).

7. U.S. Divisions began to run out of fuel. The U.S. 7th Armored became stranded 30 miles north of Verdun. When Patton discovered that U.S. Army transport had been allotted to Montgomery because "1,400 Brit three ton trucks had faulty pistons" he resorted to covertly redirecting fuel convoys destined for the British toward his own U.S. Third Army dumps. Whiting, p. 65, MHI.

8. Grow, MHI.

9. Initially, Patton had intended to surround Metz with a quick Cannae move and push on; however "some head on grappling with the forts was inevitable . . . the Metz system was too big to leave as a thorn in the line of communication." Weigley, p. 329. This is debated by J. N. Rickard, *Patton at Bay—The Lorraine Campaign* (Westport, Conn.: Praeger, 1999), pp. 129, 130.

10. Patton writing to Doolittle, 19 October 1944; quoted by D'Este in *Patton*, p. 668.

11. "Patton's operation in the vicinity of Metz in the fall of 1944 was poor and showed a lack of imaginative leadership. This lack of generalship cost the lives of American soldiers and accomplished little." Maj. E. Appleman, quoted by Gen. R. W. Grow. Grow Papers, MHI.

12. Lorraine Study—Grow: "The Mounted Attack," MHI.

13. See Oskar Munzel, *Die deutschen gepanzerten Truppen bis 1945* (Bonn: Maximilian Verlag, 1965), pp. 101–113. Munzel includes an organizational review of panzer brigades.

14. Bailey, p. 111; Weigley, p. 344.

15. Weigley, p. 338.

16. *Kriegstagebuch der Panzer-Armeeoberkommando 5;* angefangen: 9.8.44—gesschossen: 9.9.44, p. 46.

17. Maj. Gen. F. W. von Mellenthin, H. Betzler, trans., *Panzer Battles—A Study of the Employment of Armor in the Second World War* (Norman: University of Oklahoma, 1955), p. 313.

18. R. W. Grow: *Flexibility in Defense*. Special Study. 1952. MHI.

19. Anthony Kemp, *The Unknown Battle: Metz, 1944* (New York: Stein & Day, 1985), p. 83.

20. "XII Corps Offensive vs. Nancy. Corps Mission: to cross the Moselle River on a wide front, capture Nancy, and continue to the east to establish a bridge-

head over the Saar River in the vicinity of Sarreguemines. 2d Cavalry Group to pro-tect the flank of the Corps; 35th Infantry . . . to capture Nancy and continue east in the direction of Chateau Salins. 80th Infantry Division to expand shallow bridge-head over the Moselle . . . covering the north flank of the corps. . . . The 4th Armored Division to bypass Nancy in two columns to the north and south, seize the high ground in the Château-Salins area to block the exits from Nancy, and be pre-pared to continue the advance across the Saar River in the vicinity of Sarreguemines. . . . The 79th Infantry Division to move to the east in the direction of Lunéville." Nancy Bridgehead, p. 3.

21. Maj. George S. Patton Jr., Third Cavalry, "What the World War Did for Cavalry." A post–World War I article for the *Cavalry Journal* reprinted in *Armor* (May–June 1985): 8.

22. Grow, HIS 314.7, 6 October 1952, MHI.

23. Clarke came upon an ordnance team recovering a half-track under enemy attack—ignoring artillery and rifle fire, Clarke ordered them not to continue repair but to keep it in tow and head east because the advance would resume in minutes. Nancy Bridgehead, p. 25.

24. "CCB, south jaw of the pincers, gouged northeast to Chateau Salins over streams and canals. The 24th Engrs., supported by the 99th Engr. Treadway Bridge Co., floated a 168-foot bridge over the Moselle at Bayon and a 180-foot bridge over the Meurthe at Mont." *The Team: The 4th Armd Division from the Beach to Bastogne* (ETO: Published by Stars & Stripes, 1945), p. 25.

25. Nancy Bridgehead Report, and BCC Papers, MHI.

26. Memo HQ "A" 4th Armd Division 12 Oct 44. Clarke's home newspapers made him a celebrity; the clippings were passed around 4th Division HQ. BCC Papers, MHI.

27. BCC Papers, MHI.

28. Eddy generously gave Clarke an option: "'Do you think you can make it?' Clarke: 'Yes, General, I think that is the only thing to do. We can't fight the Germans on this side of the river.' General Eddy: 'Well, I will leave it up to you. If you think you can get through I'll let you go. If you think you can't make it, no blame will be attached to you.'" Nancy Bridgehead, pp. 24, 25. See also Hugh M. Cole, *The Lorraine Campaign—U.S. Army in World War II: European Theater of Operations* (Washington, D.C.: U.S. Army Historical Division, 1950), p. 86.

29. Clarke became a strong advocate of "Tri Service Doctrine." BCC Papers, MHI.

30. Nancy Bridgehead.

31. In the 48-hour period of the penetration to Arracourt, CC A had taken 1,614 POWs, inflicted 1,070 casualties, and destroyed 16 large-caliber guns, 8 tanks, and 232 miscellaneous vehicles. CC A's own costs were 3 killed, 15 wound-ed, and 4 tanks lost. CC A thoroughly impressed one of its senior prisoners of war, Standartenführer Theodore Werner, 17th SS Panzer Grenadier Division: "I would be pleased to know the commander of this particular Division . . . [he] would explain to me how this Army managed to achieve such a speed of advance which in many instances caught us completely unprepared." Nancy Bridgehead, pp. 9,17.

32. Christopher R. Gabel, *The 4th Armored Division in the Encirclement of Nancy* (Fort Leavenworth: U.S. Army Command and General Staff College, 1986), p. 16.

33. Maj. Gen. Eddy, XII Corps, Foreword, Nancy Bridgehead.

34. Gabel, p. 18.

35. Hugh M. Cole, "The Tank Battles in Lorraine," *Military Review* (1950): 3.

36. Cole, p. 4.

37. Nancy Bridgehead.

38. MS #B-472: Col. von Kahlden, "Einsatz des Panzer—A.O.K. 5 westlich der Vogesen in der Zeit vom 15.9. bis 15.10.44," U.S. Army Historical Section ETO, Allendorf, March 1947, pp. 24–25. "47 Pz Corps with 21st Pz Div, 112 Pz Bde will attack in the area of Lunéville . . . 58 Pz Corps with 111, 113 Pz Bdes will attack north across the Meurthe canal . . . recce to precede." MS #B-757: Hasso von Manteuffel, Part V: *Die Kaempfe an der Meurthe und an der Vezouse bis 23.September 1944* (ETO, Neustadt: 15 November 1947) (hereafter Manteuffel).

39. Mellenthin, p. 316.

40. Mellenthin, p. 316. "Twenty First Panzer had virtually no tanks . . . 11th Panzer was still en route . . . 112 Panzer Brigade had only a handful of tanks."

41. *Kriegstagebuch der Panzer-Armeeoberkommando 5,* 9.9.44–9.10.44, pp. 3–8.

42. Munzel, pp. 275–277.

43. Caleb Carr, "The American Rommel," *Military History Journal* 4, 4 (Summer 1992): 77.

44. Wood replaced General Baird; Bruce Clarke found Baird "sitting at his desk with his face in his hands and he was crying. . . . 'Read this letter' and this letter was from George Marshall. It said, 'You are too old to command a Division, and you are retired and ordered home.'" Baird was 62. BCC Papers, MHI.

45. Clarke: "often he [Wood] left the training of the Division to me. . . . I trained the Division, really." Interview by Col. B. Kish, BCC Papers, 1982, MHI.

46. Brig. Gen. Hal C. Pattison (one of Wood's senior staff officers) correspondence to M. R. Reed, 1971. Pattison noted that Wood "leaned heavily" on Clarke, who was a " steadying influence on Wood's sometime volatile temperament." Capt. K. A. Koyen, *The 4th Armored Division from the Beach to Bastogne* (Munich: Herder Druck, 1946), p. 101; and Hanson W. Baldwin, *Tiger Jack* (Ft. Collins, Colo.: Old Army Press, 1979), p. 100.

47. Liddell Hart's impression of Wood after spending two days with the 4th Armored Division in France. Liddell Hart, *History of the Second World War* (New York: G. P. Putnam, 1970), p. 557. Also Carr, p. 77.

48. Maj. Gen. Holmes Dager recalling overrunning a retreating German division (not specified) and its commander's statement regarding Wood. Quoted in Baldwin, p. 41. See also Carr, pp. 81, 84.

49. Manteuffel, p. 3.

50. Combat Command B comprised the 44th Armored Infantry Battalion; 69th Tank Battalion, 212d Armored Field Artillery Battalion; Reconnaissance Company and Company C, 603d Tank Destroyer Battalion; Troop B, 86th Cavalry Reconnaissance Squadron (Mechanized); Company C, 25th Armored Engineer Battalion; Battery B, 777th Antiaircraft Artillery Battalion. Edited by the staff, 6th Armored Division, *Combat History of the 6th Armored Division, 18 July–8 May 1945* (Yadkinville, N.C.: Ripple Publishing, 1947), p. 82.

51. Manteuffel. Meurthe Battles, p. 3. The second Lunéville attack was launched by the 11th Panzer Division (reinforced by the 111th and 113th Panzer Brigades and a 112th Panzer Brigade battle group). A second effort by the 111th struck the U.S. XII Corps reconnaissance group, specifically D Troop, 25th Cavalry Regiment, which "received a severe mauling at the hands of the German 11th Panzer Division in the Foret de Parroy." Nancy Bridgehead, MHI.

52. Cole, p. 6.

53. Baldwin, p. 85.

54. "The 58 Pz Korps temporarily deployed 113 Pz Bde north of the canal—the focus of the fighting." MS #B-472, Kahlden, p. 26.

55. Distributions and comments, Lorraine campaign by General Grow. Special Studies Box, WWII, Grow, OCMH Collection, MHI, 2. (Hereafter Grow, OCMH.)

56. Equipped with the M18 Hellcat mounting a 76mm gun in an open turret; it was the tank destroyer version of the Chaffee tank.

57. "Some of the tanks knocked out had fewer than a hundred miles on their odometers." War diary, *4th Armored Division,* 19 September 44, MHI.

58. Grow, OCMH, p. 3.

59. Grow, OCMH, p. 3.

60. Grow claims that the maneuver and attack was conducted by one tank company. Grow, OCMH, p. 4.

61. Cole, *Military Review,* p. 6, and Cole, *The Lorraine Campaign,* p. 225.

62. Mellenthin, p. 316.

63. War diary, 4th Armored Division.

64. "Enemy recce temporarily advanced to Dieuze." MS #B-472, p. 26.

65. Nancy Bridgehead.

66. If not *JagdPanthers* then possibly Nashorns, a reference to "mobile 88mm AT guns." War diary, 4th Armored Division, and BCC Papers, MHI.

67. Grow, MHI. The Fifth Panzer Army reported losses of eleven tanks for each side. Junghannis was cited in dispatches for this action. *Kriegstagebuch der Panzer-Armeeoberkommando 5; 9.8.44–9.9.44, 48.* CC A Operations Journal records: "Lost 12 tanks and knocked out 8 enemy"; 4th Armored After Action Report claims eighteen Panzers for only seven Shermans lost.

68. The Fifth Panzer Army considered this a major battle, though a series of battle group actions: "*Die 113. Pz. Brigade und etwa ab 20.9 auch die 111. Pz. Brigade hatten schwere Kaempfe in Raum Juvelize-Ley-Reschicourt la Petite die 4. armerik. Pz. Div.*" MS #B-472, Kahlden, p. 26.

69. Abrams was a "maneuverist." See Creighton W. Abrams, Student thesis, U.S. Army War College, 1 April 1953. "The Armored Division should be given and should use mission type orders. It is unrealistic for the corps commander to assume that he can visualize the circumstances in which the armored division will find itself three days hence and one hundred miles behind enemy lines. . . . The greatest possible latitude should be permitted the armored division commander. . . . Only then will the mobility and flexibility of armor be fully realized. Abrams, "Armor in the Team," *Armor* (June 1985), p. 32.

70. Grow, OCMH, p. 6.

71. When informed of this praise Abrams quipped: "Well, he never said that to me—and he damn well had plenty of chances." Lewis Sorley, *Thunderbolt* (New York: Simon and Schuster, 1992), pp. 95, 96.

72. *Kriegstagebuch der Panzer-Armeeoberkommando 5,* p. 46. See also Anton J. Donnhauser and Generalmajor Werner Drews, *Der Weg der 11. Panzer-Division* (Bad Worishofen: Holzman-Druck-Service, 1982). See also G. W. Schrodek, *Ihr Glaube galt dem Vaterland—Die Geschicte des Panzerregiment 15,—11. Panzer-Division* (Bad Worishofen: Schild Verlag, 1976).

73. *The Team: The 4th Armd Division from the Beach to Bastogne* (ETO: Published by Stars & Stripes, 1945), p. 27.

74. "The German losses were from TD as well as tank fire, artillery and air while American losses were primarily from tank fire." Grow, MHI.

75. Cole, *Military Review,* p. 9.

76. Manteuffel, p. 4.

77. The XV Corps (Haislip) was permitted to hold the Meurthe River line; the XII Corps held Lunéville: the 313th Infantry Regiment engaged the 21st Panzer Division at Moncel, outside the Forêt de Mondon. Luttwitz attempted to ease the pressure by attacking Lunéville with the 15th Panzer Grenadier and 21st Panzer Divisions. When the U.S. 79th Infantry Division counterattacked, Manteuffel requested permission to withdraw. Balck, citing "the clear führerbefehl [führer's order]," refused. Cole, p. 29.

78. "The back of the Fifth Panzer Army attack was broken on 29th September, nor was there any further possibility of creating a new force for continued effort to reach the Moselle." Cole, *Military Review,* p. 15. The 29 September attack cost Gen. Wend von Weitersheim (11th Panzer Division) twenty-four of his twenty-five tanks. Wood, over the area in his L-40 plane saw "burning tanks blazing all the way from the Dieuze road to the Foret de Parroy." Baldwin, p. 88.

79. "The battle at Arracourt was also a high point for TDs. Gen. Bruce's 'ideal' tank destroyer, the M18 (Hellcat) proved its worth. . . . The maneuverability of the M18 played a major role." Bailey, pp. 111–112.

80. Grow, MHI. "From 2 September–19 September the enemy launched a series of furious armored counterattacks attempting to break through to the encircled city of Nancy. In the ensuing four day tank battle, the entire German armored force in the area was depleted." After-action report, 4th Armored Division, ETO, September/October 1944.

81. MS #B-251. Gen. Horst Stumpff, the 106th Panzer Brigade. The first Panzer brigades, 101st–110th were organized as battle groups: 1 panzer battalion (30–36 Pzkw IVs or Vs), 1 panzer grenadier battalion, 1 engineer company, and 1 supply transport column. Subsequent units were generally similar. The 111th Panzer Brigade may have had a battalion of Panthers and Pzkw IVs.

82. The *Kessel* (Cauldron) and the *Rückmarsch* were the German references to the Falaise gap and the withdrawal from Normandy, respectively.

83. Hausser and Schweppenberg both had their counterattacks disrupted by tactical air, heavy artillery, and spoiling attacks.

84. *Corps Commander,* p. 53.

85. ETHINT 67, p. 3, MHI.

86. If Montgomery was frustrated at his inability to complete a perfect Cannae he seems to have sated himself by blaming Eisenhower: "His ignorance as to how to run a war is absolute and complete." Correspondence to Brooke, 14 August 1944, cited in Hamilton, p. 791. An American evaluation is closer to the truth: "21 Army Group was the best I saw in the war from a mechanical stand point. But Monty sailed off across the Channel and didn't use it. Most unfortunate." Pogue, interview with Colonel Bonesteel. Pogue Papers, MHI.

87. Operational maneuver group: an independent, corps-sized armored maneuver formation. See Chapter 14.

88. BCC Papers, MHI.

89. Liddell Hart, *Strategy* (New York: Praeger, 1954), p. 148. "Grant accepted a Napoleonic strategy of annihilation as the prescription for victory in a war of popular nationalism." Weigley, p. 143.

90. Liddell Hart, p. 148. Liddell Hart's ideal was Sherman, whom he presented as the maneuverist antithesis to Grant's alleged attritionist style. "Sherman's method was to threaten strategic points . . . [with] economy of force by maneuver . . . he maneuvered so skillfully as to lure the confederates time after time in vain attacks . . . an example of strategic artistry rarely seen in history." Pp. 150–151.

91. Weigley, p. 142.

92. Grant's instructions to Meade. Weigley, p. 145.

93. "Broad Front vs. Narrow Front," Lorraine Study—Grow campaign, HIS 314.7, MHI.

94. Orlando Ward Papers, 1941–1943, Biographic notes by Gugeler, chap. X, MHI.

95. "German Defence of Lorraine," Lorraine Study—Grow, MHI.

96. D'Este, *Patton,* p. 663.

97. Wood to Liddell Hart, p. 557.

98. Wood was considered by some to be "obstreperous, hard to handle, a difficult subordinate." Gen. Ben Lear, commander, U.S. Ground Forces Europe. Crittenberger Papers, MHI. Patton reportedly told Walker: "Johnny, I don't give a damn what you think of 'P' Wood. He was one of the best commanders I had and I want him back." See A. Harding Ganz, "Patton's Relief of General Wood," *Journal of Military History* (July 1989).

A Tiger I from the 101st Heavy Tank Battalion knocked out on Verrières Ridge during Operation Spring *(Noble, National Archives of Canada, Wilfred Laurier University, Laurier Centre for Military Strategic and Disarmament Studies)*

CHAPTER 13

"Who Killed Tiger?": The Great Tank Scandal

If we had a tank like that Tiger, we would all be home today.
—Sgt. Clyde D. Brunson, tank commander, U.S. 2d Armored Division[1]

When you consider the Tiger tank
Its conduct is in the first rank.

—Tigerfibel[2]

Allied armored doctrine, sidetracked by internecine squabbles and erroneous analysis, failed to produce a tank capable of meeting German armor on anything approaching an equal footing until 1945. The Allied inability to build a main battle tank, despite extensive experience and a wealth of technical data from two theatres, resulted in horrendous casualties to both its armored forces and the accompanying infantry. Capitalist industry's failure to forge what the Soviets and Nazis had accomplished by 1942 has been called by some the Great Tank Scandal.[3]

By the summer of 1944 Western armor had evolved, in theory, in direct reaction to German armament. In fact, it reflected the personal biases of general officers in key positions, who, rather than answer clear calls from the battlefield, ensured that their personal philosophies prevailed. In Britain, Fuller-Liddell Hart disciples and Royal Tank Corps zealots directed tank development; in the United States it was Gen. Leslie McNair, operating with the support and approval of George Marshall. It may be argued that the Soviet and German armies were even more under the aegis of their political bosses (in particular Hitler, whose meddling in the most trivial of technical decisions hamstrung both the panzer arm and the navy),[4] but it must be noted that dictatorships managed superb tank parks. Western expertise focused on the air forces, yet even here it failed to produce an operational jet aircraft like the Me 262. Operational doctrine could not be tested while saddled with inferior weapons whose tactics were based on the parry rather than the lunge. By the summer of 1944 Allied tactical creativity was stymied.

The West's armored forces had not renounced the 1930s; there were still two key armored fighting vehicles, in role, if not in type—the infantry tank and the cavalry tank. There were two types of formations—tank brigades, which operated with or under command of the infantry division, and armored divisions, capable of Operational Maneuver. The letter of the dual tank doctrine was not religiously followed. The Americans and Canadians relied on one battle tank, the M4 Sherman while the British, who could least afford it, deployed three main battle tanks—the Churchill infantry tank and two cruiser tanks, the Sherman and the Cromwell.

U.S. infantry divisions had the ubiquitous GHQ tank battalions at their disposal. The tank destroyer doctrine was given lip service to placate zealots in Washington, but most practical thinkers, and certainly all veterans of Tunisia, realized that the tank destroyer was passé as a doctrinal statement. Tank destroyers had made some initial sense as a mobile reserve capable of blocking operations against assaulting blitzkrieg columns, but they made no sense in an Allied army now committed to the offensive. Besides, when the Germans did attack, they used *Kampfgruppen,* all-arms combat teams rather than a Fulleresque "torrent of armor." Thin-skinned M3 half-tracks and M10s were marginally effective in North African defensive battles against the Afrika Korps; in the attack, tank destroyers were a liability.

Nonetheless, the Allies arrived in Normandy confident that their armored doctrine had been tested and proven. Experience in the Italian theater was not seriously considered; it had fulfilled the predictions of armored experts in that it was "rotten tank country, no place to employ armored divisions." Normandy was different. France was ideal tank country—the very theater where blitzkrieg had been force-fed to the Allies in 1940. There was every prospect of *doing it right* with armor. The problem was in combat ratio. Eisenhower's army group, in particular Montgomery's divisions, would face a sobering concentration of German armor.

Within weeks of combat in Normandy, Allied armored doctrine underwent drastic mutation. In the bocage country, U.S. and British infantry preceded all assaults in order to clear out German tank-hunting teams and lurking assault guns. In the Caen sector armor dutifully led, but every Allied operational offensive that pushed into open country was savagely hurled back despite crushing artillery and air superiority. The German defense so affected Allied doctrine that heavy bombers were pressed into service on four separate army-level breakthrough attempts, and the commander of the Canadian II Corps was forced to resort to a complex night attack in August despite the fact that his opposition had been reduced to one emasculated SS division.

It was not until Bradley's tanks had been set loose past Avranches that traditional war fighting returned. Reasons for the stalemate from 6 June to mid-August 1944 included Allied inexperience, German advantage in the defense, and the absence of Allied attack doctrine. The list is long, but one could also simply say "Tigers and Panthers." They stopped the Allies cold. Nothing could knock them out, nothing could withstand their firepower.

The Origins of the Scandal

The individual superiority of Matilda in 1939, a superiority diminished by lack of numerical strength, once lost was not regained until four years later with the 17-pounder up-gunned Sherman *in Normandy.*
                                                                —G. MacLeod Ross[5]

Why is it that I am always the last to hear about this stuff: Ordnance told me this 76 would take care of anything the German had. Now I find you can't knock out a damn thing with it.
                                                    —Dwight D. Eisenhower, July 1944[6]

The Allies had defeated Tiger tanks in North Africa in the early months of 1943; there had been nearly twelve months of battle in Italy. Tigers had been living in British captivity for well over a year. Why, suddenly did the Allies face a tank scandal? Initial contact with the Tiger suggested that it could be knocked out by the 6-pounder antitank gun: although a trial was ordered to prove these findings, it was never completed.[7]

Accordingly, after final victory in Africa, it was decided that the Sherman could do the job and the U.S. heavy tank program was stalled— the T7, ready for production in 1943 was canceled. The T7 was well armored but considered too big. The Sherman was the more logical choice if one's priority was shipping: "General Devers reflected the opinion of the Armored Force that it was preferable to use the available shipping for two 30-ton medium tanks rather than one 60-ton heavy tank."[8] Accepting Tunisian reports at face value, McNair put the U.S. heavy tank on the back burner and decided to go into Europe with his tank destroyers and the Sherman.[9]

British armor's technical inferiority to German armor was an unpleasant surprise. British industry was both not competent and too overextended by the war to give tank design any sort of priority; as a result the least skilled men ended up at the tank design bureau.

The D of M . . . steadfastly refused to stir the apathy of the General Staff in this respect, refusing to up-gun his tanks because the General Staff had not asked for bigger and better guns. Thus it came about that ignorance interposed one more obstacle in the essential liaison between those whose

SHERMAN M4

ALLIED and GERMAN
MAIN BATTLE TANKS
FRANCE 1944

Medium Tank "Sherman" M4 A1-A4
Gun: 75mm (75 Caliber Length)
Range (Eff Frontal Penetration): Mk IV to 1000m; Panther/Tiger: nil
Best Armor Penetration at 500m: 3.5"
Armor Piercing Shell Velocity m/sec: 2030fps
Armor (max): 3" Combat Weight 31 tons
Height: 287cm Speed: 25 mph (road); 20 (xcountry)
Crew: 5

FIREFLY

Medium Tank "Firefly" M4 A2
Gun: 76.2mm
Range (Eff Frontal Penetration): Mk IV to 2000m; Panther 1200; Tiger 500
Best Armor Penetration at 500m: over 6"
Armor Piercing Shell Velocity m/sec: 2030fps
Armor(max): 81mm; Combat Weight 33 tons
Height: 287cm; Speed: 25 mph (road); 15 (xcountry)
Crew: 5

M 10

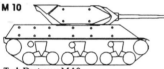

Tank Destroyer M 10
Gun: 76mm
Range (Eff Frontal Penetration): Mk IV to 1500m ;
Panther/Tiger: nil
Best Armor Penetration at 500m: 3.5"
Armor Piercing Shell Velocity m/sec: 870
Armor: 59mm; Combat Weight: 30 tons
Height: 287cm; Speed: 26 mph (road); 15 (xcountry)
Crew: 5

Killing Panther
Aim Point: Lower Gun Mantlet

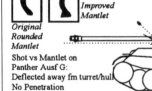

Shot vs Mantlet on
Panther Ausf D, A:
Deflected onto Hull over
driver's compartment - Kill.

Improved Mantlet

Original Rounded Mantlet

Shot vs Mantlet on
Panther Ausf G:
Deflected away fm turret/hull
No Penetration

PZKW IV

PanzerKampfWagen IV   Ausf. H
Gun: 75mm KwK 40 (48 Caliber Length)
Range (Eff Frontal Penetration):
All Allied MBT to 1500m

Armor Piercing Shell Velocity m/sec: 750 - 930
Armor (min-max): 50 - 78 mm
Combat Weight 25 tons; Height: 268 cm
Speed: 38 mph (road); 25 (xcountry); Crew: 5

PANTHER

PanzerKampfWagen V "Panther" Ausf. G
Gun: 75mm KwK 42 (70 Caliber Length)
Range (Eff Frontal Penetration):
All Allied MBT to 2000m
Armor Piercing Shell Velocity m/sec: 935 -1120
Armor (min-max): 80 - 120 mm
Combat Weight 44.8 tons; Height: 300 cm;
Speed: 46 mph (road); 24 (xcountry); Crew: 5

TIGER I

PanzerKampfWagen VI "Tiger I" Ausf. E
Gun: 88mm KwK 36 (56 Caliber Length)
Range (Eff Frontal Penetration):
All Allied MBT to 2500+m
Best Armor Penetration at 500m: over 6"
Armor Piercing Shell Velocity m/sec: 810
Armor (min-max): 100 - 110 mm
Combat Weight 55 tons; Height: 286 cm;
Speed: 38 mph (road); 20 (xcountry); Crew: 5

TIGER II
KING TIGER

PanzerKampfWagen VI "Tiger II" Ausf. B
Gun: 88mm KwK 43 (71 Caliber Length)
Range (Eff Frontal Penetration):
All Allied MBT to 2500+m
Armor Piercing Shell Velocity
m/sec: 1000-1130
Armor (min-max): 100 -150 mm
Combat Weight 69.7 tons; Height: 309 cm
Speed: 38 mph (road); 17 (xcountry) Crew: 5

duty it was to decide WHAT to build and those whose responsibility was HOW to build it.[10]

The result was the alarming state of British tanks: underarmored, undergunned, and mechanically unreliable ("with the cooling system installed backwards to suck in hot air from the engine and roast the crew . . . it took forever to perform the simplest repairs.")[11]

> The War Office . . . never tackled the many technical problems which had to be resolved before the tank really supplanted the horse on the battle-field. . . . In retrospect it becomes clear that no one in authority was giving any thought to either the technics or the tactics of the tank.[12]

The best the British could do is come up with the excellent 17-pounder gun and agree that the only decent tank to mount it on was the American Sherman. U.S. armor's attempts to create a suitable battle tank[13] were blocked by McNair and the bias of american industry and U.S. Army Ordnance against the logical Firefly (Sherman M4) solution.[14]

> There were two reasons which prevented the Americans from accepting British advice: the suspicion that the Machiavellian British had so advised because they had some ulterior and probably sinister motive, or, the fear that if an American accepted our advice he would be told by the isolation-ists that he had sold out to the Limeys.[15]

American faith in the 76mm gun and the tank destroyer would not be shaken until Normandy, when it was too late, and Bradley was reduced to begging Montgomery for Fireflies—of which the British and Canadian armored divisions had none to spare.

The tank scandal should not have come as a total surprise to Allied generals. Still, despite detailed reports from military attachés in Moscow and their own after-action reports, SHAEF was unprepared for the Tiger or Panther. There were three reasons for this. First, initial successes supported upbeat reports, and pessimistic warnings were brushed aside. Second, aborted field tests forced commanders to await detailed ordnance studies from Bovington, England, and Aberdeen Proving Ground, Maryland, whose test results arrived too late (confident initial predictions by ordnance teams testing the 76mm gun soothed misgivings and prompted the U.S. refusal to adopt the British 17-pounder as an interim solution until it became too late to do anything about it). Third, although Tigers had been captured, Panthers had not been evaluated at all. The first time the Allies met the Pzkw V Panther in actual combat was after the Allied breakout from Anzio. By then the Normandy invasion had begun. The first detailed

Panther reports read by Eisenhower's staff would be from their own troops in Normandy. The technological superiority of the Tiger and the aggressive, almost reckless way it was employed by its confident crews created a powerful legend that—despite the fact it was in the greater part myth—mesmerized Allied commands and agonized Allied armored troops.[16]

The anticipated debut of a Tiger battalion on the Western Front turned out to be a dud rather than a shock. The Afrika Korps Tigers were nailed by 6-pounder antitank guns from defilade positions that engaged the only sections of the Pzkw VI that could be penetrated, the flank and rear hull. The knocked-out monsters were examined with more curiosity than awe. Initial reports were enthusiastic: our antitank guns can kill Tiger.[17]

This was dangerously misleading. The after-action estimates were based on overoptimistic evaluations and incomplete investigations. The only attempted test (3 February 1943) ended in failure.[18] Eventually, a British technical staff field officer, Lt. Col. Neville, managed to conduct one controlled trial with plates that had been removed from Tiger by oxyacetylene cutting. The results should have set off alarms throughout the armored corps but fell through the cracks.[19] The next series of accurate tests would be conducted at Bovington, Larkhill, and Chobham. They would take months, and their results, when published, were too technical and too late to create any feverish response at SHAEF. The Allied General Staff liked what it first was told about the Tiger—that it was easy to kill. Besides, the 6-pounder gun was about to be augmented by masses of 76mm and 17-pounder guns, which, the generals were promised, would take care of any German tank. Accordingly, General McNair opposed the production of the latest U.S. heavy tank, the T26 (M26 Pershing). The AGF policy statement concluded the following:

> The recommendation of a limited proportion of tanks carrying a 90mm gun is not concurred in for the following reasons: The M4 tank has been hailed widely as the best tank on the battlefield today. . . . There appears to be fear on the part of our forces of the German Mark VI (Tiger) tank. There can be no basis for the T26 tank other than the conception of a tank-vs.-tank duel—which is believed to be unsound and unnecessary. Both British and American battle experience has demonstrated that the antitank gun in suitable numbers is the master of the tank. . . . There has been no indication that the 76mm antitank gun is inadequate against German Mark VI tank.[20]

The report was premature and served McNair's bias against the U.S. armored corps; it was also a contemptuous reply to British battlefield lessons learned and General Devers's report from North Africa. The U.S. Army was in for a tragic surprise in Normandy and the Ardennes.

The American Heavy Tank: Self-Imposed Punishment

Some things I have seen in combat that were disturbing and disgusting to any tanker. Many times I've seen our tanks engage German tanks in tank duels. Their tanks have the ups on us. . . . Give us the tanks that compare with the Jerries' tanks and we have the rest. . . . I am a tank commander and a veteran of Africa, Sicily, France, Belgium, Holland and Germany. I have been wounded once and have seen most of the action that my unit has been in. I guess I am just lucky.
— Sgt. Leo Anderson. platoon leader, 2d Armored Division[21]

During the winter of 1943, while formal tests were being conducted at Chobham,[22] one of the captured Tigers was put on public display at Horse Guards Parade in the center of London.[23] U.S. and Canadian armored officers joined British school kids climbing over the tank and were relieved to find that it was a sitting duck for any 6-pounder gun. The truth was the exact opposite. Secret trials quickly proved that although the Tiger could be killed by short-range flank fire, should it choose a less aggressive tactic and select to fight it out at long range, there was not an Allied tank in the inventory (the Red Army excepted) that could kill a Tiger. In fact, Royal Ordnance scientists discovered to their horror that the Tiger could not be penetrated at *any* range. Point-blank engagements at under 100 yards proved that 6-pounder and 75mm tank guns could not defeat the Tiger's frontal armor. The rounds simply bounced off. Controlled tests with standard Shermans and the new A4 armed with the highly touted 76mm M1A1 gun (just being delivered to select U.S. tank battalions) produced galling results. The standard Sherman 75mm, which formed the bulk of U.S., British, and Canadian tank battalions, could not engage the Tiger unless they maneuvered and closed to 100 yards, or hit the rear of the turret or the vertical plates on the flanks.[24] This was a particularly risky business because Tigers were always protected by a silent partner—another Tiger or Stug—sited in defilade.

If the Tiger got sloppy and abandoned the standard hull-down firing position, a Sherman *might* score at longer range—a pipe dream in the bocage that surrounded U.S. and British tank actions. To get close, the Sherman had to fight through hedgerows and orchards covered by antitank guns and defended by German infantry armed with the Panzerfaust. The 76mm M1A1 stood a slightly better chance, but the up-gunned Shermans were unobtainable: not a single 76mm was available on 6 June 1944. By September only 250, out of the 1,913 tanks in the 12th Army Group, were A4 Shermans.

The alternative solution was to fit a 17-pounder into a Sherman (the Firefly). It caused minor engineering problems but it worked. A 17-pounder firing armor-piercing (self-discarding sabot) could defeat a Tiger in a frontal engagement at ranges of 1,700 to 1,900 yards. The tank crews loved it. "Without doubt the Sherman Firefly was the best Allied tank of World War Two."[25] Sadly, it was not given top priority. The British lobbied to have masses of 17-pounder Shermans built in the United States, The Americans dug in their heels: British advice was suspect. The record spoke for itself. British tanks were inferior; the only reason the British had won in the desert, American tank designers said in private, was because American tanks like the Grant and Sherman arrived in time. It was American armor, not British, that won in Africa. Although exaggerated, the theory was not altogether untrue.[26]

U.S. Army Ordnance and Supply continued to concentrate on their own heavy tank; however, it was experiencing considerable teething problems. The technical delay, coupled with McNair's preference for tank destroyers and the antitank gun, ensured that the U.S. Armored Force was not to have a main battle tank capable of taking on the Panzers in Normandy. The final culprits were the indecisiveness of the ordnance team and the U.S. Armored Force itself.

Excessive confidence in the 76mm (3-inch) gun, delay in delivering the 90mm gun in quantity, and a xenophobic attitude toward anything British, denied the U.S. Army a heavy tank or a good tank-killing gun. The final verdict came from someone who should have known better—Gen. Jacob Devers, commanding general of the Armored Force. Devers returned from an inspection tour of U.S. armored units in North Africa and submitted a report to General McNair on 7 December 1942. Besides finding the tank destroyer solution impracticable, he dropped a bombshell: "Due to its tremendous weight and limited tactical use, there is no requirement in the Armored Force for a heavy tank. The increase in the power of the armament of the heavy tank does not compensate for the heavier armor."[27]

Although McNair ignored Devers's other recommendations regarding the tank destroyer program, he immediately canceled the remaining main battle tank, the T7. In recommending the cancellation of the heavy tank program Devers both played into McNair's hands and doomed the Armored Force to technical inferiority. In the winter of 1943, there was little sense of urgency in American tank development despite the cautionary advice given by MacLeod Ross (British tank expert and chief liaison to U.S. Army Ordnance) and his team of experts. The British could not even convince the Americans to build Fireflies. The 17-pounder was not considered sufficiently superior to the 76mm tank gun to warrant American production. Devers refused to attend a shooting demonstration that compared the 17-pounder with the 76mm and 90mm guns. Rejected in Detroit and Washington, Ross advised Whitehall that if the British wanted Fireflies, they would have to build them themselves. The British did that, but given the chaotic state of their industry, the best they could manage by 6 June

1944 was a 25 percent replacement. Only one out of every four tanks in an armored troop was a Firefly—not enough even for the squadron commander. By the end of June there were 109 Fireflies in France, about the strength of one German panzer regiment. In fact, until August the Canadian armor on the Caen front was actually outnumbered by the enemy (Table 13.1).

The Truth About Panzers

In my opinion the reason our armor has engaged the German tanks as successfully as it has is not due to any means to a superior tank but to our superior numbers of tanks on the battlefield and the willingness of our tankers to take their losses while maneuvering to a position from which a penetrating shot can be put through a weak spot of the enemy tank.
—Col. S. R. Hinds, CC B, 2d Armored Division[28]

The enemy tends to use his heavy tanks almost recklessly.
—First Cdn Army information bulletin October 1944[29]

The Germans continually and imprudently introduced their new tanks into combat in two conditions: unproven (still trying to overcome teething problems) or in small, ineffective groups. The Tiger was committed piecemeal; although it was impervious to Allied armor, its appreciated overall superiority produced an aggressiveness in its crews than at times defied logic and tactics, "taking risks to a degree indicating they have the utmost confidence in the vehicle."[30] The Panther's performance in its first battle, Operation Zitadelle at Kursk, was not auspicious. The haste of its development and production led to numerous problems and breakdowns. German industry immediately set to correcting the problems, and "gradually most of

Table 13.1   Panzer Battalions Versus Canadian Tank Battalions

	8 June	19 July	21 July	25 July	8 Aug
Tiger Battalion	0	1	1	3	.25
Jpz Battalion	0	0	0	1	0
Panther Battalion	1	2	3	3	.25
Pzkw IV Battalion	1	2	3	3	.50
JPz/Stug Battalion	1	2	3	4	.25
German Battalion Totals	3	7	10	14	1.25
Canadian Battalion Totals	3	3	3	6[a]	14[b]

Notes: a. 25 July includes the three tank battalions of 22d British Armored Brigade (7th Armored Division) that supported Spring and actually engaged German armor. Canadian/British tank regiments were equivalent to U.S. tank battalions.

b. Includes tank regts from recently arrived: Polish 1st Armored Division, Canadian 4th Armored Division, and Canadian 2d and British 33d Armored Brigades made available for Totalize.

the bugs were worked out, though a problem with failure of the rim bolts on the dished roadwheels persisted until the end of the war."[31] By 28 June 1944, the inspector general of panzer troops, Heinz Guderian, reported on the state of German tanks in Normandy: "The Panther appears to catch fire quickly. The lifespan of the Panther's motors (1,400 to 1,500 kilometers) is significantly higher than the Panther's final drives. A solution to the final drive problem is urgently needed."[32]

Despite the complexity and high manufacturing cost,[33] the Panther became a successful main battle tank for the Wehrmacht and gave a good account of itself in battle, particularly in the West. Compared to the Sherman the Panther was a monster. Although it weighed less than the Tiger, its armor was better distributed and the design was superior. The front glacis, side armor, and turret walls were sloped for better protection against shot and sabot rounds. The Panther demonstrated superior mobility: in fact, although it dwarfed the Sherman, it outperformed the American tank in wet and muddy terrain. By the fall of 1944, the after-action reports in Allied armies were full of bitter complaints from tank crew commanders about being outmaneuvered by the Panther on soft ground. "I saw where some MkV tanks crossed a muddy field without sinking the tracks over five inches, where we in the M4 started across the same field the same day and bogged down."[34] The Pzkw V had six distinct advantages over the Sherman:

1. Low flash powder.
2. Better gun. Its higher muzzle velocity and greater accuracy defeated all Allied armor. "The Jerries' guns didn't fail, they knocked out three of our Tank destroyers and one Sherman tank at 2800 to 3000 yards. If our tanks had been as good as the German tanks they would never had scored a hit." "I have actually seen ricochets go through an M4 at 3000 yards."[35]
3. Better armor. It defeated all Allied guns beyond 500 yards in frontal engagement: "I saw a 90mm TD shell bounce off a Mark V at approximately 1200 yards. . . . I have seen HEAT [high-explosive antitank] fired from a 105mm Howitzer at a Mark V at 400 yards. The track was hit and damaged, and a direct hit on the turret only chipped the paint."[36]
4. Superior sights. "German sights caused us much concern . . . more magnifying power and clearness than our own." "They are able to choose their power between 2 and 6 power, where ours is a stationary 3 power. The German sights have lighted graduations and can lay on a target at night." "For shooting into the sun they just flip a lever which just lets down a colored lens, reducing the glare."[37]
5. Superior flotation. "A case is cited where our tanks were mired in

mud and enemy tanks were negotiating it smoothly." "Before the addition of track extensions, our medium tanks sank 6 to 8 inches while the MkV tracks were not over 4 inches." "I noticed that the German tank had sunk into the soft ground about 3.5 to 4 inches. I also noticed the impressions left by an M4 medium tank and noticed that it had sunk about 5 or 6 inches. This was very interesting to me, as the German Mark V tank, weighing approximately 45 ton, was three times heavier than my own tank, weighing 15 ton. Our own M4 medium tank weighs 30 ton."[38]

6. Greater speed and greater mobility. "It could turn faster than the M24 light tank, move as fast as the M24." "[There is a] case of a Mark V beating an M4 around a field, making sharp swerve and reverse of direction in shorter space than M4."[39]

The Panther was actually physically larger than the Tiger (68 centimeters—2.7 inches wider, and 34 centimeters—1.4 inches higher) but it was always portrayed as the lesser tank. Its presence definitely created less panic. It was one of the curiosities of the war that the Tiger's legend grew faster than its kills. There were only three weak Tiger battalions in all of France but they were reported to be everywhere. Panthers outnumbered Tigers by at least four to one, knocked out more armor, and overran more infantry but never inspired quite the same terror.

Hard Evidence

Although the Allied armies produced a remarkable series of lessons-learned publications, operational surveys, technical liaison Letters, and superb intelligence summaries, hard statistics were not available for study until well after the Normandy and Lorraine campaigns. Armor penetration data, when offered, was taken from controlled firing tests (e.g., Aberdeen, Lulworth). Field studies based on data taken from actual engagements provide interesting information.

The combat data from western ETO tank engagements involved larger numbers of tanks than comparable studies from Italy. The highest numbers of Allied casualties occurred in the first four months of the Normandy campaign, and there were differences between the British-Canadian and U.S. wastage (tank loss figures). The U.S. AGF and Canadian Department of National Defense commissioned a series of Allied studies from Aberdeen Proving Ground, independent university scholars, and serving officers familiar with the armored operations. Among the most complete were two surveys by Professors Alvin Coox and L. Naisawald at Johns Hopkins University; a Canadian study—exclusive to Normandy—conducted by two veteran cavalry officers, Maj. N. A. Shackleton and R. P. Bourne;[40] and a comprehensive study by David C. Hardison for Ballistic Research Laboratories, Aberdeen Proving Ground.

The Hardison study gathered data from 136 separate tank engagements (based on ninety-eight battalion-combat command actions) covering the period from 15 August to 30 December 1944. Seven unit actions featured the battalions of the U.S. 3d Armored Division (Maj. Gen. I. D. White) and 4th Armored Division (Maj. Gen. J. Wood) from the breakout and pursuit operations in Normandy through the Arracourt battles and the relief of Bastogne.[41] The participating armor was primarily the M4 Sherman, although tank destroyers (M10 and M18) participated in eight engagements. The four significant findings were as follows:

1. Range. This was the determining factor and it exclusively favored the Germans.
2. Local Advantage of the Defense. In the 86 engagements in which the numbers of weapons and casualties are known, the Allies employed a total of 797 weapons and lost 149. The enemy used 327 weapons and lost 158. In the 40 considered engagements in which they were on the attack, the Allies lost 100 of 437 employed weapons, while the defending enemy lost 45 of 135. In the 37 engagements in which enemy forces were attacking they lost 83 of 138 weapons, while the Allied defenders lost 14 of 205.
3. Advantage of First Fire. Of 11 engagements in which they fired first, the attackers lost 12 of 88 weapons, while destroying 30 of 64 defending weapons. Of 57 engagements in which they fired first, the defenders lost 22 of 238 weapons, while destroying 154 of 397 weapons. Thus in 68 engagements, 34 of 326 weapons were lost by the side that fired first while destroying 184 of 461 opposing weapons.
4. Advantage of Mass. Of the 81 cases where a force of 3 or fewer weapons was employed, that force in 37 cases was annihilated. Of 91 cases in which a force of over 3 weapons was used, the force was annihilated in only 10 cases. It is interesting to note that in 100 of the considered 129 engagements, one force had no losses—in a majority of engagements, one force tended to possess an overwhelming immediate advantage.[42]

Range: The Critical Factor

We have been outgunned since Tunisia, when the Germans brought out their Mk IV Special with the long barreled 75mm gun. The higher muzzle

*velocity increases their trajectory, as range estimations are of less impor-
tance with such a flat trajectory.*

—Lt. Col. W. M. Hawkins,
commander 3d Battalion, 67th Armored Regiment[43]

Shorter engagement range frustrated Allied armor: "In a head-on one tank against one tank fight ours almost always comes out as a casualty."[44] Of the 215 tanks killed, casualties were equally distributed in the three main range categories: 0–500, 501–1,000, and 1,001–3,500 yards. Each range group accounted for approximately one-third of the tank kills, whereas German losses dropped by 50 percent at distances of over 1,000 yards. The tank scandal's immediate battlefield effects were that German guns killed at any distance, while superior armor on German tanks made them twice as safe at long range (Table 13.2).[45]

Table 13.2   Tank Losses from 136 Engagements

Range	Allied Tank Losses per Action: Out of a Total of 215 Armored Fighting Vehicles Knocked Out	German Tank Losses per Action: Out of a Total of 175 Armored Fighting Vehicles Knocked Out
0–500 yds.	73–35%	57–33%
501–1,000 yds.	65–30%	76–44%
1,001–3,500 yds.	75–35%	41–23%

Data suggest that battles of attrition would have eventually reduced the Allied armor to near impotence despite the aggregate attrition to German armor. Notwithstanding overwhelming air and tank superiority, total Allied casualties were almost three times that of the Wehrmacht. Thus the longer the ground war lasted in Europe, the greater the casualties to Allied armor. A Soviet-style strategic offensive was the only solution to the Normandy problem—the Allies had to break out and ensure that any operation victory was rapidly elevated by bold pursuit to knock the Wehrmacht out of the war quickly. Discussion of the respective values of attrition vis-à-vis maneuver must accept that in operational contests attrition precedes maneuver. Tanks and infantry had to fight through fixed defenses against sniping Panzers in order to break through.

What Killed Panzers: The German Viewpoint

On 24 May 1945, three of the principal German operational commanders in the Normandy campaign—Geyr von Schweppenburg (Panzer Group West),

Sepp Dietrich (1st SS Panzer Corps) and Paul Hausser (2d SS Panzer Corps)—joined Gen. Heinz Guderian (inspector general, panzer troops) at the U.S. Seventh Army Interrogation Center in Bavaria. During the session, this cream of panzer experience was asked what they attributed German tank losses to by percentage: air, antitank, and mechanical. And which was most feared by tank crews? All the generals were cooperative, save for Guderian, who hesitated in answering some questions, and the replies were revealing:

> Guderian: "60–70 percent through mechanical failures (Eastern Front); 15 percent A/T; 5 percent artillery; 5 percent mines; 5 percent others."
> Dietrich: "Mechanical failures, 30 percent; air 10 percent; A/T, 15 percent; tanks, 45 percent. Losses due to artillery were negligible. Most feared by crews: Allied tanks and TDs."
> Hausser: "During long movements to the zone of action, 20–30 percent of all tanks en route fall out due to mechanical failures. Considering the remainder as 100 percent, 15 percent are lost through mechanical failures; 20 percent through air attacks; 50 percent through A/T defense; and 15 percent are knocked out by artillery. Tanks and TDs are feared most by German tank crews."[46]

Geyr von Schweppenburg, who lost his entire headquarters (mostly through arrogance) to an air strike in mid-June, was understandably impressed with air power. The old hands who had suffered through the three months of Normandy knew better: tanks kill tanks. The most interesting information is the rate of mechanical breakdown: the most accomplished slayer of German panzers was German engineering.

The generals' recollections were confirmed by Allied survey teams that examined every armored fighting vehicle hulk found in Normandy. Their investigation not only chronicles in detail the actual losses caused by breakdown or crew abandonment, but fully supports Dietrich's and Hausser's indifference toward the Allied FGA threat. Battlefield inspection discovered that of the German tanks killed by direct gun fire, the overwhelming majority from tanks and tank destroyers. The remaining losses were caused by air attack, mines, and "miscellaneous, enemy action." Again, the highest single cause of German tank losses was from "miscellaneous, non-enemy action," not air attack as suggested by postwar analysts (see Table 13.3).

Normandy ended German industry's recovery in the face of increasing strategic bomber attacks and Soviet offensives. Alfred Speer's reforms could keep pace with Eastern Front wastage but were overwhelmed by the drain of the Normandy battlefield. During the first five months of 1944 production kept pace with losses: tanks (3,571) and assault guns (2,550) for a total of 6,121. For the same period, JN6 (Ordnance) recorded accepting 5,212 units from the manufacturer against a battlefield wastage of 3,119.

Table 13.3   German Tank Losses by Cause 1944–1945[47]

Cause of Immobilization	Number of Sampled Tanks	Percent of Total Known
Gunfire (75, 76, 90mm Tank Destroyer, Artillery)	520	43.2%
Hollow Charge	53	4.4%
Air Attack	91	7.5%
Mines	3	0.2%
Miscellaneous, Enemy Action	9	0.7%
Miscellaneous, Nonenemy Action	522	43.8%

This gave the Wehrmacht a net gain of 2,093 units. Before D-Day, total holdings for the German Army High Command had been increased by 36 percent.[48] This was sufficient to bring the panzer divisions up to two-thirds of their war establishment.[49] Interestingly, during this period Allied tank production actually dropped:

> Shipments of Sherman tanks have fallen over 200 below the no. required to meet our estimated wastage. . . . There is no likelihood of this sit. being remedied at an early date, in fact, it is likely to deteriorate. . . . Briefly therefore, we are short of Shermans, and we are likely to be shorter.[50]

This was understandable in Britain where the War Office decreased tank manufacture, preferring to concentrate on Firefly conversion and depend on U.S. Lend Lease M4s to equip its armored divisions, though they unacceptable for U.S. armored battalions. The price for hubris was the slapdash M26 heavy tank, which did not reach U.S. troops until well into 1945.[51]

What Killed Panzers: Allied Opinion

It has been stated that our tanks are supposed to attack infantry and should not be used tank vs. tank. It has been my experience that we have never found this ideal situation for in all our attacks we must of necessity fight German tanks.

—Lt. Col. W. M. Hawkins

The U.S. Army promptly commissioned additional detailed studies to augment the initial surveys and conclusions submitted by the 2d and 3d Armored Divisions, as well as information provided by interrogation reports. Professors Coox and Naisawald, working, as fate would have it, out of the Operations Research Office in Fort McNair, provided a conclusive analysis of Allied armor in battle. Their findings concluded the following:

- Gunfire. Both numerically and percentage wise, this exacted the highest over-all toll of tank casualties . . .
- Hollow-charge weapons. These fluctuated at a very low level of effectiveness. Toward the end of the war the incidence of tanks immobilized by panzerfaust weapons, during offensive and pursuit operations, reached the toll of 25 to 35 percent of all tank casualties.
- Land mine warfare. This indicated an increased number of mines employed by the Axis forces. The decreased tank casualties to mines in the final stages of the Western European campaign seemed to indicate that the enemy could not lay mines because so many of his troops were attempting to get out up to the very last minute.
- Nonenemy causes. (The author has added this category.) The Canadian sample provided the only detailed data from which conclusions could be drawn concerning the toll exacted by nonenemy causes. The figures show the very high proportion of tanks immobilized by this factor in relation to all other causes, during offensive and pursuit operations; thus, during the breaching of the Gustav Line in Italy, terrain and mechanical failures accounted for twice the toll exacted by the usual highest causative agent—gunfire.[52]

Coox and Naisawald cite 785 yards as the average ETO range for tank engagement; this is lower than the average range from Normandy–western France, which is 902 yards based primarily on Canadian engagements in the area around and south of Caen.[53] Specific findings by Coox and Naisawald noted that most tank gun hits were on the hull (52 percent). Studies showed that 65 percent of tanks burned when hit by gunfire, of which only 51 percent were repairable, whereas 78 percent of mined tanks and 71 percent of panzerfaust casualties could be fixed. German tank casualty data corresponded to BRL MR-798 (see chapter Note 43) findings.[54] Limited data on Allied tank crew casualties indicated that "an average of 2.0 to 2.5 crewmen per tank became casualties." Tank commanders suffered the highest overall casualty rate: 57 percent.[55]

By the summer of 1944, both Allied and German tank divisions had stabilized and both sides had reached the *point of no return* in both doctrine and tank design. Prototypes nearing production would arrive too late to make any important contribution; the M4 Sherman would bear the brunt of later operations. Although the Americans lost more tanks than the British and Canadians, the British and Canadians did it with more style. Few defeats could equal the grandeur of 500 burning hulks during Goodwood or the destruction of the British Columbian Regiment during Totalize. The U.S. commands were dissected slowly, methodically by Stugs, antitank guns, and panzerfausts. Most engagements were at short range in the bocage. Canadian tank battles occurred at best battle range and slew more armor in single engagements. Out of 2,579 U.S. tank battalion samples, half were victims of gunfire and only about 30 percent was from tank fire. Postwar studies confirmed the battlefield concerns.[56]

> In the 40 considered engagements in which they were on the attack, the allies lost 100 of 437 employed weapons while the defending enemy lost 45 of 135. In the 37 engagements in which the enemy were attacking, they lost 83 of 138 weapons while the allied defenders lost 14 of 205.[57]

In June, 85 percent of British, 73 percent of Canadian, and 50 percent of U.S. tank losses were caused by direct gunfire engagements. By August the Canadian assaults (Totalize and Tractable) through open country resulted in the continued tank casualties—70 percent. Meanwhile, British and U.S. losses to tank fire had been reduced to 55 percent and 60 percent, respectively. South of Caen, the emphasis was on gunfire.

> When the Sherman encountered a Panther in Italy and the ETO, it was so hopelessly outclassed, as to be worse than a sitting duck . . . while the Panther roamed at will with a 75mm gun that frankly outclassed the gun on the Sherman tank by a velocity of 1230 fps. It is hard for one to appreciate such a fact but it meant in simple language, practically 2 German shells could be on their way to one American.[58]

Tactics

> *I'm a gunner on a Sherman tank which mounts a 75mm gun. When the wind is blowing in the right direction while the round is being fired, we are unable to sense the round being fired. This is due to the muzzle blast and smoke which comes from the gun. This same muzzle blast makes us slow to fire at targets at extreme ranges because it immediately gives our position away.*[59]
>
> —Sgt. Michael Fritzman[60]

Despite the impressive number of training opportunities, which included field training exercises and command post exercises, Allied armor arrived in Normandy relatively unprepared. Basic training and gun camps allowed the tank crews to reach a high level of technical efficiency that stood them in good stead in fair battles against Pzkw IVs but did not prepare them for the Panther and Tiger.

> A Canadian who had fought at Caen with the Canadian 4th Armoured Brigade. . . . asked about gunnery . . . volunteered that a feature of the installation on the Shermans was the Oilgear traversing, which gave hairline laying of the gun. He added that its high speed in traversing from target to target was so much faster than the gear on the German "Tiger" tank that it was possible to catch the enemy tank off line.[61]

Allied Tank Casualties
Tanks Destroyed by Direct Gunfire Engagements
ETO   June - November 1944

Sampling
Expressed in Monthly Percentages

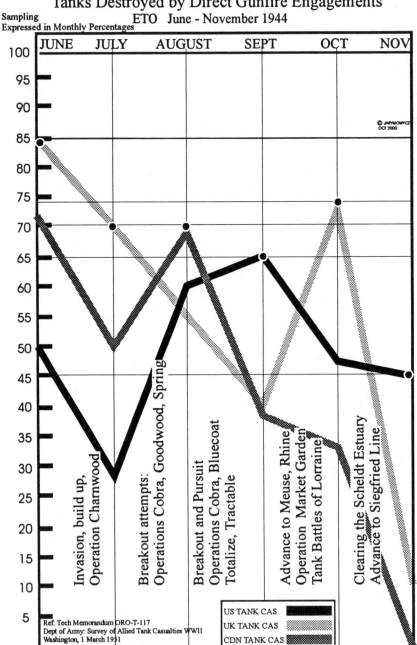

© JARYMOWYCZ
OCT 2000

JUNE | JULY | AUGUST | SEPT | OCT | NOV

Invasion, build up,
Operation Charnwood

Breakout attempts:
Operations Cobra, Goodwood, Spring

Breakout and Pursuit
Operations Cobra, Bluecoat
Totalize, Tractable

Advance to Meuse, Rhine,
Operation Market Garden,
Tank Battles of Lorraine.

Clearing the Scheldt Estuary
Advance to Siegfried Line

US TANK CAS
UK TANK CAS
CDN TANK CAS

Ref: Tech Memorandum ORO-T-117
Dept of Army: Survey of Allied Tank Casualties WWII
Washington, 1 March 1951

Killing the big cats required tactical skills that were learned on the battlefield. The Tiger and Panther crews, secure in their ability to withstand frontal hits regularly deployed forward, often in open terrain, to taunt their enemies. Openly contemptuous of the Allied 75mm gun,[62] they tempted the Shermans, daring them to advance. "The enemy showed a tendency to put his tanks on forward slopes and hold that position counting on the extreme range as a safety factor."[63]

The first Panther knocked out by the Allies in Europe was in Italy, during the attack on the Hitler Line on 24 May 1944 (two weeks before D-Day) by a Canadian crew of the British Columbia Dragoons.[64] The Allies entered the Normandy battlefield with no verified technique that would help in killing enemy main battle tanks. The unsettling realization that both German tanks were impervious to frontal engagements quickly resulted in conservative, careful tactics. A break came when tank crews from the 27th Canadian Armored Regiment (Sherbrooke Fusiliers) discovered that the Panther did have a weak spot in its gun mantlet.[65]

Early Panther models (D, A, and initial Gs) carried a rounded mantlet that, although it could not be penetrated, deflected the shot downward onto the thin upper armor that protected the driver. A good gunner with nerves of steel would aim for a 6-inch bull's eye on the lower left of the mantlet, and a hit could result in a deflection that shattered the Panther driver's overhead armor and stopped the tank cold.[66] This normally resulted in the crew's abandoning the vehicle. The technique was demanding and required a certain amount of cooperation from the Germans. If the Panther could be coaxed from a hull-down position or caught advancing, the job was easier. The oft-quoted British account gives a good example of the trauma endured:

> "And how does a Churchill get a Panther?"
> "It creeps up on it. When it reaches close quarters the gunner tries to bounce a shot off the underside of the Panther's gun mantlet. If he's lucky, it goes through a piece of thin armor above the driver's head."
> "Has anybody ever done it?"
> "Yes. Davis in C Squadron. He's back with headquarters now, trying to recover his nerve."
> "How does a Churchill get a Tiger?"
> "It's supposed to get within two hundred yards and put a shot through the periscope."
> "Has anyone ever done it?"
> "No."[67]

If the Germans stayed put, then the burden of attack was on the Sherman—which had to advance and hope for a clean line of sight. The odds were decidedly against the Allies:

At Samree, Belgium, during the attack to secure Houffalize, a precision adjustment with 8" howitzers failed to dislodge a German Mk VI tank which could not be eliminated by direct fire of any available weapon, including the 90mm T.D. This tank could not be outflanked. It had destroyed 3 of our M-4 tanks at the same range. The tank withdrew during the night.[68]

Another way to kill a Tiger was by maneuver. A troop of Shermans, having found a Tiger, would fix it with the Firefly. While the Tiger and Firefly jockeyed for position, the remaining three tanks would go around the flanks and try to close to an advantageous fire position.[69] With the Sherman's powered turret traverse matched against the Tiger's slower speed and hand-cranked traverse, the odds were on the side of the Sherman. The same was not true when attacking Panthers.

Hunting by maneuver had its own serious problems. Attack required advance, and the Germans excelled at small-unit tactics and had seen it all before on the Eastern Front. The Wehrmacht developed standard operating procedures to defeat maneuver. The most important principle was that Tiger never worked alone. Although Tigers in pairs were encountered, the common partnership was the Tiger and a Stug III (75mm self-propelled assault gun) lying silent on a flank.[70] When a Sherman troop shifted around a Tiger, they were taken in the flank by the hidden tank destroyer. If the Shermans used smoke to isolate a Tiger, they would discover a second standard operating procedure: each Pzkw VI was supported by infantry tank-killing teams armed with panzerfausts and lying in wait for advancing Shermans. The only solution was to send Allied infantry forward to clear the ground and secure dominating features from which antitank fire could be delivered. This practical tactic eventually led to considerable bad press from Allied infantry and military historians.[71]

The Sherman's high silhouette was a disadvantage: it was easily spotted from 200 to 3500 yards away. The panzers (mostly in defense in Normandy) stayed put, but when they did unmask, the German use of low-flash powder made it "very difficult for us to pick them up . . . whereas the flash of our own guns is easily discernible. . . the German guns have a much higher muzzle velocity. . . . The resulting flat trajectory gives great penetration and is very accurate."[72] Only the dust cloud made by the gun blast allowed detection by the most alert Firefly gunners.

German prisoners of war presented their own experienced views on how best to deal with panzers:

Your most effective weapon is the ability to keep still. . . . Allow the enemy tank to approach as close as possible before engaging . . . [the] British opened fire on tanks too early. . . . A tank in motion cannot shoot effectively with its cannon; the gunner can only aim accurately when the vehicle is stationary. Therefore there is no need to get "nerves" because an approaching tank swivels its turret this way and that. . . . If the tank fires its MG only you can be pretty sure you have not been spotted.[73]

Tank killing in closed terrain required a combined-arms team of artillery and infantry support. Most successful tank-infantry cooperation was achieved by outfits with mutual trust—units that had previously trained or fought together. GHQ tank battalions and Canadian regiments in independent tank brigades were shared by as many as nine battalions (thirty-six rifle companies): this gave small chance of an intimate relationship. In situations where units did know each other, an almost casual haphazard doctrine took hold. Its external nonchalance was based on an intense professionalism and battle savvy that only veterans acquire:

> Mel Gordon [regimental commander] wouldn't waste time with squadron O Groups. He knew we needed time to brief our own men—he'd take us (the Squadron leaders) to the Brigade O Group. We'd find out what we were doing and go find the infantry company we'd work with. Mel would say: "Rad, you go work with Bill, Jack, you're with Harry." We'd go and meet the battalion or company commanders and start planning.[74]

What also seemed to work against the panzers was smoke, whether fired by the infantry, tank guns, or artillery. Smoke, particularly white phosphorous (which could start engine fires) heightened the claustrophobic anxiety felt by all but the most veteran tank crews: "When we encounter an enemy tank or SP gun we cover it with smoke from hand or rifle grenades or bazooka shells. Almost invariably the tank or gun turns and runs or is abandoned by its crew. If it does neither, we close in under smoke and destroy it."[75]

Canadian tankers quickly discovered that a squadron smoke shoot permitted the Sherman to attack: a line of smoke placed along the front of an enemy position allowed them to close quickly into effective kill range. If the enemy tanks maneuvered around the smoke they would be picked up and hit in the flank; if they advanced forward to engage the advancing squadron they were perfectly silhouetted before the white smoke screen and engaged by Fireflies and artillery.[76]

Crew Protection:
German Cupola and German Engineering

The most consistently reported complaint was armor. The Sherman was constantly penetrated, while Panther's armor defeated most Allied guns. "On 5 August 1944 in the vicinity of St. Sever Calvados, France, witnessed a German Mark V tank knock out three M4 and three M5 during and after being hit by at least fifteen rounds of 75mm APC from a distance of approximately 700 yards."[77]

One of the most envied enemy equipments was the German tank crew commander's cupola. German tank cupolas were fitted with episcopes for all-round observation; the spring-loaded hatch popped up a few inches then swung to the side to permit exit. This feature gave the crew commander five inches of additional head space, permitted clear observation, and offered a breath of fresh air. Most important, it provided protection from snipers, air bursts, and shrapnel. Because the casualty rate of tank commanders was nearly 60 percent, copies of the German cupola were urgently requested. "The all around vision cupola is very much wanted; crew commanders consider that the present observation through the periscopes in the cupola is entirely inadequate . . . cas[ualties] to crew comds have been very heavy from snipers and ordinary rifle and mg fire."[78]

Despite hundreds of requests from front-line units, Allied engineering failed to come up with a comparable cupola throughout the war. Tank commanding remained the riskiest job in France.

To balance things, the panzer forces had its woes as well. German engineering proved so precise that it was a disadvantage. The engineering simplicity of the Soviet T-34 may have placed it behind the Panther in overall performance, but it proved the more reliable machine and capable of being maintained by any *kulak*. German tanks required expert care. Initially, Allied intelligence had no clear indication of this simply because most abandoned Panthers were recovered at night by German mechanical engineers. There are few records of serviceable panzers being overrun by Allied forces until the retreat from Mortain in late August 1944. Although one Pzkw V tank captured taken near Vimoutiers produced a log book that showed some impressive track mileage: the vehicle had road-marched from Paris to Verrières, then to Mortain and back again to the Falaise area. If this Panther was typical, then the panzers could continue to maneuver with Sherman as long as the battlefield remained stable and night allowed normal maintenance and repair to take place.

German tank repair was performed as far forward as possible. Specialists accompanied the troops to the combat area when enemy fire permitted.

> Damaged tanks which could not be repaired with the available means by combat units were collected by recovery vehicles and turned over to the maintenance companies of the tank regiments or to other maintenance shops. By evening, battalions or regiments had a clear picture as to the number of operational tanks, the number in need of minor repairs, the number in need of major repairs and total losses. These figures were reported through command channels. . . . During the early part of the war, 95 percent of damages were repaired by the field forces, and of these at least 95 percent within the tank regiment.[79]

M10

Tank Destroyer M 10
Gun: 76mm (Caliber Length)
Range (Eff Frontal Penetration): Mk IV to 1500m ; Panther/Tiger: nil
Best Armor Penetration at 500m: 3.5"

Armor Piercing Shell Velocity m/sec: 870
Armor: 59mm
Combat Weight: 30 tons
Height: 287cm
Speed: 26 mph (road); 20 (xcountry)
Crew: 5

Allied and German Tank Destroyers France 1944

German TD Advantage

StuG III compared to Grant

StuG III compared to Sherman

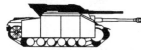

StuG III compared to M10 Tank Destroyer
Although both vehicles are "Tank Destroyers" and both
are built on the chassis of an MBT, the M10 still has its
turret. Trade-off: flexibility vs armor and high target profile.
Stug III can hide in small depressions and behind low walls.

Marder III

JagdPanzer "Marder III" Ausf M
Gun: 75mm PaK 40/3 (46 Caliber Length)
Range (Eff Frontal Penetration): all Allied MBT 1500m
Best Armor Penetration at 500m: 5.5"
Armor Piercing Shell Velocity m/sec: 795 - 933
Armor (min-max): 15 - 20 mm
Combat Weight: 10.5 tons
Height: 248cm
Speed: 42 mph (road); 15 (xcountry); Crew: 4

JagdPanther

Tank Destroyer "JagdPanther" Jgd Pz V Sd Kfz 173
Gun: 88mm PaK 43/3 (71 Caliber Length)
Range (Eff Frontal Penetration): all Allied MBT 2000+m

Best Frontal Penetration at 500m: 6" plus
Armor Piercing Shell Velocity m/sec:1000 -1130
Armor (min-max): 60 - 90 mm
Combat Weight: 45.5 tons
Height: 272cm
Speed: 46 mph (road); 24 (xcountry); Crew: 5

JagdPanzer IV

JagdPanzer Pz IV Sd Kfz 162/1
Gun: 75mm StuK 42 (70 Caliber Length)
Range (Eff Frontal Penetration): all Allied MBT 1500m
Best Armor Penetration at 500m: 3.5"

Armor Piercing Shell Velocity m/sec: 935 -1120
Armor (min-max): 45 - 90 mm
Combat Weight: 25.8 tons
Height: 185cm
Speed: 40 mph (road); 16 (xcountry); Crew: 4

StuG III

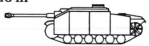

Assault Gun / TD StuG III Sd Kfz 142 Ausf B
Gun: 75mm StuK 37 (24 Caliber Length)
Range (Eff Frontal Penetration): all Allied MBT 1500m
Best Armor Penetration at 500m: 3.5"
Armor Piercing Shell Velocity m/sec: 385
Armor (min-max): 50 - 90 mm
Combat Weight   22 tons
Height: 194cm
Speed: 40 mph (road); 24 (xcountry); Crew: 4

Hetzer

JagdPanzer "Hetzer" Pz 38 t
Gun: 75mm (48 Caliber Length)
Range (Eff Frontal Penetration): all Allied MBT 1500m
Best Armor Penetration at 500m: 3.5"

Armor Piercing Shell Velocity m/sec: 750 - 930
Armor (min-max): 20 - 75 mm
Combat Weight: 18 tons
Height: 210cm; Speed: 40 mph (road); 14 (xcountry);
Crew: 4

© JARMOWICZ
OCT 2000

Tank Repairs by crews was next to impossible by 1944: most German tank crews did not have the training or mechanical skills for anything except the most rudimental maintenance.

Who Killed Tiger? Italy, 1944

Push him . . . make him run.
                        —New Zealand Army Study, 1944[80]

By the summer of 1944 the Italian campaign had been overshadowed by Normandy. The "D-Day dodgers" (the callous nickname given to Allied troops fighting in Italy by Lady Astor) had broken out of Anzio and taken Rome at about the same time that the Normandy invasion had carved out the beachhead. North of Anzio the first Panthers and Tigers were encountered: some Wehrmacht, some German air force. (The finest panzer division in Italy, oddly enough, belonged to the Luftwaffe: The Herman Göring Panzer Parachute Division). As the Germans withdrew from Rome, a technical team from the New Zealand 2d Infantry Division set about examining any Tiger tank hulks left by the retreat. The officers searched every lane and to their surprise, found twelve relatively fit Tigers. Ten had no battle damage, three had been blown up by their crews, and only two had actually been hit by Allied guns. Close inspection confirmed the dark side of the German technical superiority legend—most Tigers simply broke down. Tigers and Panthers were not the product of blitzkrieg. They were best at "sitzkrieg": long-range gunnery from hull-down positions. Tigers were "not sufficiently reliable for long marches . . . [there being] frequent suspension defects . . . [and in the] gearbox too."[81] When forced to conduct operational or even extended tactical maneuver, troubles began. The Tiger's (and to a large extent the Panther's) difficulties mounted as it was forced to move. The complexity of design and the specialization required for maintenance was more than the already hard-pressed German support system could keep up with. The experiment's concluding analysis offered a simple maxim for defeating Tiger: "Push him . . . make him run." Maneuver warfare was the kiss of death to the German Panzer arm in 1944. The final word on German technology was nailed into the concluding paragraph, which answered the keynote question: "Who Killed Tiger?—Tiger Killed Himself."[82]

Notes

1. Maj. Gen. I. D. White. Exhibit No. 2, 2d Armored Division: *Comparison of US Equipment with Similar German Equipment.* Report for Supreme Commander Allied Expeditionary Force. ETO, 20 March 1945 (hereafter White).

2. "Der Tiger ist, wenn man's bedenkt, Ein Wagen, der sich primma lenkt."
Tiger crews were given a maintenance manual, *The Tiger Primer* that included car-
toons. *Tigerfibel.* Inspector general of tank troops, 01.08.1943 (Wehrmacht
D656/27) (Stuttgart: Motorbuch Verlag).

3. See David Fletcher, *The Great Tank Scandal* (London: HM Stationery
Office, 1989).

4. See throughout, Warlimont, *Inside Hitler's Headquarters.*

5. Ross, p. 37.

6. Eisenhower quoted by Bradley, *A Soldier's Story* (New York; Popular
Library, 1951), p. 322.

7. *Report on German Pz Kw VI Tank Examined 2/3 February.* War diary.
Weapons Technical Staff, Field Force. Col. J. A. Barlow and Lt. Col. R. D. Neville,
North Africa, February 1943.

8. R. P. Hunnicutt, *Firepower—A History of the American Heavy Tank*
(Novato, Calif.: Presidio Press, 1988), p. 49. General Devers "asserted flatly, six
weeks after Pearl Harbor: 'The time has come when we should definitely insist on
the type of equipment necessary to win this war.' . . . He forthwith decided to
'secure a tough gasoline engine and stick to it.' [T]ests proved to Gen. Devers's satisfaction that the Ford GAA-V-8 engine was the single medium tank engine for
which he was looking." Orlando Ward Papers, Box 2. Correspondence, 1942–1943,
MHI.

9. The only effort made was in production of the M4A3 (76mm gun) and its
brawny cousin (178mm mantlet, 140mm nose armor, 102mm frontal plating) the
M4A3E2, appropriately dubbed Cobra King. The latter first appeared in Operation
Cobra; it was better known by the troops as "Jumbo." This was the American version of an "infantry tank."

10. Barnett, *Audit,* p. 255. See also Hancock and Cowing, *British War
Economy* (London: Collins, 1969), p. 145.

11. Barnett, *Audit,* p. 263.

12. Ross, pp. 38–39.

13. "American tank development policy seems to have been just as moribund
as the British, though with more excuse due to their isolation. . . . Between 1919
and 1938 no less than 18 types of tank were built as pilots, with none ever going to
production; a record which parallels the British." Ross, p. 255.

14. The British director general of artillery, Gen. Campbell Clarke, sent a sample 17-pounder gun to the British inspector general of armament in Canada, and the
British Technical Mission in Detroit was able to obtain dimensions and confirmed
that the Chrysler Sherman turret would accommodate the gun well enough.

15. Vivian Dykes, quoted in Ross, p. 193.

16. Tiger production began in May 1942 and continued for two years until
"King Tiger" or Tiger II replaced the Model E in August 1944. One thousand three
hundred fifty Tigers were built. See F. M. von Senger und Etterlin, *Die deutschen
Panzer 1926–1945* (Munich: J. F. Lehmanns Verlag, 1965), pp. 312–313.

17. While the Special Technical team was trying to examine the Tiger, the
British confirmed information that had already been sent worldwide by Reuters.
The *Daily Telegraph* and the *Daily Mirror* announced triumphantly: "6-Pounder
Beats New Nazi Tank—7-in Armor Pierced." 5 February 1943.

18. "8. It was decided to lay on a shot from a portee [6-pounder] at 1200 hrs.
and leave it to the discretion of the gunner officer . . . as to whether the shoot was
carried out or not. 9. The gunner officer on the spot told us that the enemy had been
shelling the area in which the tank was situated and therefore the projected shoot

was 'off.'" RG 24 BRAC *Report on German Pz Kw VI Tank Examined 2/3 February.*

19. "Carried out a firing trial against it with a 6 pdr Mk II. The plate was 102mm thick (the Brinell figure has since been ascertained to be 302), set up at approximately 21 degrees, and supported by drums filled with stones both at the back and at the front. The gun was set up 300 yds away. Two hits were obtained with the following results:

Round	Range	Angle	Result
1	300 yds	21 degrees	Shot penetrated 3 inches; plate cracked vertically. Shot turned and rebounded whole.
2	300 yds	20 degrees	Shot penetrated 3.5 inches. Bulge at back. Plate split in two.

The trial was then suspended. Owing to weather conditions and approaching darkness, photography was not possible." RG 24 BRAC Department of Tank Design, Armor Branch, "Side Armor of Pz KwVI Comments on Firing Trials Carried out in N Africa." H. Harris-Jones. Ballistics Section. 5 June 1943.

20. AGF policy statement. Chief of staff AGF. November 1943. MHI.

21. German Tanks Destroyed by XIX Corps. 15 Dec 44. Booklet Tank and SP Gun Identification. Tech Int Bulletin #8. 20 Feb 1945. ETO. MHI.

22. U.S. (Aberdeen) trials of the Tiger were under way by January 1944, with press releases ("Tamed Tiger," *Yank,* 21 January 1944:). Col. G. B. Jarrett Papers, chief of Foreign Material Branch and Ordnance Research Center, Aberdeen Proving Ground. MHI.

23. Tigers were stabled at the British School of Tank Technology at Chertsey in October. A Tiger was then placed in Horse Guards Parade for general public inspection in November 1943. The *London Illustrated News,* 4 December 1943, shows army officers and children climbing over the tank. It was then returned to Chertsey and Lulworth Camp in Dorset for gunnery trials.

24. MS #P-059, *German Tank Strength and Loss Statistics,* U.S. Army Historical Division, 9 June 1950. Statistics provided by Professor Porsche, Hermann Burkhart Mueller-Hillebrand, and Generalobst Franz Halder), p. 7. British/Canadian regiments were primarily equipped with the A4: "The decision of the US Service of Supply to allocate to the British the entire Chrysler output of Sherman (M4A4) tanks for the first quarter of 1943." Ross, p. 239.

25. A Fireflies firing "super APDS 17pdr shot" could not penetrate the frontal armor of a Tiger II, but could defeat side and rear armor on the hull and turret. RG 24 14186.

26. Brig. Gen. J. H. Collier, commander, CC A. White, Exhibit No.1.

27. "Report of the mission headed by LtGen Jacob L. Devers to examine the problems of Armored Force units in the European Theatre of Operations," RG 337 (HQ AGF), p. 3.

28. White, Exhibit No. 2.

29. RG 24 First Cdn Army Information Bulletin No. 1, 15 Oct 44.

30. RG 24 14186 (BRAC) First Cdn Army Information Bulletin No. 1. 15 Oct 44. "Who Killed Tiger." Reprint of New Zealand Army study published in British 8th Army, July 1944.

31. In grudging tribute to the design, the French army adopted the Panther as a consort main battle tank and used it at regimental level until the mid-1950s: a "most eloquent testimony to the capabilities." Bruce Culver, *Panther in Action* (Warren, Mich.: Squadron/Signal, 1975), p. 4.

32. MS #P-059, *German Tank Strength and Loss Statistics.*

33. "Instead of simplifying the design Maybach continued to turn out new, improved series—so that a tremendous variety of spare parts was required . . . cannibalization by crews was so thorough that the manufacturer would rarely receive more than an empty hull." *German Tank Maintenance in World War II,* No. 20-202 (Washington, D.C.: Department of the Army, 1954).

34. Brig. Gen. J. H. Collier; White.

35. White, Exhibits,1, 2, 3 throughout.

36. White.

37. White. Early versions of the Sherman had a periscopic sight; the British tank team visiting Washington insisted that "British" Shermans be equipped with a telescope. American engines were all superior to British models. Ross, p. 240.

38. White.

39. Ibid.

40. OPOT 117, Alvin D. Coox and L. Van Loan Naisawald. *Survey of Allied Tank Casualties in World War II,* Johns Hopkins University, 31 March 1951. Operations Research Office (cited hereafter as Coox); Maj. N. A. Shackleton and Maj. R.P. Bourne: *Analysis of Firepower in Normandy Operations of 1944* (Ottawa) (Hereafter Shackleton). *Report No. 798, Ballistic Research Laboratories,* Aberdeen Proving Ground, Maryland: David C. Hardison. *Data on WWII Tank Engagements Involving the US Third and Fourth Armored Divisions.* 1947 (hereafter BRL 798). Shackleton and Bourne examined twelve Normandy battles featuring Canadian forces at battalion level and above. Extensive graphic studies compared relative strengths and defender-attacker combat ratios. They noted several interesting tactical conclusions based on Canadian actions in Normany, including the following. Three-to-one superiority of an attacker over a defender (in subunits and weapons) was achieved only in two actions; in two of the successful attacks the defenders had no artillery support, and in a third the defenders had no tanks. In a successful attack the value of attacking artillery and mortar fire exceeded that of the defense by more than 50 percent. Except in one instance of a successful attack (Hill 140, the destruction of Columbia Regiment by Battle Group Wünsche on 9 August 1944), the value of attacking infantry exceeded that of the defense. Except in one instance, in the successful attacks, the value of the attacking armor was at least 30 percent less than that of the defense. Shackleton, pp. 2–3.

41. BRL MR-798, and White.

42. BRL MR-798, pp. 10, 13, 17.

43. White.

44. Ibid.

45. BRL MR-798.

46. Schweppenburg could not give even approximate figures. "He thinks air-tank cooperation the most deadly combination." ORO-T-117 German Estimates and Comments on Their Own Tank Casualties. Annex 2 to App. E. Seventh Army Interrogation Center, ETO, 24 May 1945 (hereafter ORO-T-117), MHI.

47. ORO-T-117. App. E, Table XXXV: 252 panzers were destroyed by their own crews; 222 were simply abandoned because of lack of spare parts, gas, recovery, or were under attack.

48. **Table 13.5   Armored Fighting Vehicles Available to the German Army High Command in 1944**

	1 January	6 June
PzMk IV	437	698
PzMk V	1,386	2,234
PzMk IV	1,558	2,048
75mm Stug	2,439	2,933
Total	5,820	7,913

49. The 1944 panzer divisions were approximately three battalions strong: a Panther battalion, a Pzkw IV battalion, and a JPz battalion based on the Stug III but being replaced by the JPz IV.

50. RG 24 14186 Canadian First Army war diary, Secret Report, Maj. Gen. Richards, RAC, Main HQ 21 Army Group, 15 August 1944.

51. **Table 13.6   Armored Fighting Vehicle Production Totals of Major Combatants, Europe, 1943–1944**

Totals	1943	1944
Germany	12,063	19,002
Soviet Union	24,000	30,000
United Kingdom	7,476	2,474
United States	29,497	17,565

52. OPO-T-117.

53. Based on study of BRL MR-798. The author selected 136 tank actions (August–December 1944) with an average Allied-to-German tank numbers of twelve tanks to four panzers. The average range of intervisibility was 1,229 yards, a distance that would have been unusual in the Italian theater for unit/subunit action.

54. **Table 13.7   Causes German Tank Losses**

	BRL MR-798	Coax/Naisawald
Gunfire	43.8%	44.0%
Abandonment	18.3%	18.4%
Mechanical	4.0%	4.1%
Self-destruction	20.7%	20.8%
Air Attack	7.5%	8.0%
Hollow-charge Rounds	4.4%	4.5%
Mines/Miscellaneous Weapons	0.9%	1.0%

55. Casualties by position in main battle tanks were commander, 57 percent; gunner, 51 percent; loader, 51 percent; bow gunner, 48 percent; and driver, 47 percent. Light tank crew casualties were higher. Coox.

56. Table 13.8   U.S. Armored Forces Engagements, August 1944–March 1945

Area	Number of Engagements	Unit	Date
Vicinity of Fromental	5	3d Arm'd Div	15 Aug.–17 Aug. 1944
Vicinity of Stollberg	8	3d Arm'd Div	15 Sept.–22 Sept. 1944
Roer to Stollberg	16	3d Arm'd Div	26 Feb.–6 March 1945
Belgian Bulge	22	3d Arm'd Div	20 Dec. 1944–15 Jan. 1945
Vicinity of Arracourt	12	4th Arm'd Div	19 Sept.–19 Sept. 1944
Sarre	20	4th Arm'd Div	9 Nov.–6 Dec. 1944
Relief of Bastogne	9	4th Arm'd Div	22 Dec.–30 Dec. 1944

Sources: BRL MR-798, and White.

57. BRL MR-798, p. 10.

58. Col. G. B. Jarrett, *Achtung Panzer—The Story of German Tanks,* unpublished manuscript, Aberdeen, Md.: 1948, p. 3.

59. Sgt. Michael Fritzman: "Exhibit No. 3. US vs. German Equipment," White, pp. 7, 8.

60. Ibid.

61. Ross, p. 248. "One of the first encounters between Panthers and 2nd Armored Division led to the report that a Sherman had been knocked out with the German 75mm round going through the transmission, through the ammunition rack on the hull floor, through the engine and out the rear!" Also, stated Sgt. F. W. Baker, 2d Armored Division: "I was tank commander of a Sherman medium tank mounting a 76mm gun. The Germans staged a counter-attack with infantry supported by at least three Mark V tanks. Ordering my gunner to fire at the closest tank, which was approximately 800 yards away, he placed one right in the side, which was completely visible to me. To my amazement and disgust, I watched the shell bounce off the side. My gunner fired at least six more rounds at the vehicle hitting it from the turret to the track. . . . I was completely surprised to see it moving after receiving seven hits from my gun." White.

62. Although the British Armament Research Establishment produced an armor-piercing discarding sabot (APDS) round for the 6-pounder gun in late 1943, an APDS round for the 17-pounder was not available until the summer of 1944. It immediately became the mainstay for Firefly and antitank troops.

63. D Hist 141.4A27013 LD2. *27 Cdn Armd Regt (Sher Fus),* after-action report, Lt. P. W. Ayriss, 31 July 1944.

64. M4 Sherman, commanded by Lt. N. C. Taylor, the gunner was Tpr. C. D. Shears. See RG 24 WD HQ 5 Cdn Armd Div. 24 May 1944. For a detailed account by Taylor himself, see Roy, *Sinews of Steel,* pp. 250-251.

65. The Sherbrooke Fusiliers' discovery may have occurred concurrently with units that began to engage the Panther's gun mantlet: there is no clear evidence which Allied unit used the technique first. Lt. Col. Mel Gordon's after-action report appears to be one of the earliest. RG 24. 27 CAR WD.

66. Interview with Gen. S. V. Radley Walters, Caen, 1991. Radley Walters explained the tactic in detail while perched on the front hull of a Panther in the Normandy Museum in Caen. See the Canadian drama-documentary: "The Horror and the Valor," segment 2, "Normandy," CBC/Gala Films, 1993.

67. Bradley, *A Soldier's Story.*

68. Lt. Col. W. M. Hawkins, commander, 3d Battalion, 67th Armored Regiment, in White, Exhibit No. 2.

69. Not always easy in a Sherman: "At Freindenhoven, Germany I saw a Mark V and Mark VI tank scarcely dig into the plowed field while the tracks of our own M-4 tanks were often deep enough in the same field to show the marks of the tank's belly dragging." S. Sgt. Alvin G. Olson, platoon sergeant 2d Armored Division, in White.

70. "Tigers usually well enough sited to make deployment of a sniping anti-tank gun, M 10 or towed gun for stalking purposes, difficult." RG 24 14186 BRAC Ln Letter 15 Oct 44. "When we encounter an en tk or SP gun we cover it with smoke from hand or rifle grenades or bazooka shells. Almost invariably the tank or gun turns and runs or is abandoned by its crew. If it does neither, we close in under smk and destroy it." "ETO Battle Experiences." Maj. Gen. A. C. Gillem Jr. July 1944–April 1945. Gillem Papers, MHI.

71. English, pp. 214, 312–313.

72. Brig. Gen. J. H. Collier, CC A, White, Exhibit No. 1.

73. RG 24 10553 CMF Info Letter No. 10, "How to Deal With Panzers—A German View."

74. Interview with Gen. S. V. Radley Walters, 1992.

75. "ETO Battle Experiences Jul 44–Apr 45," Gillem Papers, MHI, p. 14.

76. Interview with S. V. Radley Walters, 1992.

77. Thomas L. Jentz, *Germany's Panther Tank—The Quest for Combat Supremacy* (Atglen: Schiffer Military, 1995), pp. 155–156.

78. RG 24 10460 2 CAB WD "Reply to DTD Tk Gunnery Questionnaire"; RG 24 10457 Report on RAC Weapons HQ 1st Cdn Army; and RG 24 10925 3 Cdn Inf Div Lessons Learned—3 Div Questionnaire Appx D.

79. MS #P-059, p. 15; and Military Training Pamphlet No. 20-202 *German Tank Maintenance during World War II,* June 1954, p. 14. MHI.

80. RG 24 14186 (BRAC) "Who Killed Tiger." New Zealand army study published by 2d New Zealand Division intelligence for British 8th Army, July 1944, based on tanks discovered "near Rome and the Alban Hills."

81. RG 24 14186 (BRAC).

82. RG 24 14186 (BRAC).

CHAPTER 14

Stavka in Normandy

Many Westerners believe the Russians to be technically backward, and less gifted. Here a clear warning is required. . . . Nothing would be worse than to underrate the strength of a great nation as full of life as the Russians.

—Col. Gen. Heinz Guderian[1]

By the late 1980s Western Military Historians and analysts came to appreciate the enduring contributions of Soviet Military Art and Science to the conduct and study of War at the Operational Level—that is, at echelons above corps and on the scale of theatre-strategic campaigns . . . this was before being dismissed by Western scholars as mere pretension and an artificial creation imposed between tactics and strategy.

—W. C. Frank and P. S. Gillette, *Soviet Military Doctrine*[2]

Produmaem eshche.

—Stalin to the Stavka, April 1944[3]

A comparison of Soviet, German, and Western doctrines is difficult to resist. While there are many similarities at the troop-combat team level, there are several clear differences: *auftragstaktik,* the battle group doctrine, and, most significant, the Soviet strategic offensive. The former are aspects of operational art, the latter is the sum total of the operational art. The preceding chapters have been somewhat critical of the Allied military craft and certain Allied commanders. But before accusing the Western Allies of malpractice, it would be judicious to determine the correct procedure in the theaters of operations. A review of operations in Europe will determine that the state of the art was the Eastern Front and the most skilled practitioners were the Soviet.

If German doctrinal superiority at the battle group to corps level is (deservedly) acknowledged, then it must also be recognized that by 1944, particularly at the theater level, the Soviets had no peers, indeed, were echelons *above* anything the Western or the Third Reich's general staffs could produce. Soviet military skills have been both misunderstood and misrepresented, particularly by their former Allies.

Western Allies Strategic Offensive

The best example of the Allied strategic offensive par excellence is the Normandy invasion. It is doubtful that the Russians could have managed a D-Day. The remaining theater offensives, beginning with Monte Cassino and extending to Goodwood and Cobra, featured the stamp of a substantial Allied effort, strategic air attack. Kluge's first question when he arrived at Dietrich's headquarters during Operation Spring was "Where are the heavy bombers?" When he was told there were none, he promptly released the 1st SS Panzer Corps operational reserve to Dietrich and went back to his headquarters to closely follow Cobra. It was clear by the middle of July that if the Allies seriously meant to attack, they would use USAAC and RAF resources.

The Allied strategic offensives followed a strategical path in the most general terms, despite ex post facto arguments. Montgomery demonstrated considerable difficulty in behaving like the complete strategic commander: his operations reflected a general subscription to an overall campaign plan, but many ventures were simply reactive directives to failed schemes. Operations Spring and Totalize are good examples. The series of contradictory instructions dealing with the Falaise problem ended with Montgomery, the theater operational commander, directing the operations of a *single* division (Maczek's Polish 1st Armored) to close the gap.

The Allied strategic offensive formula began with a massive air attack by heavy bombers, heavy artillery concentrations, tactical airstrikes, and an attempt to penetrate the German defense with first-echelon assault divisions. Frontages were narrow; in some cases, though theoretically of division level, the thrusts were on narrow brigade, or often battalion, and even company, frontages (i.e., Goodwood, Atlantic, Spring, Totalize). Penetration was followed by a prolonged break-in battle that generally exhausted the enemy but did not annihilate him. In contrast, the Soviet strategic offensive destroyed enemy defenses completely and quickly tore the front apart to expose, engage, and overwhelm enemy operational reserves.[4] Once a breakthrough was achieved, and the Soviet tank armies acquired operational maneuver, there was little the Germans could do except give ground and wait for exhaustion and logistic difficulties to stop the Russians.

Glubokii Boi

The Soviet Republic needs to have a cavalry force.
Red Cavaliers, forward! Proletarians, to horse!

—Leon Trotsky, 1919[5]

Wide sectors of the enemy frontage were to be amused and held down by
the weak forces of the pinning group (skovyvayuschaya gruppa) *while at*
least two-thirds of the combat strength was focused in the "shock group"
(udarnaya gruppa).

—Christopher Duffy[6]

The Soviet strategic offensive evolved from the 1920 campaign against
Poland to the Great Patriotic War (World War II). General Budenny's
16,000 cossacks,[7] initiated classic *glubokii boi* by marching from Tsaritsyn
to Warsaw, and creating havoc in the newly raised Polish army:

For our troops who were not prepared to meet this new offensive weapon,
Budenny's cavalry became an invincible, legendary force. And it should
be remembered that the farther in rear one goes, the more does such
obsession escape all reason—to become all powerful and irresistible.[8]

M. N. Tukhachevskii and V. K. Triandafilov developed deep battle
concepts in the 1930s. The evolution of the Soviet art of war had to endure
failure in Finland and the shock of German Operation *Barbarossa* before
the slavophiles predominated over the tactical westernizers. Only then were
early Field Regulations (PU-29 and PU-36) resurrected and updated, resulting in PU-41, a blueprint for victory. Experimentation in grand strategic
offensives finally produced PU-44, the formula that crushed the
Wehrmacht. Battlefield expertise was bought with time and great human
cost. At first the Russians simply attacked. Then they tried a form of
blitzkrieg and predictably failed against their Wehrmacht opponents.

The German response to the Soviet 1941, 1942, and 1943 counteroffensives was a classical blueprint later attempted in the Falaise gap and
used successfully by General Hodges in the Ardennes: Hold the shoulders
of the break-in, and fix and channel the enemy via blocking positions and
obstacles—force him to penetrate into ground of your choosing. When he
has exhausted himself or reached his "culmination point," counterattack his
flanks, cut off his head, and restore the main battle position. The plan
required refined command, trained staffs, and combat-experienced officers
to execute it. The Germans had plenty of these.

The Soviet solution to the strategic offensive has been dismissed as a
simple assault that overwhelms a sophisticated enemy by numbers, and
eventually gallant Western culture is somehow overwhelmed by crude bar-

baric hordes that triumph by artless mass. "The simile of the steamroller is, however, excellent as a description of the way in which the Red Army performed in the Second World War."[9] Variations of this interpretation were accepted by many Western military historians and their armies for many decades. Liddell Hart's "The Other Side of the Hill" and "The Red Army" encouraged similar publications by senior German officers, who received a sympathetic Western audience during the Cold War.[10] "Believe us, they are masses and we are individuals. That is the difference between the Russian soldier and the European soldier."[11] That all of the major essays featured in "The Red Army" were written by Germans did not appear to bother Liddell Hart or his reviewers. In point of fact, there is little evidence to show that German skills, which appeared brilliant at the tactical and grand tactical level (former Wehrmacht generals were regularly invited to show NATO planners how to beat the Soviets), extended to the strategic level. But this is the area in which the Soviets were most dangerous and where they ultimately destroyed the German eastern armies.

Whether through Prussian arrogance or refusal to take their own intelligence reports seriously, the German General Staff scorned Soviet leadership. The Germans were almost totally ignorant of the Red Army (i.e., Soviet army) leaders who did not attend the Kriegsakadamie—the names Konev, Zhukov, Rokossovskii, or Vasilevskii meant little to them: "They exchanged glances but said nothing. After a moment's silence General Lasch said somewhat bashfully that he had not heard of Marshal of the Soviet Union Vasilevskii before his name was mentioned in the ultimatum to the Königsberg garrison."[12]

It was wishful thinking, but NATO found it easier to accept that sheer numbers and a barbaric disdain for human casualties had achieved victory over an exhausted Germany being battered into submission by the Allied bomber offensive than to accept that the Bolsheviks were a formidable foe that had beaten the best the Third Reich had.

Soviet Military Doctrine, 1917–1945

Soviet military doctrine evolved through three stages. The first was a political and technical phase that emphasized readiness for war, modern equipment, and fundamentals based on reality during 1917–1928. The second stage, 1929–1941, was based on the decision to achieve superiority in three decisive weapons systems: tanks, artillery, and aircraft. The early 1930s witnessed the introduction of mass production and the experimentation with a mechanized corps. The 1934 Provisional Field Regulations of the Red Army stressed the need for a tank corps and experimented with the concept of the deep battle. Soviet chief of general staff, B. M.

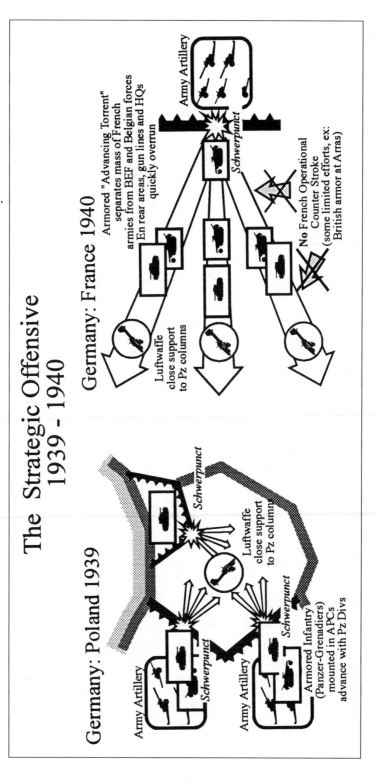

The Strategic Offensive
1939 - 1940

Germany: Poland 1939

Schwerpunct

Schwerpunct

Schwerpunct

Schwerpunct

Luftwaffe
close support
to Pz column

Army Artillery

Army Artillery

Armored Infantry
(Panzer-Grenadiers)
mounted in APCs
advance with Pz Divs

Germany: France 1940

Armored "Advancing Torrent"
separates mass of French
armies from BEF and Belgian forces
En rear areas, gun lines and HQs
quickly overrun

Army Artillery

Schwerpunct

No French Operational
Counter Stroke
(some limited efforts, ex:
British armor at Arras)

Luftwaffe
close support
to Pz columns

Shaposhnikov wrote that "the operational staff must be become the brain of the Red Army." The writings of the early Soviet military thinkers "contain the most precisely formulated fundamental positions on Soviet military-theoretical thought."[13] The 1920s and 1930s produced creative thinkers like Shaposhnikov and M. N. Tukhachevskii,[14] under whose inspired leadership emerged the concept of deep battle. The philosophy of "deep operations" was formalized in 1933 with the publication of "Temporary Instructions on the Organization of *Deep Battle*." These were initially ignored by the West, even after the Soviet victory in 1945, and particularly during the Cold War, when Soviet military histories, operational studies, and philosophy were dismissed as propaganda.

The Red Army set aside the 1936 Field Regulations when the Communist Party began its political purges of the Soviet High Command (Stavka). Stalin's 1937 purges removed much of the intellectual leadership: Gen. A. I. Kork, head of the Frunze Academy was shot; Tukhachevskii, Uborevich, and Svechin were also executed.[15] The entire concept of deep operations was ignored as revisionist and fascist-inspired. Military concepts pioneered by Tukhachevskii were abandoned.[16]

Until the purges, the Red Army was basically a czarist organization wearing communist uniforms. The Civil War did not produce sufficient numbers of committed Bolsheviks with the expertise to direct operations. The youngest General Staff officers were trained by the German army, and these too were removed in the 1937 purges. That left an army whose leadership was composed of politically acceptable generals or young communist officers who knew no national leader but Stalin: "even while cowing the Red Army and its leaders, Stalin had not forfeited the loyalty of the army. . . . This was no blind, bloody and aimless killing. On the contrary, it was the most delicate piece of surgery which Stalin carried out on the Soviet Body politic."[17]

The purges left three types of acceptable senior officers. First was the original 1917 Bolshevik who had learned his trade in the czar's army or the field (there were very few of those). Second, there were the loyal, albeit German-trained, staff officers (the few that survived received army groups to command and soon met their former teachers during *Barbarossa*). Third were the unobtrusive political toadies who could not possibly lead the Red Army to operational victory.

Experiments in Spain and Finland quickly proved that Western technology and tactics still had an edge. The doctrine of maneuver warfare appealed to an army whose cossacks had chased Napoleon out of Russia, but it was still left in limbo. A less proficient Stalinist officer corps drew incorrect lessons from the Spanish Civil War (1936–1939) and Russo-Finnish War of 1939–1940. Zhukov's campaign in Manchuria against the

Japanese again confirmed the future path for Soviet doctrine: Khalkin Gol was won by boldly used armor.

Barbarossa

We are being fired on. What shall we do?
—Red Army radio signal, dawn, 21 June 1941[18]

Once the German invasion began, the third and final stage of Soviet doctrine development (1941–1945) commenced. The shock of defeat forced revision. The Red Army resurrected the tank corps and reintroduced deep operations. The guiding factors for operational development were stability in the rear, morale of troops, quantity and quality of divisions, and emphasis on the organizational ability of command personnel. The first step was the creation of mobile groups (*podvizhnye gruppy*) to conduct operational maneuver, first at army level (operational grouping of army corps), and subsequently at front level (operational grouping of armies).[19]

To suggest that the Soviet army learned as it fought is simplistic; the ability to defeat both *Barbarossa* and the 1942 offensive on a front stretching from the Baltic to the Black Sea speaks for itself. Throughout these desperate battles the Red Army raised new formations, supplied its field armies, conducted counteroffensives, and continued to mass-produce weapons whose quality shook the German High Command and arms industry. The Soviet staff that survived the purges to serve the Stavka was remarkably—Allied and German staffs might say surprisingly—skilled at organization and control.

Problem Solving

Mnogo raz podumat'.
—Stalin to the Stavka[20]

On 21 June 1941, in Operation *Barbarossa* three attacking German army groups easily penetrated the Red Army's operational depth. The Wehrmacht's expertise at operational maneuver produced astounding encirclements of hundreds of thousands (the Kiev envelopment alone netted half a million Soviet prisoners). The Red Army counterattacked courageously but could not slow the blitzkrieg.[21] Suddenly, as the panzer divisions penetrated into the central steppes and beyond the Prut River, the Soviet second-echelon corps appeared. These held Stalin's operational reserves and his best tanks. Initial contact with the KV and T-34 series of tanks shocked the

German army into a frenzied development program to produce a main battle tank capable of defeating its Soviet counterpart.[22]

Tigers and Panthers were rushed into battle but never really recovered from their curtailed shake-out period.[23] The German army basically played catchup with the Soviets, particularly in artillery and armor.[24] The doctrinal evolution on the battlefield went through rapid evolution as senior Soviet officers were captured, killed, or removed by the Stavka for lack of enthusiasm or exhibiting fear instead of confidence. The great encirclements of the 1941–1942 campaign saw the German generals eliminate most of their former students[25]—it was really a practical extension of a Berlin senior staff course, and the price for failure was cruel. Having survived the onslaught, the Stavka now turned to the problem of the counterattack. Solutions were initially imitations of the German technique: spearhead penetrations and the deep envelopment. These did not do well against those who had invented them in the first place.

The problem facing the Stavka was essentially how to throw the German army out of the Soviet Union. The answer was simple: attack and annihilate. Attack posed its own problems; the German defense system was based on depth, local counterattack, and counterstrokes by operational and strategic reserves. The battlefield was dominated by long-range antitank weapons and artillery that used natural and military obstacles to draw the attacker into killing zones of ever increasing size. Then the attacker, if he broke through, soon found himself facing new blocking positions and an armored counterattack just as he was losing momentum: "The highest expression of activity in defense is the conducting of counterattacks and counterstrikes."[26] The problem was thus threefold: one, break through the initial defense zones and avoid the dogfight that slows the attack; second, defeat the operational reserves; and, third, prevent the strategic reserves from blocking and destroying the force of penetration before it can accomplish strategic (or political) results. Strategic results were considered the only justification for attempting a strategic offensive.[27]

The Strategic Offensive

Offensive is everything in the Red Army—it is initiative.
—Reznichenko[28]

If the enemy keeps his flanks closed and it is not possible to envelop them, the enemy battle formation must be crushed by a deep strike from the front.
—Marshal Mikhail Tukhachevskii[29]

Because operational battles gained limited terrain, and dealing with them was well within German capabilities, the answer had to be strategic

offensive: big forces, big kills, big gains. This type of effort is most complicated, requiring the most detailed staff work, dynamic leadership at all levels, trained formations, and a sophisticated supply system to maintain
momentum. The first Soviet army attempts were desperate mass assaults
that quickly failed. The first true strategic offensives began in 1943
(Operation *Zvezda,* the Kharkov-Kursk counteroffensive).[30] Strategic plans
included a temporary strategic defense to weaken German attacker—
"diversionary attacks to draw German operational reserves to other sectors
. . . and two major counteroffensives against weakened German forces."[31]
After initial success, the attacks were defeated because the Germans kept
cool and retained operational maneuver. The shoulders of the penetration
were held and, at Kharkov, for example, Manstein was able to successfully
counterattack with the SS panzer corps. This highlighted the final but
essential goal of a successful offensive: deny the German panzer reserves
operational maneuver. "Operational Maneuver is the organized shifting of
distinct groups of forces during an operation to achieve a more favourable
position with regards to an enemy in order to strike a blow against him or
to repel and enemy attack."[32]

There is no evidence to suggest that Montgomery conceived
Goodwood, Spring, Bluecoat, and Totalize in classical Soviet terms. The
offensives were part of a loosely organized strategy in that they followed
each other. None of the Montgomery breakouts husbanded all available
operational resources to achieve a strategic result; instead they were rather
democratic. Each national group was given a kick at the can and shared the
strategic bombers. SHAEF was not able, despite Eisenhower's general urg-
ings for audacity, to arrive at a successful formula throughout the
Normandy campaign. The Wehrmacht's defense in Normandy was the same
standard formula it had used on the Eastern Front: three lines of defense
and operational reserves to seal off and then decapitate the penetration.

After reviewing the teething problems of the first offensives, the
Stavka was urged to "think further" (*produmaem eshche*) by Stalin. The
Soviet military mind is a curious collection of the chessmaster's simple but
deadly moves, the technical execution of the Kirov Ballet, the passion of
folk dances, and the savage ruthlessness of a cossack horde. The Soviet
attack is at once ultrasophisticated and pathetically crude. Tactically, there
was no contest against the Wehrmacht at the platoon to brigade level.
Soviet divisional staffs were decidedly inferior. German officers prided
themselves on their instinctive sixth sense for terrain and tactics.[33] The
German army operated by its *auftragstaktik:* mission orders, or general
guidelines for independent tactical initiative by subordinates who understood clearly what the next higher commander would do when faced with
the same tactical problem.

German generals who had taught the senior staff course to Red Army
officers before World War II recalled the long and ponderous attempts by

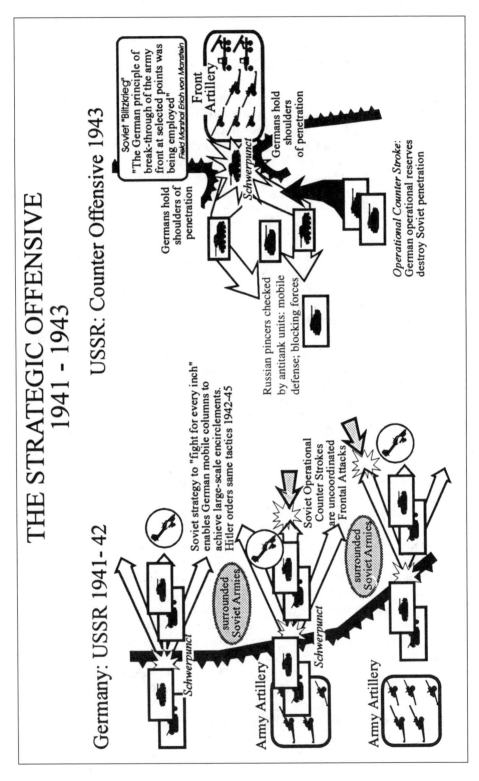

their Soviet students to write a page-long operational order. "In the mean-time, their troops waited for their maps whereas we were already on the move for hours."[34] Although German superiority below army level was considerable, and in most cases unchallenged, an amazing transition occurred at the front and theater level, where there appeared the Russian genius that had produced Frunze and Tukhachevskii. The simplicity of the Red Army's Field Service Operations (PU-44) masked the sophistication required to carry them out.

The Soviet approach was direct. First, eliminate the dogfight for suc-cessive defense lines; second, and most important, cut out the shoulders of the breakthrough; and, finally, restore the deep battle: kill off headquarters and operational reserves before they arrive at the front. The method was elemental—destroy everything. Do not attack hoping for a spearhead and then pour troops through the breach as in France in 1940; instead, rip out a chunk that is 35 to 75 miles (60–120 kilometers) wide.[35] The enemy cannot hold the shoulders if your initial attack destroys his entire upper torso, with "large scale enemy losses . . . [the] enemy . . . not [able to] close the gaps . . . [and] forced to execute the maneuver of deep reserves and take forces from strategic directions."[36] The Soviet strategic offensive solved the prob-lem with chess-like precision, simply, elegantly, and savagely: tear away a 60 miles of front, insert a massive second echelon, and tear away another 125 miles of rear areas and operational reserves. Simultaneously, send out OMGs to keep the operational and strategic counterplans irrelevant.

The challenge was perfecting the mechanics of the Offensive. Tearing apart the front on a gigantic scale demanded outstanding staff work to col-lect the concentration of firepower and logistic support. The "one big strike" was the key, based on massive artillery fire by gun concentrations unheard of in the West, and certainly never attempted in the Soviet way until the Rhine crossings of 1945. There were twelve Red Army strategic offensives from 24 December 1943 to 12 May 1944.[37] Allied offensives were divided between Italy and Normandy, and, further, Montgomery per-mitted separate offensives by 12th and 21st Army Groups.

Breakthrough Artillery

The final goal of the Red Army attack doctrine is the immediate develop-ment of the tactical breakthrough into an operational breakthrough.
—Soviet Field Regulation, PU-44

Stalin ordered an artillery offensive in January 1942. Within months, Soviet FOOs were advancing with the infantry and armor mounted in their own radio-equipped tanks—a full two years before the idea dawned on Bradley and Quesada. The BM-31 "Katyusha" multiple rocket launcher with its twelve 300mm free-flight rockets was introduced in late 1942: their coordinated moving barrages and successive concentrations were used during the Battle of Stalingrad. Soviet commanders quickly acquired the skills to allow a totally flexible response to new battle situations. By 1943 the first "breakthrough artillery corps" (AKP) was organized. It consisted of two breakthrough divisions and one rocket launcher division (the equivalent of 1,000 guns). Ten complete AKPs were formed before the war ended, and by the summer of 1943 a front counterbattery group was formed.

Soviet artillery resources became centralized: by 1945 35 percent of Red Army artillery was in High Command reserve. The aim of Soviet artillery fire was to neutralize both defenses and local reserves: the only solution was early counterbattery fire or Luftwaffe airstrikes, but by 1944 this was no longer possible.

Soviet forward observers adjusted counterbattery fire before and during offensives so effectively that early unmasking by German gunners meant their certain death. Air parity, and in some cases air superiority, was achieved by the Red Army Air Force during 1943 and 1944 despite early German use of radar.[38] Thereafter, from December 1943 through August 1944 the Stavka was able to concentrate its forces against single German army groups, severely damaging each in succession as follows:

- December 1943–April 1944: Army Group South
- June–July 1944: Army Group Center
- July–August 1944: Army Group North Ukraine
- August–September 1944: Army Group South Ukraine

Soviet strategic planning "tested the limits of German endurance."[39] As already noted, Soviet offensives were conducted on wide fronts of 35 to 75 miles; tactical breakthroughs were 3 to 8 miles wide and prevented the defender from establishing effective shoulders from which to contain penetration. Three miles was the minimum width allowable. The average was about 6 miles, and, since there were at least two breakthroughs occurring simultaneously, the enemy front was not just ruptured but was razed beyond the operating boundaries of the defending depth formations—and quickly exposed its operational reserves to second-, often first-echelon tank armies.

Attack density and artillery preparation changed as Red Army experience grew. Initial preparatory fires used on average two and a half hours, with a density of 233 guns and rockets per kilometer in an average breakthrough sector of 9 to 20 miles (see Table 14.1).

Table 14.1   Soviet Army Preparatory Fire Times[40]

Date	Strategic Offensive	Preparatory Fire[a]
1942/1943	Stalingrad	70 minutes
July 1943	Kursk	160 minutes
August 1943	Kharkov	160 minutes
January 1944	Korsun-Shevchenkovskii	20 minutes
June 1944	Beloruss	160 minutes
July 1944	Lvov	100 minutes
August 1944	Jassy	100 minutes
October 1944	Petsamo	150 minutes
January 1945	East Prussia	120 minutes
January 1945	Vistula	120 minutes
February 1945	East Pomerania	50 minutes
April 1945	Berlin	160 minutes

Sources: Chris Bellamy, *The Evolution of Modern Land Warfare* (London: Routledge, 1990) and *Red God of War* (London: Brassey's, 1986).
Note: a. Average 2.5 hours preparatory fire, total time only. Actual fire by armies with strategic offensives averaged 10-minute barrages.

A strategic offensive would open fire on at least two such sectors simultaneously. Compare this with the Allied artillery density for Goodwood and Spring of approximately eighty guns per kilometer. The heavy bombers are not included in artillery density calculations, but the bomber strike accounts for one continuous stream (fifteen to thirty minutes) of individual bombers dropping single loads. Artillery fire is capable of being repeated, shifted, and accurately concentrated during an operation. Heavy bombers attack once and, as Cobra, Totalize, and Tractable proved, often miss. However, "the Army having been drugged with bombs, it is going to be a difficult process to cure the drug addicts."[41]

By August 1944 the Red Army orchestrated breakthrough frontages of 9, 11, and 28 miles. The Jassy offensive (Romania) of 20 August 44 included 6,200 guns and 460 Katyushas.[42] The attack included formal deception practiced operationally (which was also used successfully by the Allies)[43] as well as penetration by OMGs (not used by the Allies). The use of deception was best illustrated during the summer offensive against German Army Group Center in July 1944 (corresponding to Goodwood, Spring, and Cobra). The Soviets conducted an artillery maneuver moving 3,500 guns and 35,000 vehicles over 410 miles to redeploy (in total surprise) on the northern sector of Army Group Center. The sophisticated planning and technical efficiency required to move a strategic mass of artillery from one front flank to another without German knowledge is staggering. Artillery concentrations were increased from 5,500 to 9,000 guns along the attacked sector.

Goodwood: Soviet Disapproval

By comparison, Goodwood, Spring, Cobra, and Totalize were sent in along frontages of 4, 3.75, 4, and 3 miles, respectively. These were noted with disapproval by the Soviets as examples of unsuccessful offensive operations.

The Lvov offensive took place at the same time as Goodwood. The Stavka concentrated 68 percent of Red Army divisions for the attack, including 80 percent of armored fighting vehicles, 65 percent of the artillery, and 100 percent of the aircraft. The breakout sector was 16 miles wide, the offensive front extended 273 miles. Soviet ratios were difficult to achieve for Western Allied corps fighting isolated breakthrough battles. However, since Montgomery had access to all the artillery and armor of the Normandy front, it is regrettable he opted for an all-British show in Goodwood, Totalize, or Tractable rather than create a powerful second echelon based on a U.S. armored corps.

There was no operational breakthrough plan for Operation Spring or Totalize; conversely, during Totalize Simonds actually contrived to stop the entire offensive to wait for a heavy-bomber attack. The last two operations, contrasted to Soviet breakouts appear amateur and, in Totalize's case, absurd.[44] There is little doubt that the Western Allies could have duplicated the artillery concentrations used by the Russians. Western Allied artillery control, particularly British/Canadian, was tactically superior to that of the Soviets. There were over 500 guns in the Simonds's corps alone; Montgomery controlled over 3,000 guns, not including thousands of medium and heavy mortars, tank guns, rocket batteries, and antitank regiments.

At issue was the requirement for specific doctrine for the breakout—all that existed was the North African example, and this was in essence attrition warfare. From Montgomery's initial briefing at St. Paul's School, it was simply assumed the Western Allies would somehow break out in Normandy. Western Allied strategic planning does not seem to have accounted for the actual mechanics of the campaign. The idea of Simonds's sitting alone in his trailer dreaming up a new method for breaking through Dietrich's defenses, would have been so out of place in the Soviet system as to be completely ludicrous. But in Normandy, each commander did his own thing.

Breakthrough Operations and Operational Maneuver

Battle is the means of the operation. Tactics are the material of operational art. The operation is the means of strategy, and operational art is the material of strategy.

—A. A. Svechin[45]

One of the Red Army innovations that was particularly suited to strategic operations was the operational maneuver group.[46] The OMG was a mobile, totally mechanized assault unit no smaller than a division, and usually a tank corps, whose mission was to quickly penetrate frontal defenses by avoiding all contact and enemy fire in order to reach the enemy's operational depth. There the formation would again ignore any ad hoc blocking positions or meeting engagements, seeking instead political, operational, or even strategic objectives. OMG missions included Luftwaffe airfields, communication centers, high-level headquarters, and urban centers. The group could be called upon to encircle or conduct a meeting engagement, but this was rare. OMGs were a one-way operation. The tanks, armored personnel carriers, and self-propelled artillery, including mobile supply columns, raced to their objectives using any available approach until they captured the objective or ran out of supplies. The devastating effect of independent formations loose in rear areas but not conforming to predicted movement created immense headaches for defending staffs. OMGs drew away strategic reserves, totally disrupted communications, and, most important, denied the enemy operational maneuver in his own rear areas.

> Maneuver is one of the most important conditions for achieving success. Maneuver consists of the organized movement of troops for the purpose of creating the most favorable grouping and in placing this grouping in the most favorable position for striking the enemy with a crushing blow to gain time and space. Maneuver should be simple in conception and be carried out secretly, rapidly, and in such a way as to surprise the enemy.[47]

During the Kursk-Orel campaign, the attacks were extensively supported by mechanized artillery that advanced with the armor and fired in direct engagements.[48] In most successful operations, the Russians had one self-propelled gun to every two tanks. The actual assault was preceded by a double barrage. Insertion of mobile formations whose orders were to penetrate beyond the defensive depth and avoid local engagements quickly brought about meeting engagements with operational reserves that were quickly overwhelmed.[49] German capacity for counterattack was severely curtailed by the big strike of the breakthrough: 89 percent of counterattacks were received beyond front-line defenses. The Soviet tank armies led operations with one forward detachment, a reinforced tank brigade, for each forward corps "to perform tactical maneuver. . . . These forward detachments were tasked with securing key objectives, obviating defenses, and facilitating the advance of their parent units (later also a deep function)."[50] (The British Columbia Regiment's thrust during Totalize would in Soviet doctrine have been a forward detachment.)

The Russian terminology for the armored breakthrough is particularly descriptive and certainly more savage than the low-key terms used by

Canadians in imitation of the casual, antithetical language of the British officer class.[51] The aim of the offensive was not merely to break in, conduct a dogfight, and break out but to *razryvat'* (tear apart) the enemy. From the Red Army Field Manual of 1936 to PU-44 the tone is definitive: "In the meeting encounter one must strive for a rapid . . . tearing apart of the enemy deployment into separate disconnected groupings." To illustrate the total Western miscomprehension of what was happening on the Eastern Front, the No. 10 Liaison Letter (July 44) distributed throughout the 21st Army Group HQ stated that military reports showed "the remarkable parallel between British and Soviet tank tactics."[52]

Operational Reconnaissance

The Soviet concept of battlefield reconnaissance was totally different from Western doctrine. Western corps and infantry division's reconnaissance formations' tactics were still devoted to observation and reporting. "Recce in force" was considered and available since both the British and Canadians reconnaissance regiments were equiped with main battle tanks and capable of fighting for information. British and Canadian staffs virtually abandoned operational reconnaissance in favor of using the heavy divisional reconnaissance regiment simply as another armored unit and forming battle groups tasked with missions well outside their proper role.

When they were conducted (normally by the corps armored car regiment) Western reconnaissance missions were assigned fixed, limited aims and controlled by phase lines. Mission-directed reconnaissance did not appear until the U.S. Third Army began to sweep toward Le Mans. Western operational reconnaissance was surrendered to the tactical air and the reconnaissance squadrons of the RAF or USAAC.[53]

Soviet operational reconnaissance preceded corps tactical reconnaissance and was based on the reconnaissance group. Both types of Soviet reconnaissance employed tank and mechanized units to maintain momentum. Reconnaissance was continuous, conducted day and night, and attempted to maintain continuous contact with a mobile enemy force.[54] The forward units

> performed reconnaissance while moving. . . . Soviet reconnaissance detachments do not operate like their British counterparts . . . sit down and observe and report and observe again. . . . They observe what they can and report what they can while continuing with their advance.[55]

The mission of the Red Army's reconnaissance units was to find the enemy's operational armored mass and alternative routes around blocking positions to enable OMGs and tank armies to maintain momentum. The British/Canadian tactics required reconnaissance to report accurately as well as place pickets near the enemy position to allow a controlled *hand-over* to the follow-on battlegroup. Soviet reconnaissance operated miles ahead of main bodies and reported while en route, never halting the advance so as to further develop contacts. The trade-off was time for accurate information. At the operational level, the Soviets were prepared to make sacrifices for speed.[56]

Mass

The worth of a mechanized unit shows itself in the highest degree when the enemy has not yet had time to organize antitank defense.
— Gen. K. B. Kalinovskii[57]

The main and decisive force in exploiting the success after the break-through were the tank armies and the detached tank and mechanized corps. In cooperation with the air force, like a fast-moving ram of colossal power, they cleared the way for field armies.
— Marshal Zhukov[58]

The Soviet tank attacks overwhelmed German armor by closing rapidly and boldly while being supported by extensive fire from heavier gunned T-34/85s, KVs, and SU-85 and SU-100 companies.[59] The assault was part of a combined-arms philosophy: the Russians raised combined-arms corps[60] and combined-arms armies to ensure a constant balance and eliminate the

Table 14.2   Combined-Arms Organization

	Soviet Tank Army				Soviet Tank Corps			
	1943	1944	1945		1942	1943	1944	1945
Tanks	500+	600+	700	Tanks	168	208	207	228
Self-Propelled Guns	25	98+	250	Self-Propelled Guns	—	49	63	42
Artillery/				Artillery	12	12	36	56
Mortars	500+	650+	850	Heavy Mortars	18	48	94	94
				Multiple Rocket Launchers	8	8	8	8
Personnel	40,000	48,000	50,000	Personnel	7,000	10,000	12,000	11,788

Notes: March 1942: Four tank corps formed (each two tank brigades) "lacked operational, tactical self-sufficiency." The 1944 Soviet tank army had more than twice the number of tanks as a Western armored division (600 vs. 240); a Soviet tank corps was smaller than a Western armored division but larger than a German panzer division (207 vs. 245).[61]

need to regroup into a German *Kampfgruppe* system, which their lower echelons would have found difficult to successfully duplicate. However, it was common to reorganize any formation and reinforce it with the required units estimated as needed for a successful assault (see Table 14.2).

The Soviet offensive philosophy was based on both concentration of all means in one operation as well as several coordinated tactical incisions within the actual attack: "An enemy front capable of enduring dozens of small strikes may be broken by one big strike. In certain conditions, a certain mass (*massivnost*) of operation is necessary in order to obtain even minimum results."[62] There was no breakout phase or planned pursuit stage. The Red Army offensive maintained momentum by introducing second-echelon formations, as required, to prevent the enemy from catching his breath. "The uninterruptedness of pursuit was attained . . . above all by the periodic interchange of the pursuing troops by bringing Second Echelon reserves into battle."[63] During the Weichsel-Oder operation the advance detachments of the Third Guards Army were changed five times in eleven days. The uninterrupted combat action of tanks in advance units rarely exceeded two to three days. The aim was to produce a temporary cessation of the enemy's capacity for combat by quickly producing irreparable losses in selected areas.[64] These losses exercised a greater impact on morale than losses during a protracted period. The formula was simply stated: "The higher one's ability to concentrate in both time and space—the greater one's assurance of victory over supreme forces."[65]

Compare this doctrine to Operation Spring's attachment of tank squadrons to brigades or Simonds's feeding the British 7th Armoured Division into the battle against the 1st SS and 9th SS Panzer Divisions a squadron at a time. Operation Spring demonstrated a timid and indecisive use of armor by the Canadian II Corps. This was to be repeated in Totalize and Tractable: although the armor was massed at the outset, it was hamstrung by a doctrinal inability by armored brigade or division commanders to get their tanks to move. Bypassing points of resistance was demanded by Simonds, Kitching, and Maczek, but it was left to brigade and regiment commanders to bring it about. The wartime restrictions governing maneuver in English farmlands and the paucity of divisional exercises produced an armored force incapable of armored offensives. Western Allied armored battles invariably became uncoordinated piecemeal efforts. Simonds's frustrations at Totalize were foreseen by the Soviets[66] whose operational instructions emphasized "one strike after the other . . . it is not permitted to stop."[67] The emphasis on speed and violence generally brought immediate results: "Russians broke into our position even before the end of the artillery fire."[68]

By the winter of 1943–1944 the Soviet strategic offensive had evolved to a stage where the German army could not afford to practice its own

The Strategic Offensive 1944 - 1945

USSR: Soviet Strategic Offensive 1944 - 1945

Germany: Ardennes 1944

Front Artillery

"One Big Strike"

High Density: massed Artillery plus several echelons of Mech and Tank Armies

Front Artillery

"One Big Strike"

© Roman Jarymowycz Oct 2000

Strategic Offensives destroy vast sections of front (150 km+): each Operation (10 - 30 km frontage) overwhelms German Operational Reserves then quickly fixes and wears away Strategic Reserves. Wehrmacht cannot "hold the shoulders" because Red Army attack destroys, at once, the upper torso.

German *Neo Blitzkrieg* Renaissance of *Hutier Taktik* Infiltration and penetration to rear areas

Front Artillery

Americans hold shoulder and key road center

Operational Maneuver: Divs fm 21st Army Group deploy to block German penetration

Allied Air Attack: interdiction and "tank busting"

Operational Maneuver and Counter Stroke: Americans use ad hoc Strategic Reserve: Patton's 3d Army doctrine. The only defense against the Soviet strategic offensive was to not defend. A successful defense on the Eastern Front required total operational maneuver in a mobile defense capable of trading ground for operational advantage. Hitler would not hear of this. The Wehrmacht was ordered to dig in and fight for every inch of Mother Russia. This politically sound but militarily stupid strategy eventually gave rise to the "we could have defeated them if Hitler had let us" argument.[69] It is a moot point.

Western Operational Warfare

I repeatedly urged Montgomery to speed up and intensify his efforts to the limit. He threw in attack after attack, gallantly conducted and heavily supported by artillery and air, but German resistance was not crushed.
                                                        —Dwight D. Eisenhower[70]

The Americans and British shared the Russians' problem in defeating the German army's three-zone defense. The Western Allies attempted to trade technology for a quick victory. Poor strategic planning (getting involved in an Italian campaign) and weak operational leadership (Montgomery, and eventually Eisenhower) resulted in high casualties and a long, costly war. The Soviets' solution was expensive but it worked: besides, they were fighting to liberate their homeland. The Western Allies, who were liberating someone else's homelands, were free to experiment with grand tactics and their overwhelming technological edge. By the winter of 1943–1944 the Soviet armies had perfected their strategic *métier:* the 1944 summer offensive destroyed an entire German front. In retrospect, it could be argued that the 1944 Soviet strategic offensive took about the same time and produced the about same results as the Normandy campaign. The destruction of German Army Group Center (June–August 1944) included an advance of 450 miles into German-held territory. Normandy lasted about eighty-six days and pushed the Germans from the bocage to the Scheldt, the Ardennes, and Lorraine, about 350 miles. The Red Army destroyed over sixty Axis divisions. Conversely Model got most of his armies across the Seine, lost no panzer divisions, not a single one, and was able to defeat Montgomery's next strategic offensive, the pathetically planned and tragically executed Operation Market Garden.[71]

An adaptation of the Soviet system may have been the answer to the Allied frustrations in Normandy. Goodwood should have worked, but Montgomery tore away only a small part of the front; the stone villages in the path of his tanks held fast and soon stopped Goodwood cold in an armored dogfight. A British success could have resulted in a reversed Cobra but the 21st Army Group had no second-echelon armored corps ready to overwhelm Dietrich. It will be remembered Montgomery decided early against using additional tank formations. It has been argued in defense of the Western Allies that the German defense in Normandy was more complex than anything on the Eastern Front. "German density in Normandy is 2 1/2 times that on the Russian front, whilst our superiority in strength was only in the nature of some 25 percent as compared to 300 percent Russian superiority on the Eastern front."[72] Actually, German density in Normandy varied constantly: most panzer divisions were forced to hold the line, making the creation of operational reserves very difficult.

On the Eastern Front, vast Soviet supremacy occurred because the Red Army senior staff planned for it. Coalition warfare produced dramatically less effective approaches to operations at the army group level. A certain disdain for the foreign, allegedly barbaric nature of Soviet doctrine may have dissuaded U.S., British, and Canadian staffs from studying the lessons learned.[73] An early misinterpretation of the effect of air power (tactical and strategic) coupled with an unrealistic transfer of North Africa experience debilitated the evolution of Western Allied operational art. Although leadership was centralized, the most senior military leaders were not held accountable for their failures. Indeed, style appears to have counted for more than sober evaluation of the mechanics of war. It was simply accepted that, once ashore, Montgomery would defeat the German armies. How he proposed to accomplish this (there were no operational maneuver plans save such phase lines as "D+10 or D+90.") does not appear to have been challenged except by the Air Marshal Tedder clique.[74]

SHAEF's operational art did not employ key Soviet principles: concentration of all resources, overwhelming superiority and, deep battle. Montgomery (and, in fairness, Eisenhower) demonstrated at best a vague understanding of deep operations. Eliminating the common factor of strategic bombing, the major British, Canadian, and U.S. offensives were uncoordinated, poorly supported, and too individual in nature to suggest the guiding hand of a great captain. Some, like Totalize and Tractable, were, from an armored, and certainly from a Soviet point of view, inane. The fact that Spring and Totalize were loose parts of a strategic effort that only succeeded because of Cobra, should not obscure the fact that there was no actual strategic offensive, but rather a series of reactions to Goodwood's failure.

Bradley and Montgomery's operational art was to claw away until something gave. Clearly, the spot for the strategic offensive was the Caen area and not the U.S. Army's bocage-cursed front. Deep operations appeared after Avranches, but were initiated by divisional commanders and immediately made Montgomery, and especially Bradley, apprehensive. Patton radiated a sense for the operational situation but lacked the horses to carry it out. When he did try, it was under the conservative rein of his boss. Senior Western generals were not as good as their Soviet counterparts. It will be suggested that the Soviets had had four years to practice.[75] It should be noted the Western Allies had had six.

Notes

1. Guderian in B. H. Liddell Hart, ed., *The Red Army* (Gloucester, Mass.: Peter Smith, 1968).
2. W. C. Frank Jr. and P. S. Gillette, *Soviet Military Doctrine from Lenin to Gorbachev 1915–1991* (Westport, Conn.: Greenwood Press, 1991).
3. "Let's think this over." John Erickson, *The Soviet High Command: A Military Political History, 1918–1941* (London: Macmillan, 1962).
4. By strategic reserves is meant armored forces directly under Hitler's command and not within the immediate operational area or within the control of the operational commander (Kluge). German panzer divisions pulled out of different army units in the West during the Normandy campaign around August (116th Panzer Brigade, 9th and 11th Panzer Divisions) became strategic reserves and most were eventually committed to Normandy. The 9th and 10th SS Panzer Divisions were seconded to the Eastern Front to fight in the Brody area, released to the strategic reserve, and then reassigned to Normandy.
5. Ellis, pp. 160, 173.
6. Christopher Duffy, *Red Storm on the Reich* (New York: Athenaeum, 1991).
7. The Tsaritsyn (later Stalingrad)/1st Cavalry Group became the cadre associated with Budenny's First Cavalry Army—a Communist Party old boys' association. Stalin was its political commissar, Kulik had been an officer, and even Zhukov had been a troop sergeant. Budenny's Konarmyia is best remembered as the fulfillment of Trotsky's "proletarians to horse" vision.
8. Marshal Pilsudski, as quoted by J. F. C. Fuller, *The Decisive Battles of the Western World Vol II* (London: Paladin, 1970), p. 410.
9. Field Marshal Erich von Manstein, *The Development of the Red Army 1942–1945*. Chapter 13 in Hart, ed., *The Red Army*. Manstein notes "a lack of ability and of initiative, as well as the lack of readiness to accept responsibility on the part of higher, intermediate and subordinate officers . . . [and] Russian soldiers' need for fewer supplies than Western soldiers." Manstein grew passionate in his analysis of the German defeat: "Never, not even during the first years of the war, were Soviet commanders compelled to fight against superior numbers. Never were they asked to win a victory against an enemy superior in numbers."
10. Liddell Hart, *Red Army*. Of thirty contributors, only three were Red Army officers: two had been taken prisoner by the Germans and the third deserted to the underground, being "disillusioned" with Stalin. Nine of the contributors are German officers. Guderian's effusive praise of Liddell Hart in the foreword to *Panzer Leader* is now generally accepted as perceived political correctness and economic savvy. Compare this with the more balanced L. Hanset; W. C. Frank Jr. and P. S. Gillette; and W. Schneider, *Soviet Ground Forces—An Operational Assessment* (London: Croom Helm, 1986); and, of course, John Erickson's superb works.
11. Mellenthin, quoted in *Generals Balck and von Mellenthin on Tactics: Implications for NATO Military Doctrine* (McLean, Va.: BDM Corporation, 1980), p. 12.

12. Marshal I. K. Bagramyan, quoted in John Erickson, *The Road to Berlin. Stalin's War with Germany,* vol. 2. (London: Weidenfeld & Nicolson, 1983), p. 234.

13. Marshal V. A. Zakharov, in Harriet Fast Scott and William F. Scott, eds., *The Soviet Art of War, Strategy and Tactics* (Boulder, Colo.: Westview, 1982), p. 18. M. V. Frunze succeeded Trotsky as head of the Red Army in 1925 and went on to dominate Soviet operational development. The only early Soviet work of consequence was A. A. Svechin's 1927 publication, *Strategy.* See A. I. Radzievskii, ed., *Akademiya Imena M. V. Frunze* (Moscow: Voenizdat, 1972).

14. Tukhachevskii was a Soviet Patton—criticized for "reckless advance . . . ignoring logistics"—nevertheless he was praised by his Polish opposite number, Pilsudski. During his trial Tukhachevskii was described as a "Bonapartist type, an adventurer, an ambitious man who strove not only for a military but also military-political role." See also R. Simpkin, *Deep Battle: The Brainchild of Marshal Tukhachevskii* (London: Brassey's, 1982).

15. Soviet senior officers' writings may have been influenced by German "Western" thinking. Tukhachevskii, Uborevich, and others attended staff college and field training in Germany. They had served under German advisors in the Soviet Union after the Treaty of Rapallo. The Red Army also had an impressive catalog of military works from the West, including the U.S, Army's *Infantry in Battle,* Fuller's *Operation of Mechanized Forces,* de Gaulle's *Toward a Professional Army,* Machiavelli's *Art of War,* Eimansberger, and Clausewitz. These may have been translated under the direction of Kork and Tukhachevskii.

16. William J. McGranahan, "The Fall and Rise of Marshal Tukhachevsky," *Parameters* (July 1978): 62–72. David Glantz and Jonathan House, *When Titans Clashed: How the Red Army Stopped Hitler* (Lawrence: University Press of Kansas, 1995).

17. Three of the "first five marshals of the Soviet Union" were shot. Hundreds of senior officers shared their fate. Erickson, pp. 505, 506.

18. Erickson, p. 565.

19. W. C. Frank, Jr. and P. S. Gillette, *Soviet Military Doctrine from Lenin to Gorbachev, 1915–1991* (London: Greenwood, 1992), p. 135. The evolution of mobile groups first appeared in late 1941 and "reached a pinnacle of success" in late 1944 and 1945.

20. "Let's think about this one more time." Quoted in David M. Glantz, *The Soviet Conduct of Tactical Maneuver* (London: Frank Ross, 1991), p. xxi.

21. The Red Army armor force comprised 7 tank divisions, 79 independent tank brigades, and 100 independent tank battalions by December 1941. "Although Soviet defensive (and counteroffensive) concepts appeared theoretically realistic, in practice they were disastrous." Gillette, p. 138.

22. The KV was a nasty surprise. A single KV-I, parked in place, held up a panzer division for most of the day. Impervious to German main battle tanks, the divisional antiaircraft unit was sent up to dispatch it with 88mm guns. Douglas Orgill, *T-34 Russian Armor* (New York: Ballantine, 1971). The T-34's origins extended to the U.S. Army and J. Walter Christie's original design. Two models ended up in the Soviet Union and were tested in Voronezh. The Bt and T series soon followed—all Christie tank siblings.

23. Marshal Vatutin noted that "it was not a secret that the 88mm gun of the 'Tigers' and 'Ferdinands' could penetrate the armor of our tanks at a distance of two kilometers. . . . But the heavy tanks of the enemy had a disadvantage—their bad

maneuverability. . . . Before the steel colossi could turn their turrets around, the easily maneuverable 34s could fire on them." N. Leites, *Soviet Style in War* (New York: Crane Russak, 1981).

24. "As for the quality of the Tigers and Ferdinands, German hopes proved unjustified (as on a small scale they had already proven in Tunisia); this Tactical Gambling brought no profit." W. E. D. Allan, *The Russian Campaigns of 1941–43* (New York: Penguin, 1944), p. 148. The Tiger's appearance briefly restored tactical armored ascendancy. The advent of the Stalin tank evened things out, although the Russians withdrew the Stalins when Tigers were seen because of "the Stalin's slow rate of fire." The Stalin's frontal armor was only penetrated by Tiger cannon fire from less than 600 yards. Still, Guderian noted that "the Tiger can no longer afford to ignore the principles practiced by normal tank units. Tigers can no longer show themselves 'to have a look around' but must behave like other tanks." RG14186: App. H to CAC Bulletin No. 5, Feb 45: "*Nachrachtenblett der Panzer truppen,*" extract.

25. In May 1942 the Germans counterattacked a southwestern front offensive and encircled three Soviet armies, two tank corps, and three cavalry corps: approximately 200,000 troops and 500 tanks.

26. A. I. Eremenko, *Zapiski Komanduyushchaegom Frontom* (Moscow: Voenizdat, 1961), p. 298.

27. See Harriet Fast Scott and W. F. Scott, *Soviet Military Doctrine: Continuity, Formulation, and Dissemination* (Boulder, Colo.: Westview, 1988); Scott and Scott, eds., *Soviet Art of War;* D. T. Yazov, "On Soviet Military Doctrine," *RUSI Journal* 134 (Winter 1989).

28. V. G. Reznichenko, "Tactics," in Scott and Scott, eds., *The Soviet Art of War,* p. 235.

29. M. K. Tukhachevskiy, "What Is New in the Development of Red Army Tactics." Scott, p. 56.

30. The first use of a "front mobile group" occurred in January 1943 when Vatutin placed four tank corps (the 3d, 10th, 18th, and 4th Guards) under a single headquarters. To augment infantry mobility he attached truck-carried rifle divisions to each tank corps. see W. C. Frank, V. A. Zakharov, A. A. Sidorenko, *The Offensive* (Moscow: Defense Ministry, 1970); A. N. Radzevskii, *Tankovyi Udar* (Moscow: Defense Ministry, 1977).

31. Frank and Gillette, p. 142. The Allied invasion of Sicily also served to draw off considerable German resources from the Eastern Front. See Manstein, p. 229, and Carlo D'Este, *Bitter Victory* (New York: Harper, 1988).

32. B. Arus Hanian, "Manevr v nastupatel'nykh operatsiyakh Velikoy Oechestvennoy Voiny," *Soviet Military Doctrine* 12h, 12 (December 1963): 3.

33. When challenged by the American historian, General DePuy with, "Out of every one hundred German generals [how many] had *Fingerspitzengefühl?*" General Balck replied, "Three or four, but they were unrecognized." Mellenthin. BMD 21.

34. ETHINT MS #303 General Blumentritt. *Technique of Command.* 27 January 1947, MHI 13.

35. Broad-front attacks by the Russians/Soviets are part of their military history: the Brusilov offensive, 1916 290-mile front; Civil War, 1920, 250-mile front; Stalingrad, 1941, 400-mile front; Belorussia, 1943–1944, 415-mile front; Baltic, 1944, 310-mile front; Berlin, 1945, 280-mile front.

36. A. A. Sidorenko, *The Offensive* (Moscow: 1970); Stalin personally urged "a single main blow" for the offensive but finally agreed with Rokossovskii to accept more than one operational attack to form a strategic offensive. See John

Erickson, *The Road to Berlin. Stalin's War with Germany* Vol. 2 (London: Weidenfeld & Nicolson, 1983), p. 203. See also David M. Glantz, "The Nature of Soviet Operational Art," *Parameters* XV, 1 (1985): 2–12. Earl F. Ziemke, "The Soviet Theory of Deep Operations," *Parameters* (June 1983): 23–33.

37. Followed by Lwow-Sandomierz (13 July–31 August), Baltic (5 July–1 October), and Jassy-Kishinev (20–29 August). The total was nineteen offensive operations and one defensive strategic operation. The grand total for the four years was fourteen defensive and forty-one offensive strategic operations. Scott, p. 121.

38. Early warning by Freya radar alerted the IV Air Fleet of a powerful pre-emptive strike by the entire Soviet air front. Quick reaction scrambled all Luftwaffe squadrons in the area. Fighters intercepted and shot down 400 (claimed) Soviet aircraft and denied the Soviets air superiority. See G. Jukes, *Kursk* (New York: Ballantine, 1968), and A. Price, *Luftwaffe* (New York: Ballantine, 1969).

39. David M. Glantz, "Soviet Military Strategy during the Second Period of War (Nov. 1942–Dec. 1943), a Reappraisal," *The Journal of Military History,* 60 1 (January 1996): 150.

40. See Bellamy, *Red God of War,* p. 198.

41. Air Marshal Tedder, commenting on yet another bombers-as-artillery scheme: Simonds's attack against Walchern Island, October 1944. Tedder's protest against this "misuse" of strategic airpower began with Goodwood and carried on through Cobra, Totalize, and Tractable. See: Lord Tedder, *With Prejudice* (London: Cassell, 1966), p. 606.

42. The plan called for three phases: (1) initial penetration: 6 to 7 miles; (2) "insertion of Front's mobile formations"; (3) extending the battle "into the Operational Depth." The Vistula Offensive (12 January 45) conducted a one-hour, forty-seven-minute preparatory fire including a seven-minute "fire strike" on German batteries, antitank guns, and artillery positions.

43. A massive strategical deception plan regarding the D-Day invasion area totally misled the German High Command (War and Army) and, partly, Hitler. Weeks after the Allies' establishment in Normandy most of the German Fifteenth Army, including reserve Stug brigades and the 116th Panzer Division, were kept north of the Seine awaiting the invasion at Pas-de-Calais predicted by a deceived German intelligence staff.

44. By the end of the summer of 1944 there were "hardly more than 10 or 12 Panzer and motorized divisions left. . . ". H.S. Scheibert and U.E. Elfrath, *German Armored Forces on the Eastern Front 1941–44* (Dorheim: Almark Podzun Verlag, 1971).

45. A. A. Svechin, *Strategiya v Akademicheskoi Postanovke ,Voina i Revolyutsiya* (Moscow: Voyennyi Vestnik, 1928).

46. Russian "cavalry raids" are traditional and were effectively used against Napoleon; the First Horse Army's raid in 1920 is another example; see P. A. Rotmistrov, *Vremya i Tanki* (Moscow: Voenizdat, 1972); A. Kh. Babadzhanyan, *Tanki i Tankovye* (Moscow: Voenizdat, 1980); V. Ye. Savkin, *Osnovnye Printsipy Operativnogo Iskusstva i Taktiki* (Moscow: Voenizdat, 1972); and Christopher Bellamy, pp. 198–199.

47. Red Army Field Regulations (PU-44).

48. Col. B. Frolov, "Tankovoye srazheniye v Rayone Bogodukhova. Voyenno-istoricheskiy zhurnal," *Military History Journal* (9 (September 1978): 18–24.

49. "Practically every Russian attack was preceded by large-scale infiltration, by an 'oozing through' of small units." German after-action report, in N. Leites, *Soviet Style in War* (New York: Crane Russak, 1990), p. 300.

50. Frank and Gillette, p. 142. Forward detachments (which were *not* OMGs), which had about sixty tanks each and operated up to 13 miles in front of the main body, were initially easily destroyed by German battle groups. "The Soviets later remedied this problem by better tailoring the composition of detachments (principally with antitank and artillery means) and matching the distance of advance to enemy strength and terrain." See also A. N. Radzevskii, *Tankovyi Udar* (Moskva: Defense Ministry, 1977).

51. For example: "write down," "write off," "bump," "push through," "engage," "sort out," "smash," and "bash" compare with Soviet terms like *razdrobit'* (smash to pieces), *razdirat'* (rip apart), and the very apt *razryvat*.

52. Liaison letter No. 10. July 1944. D Hist 141,009 D116. *Comparison of Soviet and British Tank Tactics.*

53. See Brereton, Greenhous et al., *The Crucible of War—The Official History of the Royal Canadian Air Force* Vol. 3 (Toronto: Toronto University press, 1993). Also see Lt. Gen. R. Rhomer, *Patton's Gap.*

54. See *1944 Combat Regulations for Tank and Mechanized Forces: Reconnaissance.*

55. Andreas Rezpniewski, *Armaments Development Tendencies During the Second World War* in W. Bieganski, *Military Technique Policy and Strategy in History* (Warsaw: Ministry of National Defense, 1976). See also V. G. Reznichenko, ed., *Takitka* (Moscow: Voenizdat, 1966), and P. M. Vigor, "Soviet Reconnaissance," *RUSI Journal* 4 (1975).

56. Mellenthin noted that when fighting Soviet mobile columns, the German staffs normally had "about five minutes" to make tactical decisions. BDM 25.

57. Leites, p. 240.

58. Marshal G. K. Zhukov, *Vospominania i Razmyshlenyi* (London: Macdonald, 1969).

59. A. N. Radzevskii. The bulk of supporting artillery accompanied the armor after the breakin and engaged blocking positions with direct 76mm or 152mm fire while the T-34s and SU-85s or SU-100s maneuvered toward the rear. See Derek Leebaert. *Soviet Military Thinking* (London: George Allen & Unwin, 1981).

60. The 1943 Field Regulation *Polevoy ustav—1943,* stipulated that interarms cooperation "should be managed in the interests of the infantry." It became clear that winning the firefight (*ognevoy boy*) was the decisive factor in tactical encounters. Strengths of the Soviet rifle division: 1941, 14,483; 1943, 9,380 (low point); 1945, 11,780. J. Erickson, L. Hansen, and W. Schneider, *Soviet Ground Forces—An Operational Assessment* (Boulder, Colo.: Westview, 1986), p. 16.

61. Soviet battle divisions establishment: (1) rifle division: foot, horse-drawn, or motorized; (2) tank division: medium/heavy main battle tanks, mechanized or motorized infantry; (3) mechanized division: the "combined-arms infantry-tank team"—one mechanized regiment, three rifle battalions, one tank battalion, one extraheavy tank/self-propelled gun regiment (each included a motorized rifle battalion); (4) artillery division (also heavy "breakthrough" division, varied to "suit particular operational assignments")—light gun brigade, howitzer brigade, medium howitzer regiment, medium gun regiment, MRL brigade, heavy mortar brigade—nearly all towed or mechanized; (5) antiaircraft division; and (6) a cavalry division.

62. A. A. Svechin in A. V. Kadishev, *Readings in Strategical and Operational Soviet War Doctrine.* (Moscow: Voenizdat, 1965), p. 257.

63. Reznichenko, p. 317.

64. When asked "which did General Balck and General von Mellenthin consider the most difficult to defend against?" Balck replied, "speed." BDM 14.

65. Reznichenko, p. 318.

66. "If you press on him (a subordinate officer) he attacks. If you leave him out of your sight, he stops." N. K. Popel, *Tanki Dovernuli na Zapad* (Moscow: Voenizdat, 1960), p. 120. "Let there be fewer unjustified pauses." Col. S. Smirnov, *Voennyi Vestnik* 9 (1977): 58.

67. *1944 Combat Regulations for Tank and Mechanized Forces.* "A tank attack must be carried out without stopping . . . it is forbidden . . . to partition a combined arms formation assigned to a tank brigade." Chap. 1.

68. German after-action report, Leites, p. 301.

69. Duffy, p. 362, notes that beside Hitler's persistent meddling in deployment, operations, tactics, even in the movement of a tank train, "Stalin was Olympian and detached in comparison." See Warlimont for detailed examples of Hitler's obsession with military trivia during conferences.

70. General Dwight D. Eisenhower, *Crusade in Europe* (New York: Doubleday, 1948), p. 267.

71. The German unit most responsible for destroying the British airborne units in Arnhem was Montgomery's old friend, the 9th SS Panzer Hohenstauffen Division, which was "resting and reforming" near the city after escaping from Falaise.

72. Brooke, in Hamilton, p. 766, and Montgomery, p. 261.

73. Doctrinal support for the Soviets was strongest within the old guard writing for the *Cavalry Journal.* General Hawkins was still lobbying for a cavalry division as late as 1945. Throughout 1944–1945 no fewer than thirty-one articles dealing with horsed cavalry appeared, including: "The Tank Cavalry Team," Jan.–Feb. 1944; "Air Support of Cavalry and Tanks," Mar.–Apr. 1944; "Need for Horses in Italy," and "Vital Role of Soviet Cavalry."

74. There was a distinct RAF cabal, led by Marshal Tedder, in opposition to Montgomery's generalship during the Normandy campaign. See D'Este, *Decision in Normandy.* pp. 394–396, 472.

75. Earl F. Ziemke suggests that reasons for a Soviet victory over the Germans include a single theater (no threat from the Japanese); no contribution to the naval war and only tactical/operational effort in the air war; and no strategic effort save within the Soviet zone; further, the Red Army paid extremely heavy prices in men and material. "The Soviet Command planned its operations as if under compulsion to legalize every territorial acquisition by actual military conquest." E. F. Ziemke, *Stalingrad to Berlin: The German Defeat in the East* (Washington: Army Historical Series Office of the Chief of Military History, 1968), p. 504.

Generals of the 1st Canadian Army Headquarters, 1945, including: Seated—Maczek, 1st Polish Armored Division, (first on left), Simonds (third from left), Crerar (center), Foulkes (fifth from left), Hoffmeister, 5th Canadian Armoured Division (sixth from left); Standing—Kitching, 4th Canadian Armoured Division, (fourth from left), Burns (seventh from left), Foster, (eighth from left), Moncel (ninth from left) *(Bell, National Archives of Canada, Wilfred Laurier University, Laurier Centre for Military Strategic and Disarmament Studies)*

CHAPTER 15

Conclusion:
The Allied Operational Art

There is an unfortunate tendency of late to ignore mounted combat as if it were a relic of the past that died with the horse. . . . Although there was not a horse in the American Army in Europe, there was plenty of cavalry action.
        —Maj. Gen. R. W. Grow, U.S. 6th Armored Division[1]

Penetrating and merciless analysis and criticism of our military experience is needed if our armed services are to grow better rather than worse. We cannot afford to have any protected "heroes."
        —Maj. P. E. Appleton, U.S. Cavalry[2]

The introduction of tanks in World War I appeared to end cavalry operations. Although mounted formations fought spirited campaigns during the Russian Civil War and the Polish campaigns, the future lay in mechanization. Early sages were zealots, and their predictions insulted both the competence and traditions of the older combat arms. The J. F. C. Fuller–B. H. Liddell Hart solutions to future war ("torrents of armor," "all-tank armies") were debated by professionals and rejected for a number of reasons, the principal ones dealing with the mechanical unreliability of the tank and parochial reaction against young Turks who threatened to dominate the military establishment.

Both infantry and cavalry attempted to absorb the tank. The cavalry intended to bring it under control as a stablehand to the horse, and the infantry was determined to use armor as a mobile machine gun platform moving at a soldier's pace. The "apostles of mobility" demanded their own separate arm. This was successfully resisted in the United States but not in the Soviet Union, Germany, and Britain. The creation of the Royal Tank Corps was not a step forward for armor, it merely concentrated the converts and made them easier targets.

European and U.S. cavalry hierarchies generally misunderstood the tank, attempted to subvert mechanization, and succeeded in creating an interim modern doctrine that effectively reduced the cavalry to secondary roles of mounted infantry and scouting cavalry. As late as 1939, the cavalry was still hesitant to adopt the mantle of armor. The opposition came principally from senior generals, for most horsed regiments were quite prepared to mechanize. The professional cavalry readily agreed that their faithful steeds were better off patrolling frontiers and playing polo than advancing against artillery and machine gun fire. Modern cavalry officers, even those who embraced the new order, were careful to point out subtleties: "We must be careful not to confuse 'transportability' with 'mobility.' The latter refers to the battlefield. It is the difference between mounted combat and dismounted combat."[3]

The bedrock of any armored force is a virile doctrine. Doctrine in its essence is simply a clear explanation of "how we fight." Oversophisticated doctrines are ineffectual because they are not easily understood by the troops who must actually carry them out. Still, new doctrines cannot be simplistic if they are to produce results on the battlefield. They require a three-part agenda.

The first phase consists of a doctrine for fighting troops. "How we do things" primers in plain terms that allow soldiers to effectively take part in battle, are necessary. The selection of a doctrine invariably rises out of past battle experience. Since philosophes often have different paths to conversion, there is always a bit of Calvin versus Zwingli in the officer corps. The key difference between the Western Allies and Europe's totalitarian regimes was that liberal democracies insisted on an egalitarian doctrine that forced their general staffs to consider the welfare of every single soldier in all aspects of war. It did not mean that Western generals did not waste their men as uselessly and awkwardly as autocratic powers, merely that general staffs desired an amicable doctrinal unity in their combat arms and were prepared to entertain debate. This cost time.

Totalitarian regimes imposed doctrinal solutions with determined and exacting discipline. The Soviets, and to some extent the Germans, developed an operational doctrine that to the untrained observer was a crude, Mongol-like tearing at an enemy wherein overwhelming numbers eventually wore down a gallant but spent foe. In fact, the highest level of doctrinal art was reached on the Eastern Front, where doctrine achieved both the commonest tactical simplicity (for the soldier) and featured the most intricate chess-like planning and sophisticated strategic execution.

The second phase comprises a doctrine for the general staff. It is the same doctrine, but complete in operational and strategical aspects. This must be somewhat complex if it is to overcome a sophisticated enemy. If totally new, it usually demands new technology. Command and control procedures must be perfected at the senior staff level. This requires war gaming to perfect the art. Thus, an experimental formation is vital for any army in order to remain intellectually and tactically au courant. In the 1930s, the major players produced exotic tank outfits and conducted trial maneuvers in Grafenwöhr, Salisbury Plain, Verdun, Kiev, and Louisiana. These allowed the staffs to "test" before they began to teach.

The third phase, education, is relatively simple. Set up a teacher's college to educate the officers, who in turn will indoctrinate the masses through combat arms schools and purge anyone who does not profess the faith. The final stage of conversion is practice—Sir Francis Tuker called it "the approach to battle." The more often the battle formations and their support groups execute the new principles, the easier the fighting—Suvorov's maxim of "Train hard, fight easy." Despite the pioneer experimentation of the British army, European mechanization succeeded primarily because of political reasons. The ardent support of totalitarian despots made tank armies a reality and forced the Western democracies to create parallel organizations. Notwithstanding test campaigns in Spain and Manchuria, mechanization was unconditionally accepted only after the 1939 invasion of Poland. France and Britain did not organize armored divisions until the winter of 1939, and the Canadian and U.S. armored forces were created only after the German invasion of France.

U.S. and Canadian Armies

The revolution wrought by Abrams and others in the field when they made up what was to become armored forces [doctrine] . . . They had not been taught this, they invented it.

—Gen. Bruce C. Clarke[4]

The Canadian cavalry was too small to effectively participate in the mechanization debate. The Canadian motorized brigade and tank battalions were disbanded after World War I, and the cavalry reverted to a decentralized mounted force. Debate was exclusively intellectual and conducted principally by noncavalry officers. The transition to armor was effortless because the European campaigns had de facto refuted all rebuttal. The Canadian Armoured Corps leadership was not developed in major theaters. Experienced cavalry or armored commanders were not promoted, leaving Canadian armor under the direction of artillery, engineer and infantry-trained commanders. Despite a British Empire tradition and regimental system, in many ways the Royal Canadian Armoured Corps mirrored the U.S. Army Ground Forces (AGF) more than its British brothers.

The U.S. tank corps, although buttressed by combat experience and a sophisticated industrial base, was soon retarded by a bitter mechanization debate. Fortunately, pioneering efforts by Van Voorhis and Edna Chaffee ensured that both experimentation and cross-training among the officers occurred. The resistance by the U.S. Cavalry was ill conceived and eliminated this corps from a decisive role in World War II. The War Department adopted the least complicated solution to the problem in 1940 and, rather than award control of armor to either the infantry or cavalry branches, created the U.S. Armored Force. The break between cavalry and armor was unnatural and should have been mended before it was too late. General Herr was eventually simply ignored by Marshall and McNair; the cavalry was doomed to never recapture its former stature. Marshall then ordered Embrick to organize the Louisiana maneuvers, which served to further define national war-fighting techniques. The cavalry entered the war on the periphery of doctrine, relegated to reconnaissance duties at the squadron level.

The U.S. Armored Force faced a daunting challenge; having neutered the cavalry and its grand history, it was forced to create an armored ethos. The new tank formations could not invoke the spirits of battles past. Save for the few battalions that fought under Patton in 1918, U.S. armor had to define itself. Far younger than the Royal Tank Corps, not as brassy or confident, but with better equipment and a homegrown doctrine, the U.S. tank force was a working-class experiment within the tenets of mechanized war. By grouping all it had, the American *jeune école* exercised the opportunity to test the variety of warring branch doctrines. The results were conclusive: in any tactical problem where pure armor was pitted against horsed or partly mechanized horse formations, the armored force succeeded hands down. It was not simply a question of trying to put the old school in its place; Louisiana allowed U.S. armor to find its legs. "[Louisiana] indicated a definite change in policy in so far as Infantry Tank units were concerned. Prior to this time we had separate tank platoons, companies and battalions widely dispersed over the country."[5] The eventual result was FM 100-5 *The Armored Division*. The first draft appeared on 20 October 1940 and was remarkably bold. Yankee common sense and blitzkrieg models in Poland and France expeditiously produced the kind of thinking that had been only discussed by Fuller and Tukhachevskii: "[The] prime role is in offensive operations against tactical or strategical objectives deep in the hostile rear. . . . Opposed by superior forces, the division avoids decisive combat if its mission permits. . . . The main attack is rapid, deep and sustained until the decision is won."[6]

This was well on the path to deep battle. The important factor was to separate armor in mass from infantry tasks. FM 100-5 was a rough tactical primer, but really directed toward the post-spearhead operations within the corps area. The AGF was on the cusp of admitting that the armored division, as part of an armored corps, was an operational weapon capable of strategic decision.

Active U.S. participation in North Africa at the company level at El Alamein and at division and corps level in Tunisia polished technical skills and further refined existing doctrine. Gen. Orlando Ward may have been unfairly sacked but overall, 1st Armored Division was eventually a better division despite the Kasserine Pass disaster. Although U.S. armor endured the same teething troubles as Canadian armor, it appeared to perform better at the division and corps level. This can be traced directly to leadership and experience.

The U.S. Army entered World War II with inferior equipment:

> [The] culminating phase of 3rd Army maneuvers was designed to illustrate the action of a large contingent of tanks to execute a breakthrough . . . the attack area was drenched by heavy a rain storm . . . the tank attack was launched with disastrous results. Not over 20% of the tanks reached their objectives. . . . They were impotent, faulty in design, of questionable military value.[7]

The ability of American industry to create a speedy, mechanically reliable vehicle was only a partial victory. Selecting the M4 Sherman was a stopgap solution—There were supposed to be better tanks down the production line.[8] The Sherman eventually won its campaigns but at considerable cost to men and machines. Further, while the staff at Aberdeen Proving Ground was fiddling with experimental armor, the Armored Force was being subverted from within. The artillery and infantry generals appointed by Gen. George Marshall to create the AGF were seduced by the antitank gun, and conducted a crusade against maneuver warfare. The result was that the Armored Force did not have a principal tank that could meet the enemy on equal terms until 1945. In fact, the U.S. Army would not have a main battle tank that replicated the psychological and technical superiority of the German King Tiger until it fielded the M1 Abrams in the early 1980s.

Technical shortcomings were not limited to the West. The German army's tank development program looked good on paper but it was, in some ways, a sham. The folks who produced the Volkswagen could not manufacture a main battle tank able to move on the battlefield without a coterie of mechanics and spare parts. The Panther and Tiger were deadly killing machines but absolute mechanical nightmares invented by engineers with a surprising inability to correct breakdowns. Worse, the tanks arrived late—they were a response to Red Army armor. The Russians had fared better: their tanks were simple. They worked and had big guns. When bigger tanks with bigger armor and bigger guns were needed, Soviet industry

promptly provided them. That the German Panther and Tiger were generally superior to the T-34 or KV, when they finally reached the battlefield, is
incidental. The Red Army was not jousting. The Soviet strategic offensive
required a mass of armor to execute deep battle: thousands of long-range
tanks that moved quickly and required only elementary maintenance. The
Red Army did brilliantly. Its accomplishments were nevertheless dismissed
in a series of published apologias by German generals and a Cold War
Western military content to believe that the Soviets achieved success only
through crude mass.

An Armored Doctrine

Use 'em all and give 'em hell.
                    —Gen. William D. Crittenberger[9]

Doctrine development required definition of first principles—primarily, What is a tank? More important, What are tanks? The difference is crucial to the creation of an armored force. An armored division required a
doctrine integrally distinct from that of an infantry division. This was interpreted in various ways. The British and French convinced themselves that
there was a requirement for two different types of tanks, infantry tanks and
cavalry tanks. However, by 1945, even Montgomery was convinced that:
"we require one tank which will do both jobs."[10] The definition of what a
tank is was quickly realized in combat: the tank (specifically, an armored,
tracked vehicle mounting a powerful gun) could fight in any terrain, in any
conditions, in any climate, singly or in small groups. The tank excelled in
the attack but was also deadly in the defense. It best supported the infantry
but could fight independently. There was simply nothing the tank, accepting its utter dependability on petrol, oil, and logistics, could not do.

The second question of what tanks are (massed armor) revealed a very
different doctrinal mission. Chedéville's lament that: "the tank is very delicate" is best applied to the armored division, corps, or tank army. Massed
tanks are not capable of operations in closed terrain or urban areas and
should not attack prepared defenses or fortifications.[11] Massed armor was
reserved exclusively for the breakout and pursuit. Combat doctrine soon
determined that tanks must fight tanks but, specifically, they must maneuver. Armored corps, conducting operational maneuver can achieve strategic
results; massed armor, maneuvering in deep battle, is therefore a strategic
arm. This was realized in principle by most general staffs, but only effectively practiced by the German and Soviet high commands.

The experimentation with numerical ratios created different solutions,
each representing the particular doctrinal catechism of the general staff

responsible. In their respective armored divisions, the French tanks out-numbered infantry by two to one, while for the British, still influenced by Fuller and Liddell Hart, tanks well-nigh suffocated balance and the all-arms team solution and the ratio was six to one. By midwar the German ideal panzer division had a reconnaissance battalion, two tank battalions, a mechanized antiarmor (Jagdpanzer) battalion, six panzer grenadier battalions (of which one or two could be transported in armored personnel carriers) and two battalions of motorized artillery.[12] The changes in U.S. armored organizations were less radical than with the British.[13] Although there were still two heavy armored divisions (the 2d and 3d) in 1944, massed armor in an average U.S. armored division really meant about 250 tanks. The Americans began operations with a balanced armored division of triplicates: three tank battalions, three armored infantry battalions, and three self-propelled artillery battalions. It proved an effective weapon, but still required some calibration by expert craftsmen.

The final solution for the perfect tank formation fixed by the Armored Division Committee (ETO, 7 November 1945) is interesting—it proposed a battle-proven U.S. armored division based on *imbalance*: 3 regiments, each with 1 tank battalion and 2 infantry battalions supported by 5 battalions of self-propelled artillery (3 medium and 2 heavy).[14] The final solution had infantry outnumbering tanks by three to two. So much for Fuller and Liddell Hart.

The panzer division was a better fighting machine than the tribal systems of the Canadian armies or the bureaucratic evolution of U.S. combat commands. *Auftragstaktik,* as in, "Above all, orders are to avoid going into detail when changes in the situation cannot be excluded by the time they are carried out," proved doctrinally superior.[15] This was also true for the battle group system.[16] Both were better than the U.S. combat command system because this model was made unnecessarily rigid in its application. U.S. commanders who trained under Chaffee understood his intent and used the system correctly. In the end, the German battle group approach proved to be about as effective as the combat commands but did not require three extra headquarters.

The British, and therefore the Canadian, solution to the armored division was based on two formations: an armored brigade and an infantry brigade—the organization often operated as two (very Canadian) solitudes. The Royal Canadian Armoured Corps failed to produce its own distinctive doctrine. With no experience in North Africa, it was content to emulate British desert doctrine, despite clear indications that it was inferior to German methods. Canadian and British high commands had no realistic concept of deep battle or armored operations in a major offensive. Because of the emphasis on seaborne assault, Western Allied strategic offensives were principally ultrasophisticated amphibious operations. The only model of a successful Allied strategic ground offensive, was unfortunately at El Alamein. This was to dominate disproportionately the Allied doctrinal planning.

Although they had beaten the Germans in Africa, Italy, Normandy, and again in the Ardennes, the Americans remained on the periphery of an operational philosophy for maneuver warfare. Deep battle was to remain a Soviet art until it was discovered by the Pentagon in the late 1970s. But then, the Americans could argue they already intuitively understood deep battle. Despite General Wood's reference to Grant, the U.S. Army proved to be quite comfortable with deep and sweeping operations, and in fact had been bred on them. Sherman's march to the sea or Lee's attack into Pennsylvania were classic examples of deep battle. With traditions like that U.S. generals, if given the chance, would naturally and effortlessly excel in operational maneuver.

Lessons Not Learned—Technology and Tank Scandals

Blitzkrieg made conscientious conversion unnecessary because it articulated the self-evident: armor is cavalry. Better still, the armored division was the resurrection of heavy cavalry, the traditional arm of decision. Post-World War I cavalry had been limited to liaison and covering force missions. Panzer divisions restored to the cavalry its former position of preeminence. The British cavalry arrived in the western desert prepared to retrieve glory of old. It received a rude awakening. The doctrinal answer was that Fuller, Liddell Hart, and Hobart were wrong. Guderian was right, and what the Germans meant all along was not the supremacy of armor, but of combined arms: a cocktail of armor, armored infantry, mechanized artillery and armored engineers, all supported by tactical air attack.

In general, Axis and Allied armies mirrored basic principles, but the Germans were considered better led. Maneuver was enthusiastically attempted and reached competence at corps levels by both sides, although the Germans (the Rommel effect) were the more creative. The North African experience, although important preparation for staffs and soldiers, proved to be a doctrinal detriment to formations training in Europe. British battle schools and war colleges continued to stress desert tactics: "the defensive box," "brigade fortress," and the "pivot" were taught to Allied armored divisions preparing for Normandy, all of which which turned out to be a waste of time. The essence of maneuver warfare was overshadowed by Montgomery's "set piece battle" and interest in Waterlooesque defensive victories.

Rommel had taught most of his lessons to the British desert army before Montgomery arrived. Success at El Alamein and Médenine deflected criticism of Montgomery's handling of armor in the pursuit. Montgomery, a limited commander, became a doctrinal *dictum imperatur* for the British and Canadian armies. This egotistical figure would enjoy an unrealistically strong influence on Allied strategic operations.

Main Battle Tanks

The tactical impact of the Tiger tank was misinterpreted and incompetently reported after incomplete tests in Tunisia. The need for a new main battle tank was forgotten in the delirium of final victory in Tunisia and Sicily. The Allies, convinced that the Sherman would do the job nicely, were not prepared to introduce an effective gun tank (the Firefly) until the summer of 1944. This eventually led to the Allied tank scandal.

Allied development of heavy tanks was lax. Lessons from the Eastern Front and North Africa had little effect. Parochial infighting, interdepartmental competition, and bureaucracy delayed the appearance of a suitable heavy tank until 1945. Chauvinism, the "not invented here" syndrome prevented the U.S. Army from mounting the British 17-pounder gun on U.S. Shermans. The much anticipated U.S. 76mm gun quickly proved a disappointment, and the Firefly remained the only effective tank killer in Normandy. Shaken awake by the reality of the battlefield, Bradley finally requested Fireflies—but there were none to be had. Allied tanks were outgunned, outarmored, and outmaneuvered by German tanks.

The tank destroyer doctrine imposed by General McNair quickly proved flawed and served to further muddy U.S. war-fighting dogma. As late as 1944 infantry generals debated which was superior, towed or self-propelled antitank guns. The proposed solution, the M10 tank destroyer mounting a 90mm gun, was not effective against Panthers or Tigers and was so inadequately armored that both Pzkw IVs and mortars could stop them. The Allies eventually survived two serious tank scandals. Normandy was kept quiet because there were few U.S.-German tank versus tank contests, and eventually the Allies were successful. The Ardennes operations spotlighted Allied inadequacy when Tiger IIs ripped through U.S. units, but again Patton's dramatic victory removed rancor from the headlines.[17]

Lessons from the ETO: Allied Doctrinal Separatism

The initial tactics during a breakthrough operation are designed to accomplish one purpose: secure operational maneuver room for armor in the enemy rear areas.
      —Lt. Col. George B. Pickett Jr., 11th Armored Division

Based on a comparison of Operations Totalize and Tractable with Cobra and the Arracourt operation, it could be argued that U.S. division commanders were superior to their Canadian peers. Maczek and Kitching might have performed well in Lorraine, but Canadian armor would never again have the opportunity to conduct maneuver operations. Sentenced by Montgomery to fight in the flooded *polders* of Holland, it was denied a second chance. In hindsight, a Canadian armored battle group should have been sent to North Africa in 1942, certainly in 1943, to acquire combat experience. The Canadian II Corps failure during Totalize, despite a successful breakthrough and an armored superiority in excess of four to one, indicated that the application of doctrine was a serious problem. It should be noted that the Germans maintained operational maneuver throughout the the Goodwood, Spring, Bluecoat, Totalize, and Cobra offensives until forced by Hitler to concentrate and attack inside the growing Falaise pocket.

The pursuit during Cobra was spectacular but overrated. It was, at last, operational maneuver, but the U.S. Third Army was not challenged by German operational reserves and it did not create the sort of panic in the German High Command that had doomed the French army in 1940. As key strategic prizes were ignored, U.S. armor picketed Brittany and drove by Falaise rather than slamming the door shut. It should be noted that it was a U.S. infantry division that met Maczek's Polish 1st Armored Division to finally close the gap at Chambois.

Properly handled, as demonstrated in Lorraine, Shermans could defeat Panthers. But it must be recognized that the tank battles fought by Canadian regiments from 11 June to 5 August 1944 were fought at both technological (Panther versus Sherman) and numerical disadvantage, even though there were a number of splendid squadron actions where determined, imaginative commanders prevailed.[18] Operationally, Totalize was inadequately supported by its own army group and failed to employ mass against an armored foe ready to be destroyed.

Thanks to Overlord's success, Montgomery began the Normandy campaign with the opportunity to seek a battle of annihilation. But before long, his (and Eisenhower's) inability to orchestrate such a battle of proportions as understood by the Stavka resulted in a front fixed in attrition warfare.[19] Montgomery courted the operational art with apathetic methods: seeking operational maneuver via operational exhaustion.

A comparison of the Soviet strategic offensive with Montgomery's corps battles in Normandy illustrates the Allied requirement for a pragmatic breakout philosophy. Despite his empirical guise, Montgomery did not pool his strategic resources. He perpetuated doctrinal separatism—a democratic procession of regional initiatives with each commander inventing his own doctrinal solutions, which were then tested by U.S., British, and Canadian offensives. Although he ruled with an iron fist and meddled in the most trivial affairs, once the armored pursuit began Montgomery left the Americans operationally alone and permitted incredible freedom of action late in the campaign.[20] In like manner, save for a string of contradiction instructions, he also ignored the Canadians: "In the final stages Montgomery had British divisions to spare, but Simonds was not reinforced."[21]

Despite his black beret, Montgomery did not really understand what to do with tanks. His first major failure, Goodwood, forced him to declare a strategy based on attritional breakout through the bocage. Montgomery's inability to understand the use of armor resulted in wasted time: "Monty's trouble was that he never rose to Army Group Commander level. He was a corps commander or an army commander."[22] The Third Army staff agreed: "Actually from the time of breakthrough we called the shots and dragged the British along with us."[23] Montgomery's ex post facto insistence that he was following a master plan does not stand up to critical analysis.

When Bradley's conservatism during Cobra prevented a complete strategic victory,[24] Eisenhower should have taken complete operational command—ideally as soon as the Cobra breakout. He could not have possibly done worse than Montgomery, who spent much of his time racing Bradley and criticizing his chief: "As a commander in charge of the land operations, Eisenhower is quite useless. There must be no misconception on this matter; he is completely and utterly useless."[25] Eisenhower put up with too much from Montgomery. He waived taking personal action even after it became apparent that Montgomery was prepared to invent excuses to justify failure: "Monty's talk of his original plan to hinge on Caen is absolutely balls. When he was checked in his original intent of taking Caen he had the idea of doing the other op. I believe the second shows greater insight. I don't see why he doesn't tell the truth."[26] Attempts to work with his British prima donna only increased Eisenhower's frustration: "Steady Monty, you can't talk to me that way, I'm your boss."[27] Perhaps Marshall was right when he stated that a democracy could not fight a Seven Years' War.

As an armored maneuverist, Montgomery was to prove no different from his disdained American lieutenant, Omar Bradley. Both were attritionists. Unfortunately they emulated Grant's operational style, not his generalship as commander in chief:

> The strategy of annihilation became characteristically the American way in war. . . . Grant proposed a strategy of annihilation based on the principle of concentration and mass, hitting the main Confederate armies with the concentrated thrust of massive Federal forces until the Confederate armies were smashed into impotence.[28]

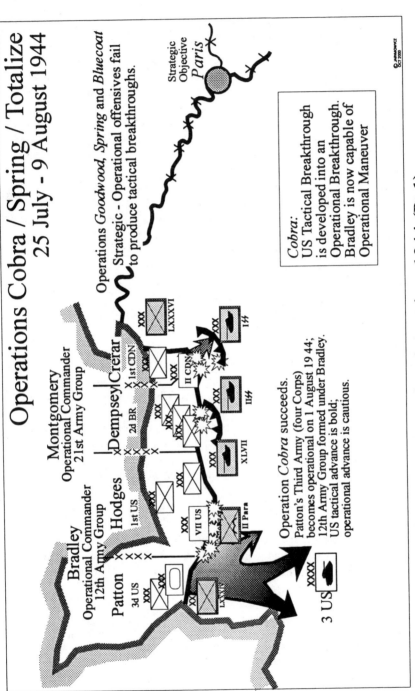

Operations Cobra / Spring / Totalize
25 July - 9 August 1944

Operations *Goodwood*, *Spring* and *Bluecoat*
Strategic - Operational offensives fail
to produce tactical breakthroughs.

Montgomery
Operational Commander
21st Army Group

Dempsey Crerar

Bradley
Operational Commander
12th Army Group

Patton   Hodges

Strategic
Objective
Paris

Cobra:
US Tactical Breakthrough
is developed into an
Operational Breakthrough.
Bradley is now capable of
Operational Maneuver

Operation *Cobra* succeeds.
Patton's Third Army (four Corps)
becomes operational on 1 August 1944;
12th Army Group formed under Bradley.
US tactical advance is bold;
operational advance is cautious.

The Allied Operational Art circa 1944 (Pt 1)

Cultural Doctrine

Warfare is an art in which clarity of appreciation and boldness of decision constitute essential elements. An art which could find success only in mobile operations.
—Field Marshal Erich von Manstein[29]

The evolution of armored doctrine more reflected cultural traits rather than tactical science. Blitzkrieg may have had its roots in the Great War's tactics but it was disciplined risk-taking audacity and a predilection for auftragstaktik that ensured success. The Russians' psyche more than technical expertise allowed them to excel in the operational art. Individual penchants could not overcome national character and embedded temperament. Armor enjoyed unrivaled operational dominance from 1939 to 1945. Initially, the French and British struggled within their doctrine as did the Americans, who had to overcome the McNair clique's tank destroyer theories and a conservative hierarchy. U.S. armor succeeded despite direction from Bradley, Montgomery, and Eisenhower.

At mid-1944 the Germans were not superior to the Allies operationally nor necessarily better led at the tactical level. The Germans did have certain advantages of combat experience, fighting in defense, and superior tanks, but the decisive factor lay in the Wehrmacht's doctrine. German armored doctrine was no different from German infantry doctrine, which consisted of a logical, systematic approach based on disciplined initiative. "The German method is really rooted in the German character, which—contrary to all the nonsense talked about 'blind obedience'—has a strong streak of individuality and—possibly as part of its Germanic heritage—finds a certain pleasure in taking risks."[30] Audacious techniques were possible only in an army that was instinctively comfortable with both tactics based on individual initiative and those based on orders. The cultural difference between the Germans and the Allies may have been more of a factor than a dogmatic conversion to technical war-fighting directives or better tanks.

Normandy has been misinterpreted, and there are many myths that still persist. The tactical issue was gunnery and armor. All the Allied armored offensives in the Caen sector were defeated by long-range tank fire. The Sherman's inferiority soon led to the "infantry must lead," solution and some have chided Allied armor commanders for holding back out of respect for (one might almost say fright) German main battle tanks:[31] "Without question, the tank arm remained the weakest link in the Anglo-Canadian order of battle."[32] However, a close study of the great armored battles (Goodwood, Totalize, Tractable, Cobra, and Arracourt) shows the very opposite. When ordered to attack, Allied armored divisions led throughout and regularly demonstrated aggressiveness to the point of recklessness.

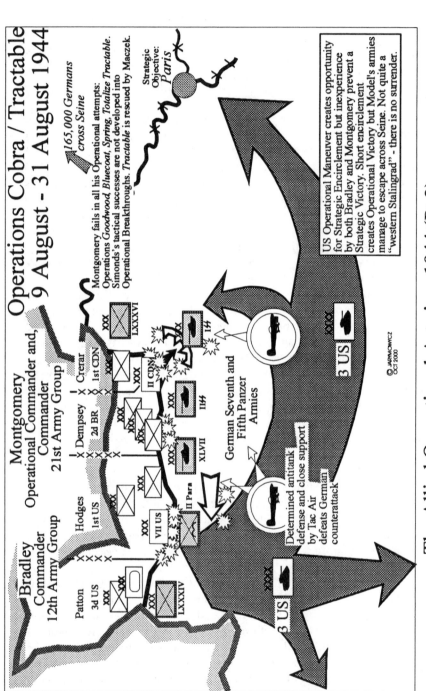

Operations Cobra / Tractable
9 August - 31 August 1944

Bradley
Commander
12th Army Group

Montgomery
Operational Commander and,
Commander
21st Army Group

Patton   Hodges   Dempsey   Crerar
3d US   1st US   2d BR   1st CDN

VII US

II Para   II CDN   LXXXVI

German Seventh and
Fifth Panzer Armies

LXXXIV

XLVII

Determined antitank
defense and close support
by Tac Air defeats German
counterattack

Montgomery fails in all his Operational attempts:
Operations *Goodwood Bluecoat, Spring, Totalize Tractable.*
Simonds's tactical successes are not developed into
Operational Breakthroughs. *Tractable* is rescued by Maczek.

165,000 Germans
cross Seine

Strategic
Objective:
Paris

US Operational Maneuver creates opportunity
for Strategic Encirclement but inexperience
by both Bradley and Montgomery prevent a
Strategic Victory. Short encirclement
creates Operational Victory but Model's armies
manage to escape across Seine. Not quite a
"western Stalingrad" - there is no surrender.

3 US

3 US

© JARMOWICZ
OCT 2000

The Allied Operational Art circa 1944 (Pt 2)

The fact that Simonds and Kitching had not exercised their commands before Normandy is disquieting and creates serious questions about planning at Canadian Army HQ. However, training by itself would not have guaranteed success. U.S. armored divisions were not always led by cavalry officers, but often by soldiers who had become cavalrymen in temperament and style.[33] The distinction between the two, carried over from the 1930s, became nebulous in battle, though some postwar analysis did try to clarify the issue:

> The modern version of cavalry—miscalled "Armor"—is trained and equipped to fight mounted while equally capable of fighting dismounted when demanded by the situation and switching rapidly from one to another. Tanks, a form of armor, are essential to both, but the unwary student must not be confused into thinking that "tanks" and "armor" are synonymous.[34]

Many of the most successful North American armored officers came from varied backgrounds—Wood was a gunner, Clarke an engineer, and Maj. Gen. B. M. Hoffmeister, perhaps Canada's best tank commander, who commanded the Canadian 5th Armored Division in Italy, was an infantry officer.[35] Patton was both a tanker and a cavalry officer. His competence in leading armor rested more on his ability to function within the art of maneuver than application of scientific principles. Perhaps the final word on the cavalry-armor debate was written by Robert Grow, a cavalier and a successful tank division commander: "Cavalry is not simply an arm—it is a state of mind."[36]

Notes

1. Grow, HIS 314.7, Special Studies "Mounted Attack," 18 November 1952. Grow Papers, MHI.
2. Maj. Roy E. Appleton, Cavalry. Written comments regarding Grow's Special Study: "Broad Front vs. Narrow Front—Lorraine Campaign," HIS 314.7. Grow Papers, MHI.
3. Grow Papers, MHI.
4. BCC Papers, "The Liberation of Orleans," MHI.
5. "Lessons Drawn from a Concentration of the Provisional Tank Brigade." Presented to Officers of the 2nd Armored Division, 7 October 1940. Gillem Papers, MHI.
6. "The second phase of Louisiana was utilized to test the organization and operations of a Mech Force . . . given 48 hours to organize a provisional Mech Force, move 75 miles into an offensive action." "Lessons Drawn." Gillem Papers, MHI.
7. "Lessons Drawn," Gillem Papers, MHI.
8. See R. P. Hunnicutt, *Sherman—A History of the American Medium Tank*

(Belmont, Calif.: Taurus, 1978); Charles M. Bailey, *Faint Praise: American Tanks and Tank Destroyers During World War II* (Hamden: Archon, 1983); Peter Chamberlain and Chris Ellis, *British and American Tanks of World War II* (New York: Arco, 1969).

9. Gen. William D. Crittenberger Papers, MHI.

10. Speech to Royal United Service Institution, November 1945. Quoted in *Cavalry Journal* (January 1946).

11. The limits of armor in urban-area operations is relative: "Don't tell me that I shouldn't have used armor in a city. I knew that but in war you use what you have and not what you would like to have." Haislip Papers, p. 12.

12. Self-propelled artillery (Wespe, Hummel) was gradually introduced in 1943 but seldom reached battalion strength.

13. Chaffee was suspicious of "new" infantry terminology: "I do not like the words 'Combat Team' applied to armored for in the Army at large, it refers primarily to the infantry regiment and its associated battalion of artillery in the Triangular Division." Lecture given by Adna R. Chaffee to the Officers of the Armored Force at Fort Knox, 13 September 1940. WDC Papers. Nevertheless, terms like "combat team" and "frag orders" began to be used with regularity in the Armored Force as early as 1940 and 1941.

14. "Proper Missions Armored Division," U.S. Army, ETO General Board (June–November 1945). Study No. 48. File R 320.2/3. MHI.

15. Martin van Creveld, *Fighting Power and US Army Performance, 1939– 1945* (Westport, Conn.: Greenwood, 1982).

16. "The influence of *Auftragstaktik* was by no means always good, but it undeniably encouraged initiative, and its survival (although downgraded by the heavy losses among commanders) gave German officers and NCOs an almost unique facility to meet unexpected emergencies. Scratch forces were thrown together at a moment's notice, which permitted the Germans to deliver counterattacks or fight their way to safety when other troops might have broken or surrendered." Christopher Duffy, *Red Storm on the Reich* (New York: Da Capo Press, 1993), p. 55.

17. A capsule summary of the tank scandal's demise is Berryman's cartoon in the Washington, D.C. *Evening Star,* 25 March 1945. Berryman (misquoting Forrest) has Patton as the key defense witness in a "tank trial." The accused, U.S. tank policy, is declared innocent on Patton's testimony: "Your honor, the defendant got there fustust with th' mostest . . . the indictment should be dismissed."

18. An inspiring example of properly handled Shermans defeating Panthers in tank country is Gen. S. V. Radley Walter's (then a major commanding a Sherman sqn in 27th CAR) defense of St. André against three panzer battle groups in the last days of Operation Atlantic. Individual squadron actions during Totalize and Tractable merit study. See the regimental histories of regiments in the Canadian 2d Armoured Brigade: Sherbrooke Fusilier Regiment, Fort Garry Horse Regiment, and the 1st Hussars; Canadian 4th Armoured Brigade: Canadian Grenadier Guards, Governor General's Horse Guards, and British Columbia Regiment. Superior subunit accounts and excellent after-action reports are in the RG 24 WD of the Canadian 27th Armoured Regiment (Sherbrooke Fusiliers).

19. Delbrück referred to *stellungs und ermattungskrieg,* a war of operational attrition. An annihilating Cannae type of battle, *niederwerfungsstrategie* ("A strategy which intends to force the decision, must do it where the first successful blow is struck") eluded all the Allied forces save Stalin's armies. See Delbrück, p. 276.

20. "He tended to leave Bradley alone." Lt. Gen. Walter Bedell Smith, chief of staff, SHAEF. Interview, Pogue Papers, 8 May 1947, MHI.

21. Wilmot, p. 424.

22. Bedell Smith, 8 May 1947, MHI.

23. Hansen Diary, pp. 22-a, 5–6, MHI.

24. Yet Bradley appeared quite aware of the historical significance of Cobra: "[such] an opportunity comes to a commander not more than once in a century. We're about to destroy an entire hostile army." Alister Horne, "In Defence of Montgomery," *Quarterly Journal of Military History* 8, 1 (Autumn 1995): 60.

25. Montgomery to Viscount Alanbrooke, 1944. Eisenhower's later evaluation of Montgomery was terse: "Just a little man—he's just as little inside as he is outside." Glenn LaFantasie, "Monty and Ike Take Gettysburg," *Quarterly Journal of Military History* 8, 1 (Autumn 1995): 68, 73.

26. Bedell Smith, Pogue Papers, 12 February 1947, MHI.

27. Wilmot, p. 489. Montgomery was not without defenders. Winston Churchill stood on his behalf: "I know why you all hate him. You are jealous: he is better than you are." Alister Horne, *Journal of Military History,* 66.

28. Weigley, pp. xiv, 142.

29. Manstein, pp. 380–383.

30. Ibid., p. 383.

31. Modeled after Lieutenant General Crocker's ruminations on Maj. Gen. R. F. H. Keller. RG 24 NAC DHist 514 Crerar documents: correspondence between Crocker and Crerar, 5 July 1944.

32. English, p. 312.

33. It is interesting to note that even Patton added fuel to Hawkins's pro-cavalry fires: "If I'd had a division, or even a brigade, of horse Cavalry in Tunisia and Sicily . . . the bag of Germans would have been a great deal larger. Very few would have escaped, because Cavalry can conduct a pursuit much faster than tanks under certain conditions." Col. R. S. Allen, *Lucky Forward. The History of Patton's Third US Army* (New York: Vanguard, 1947), p. 169. There is no record of Patton wanting cavalry in Normandy, although he did say, oddly enough, "There is no question that horsed Cavalry would have been of tremendous value in the Saar Campaign."

34. Grow memorandum to Gen. Orlando Ward, 10 November 1950. Grow Papers, MHI.

35. The commanders of "elite" tank divisions were from varied backgrounds: Brig. Gen. H. W. Baird (1941–1942) was cavalry; Lt. Gen. E. L. M. Burns and Maj. Gen. Hogue and Clarke were engineers; Maj. Gen. G. Kitching was a infantry; Maj. Gen. J. Wood was artillery, as was his successor, Maj. Gen. H. J. Gaffey.

36. Grow, "Mounted Attack," MHI.

Allied Tanks of World War I

Data	France Renault	USA M-1917	Britain Mark V	Britain Mark V Star	USA Mark VIII	France Schneider	France St. Chamond
Armament	1x37mm or 1x8mm[a]	1x37mm or 1x.30 cal[a]	2x6pdr 4x8mm	2x6pdr 5x8mm	2x6pdr 5x.30 cal	1x75mm 2xHMG	1x75mm 4xHMG
Speed	6 mph	5.5 mph	4.6 mph	4 mph	6.5 mph	5 mph	5 mph
Range	24 miles	30 miles	25 miles	40 miles	50 miles	25 miles	37 miles
Crew	2	2	8	8	11	6	9
Length	16'5"	16'5"	26'5"	32'5"	34'2.5"	19'8"	28'10"
Width	5'8"	5'10.5"	13'6"	13'6"	12'5"	6'7"	8'9"
Height	7'6.5"	7'7"	8'8"	8'8"	10'2.5"	7'10"	7'8"
Plate	0.3-0.6"	0.25-0.6"	0.2-0.47"	0.24-0.59"	0.236-0.63"	0.2-0.95"[b]	0.2-0.67"
Weight	7.4 tons	7.25 tons	31.9 tons	37 tons	43.5 tons	14.9 tons	25.3 tons
Wall	24"	36"	59"	58"	54"	31"	15"
Obst	6.5'	7'	10'	14'	16'	5'10"	8'

a. Renault / M-1917 were the same tank; gun or heavy machine gun was mounted in a fully traversing turret.

b. Schneider had an early version of spaced armor—double plates, 1.5" space on front, sides, and top. The British 6-pounder was equivalent to 57mm; all 8mm weapons were HMG (heavy machine guns).

Plate: Armored Plate thickness; Obst.: width of trench tank capable of crossing; Wall: Height of vertical wall tank can climb

Allied Armored Formations, ETO

Canada

4th Armoured Division	(1942)	Normandy—Cobra/ Tractable; Germany
5th Armoured Division	(1941)	Italy, Holland, Germany

United Kingdom

1st Mobile Division	(1937)	
1st Armoured Division	(1938/1939)	
Mobile Division Egypt	(1938—became 7th Armd Division)	
2d Armoured Division	(1939/1940)	
6th Armoured Division	(September 1940)	
7th Armoured Division	(September 1940)	Normandy—Cobra/ Bluecoat; Germany
8th Armoured Division	(November 1940)	
9th Armoured Division	(December 1940)	
10th Armoured Division	(August 1941—from 1st Cavalry Division)	
11th Armoured Division	(March 1941)	Normandy—Cobra/ Bluecoat; Germany
Guards Armoured Division	(June 1941—from Guards Brigade)	Normandy—Cobra/ Bluecoat; Germany
42nd Armoured Division	(August 1941—from infantry)	
79th Armoured Division	(September 1942)	Normandy; Germany

United States

1st Armored Division	(1940) "Old Ironsides"	North Africa; Italy
2d Armored Division	(1940) "Hell on Wheels"	North Africa; Normandy—Cobra; Germany
3d Armored Division	(1941) "Spearhead"	Normandy—Cobra; Germany
4th Armored Division	(1941) "Breakthrough"	Normandy—Cobra; Germany
5th Armored Division	(1941) "V for Victory"	Normandy—Cobra; Germany
6th Armored Division	(1942) "Super Sixth"	Normandy—Cobra; Germany
7th Armored Division	(1942) "Lucky Seventh"	France/Germany
8th Armored Division	(1942) "Iron Snake"	France/Germany
9th Armored Division	(1942) "Phantom"	France/Germany
10th Armored Division	(1942) "Tiger"	France/Germany
11th Armored Division	(1942) "Thunderbolt"	France/Germany
12th Armored Division	(1942) "Hellcat"	Germany
13th Armored Division	(1942) "Black Cat"	Germany
14th Armored Division	(1942)	Germany
16th Armored Division	(1943)	Germany
20th Armored Division	(1943)	Germany

Other Allied Armored Formations

| 1st Polish Armored Division | (1942/1943) Normandy—Cobra/Tractable; Germany |
| 2d French Armored Division | (1942/1943) Normandy—Cobra; Germany |

APPENDIX C

The M4 Sherman Tank

M4: Wright-Continental R-975 Whirlwind radial aircraft engine; British designation Sherman I: 75mm gun

M4A1: Wright-Continental (in some Canadian armored regiments); British designation Sherman II: 75mm, last series, 76mm gun

M4A2: Diesel-powered General Motors Twin 6-71 (found in some Canadian units, particularly Canadian 2d Armoured Brigade; mostly in U.S. Marine Corps and Red Army formations); Sherman III: 75mm; Sherman IIIA: 76mm gun

M4A3: Ford GAA (mostly in U.S. Army tank battalions); Sherman IV all: 75mm gun

M4A4: Chrysler A-57 multibank: four automobile engines mated together, lengthened rear hull (manufactured almost exclusively for British/Canadian armored units); Sherman V: 75mm gun

M4A5: Designation for Canadian Ram tank: only in Canadian units; one Ram I tested by U.S. Army

Firefly: 17-pounder gun; (British/Canadian armored units only). Nearly all models of Shermans were converted to Firefly but most numerous was Sherman V. When fitted with the 17-pounder the suffix C was added, i.e. Sherman IC, IIC, IIIC, IVC, and Sherman VC (most numerous).

APPENDIX D

Armored Corps Casualties

Canadian Armoured Corps (CAR) Casualties

May 1940–April 1945

Unit	Regiment	KIA	Total
10th Armoured Regiment	*FGH*	86	402
12th Armoured Regiment	*Three Rivers*	67	382
6th Armoured Regiment	*1 H*	105	344
8th Reconnaissance	*14 CH*	50	308
27th Armoured Regiment	*SHER FUS*	66	287
14th Armoured Regiment	*CALG R*	44	273
28th Armoured Regiment	*BCR*	35	270
7th Reconnaissance	*17 DYRCH*	49	269
2d Armoured Regiment	*LDSH*	59	268
29th Reconnaissance	*S ALTA*	49	259
11th Armoured Regiment	*ONT R*	30	258
22d Armoured Regiment	*CGG*	57	250
3d Reconnaissance	*GGHG*	39	246
9th Armoured Regiment	*BCD*	48	245
1st Reconnaissance	*RCD*	24	230
21st Armoured Regiment	*GGFG*	58	204
5th Reconnaissance	*8 PLNBH*	27	179
18th Reconnaissance	*XII MAN D*	31	147
4th Reconnaissance/Infantry	Princess Louise's Dragoon Guards	127	802[a]

a. The high casualties attributed to the Princess Louise's Dragoon Guards, 4th Reconnaissance Regiment, occurred after the unit had been converted to infantry and sent into action before it had been sufficiently trained.

U.S. Armored Force Casualties

Unit	Total
1st Armored Division	6,596
2d Armored Division	5,740
3d Armored Division	9,189
4th Armored Division	5,907
5th Armored Division	3,152
6th Armored Division	4,655
7th Armored Division	4,899
8th Armored Division	2,039
9th Armored Division	2,973
10th Armored Division	3,883
11th Armored Division	2,912
12th Armored Division	3,141
13th Armored Division	1,165
14th Armored Division	2,515
16th Armored Division	23
20th Armored Division	293

Sample of Allied Tank Casualties by Theater

Theater of operations	Total Sample	Total Known Casualties	Gunfire		Nonenemy	
Western Europe						
United States—1944	2,579	2,065	1,051	50.9%	292	14.1%
United Kingdom—1944	1,103	1,048	621	59.2%	21	2.0%
Canada—1944	473	294	161	54.8%	66	22.4%
North Africa						
United States—1942	72	37	23	62.2%	12	32.4%
United States—1943	205	81	36	44.4%	14	17.3%
United Kingdom—1942	1,123	1,123	884	78.7%	1	0.1%
United Kingdom—1943	182	182	140	76.9%	0	
France—1943	39	39	30	76.9%	unknown	
Sicily						
United States—1943	58	21	10	47.6%	4	19.0%
United Kingdom—1943	31	31	23	74.2%	0	
Canada—1943	20	20	6	30.0%	4	20.0%
Italy						
United States—1943	55	44	18	40.9%	17	38.6%
United States—1944	471	407	180	44.2%	103	25.3%
United Kingdom—1943	128	109	60	55.0%	6	5.5%
United Kingdom—1944	652	521	309	59.3%	18	3.5%
Canada—1943	73	66	21	31.8%	22	33.3%
Canada—1944	631	488	146	29.9%	246	50.4%

Source: ORO-T-117 Tables I, II: "Sampling of Allied Tank Casualties to All Causes."

Tiger Versus Allied Armor: Penetration Tables

Tiger versus Sherman A2 (75mm M3 Gun) and Sherman A4 (76mm M1A1 Gun)[a]

		Tiger I vs. Sherman A2	Sherman A2 vs. Tiger I	Tiger I vs. Sherman A4	Sherman A4 vs. Tiger I
Front:	Turret	1,800 meters	0 meters	1,800 meters	700 meters
	Mantle	200 meters	0 meters	200 meters	100 meters
	DFP	0 meters	0 meters	0 meters	600 meters
	Nose	2,100 meters	0 meters	2,100 meters	400 meters
Side:	Turret	3,500 meters+	100 meters	3,500 meters+	1,800 meters
	Super	3,500 meters+	100 meters	3,500 meters+	1,800 meters
	Hull	3,500 meters+	900 meters	3,500 meters+	3,200 meters
Rear:	Turret	3,500 meters+	100 meters	3,500 meters+	1,800 meters
	Hull	3,500 meters+	0 meters	3,500 meters+	1,700 meters[b]

Tiger versus Cromwell / Churchill (75mm M3 Gun)

		Tiger I vs. Cromwell	Cromwell vs. Tiger I	Tiger I vs. Churchill	Churchill vs. Tiger I
Front:	Turret	2,000 meters	0 meters	1,700 meters	0 meters
	Mantle	2,700 meters	0 meters	1,400 meters	0 meters
	DFP	3,500 meters	0 meters	1,300 meters	0 meters
	Nose	2,400 meters	0 meters	1,100 meters	0 meters
Side:	Turret	3,400 meters+	100 meters	1,700 meters+	100 meters
	Super	3,500 meters+	100 meters	3,000 meters+	100 meters
	Hull	3,500 meters+	900 meters	3,000 meters+	900 meters
Rear:	Turret	3,500 meters+	100 meters	2,600 meters+	100 meters
	Hull	3,500 meters+	0 meters	3,500 meters+	0 meters

a. All figures are meters.

b. Tom Jentz and Hilary Doyle, *Tiger 1 Heavy Tank, 1942–1945* (London: Osprey, 1993), p. 19.

APPENDIX G

Analysis of Allied Tank Casualties in Normandy, 6 June–10 July

Analysis of Sherman Casualties: 6 June–10 July[a]

(I) Total Tank Casualties Analyzed		Proportion of Total Tanks
(a) Number penetrated by German armor-piercing shot	40	89%
(b) Number mined	4	9%
(c) Number damaged, unidentified but "brewed up"	1	2%
(II) Total "Brewed Up":	37	82%
(a) Number penetrated by shot and "brewed up"	33	73%
(b) Number mined and "brewed up"	3	7%
(c) Number "brewed up" by unknown causes	1	2%

Note: In several cases it is difficult to distinguish between penetrations of 75mm and 88mm, particularly after the tank had "brewed up." Too much reliance must not be placed on the proportion of such penetrations, though the proportion given agrees well with the estimated occurrences of such guns given by Canadian 2d Army, Main HQ. Estimates by fighting soldiers were found to be unreliable since many reported they had been knocked out by 88mm, when in fact it had been 75mm shot, while the reverse mistake has not yet been discovered.

(III) Tanks Penetrated by German Armor-Piercing Shot

Proportion of
Total Hits

		Proportion of Total Hits	
(a)	Total Hits Recorded	65	
(i)	75 mm	53	82%
(ii)	88 mm	12	18%
(b)	Number of Penetrations	62	95%
(i)	75 mm	50	77%
(ii)	88 mm	12	18%
(c)	Number of Failures to Penetrate	3	5%
(i)	75 mm	3	5%
(ii)	88 mm	—	0%

Distribution of Hits

	Front	Side	Rear
Hull	7	24	6
Turret	12	12	4
Total	19	36	10

Distribution of Number of Hits Required to Knock out Each Tank

Number of Hits	1x hit	2x hits	3x hits	4	5	6	7	8x hits
Tanks Knocked Out	25	11	2	1	-	-	-	1

Distribution of Hits

Angle of Penetration	0–9	9–30	30–90 (degrees)
Hull	32	19	8
Turret	19	16	3

Further Study of Tanks Hit but not Penetrated and Remained in Action

Total Tanks Inspected	124
Hits Failing to Penetrate	83

a. RGd 24: Report No. 12: Canadian 2d Army: Analysis of 75mm Sherman Tank Casualties Between 6th June and 10th July.

Selected Bibliography

Primary Sources Unpublished

Government Records, Personal Papers, and Manuscript Collections

Abteilung MA (Militärarchiv) des Bundesarchivs, Freiburg.

Bradley papers, Gen. Omar N.: MHI.

Chaffee papers, Gen. A. R.: The Patton Museum Library.

Crerar papers, NAC.

Crittenberger papers, Maj. Gen. Willis D.: MHI.

Grow papers, Gen. Robert W. Grow.: Special Studies, World War II Office of Chief of Military History (OCMH) Collection, MHI.

Haislip papers, Gen. Wade H.: MHI.

Hansen papers, Col. Chester B.: Hansen Diary, MHI.

Harmon papers, Col. Ernest Nason: MHI.

Heiberg papers, Col. Harrison H. D.: Patton Museum Library.

Jarrett papers, Col. George B.: MHI.

Military Documents, Directorate of History, National Defence Headquarters (NDHQ), Ottawa.

Military Documents, U.S. Army Military History Institute (MHI), Carlisle Barracks.

Military Documents, U.S. Armored Corps Museum Library, Fort Knox.

Newton papers, Brig. Gen. Henry C.

Pogue Manuscripts, Dr. Forrest C.: Patton Museum Library.

Record Group 24, National Defence 1870–1981, National Archives of Canada (NAC), Ottawa.

Stearns papers, Capt. Marshal: Correspondence between Prof. Reginald Roy and Marshal Sterns.

Ward papers, Gen. Orlando: MHI.

White papers, Maj. Gen. Isaac: MHI.

Primary Sources Published

Blumenson, Martin. *Breakout and Pursuit, United States Army in World War II, The European Theater of Operations,* Washington: Office of the Chief of Military History, Dept. of the Army, 1961).

Ellis, Maj. L. F. Official History of the British Army *Victory in the West, Vol. I: The Battle of Normandy.* London: HMSO, 1962.

Office of the Chief of Military History, Washington, D.C.: Department of the Army, 1961.

Stacey, Col. C. P. *Official History of the Canadian Army in the Second World War, Volume III, The Victory Campaign: The Operations in North-West Europe, 1944-1945.* Ottawa: Queen's Printer, 1966.

————. *Official History of the Canadian Army in the Second World War, Volume I, Six Years of War: The Army in Canada, Britain and the Pacific.* Ottawa: Queen's Printer, 1966.

Manuals and Pamphlets

AGF Report. Employment of Four Tank Destroyer Battalions in the ETO. Officers' Advance Course, Comm. 24, Armored School, Fort Knox, 1950.

AGF Report. Hardison, David C. *Data on WWII Tank Engagements Involving the US Third and Fourth Armored Divisions.* ETO, 1947.

AGF Report. Hinds, Col. I. S., Comd CCB, 2d Armd: *Comparison of US Equipment with Similar German Equipment.* Exhibit No. 2, 20 March 1945.

AGF Report. McNair, Gen. Lesley J., *Notes for Special Critique for General Officers Only,* 11 September 1941.

AGF Report. A Report on United States vs. German Armor—Prepared for General of the Army Dwight D. Eisenhower, Supreme Commander Allied Expeditionary Force. Maj. Gen. I. D. White, CO 2d Armored Division, 1945.

AGF Report. Rockenbach S. D., *Report of Chief of the Tank Corps,* 13 October 1919. MHI.

AGF Report. White, Maj. Gen. I. D., 2d Armored Division. *A Report on United States vs. German Armor.* ETO, 1945.

AGF Study No. 1. U.S. Army 1946, *Origins of the Army Ground Forces,* General Headquarters, U.S. Army, 1940–1942.

AGF Study No. 11, 16. *Armor—After Action.* U.S. Army Historical Section-Army Ground Forces, 1948.

AGF Study No. 20-202 *German Tank Maintenance in World War II.* Deptartment of the Army. Washington, D.C., 1954.

AGF Study No. 29. Dunham, Emory A. *Tank Destroyer History.* Historical Section, Army Ground Forces, 1946.

AGF Study No. ORO-T-117 *German Estimates and Comments on Their Own Tank Casualties.* Annex 2 to Appendix E. Seventh Army Interrogation Center, ETO, 24 May 1945.

AGF Study No. 319.1. *After Action Report Sept/Oct 1944.* 4th Armored Division Papers.

AGF Study No. 798 BRL MR-798 *Data on WWII Tank Engagements Involving the US Third and Fourth Armored Divisions.* Ballistic Research Laboratories, Aberdeen Proving Ground, Md. 1 April 1947.

AGF Study. Coox, Alvin D. and L. Van Loan Naisawald. *Survey of Allied Tank Casualties in World War II.* Operations Research Office, Johns Hopkins University, 31 March 1951.

Armored Warfare in World War II Conference featuring F.W. von Mellenthin, Major General German Army. Battelle Columbus Laboratories, Tactical Technology Center, Columbus, Oh., 10 May 1979.

BDM Corporation. *Generals Balck and von Mellenthin on Tactics: Implications for NATO Military Doctrine.* 19 December 1980.

Barlow, Col. J. A. and Lt. Col. R. D. Neville *German Pz Kw VI Tank Examined 2/3 February.* War Diary. Weapons Technical Staff, Field Force, North Africa, February 1943.

Field Regulations USSR (FR Soviet): Provisional Field Regulations—Vremennyi polevoy ustav RKKA 1936 (PU-36), Moscow, 1937.

Final Report, Third Army Maneuvers, 5–25 May 1940, Vol. III, Anx. 21, Final Critiques. MHI.

FM 17-32 *Armored Force Field Manual* Aug. 1942.

FM 17-33 *The Tank Battalion.*

FM 17-36. *Employment of Tanks with Infantry.* U.S. Armor School. 7 February 1944.

FM 17-100 (Tentative) *Employment of the Armored Division* 29 Sept. 1943.

FM 17-100 *The Armored Division* 1944.

FM 100-5 *The Armored Division,* stated: Draft copy dated 24 January 1941.

FM 101-10. *The Corps.*

FR Soviet. Instrukstii po glubokomu boiu (*Instructions for Deep Battle*), 1935.

FR Soviet. Polevoy ustav 1944—1944 Field Regulations, 1944.

FR Soviet. 1944 Combat Regulations for Tank and Mechanized Forces: Reconnaissance.

G2 Periodic Report No. 229. Translated from *1 SS LAH Pz Div Int Bulletin.*

Gabel, Dr. Christopher R. *Seek, Strike, and Destroy: US Army Tank Destroyer Doctrine in World War II.* Leavenworth Papers, No. 12. Combat Studies Institute, USACGSC, Fort Leavenworth, 1985.

IX Tactical Air Force: *Mortain Operations.* August 1944, MHI.

Lessons from the Tunisian Campaign, War Department, Washington, D.C., 1943.

Military Training Pamphlet No. 2. *The Offensive.* War Office, June 1943.

Military Training Pamphlet No. 3. *The Defense.* War Office, June 1943.

Military Training Pamphlet No. 20-202. *German Tank Maintenance in World War II.* War Office, June 1954.

Military Training Pamphlet No. 20-233. *German Defense Tactics against Russian Break-Throughs.* War Office, October 1951.

Military Training Pamphlet No. 63. *The Cooperation of Tanks with Infantry Divisions.* War Office. May 1944.

NAC. *After Action Reports 44–45 6 Armd Div* Files. Box. George Hoffman Collection.

NAC Report. C1-279: *Operations of 6th Armd Div Trains During the Brittany Campaign.* 26 August 1944.

NDHQ Report. Bourne, Maj. R. P and Shackleton, Maj. N. A.: *Analysis of Firepower in Normandy Operations of 1944.* Ottawa.

Report of Observers ETO, 1944–1945 Vol. II (19 June–11 October 1944) U.S. Army Observer Board ETO.

Operational Research Unit Report No. 4 *Air Attacks on Enemy Tanks and Motor Transport in the Mortain Area,* August 1944.

Technical Intelligence Bulletin No. 8. *German Tanks Destroyed by XIX Corps. 15 Dec 44.* ETO, 20 February 1945.

United Kingdom Military Training Pamphlet (UK) No. 22 *Tactical Handling of Army Tank Battalions Part II. Battle Drill and Manoeuvre.* War Office, 1939.

UK No. 2. *The Offensive.* War Office, June 1943.

UK No. 3. *Handling of an Armoured Division.* War Office, 1941.
UK No. 12. *Doctrine for the Tactical Handling of the Division and the Armoured Division.* War Office, 1941.
UK No. 41. *The Tactical Handling of the Armoured Division and Its Components.* War Office, July 1943.
White, Jam. Gen. I. D. 2d Armored Division *US vs. German Equipment.* Brig./Gen. J. H. Collier, Comd CC A. Exhibit No. 1, 1945.
White, Maj. Gen. I. D. Exhibit No. 2; Col. I. S. Hinds, Comd CCB, 2d Armd: *Comparison of US Equipment with Similar German Equipment,* 20 March 1945.
Wright, Capt. H. B. and Capt. R. D. Harkness. *A Survey of Casualties Amongst Armoured Units in Northwest Europe.* Medical Research Team, British 21 Army Group (No. 2 ORS), January 1946.

Memoirs, Journals, and Accounts

Bradley, Omar N. *A Soldier's Story.* New York: Henry Holt, 1951.
Horrocks, Sir Brian. *Corps Commander.* New York: Charles Scribner's Sons, 1977.
Kitching, George. *Mud and Green Fields. The Memoires of Maj. Gen George Kitching.* St. Catherine's, Ont.: Vanwell, 1993.
Maczek, Gen. Stanislaw T. *Avec mes Blindés.* Paris: Presses de la Cité, 1967.
Martel, Lt. Gen. Sir Gifford le Q. *Our Armoured Forces.* London: Faber and Faber, 1945.
Mellenthin, Maj. Gen. F. W. von. *Panzer Battles: A Study of the Employment of Armor in the Second World War.* trans. H. Betzler, ed. L. C. F. Turner. Norman: University of Oklahoma Press, 1983.
Montgomery, Field Marshal The Viscount. *Memoires.* London: Collins, 1958.

Books and Monographs

Bailey, Charles M. *Faint Praise: American Tanks and Tank Destroyers During World War II.* Hamden: Archon, 1983.
Blumenson, Martin *The Battle of the Generals. The Untold Story of the Falaise Pocket.* New York: William Morrow and Company, 1993.
Copp, Terry *Brigade,* Stoney Creek, Ontario: Fortress Press, 1992.
Corum, James S. *The Roots of Blitzkreig—Hans von Seeckt and German Military Reform.* Kent: University of Kansas Press, 1992.
D'Este, Carlo. *Decision in Normandy.* New York: HarperCollins, 1983.
English, J. A. *The Canadian Army and the Normandy Campaign—A Study of the Failure of High Command.* New York: Praeger, 1991.
Frank Jr., W. C. and P. S. Gillette, *Soviet Military Doctrine from Lenin to Gorbachev 1915–1991.* Westport, Conn.: Greenwood Press, 1991.
Granatstein J. L. and Desmond Morton, *Bloody Victory.* Toronto: Lester & Orpen Dennys, 1984.
Hamilton, Nigel *Master of the Battlefield Monty's War Years 1942–44.* New York: McGraw-Hill, 1983.
Harris, Stephen J. *Canadian Brass: The Making of a Professional Army, 1860–1939.* Toronto: University of Toronto Press, 1988.

Larson, Robert H. *The British Army and the Theory of Armoured Warfare 1918–1940.* Newark: University of Delaware Press, 1984.

Meyer, Hubert. *Kriegsgeschichte der 12.SS-Panzerdivision "Hitlerjugend."* Osnabrück: Munin Verlag, 1987.

Radzievskii, A. I. *Tankovyi Udar.* Moscow: Voenizdat, 1977.

Ross, G. Macleod, with Maj. Gen. Sir Campbell Clarke. *The Business of Tanks 1933 to 1945.* Devon: Arthur H. Stockwell, 1976.

Roy, Reginald H. *Normandy 1944.* Toronto: Macmillan, 1984.

Scott, Harriet, Fast and W. F. Scott, eds. *The Soviet Art of War, Strategy and Tactics.* Boulder: Westview. 1982.

Smithers, A. J. *Rude Mechanicals—An Account of Tank Maturity During the Second World War.* London: Leo Cooper, 1987.

Weigley, Russell F. *Eisenhower's Lieutenants.* Bloomington: Indiana University Press, 1990.

Wilmot, Chester. *Struggle for Europe.* London: Collins, 1952.

Winton, H. W. *To Change an Army—General Sir John Burnett-Stuart and British Armoured Doctrine, 1927–1938.* Lawrence: University Press of Kansas, 1988.

Index

Abrams, Gen. Creighton W., 243; crosses Moselle, 228; grouping 22 Sept, 242; Mannecourt Hill, 240
Air Force: U.S. IX, 154; RAF Typhoons at Totalize, 177; U.S. VIII, 171
Alexandria Recommendations, 68–69
Allen, Maj. Gen. R.H., orders T1 light tank, 27
Allied armored formations, ETO, 333; Allied tanks World War I, 331
Amiens tank attack, 14
Andrews, Maj. Gen. F.M.: recommends Armor as separate arm, 31; supports Chaffee, 71
"apostles of mobility," armor *philosophes*, 313–314
Argentan, 155
armor: Allied outclassed, 271; Allied reduced production 1944, 269; Allied tank crew casualties, 270; Allied tank losses by cause, 270, 272; as a strategic arm, 316
army group: 21st Army Group gathers laurels after Cobra, 221; ignores eastern flank, 186
Arracourt, 229, 234, 237
artillery: 2 AGRA (Army Group Royal Artillery), 116, 171; 9 AGRA, 171; set piece attack, 14
attrition warfare vs. maneuver, 10, 11
auftragstaktik, 57, 120; adoption before 1914, 57; Allied failure during Cobra pursuit, 155; comparison Western to Soviet doctrine, 285; cultural rather than technical, 217; definition by Manstein, 84; difficulty in British/Canadian system, 170; in combat commands, 319; German concept vs. Soviet operational art, 293; mobility doctrine, tactical principles, 50, 57–59, 206; suited to German character, 325; Task Force Hunter at Arracourt, 237

Balck, Gen. Pz. Tps. Hermann, 240, 241
Battle of France 1940: legitimizes mechanization, 83
Bayerlein, Lt. Gen. Fritz, Panzer Lehr, 138
Bechtolsheim, Capt, visit to U.S., 57
Bezange-la-Petite, 235
Blanchard, Maj. Gen. Wendell, 234
Blaskowitz, Col. Gen. Johannes, 225, 229; relieved by Hitler, 241
Bocage: Bradley comment, 113; obstacles to maneuver, 112
Bombers, big-time fratricide, 186; effects during Operation Goodwood, 115; strategic arm as heavy artillery, 113, 114, 149, 185, 187, 286
Booth, Brig. E.L.: 4th Armored brigade at Totalize, 173
Bradley, Gen. Omar N., 111, 114, 141, 148–149, 163; anger toward Dempsey, 161, avoids *auftragstaktik* "mission command," 155; conservatism prevents complete victory, 323; conservative after Avranches,

350

About the Book

An operational critique of the art of war as practiced by U.S. and Canadian tank commanders in France in 1944, *Tank Tactics* also traces the evolution of North American armored doctrine.

Jarymowycz draws on after-action reports, extensive battlefield reconnaissance (involving both Allied and German veterans), and recently discovered battle performance reviews, as well as Allied and German interrogation reports, war diaries, and technical evaluations, to compare and evaluate combat success and failure. He provides detailed tactical diagrams and analyses of tank versus tank engagements—and illustrates the frustrations of commanders attempting maneuver warfare under the exasperating caution of Bradley and the questionable direction of Montgomery.

This penetrating analysis features a review of tank battles in Lorraine, where the U.S. Third Army commanders demonstrated mastery of mission command doctrine. Jarymowycz concludes by comparing U.S. and Soviet approaches to operational maneuver, describing creative tactical mixes found in combat commands well before battle groups became common in NATO parlance.

Lt. Col. Roman Johann Jarymowycz is dean of the Canadian Militia Staff College, Kingston, Ontario.

Stackpole Military History Series

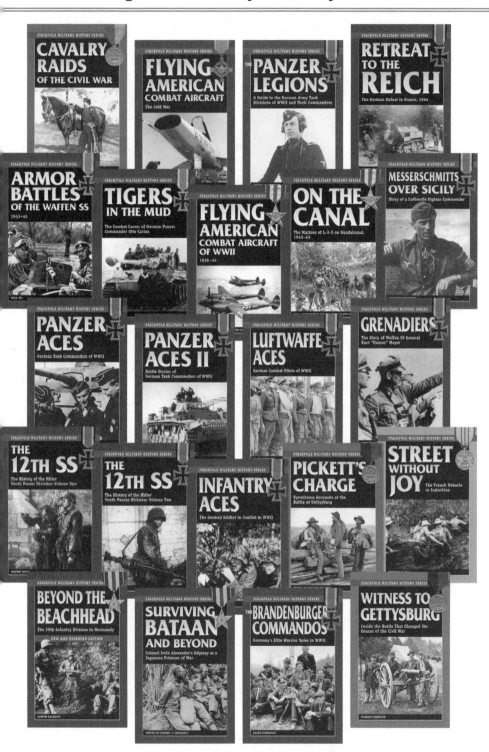

Real battles. Real soldiers. Real stories.

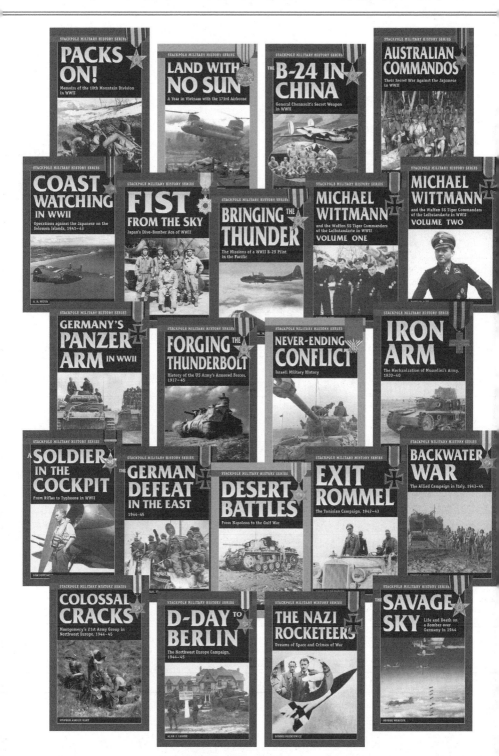

Stackpole Military History Series

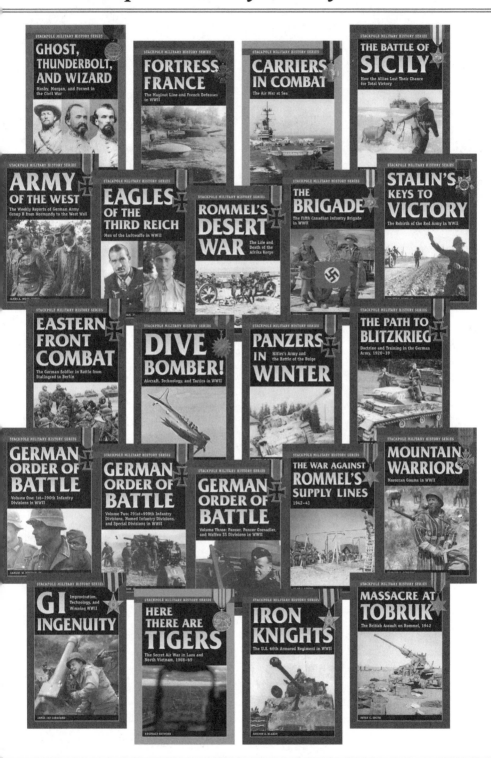

Real battles. Real soldiers. Real stories.

Stackpole Military History Series

STACKPOLE MILITARY HISTORY SERIES

PANZERS IN NORMANDY
General Hans Eberbach and the German Defense of France, 1944
SAMUEL W. MITCHAM, JR.

STACKPOLE MILITARY HISTORY SERIES

TRIUMPHANT FOX
Erwin Rommel and the Rise of the Afrika Korps

STACKPOLE MILITARY HISTORY SERIES

TANK TACTICS
From Normandy to Lorraine

STACKPOLE MILITARY HISTORY SERIES

ROMMEL'S LIEUTENANTS
The Men Who Served the Desert Fox, France, 1940

STACKPOLE MILITARY HISTORY SERIES

WOLFPACK WARRIORS
The Story of WWII's Most Successful Fighter Outfit
ROGER A. FR

NEW for Spring 2009

STACKPOLE MILITARY HISTORY SERIES

ARMOURED GUARDSMEN
A War Diary from Normandy to the Rhine
ROBERT BOSCAWEN

STACKPOLE MILITARY HISTORY SERIES

DOUGHBOY WAR
The American Expeditionary Force in WWI
EDITED BY JAMES H. HALLAS

STACKPOLE MILITARY HISTORY SERIES

PHANTOM REFLECTIONS
An American Fighter Pilot in Vietnam
MIKE McCARTHY

Real battles. Real soldiers. Real stories.

STACKPOLE MILITARY HISTORY SERIES

GOODWOOD
The British Offensive in Normandy, July 1944

IAN DAGLISH

STACKPOLE MILITARY HISTORY SERIES

DESTINATION NORMANDY
Three American Regiments on D-Day

STACKPOLE MILITARY HISTORY SERIES

EXPENDABLE WARRIORS
The Battle of Khe Sanh and the Vietnam War

BRUCE B. G. CLARKE

STACKPOLE MILITARY HISTORY SERIES

D-DAY DECEPTION
Operation Fortitude and the Normandy Invasion

STACKPOLE MILITARY HISTORY SERIES

RED STAR UNDER THE BALTIC
A Soviet Submariner in WWII

NEW for Spring 2009

STACKPOLE MILITARY HISTORY SERIES

HITLER'S NEMESIS
The Red Army, 1930–45

WALTER S. DUNN, JR., WITH A FOREWORD BY DAVID GLANTZ

STACKPOLE MILITARY HISTORY SERIES

PENALTY STRIKE
The Memoirs of a Red Army Penal Company Commander, 1943–45

ALEXANDER V. PYL'CYN

Stackpole Military History Series

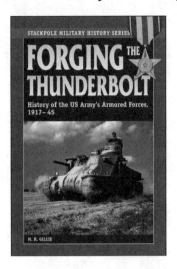

FORGING THE THUNDERBOLT
HISTORY OF THE U.S. ARMY'S ARMORED FORCES, 1917–45
M. H. Gillie

In less than thirty years, the U.S. Army's armored force rose from humble beginnings in borrowed tanks in World War I to a thundering crescendo of tactical prowess and lethal power during the liberation of Western Europe in World War II. M. H. Gillie's classic study recounts this stunning achievement: the bitter internal debates, the technological innovations, and the live-or-die battles with German panzers.

$19.95 • Paperback • 6 x 9 • 320 pages • 26 photos

WWW.STACKPOLEBOOKS.COM
1-800-732-3669

Stackpole Military History Series

IRON ARM
THE MECHANIZATION OF MUSSOLINI'S ARMY, 1920–1940
John Joseph Timothy Sweet

Though overshadowed by Germany's Afrika Korps, Italian
tanks formed a large part of the Axis armored force that
the Allies confronted—and ultimately defeated—in North
Africa in World War II. Those tanks were the product of
two decades of development that put Italy near the fore of
the world's tank forces. For a time, it stood second only to
Germany in number of tank divisions and was the first to
establish an armored corps. Once war came, however,
Mussolini's iron arm failed as an effective weapon.
This is the story of its rise and fall.

$16.95 • Paperback • 6 x 9 • 240 pages
23 photos, 4 maps, 2 diagrams

WWW.STACKPOLEBOOKS.COM
1-800-732-3669

Stackpole Military History Series

GERMANY'S PANZER ARM IN WWII

R. L. DiNardo

No twentieth-century military organization has been
as widely studied as the German war machine in
World War II, and few of its components were as
important, influential, or revolutionary as its armored
force. Nevertheless, there are almost no truly
integrated studies of the organizational, economic,
personnel, doctrinal, and tactical factors that affected
the panzer arm's performance. Drawing on military
documents, memoirs, battle reports, and other
original sources, DiNardo fills that gap with this
detailed look at the rise and fall of German armor.

$16.95 • Paperback • 6 x 9 • 224 pages • 27 photos • 17 diagrams

WWW.STACKPOLEBOOKS.COM
1-800-732-3669

Stackpole Military History Series

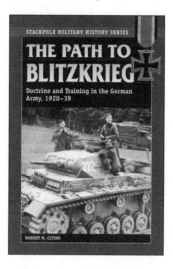

THE PATH TO BLITZKRIEG
DOCTRINE AND TRAINING IN THE GERMAN ARMY,
1920–39
Robert M. Citino

In the wake of World War I, the German Army lay in ruins—defeated in the war, sundered by domestic upheaval, and punished by the Treaty of Versailles. A mere twenty years later, Germany possessed one of the finest military machines in the world, capable of launching a stunning blitzkrieg attack that shredded its opponents in 1939–40. Distinguished military historian Robert M. Citino shows how Germany accomplished this astonishing reversal and developed the doctrine, tactics, and technologies that its army would use to devastating effect in World War II.

$19.95 • Paperback • 6 x 9 • 320 pages • 10 photos

WWW.STACKPOLEBOOKS.COM
1-800-732-3669

Stackpole Military History Series

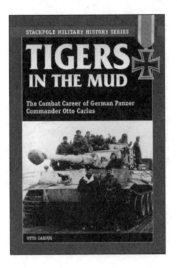

TIGERS IN THE MUD

THE COMBAT CAREER OF GERMAN PANZER
COMMANDER OTTO CARIUS

Otto Carius,
translated by Robert J. Edwards

World War II began with a metallic roar as the
German Blitzkrieg raced across Europe, spearheaded
by the most dreadful weapon of the twentieth century:
the Panzer. Tank commander Otto Carius thrusts the
reader into the thick of battle, replete with the
blood, smoke, mud, and gunpowder so common
to the elite German fighting units.

$19.95 • Paperback • 6 x 9 • 368 pages
51 photos • 48 illustrations • 3 maps

WWW.STACKPOLEBOOKS.COM
1-800-732-3669

Stackpole Military History Series

ARMOR BATTLES
OF THE WAFFEN-SS
1943–45

Will Fey, translated by Henri Henschler

The Waffen-SS were considered the elite of the
German armed forces in the Second World War and
were involved in almost continuous combat. From
the sweeping tank battle of Kursk on the Russian
front to the bitter fighting among the hedgerows
of Normandy and the offensive in the Ardennes,
these men and their tanks made history.

$19.95 • Paperback • 6 x 9 • 384 pages
32 photos • 15 drawings • 4 maps

WWW.STACKPOLEBOOKS.COM
1-800-732-3669

Stackpole Military History Series

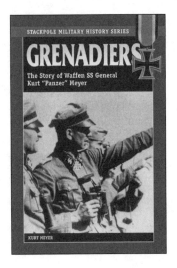

GRENADIERS
THE STORY OF WAFFEN SS GENERAL
KURT "PANZER" MEYER

Kurt Meyer

Known for his bold and aggressive leadership, Kurt
Meyer was one of the most highly decorated German
soldiers of World War II. As commander of various
units, from a motorcycle company to the Hitler Youth
Panzer Division, he saw intense combat across Europe,
from the invasion of Poland in 1939 to the 1944
campaign for Normandy, where he fell into Allied
hands and was charged with war crimes.

$19.95 • Paperback • 6 x 9 • 448 pages • 93 b/w photos

WWW.STACKPOLEBOOKS.COM
1-800-732-3669

Stackpole Military History Series

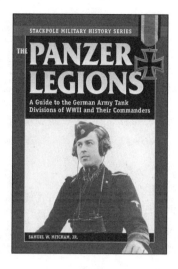

THE PANZER LEGIONS
A GUIDE TO THE GERMAN ARMY TANK DIVISIONS OF WWII AND THEIR COMMANDERS

Samuel W. Mitcham, Jr.

Drawing on years of research and covering all of the German Army's panzer divisions from their creation through their destruction or surrender, Samuel Mitcham chronicles the combat histories of the tank units that formed the backbone of the Nazi war machine. He also details the careers of the divisions' commanders, men like Erwin Rommel and Heinz Guderian who revolutionized modern warfare. In-depth and comprehensive, this is an essential resource on German armor in World War II.

$19.95 • Paperback • 6 x 9 • 352 pages • 30 b/w photos • 8 maps

WWW.STACKPOLEBOOKS.COM
1-800-732-3669

Stackpole Military History Series

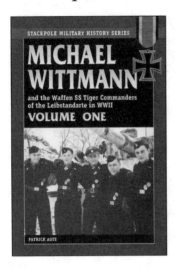
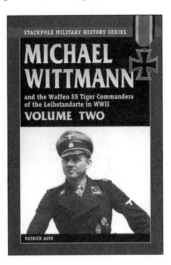

MICHAEL WITTMANN AND THE WAFFEN SS TIGER COMMANDERS OF THE LEIBSTANDARTE IN WORLD WAR II

Patrick Agte

By far the most famous tank commander on any side in World War II, German Tiger ace Michael Wittmann destroyed 138 enemy tanks and 132 anti-tank guns in a career that embodies the panzer legend: meticulous in planning, lethal in execution, and always cool under fire. Volume One covers Wittmann's armored battles against the Soviets in 1943–44 at places like Kharkov, Kursk, and the Cherkassy Pocket. Volume Two picks up with the epic campaign in Normandy, where Wittmann achieved his greatest successes before being killed in action. The Leibstandarte went on to fight at the Battle of the Bulge and in Austria and Hungary before surrendering in May 1945.

Volume One: $19.95 • Paperback • 6 x 9 • 432 pages
383 photos • 19 maps • 10 charts
Volume Two: $19.95 • Paperback • 6 x 9 • 400 pages
287 photos • 15 maps • 7 charts

WWW.STACKPOLEBOOKS.COM
1-800-732-3669

Stackpole Military History Series

THE 12TH SS
THE HISTORY OF THE HITLER YOUTH PANZER DIVISION
Hubert Meyer

Recruited from the ranks of the Hitler Youth, the elite
12th SS Panzer Division consisted largely of teenage
boys who were fanatically devoted to the German cause.
Volume One covers the division's baptism of fire in
Normandy, including its bloody battles for the city of
Caen. Volume Two picks up with the conclusion of the
Normandy campaign, recounts the Battle of the Bulge,
and follows the 12th SS into Hungary for its final stand.

Volume One: $19.95 • Paperback • 6 x 9 • 592 pages
113 photos, 5 illustrations, 13 maps
Volume Two: $19.95 • Paperback • 6 x 9 • 608 pages
60 b/w photos, 4 maps

WWW.STACKPOLEBOOKS.COM
1-800-732-3669

Stackpole Military History Series

THE GERMANS IN NORMANDY
by Richard Hargreaves

Richard Hargreaves recounts the Normandy campaign
from the perspective of the German soldiers who
manned the Atlantic Wall when the Allies invaded
France in June 1944 and then put up a bitter but
ultimately hopeless defense throughout that horrific
summer. These are the stories of the troops—like
Michael Wittmann, Kurt Meyer, and the boy soldiers of
the 12th SS Panzer Division—who looked out from
pillboxes on Omaha Beach, fired machine guns over
hedgerows, commanded panzers, defended the
bombed-out ruins of St. LÙ and Caen, and suffered
through the nightmare of the Falaise Gap.

$19.95 • Paperback • 6 x 9 • 320 pages • 19 b/w photos, 2 maps

WWW.STACKPOLEBOOKS.COM
1-800-732-3669

Stackpole Military History Series

PANZER ACES
GERMAN TANK COMMANDERS OF WORLD WAR II
Franz Kurowski

With the order "Panzers forward!" German tanks
rolled into battle, smashing into the enemy with
engines roaring and muzzles flashing. From Poland
and the Eastern Front to the Ardennes, Italy, and
northern Africa, panzers stunned their opponents—
and the world—with their lightning speed and raw
power, and the soldiers, like Michael, who manned
these lethal machines were among the
boldest and most feared of World War II.

$19.95 • Paperback • 6 x 9 • 480 pages • 60 b/w photos

WWW.STACKPOLEBOOKS.COM
1-800-732-3669

Stackpole Military History Series

RETREAT TO THE REICH
THE GERMAN DEFEAT IN FRANCE, 1944
Samuel W. Mitcham, Jr.

The Allied landings on D-Day, June 6, 1944, marked the beginning of the German defeat in the West in World War II. From the experiences of soldiers in the field to decision-making at high command, military historian Samuel Mitcham vividly recaptures the desperation of the Wehrmacht as it collapsed amidst the brutal hedgerow fighting in Normandy, losing its four-year grip on France as it was forced to retreat back to the German border. While German forces managed to temporarily halt the Allied juggernaut there, this brief success only delayed the fate that had been sealed with the defeat in France.

$17.95 • Paperback • 6 x 9 • 304 pages • 26 photos, 12 maps

WWW.STACKPOLEBOOKS.COM
1-800-732-3669

Stackpole Military History Series

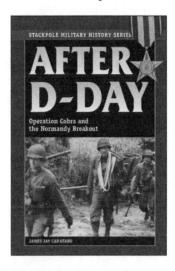

AFTER D-DAY
OPERATION COBRA AND THE NORMANDY BREAKOUT
by James Jay Carafano

After storming the beaches on D-Day, June 6, 1944, the
Allied invasion of France bogged down in seven weeks
of grueling attrition in Normandy. On July 25, U.S.
divisions under Gen. Omar Bradley launched
Operation Cobra, an attempt to break out of the
hedgerows and begin a war of movement against the
Germans. Despite a disastrous start, with misdropped
bombs killing more than 100 GIs, Cobra proved to be
one of the most pivotal battles of World War II,
successfully breaking the stalemate in Normandy and
clearing a path into the heart of France.

$19.95 • Paperback • 6 x 9 • 336 pages • 31 b/w photos, 10 maps

WWW.STACKPOLEBOOKS.COM
1-800-732-3669

Stackpole Military History Series

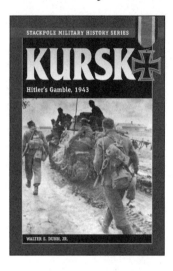

KURSK
HITLER'S GAMBLE
Walter S. Dunn, Jr.

During the summer of 1943, Germany unleashed its last major offensive on the Eastern Front and sparked the epic battle of Kursk, which included the largest tank engagement in history. Marked by fiery clashes between German Tigers and Soviet T-34s in the mud and dust of western Russia, the campaign began well enough for the Germans, but the Soviets counterattacked and eventually forced Hitler to end the operation. When it was over, thousands lay dead or wounded on both sides, but the victorious Red Army had turned the tide of World War II in the East.

$16.95 • Paperback • 6 x 9 • 240 pages • 9 photos, 1 map

WWW.STACKPOLEBOOKS.COM
1-800-732-3669

Stackpole Military History Series

SOVIET BLITZKRIEG
THE BATTLE FOR WHITE RUSSIA, 1944
Walter S. Dunn, Jr.

On June 22, 1944, the third anniversary of the German
invasion of the Soviet Union, the Red Army launched
Operation Bagration, its massive attempt to clear
German forces from Belarus. In one of the largest
campaigns of all time—involving two million Soviets
and nearly a million Germans—the Soviets recaptured
hundreds of miles of territory and annihilated an
entire German army group in two months of vicious
fighting. Bagration crippled the Germans in the
East and helped turn the tide of the war.

$16.95 • Paperback • 6 x 9 • 288 pages • 18 b/w photos • 12 maps

WWW.STACKPOLEBOOKS.COM
1-800-732-3669

Also available from Stackpole Books

FIGHTING MEN OF WORLD WAR II
VOLUME 1: AXIS FORCES
VOLUME 2: ALLIED FORCES
David Miller

These comprehensive volumes present a full-color
look at Axis and Allied soldiers in World War II,
covering their weapons, equipment, clothing,
rations, and more. The Axis volume includes Germany,
Italy, and Japan while the Allied volume presents
troops from the United States, Great Britain, and the
Soviet Union. These books create a vivid picture of
the daily life and battle conditions of the fighting
men of the Second World War.

$49.95 • Hardcover • 9 x 12 • 384 pages • 600 color illustrations

WWW.STACKPOLEBOOKS.COM
1-800-732-3669